# CONTEMPORARY
# TEACHING OF
# SECONDARY SCHOOL
# MATHEMATICS

# Contemporary
# TEACHING OF
# SECONDARY SCHOOL
# MATHEMATICS

## STEPHEN S. WILLOUGHBY

*Division of Science and Mathematics*
*School of Education*
*New York University*

*John Wiley & Sons, Inc.*
NEW YORK   LONDON   SYDNEY

*To Sali, Wendy, and Todd, who put up with,*
*and without me, for so long so that this*
*book might be published*

Library of Congress Catalog Card Number: 66-26762
Printed in the United States of America

# PREFACE

This book is addressed to the following three audiences:

First, experienced mathematics teachers who have not been able to keep abreast of all recent developments in mathematics education. To these teachers, the book presents and explains important new ideas and proposes methods of teaching specific subject matter.

Second, inexperienced teachers with a strong, recent background in mathematics. For these novices, the book relates concepts learned in pure mathematics courses to what happens in the classroom; it suggests which concepts will be the most important in developing their pupils' comprehension as well as ways to teach and use these concepts. The beginning teacher should find Chapter 3, on classroom management and techniques, of particular interest.

Third, prospective teachers who do *not* have an adequate background in mathematics. It is hoped that this is a vanishing breed. No single book or course could enable teachers who are unprepared to do a competent job of teaching mathematics, but this book can give them some information about where their major weaknesses are and what they must do to remedy their shortcomings.

The substantial amount of mathematics in this book is not meant to replace a strong, formal mathematical education. Rather, the mathematics discussed here is meant to supplement the standard mathematics courses by both considering mathematical principles in the context of the secondary school curriculum and by considering mathematical topics which are important to a teacher but not ordinarily taught in college mathematics courses (for instance, mathematical explanations of common algorithms, use of field properties to help pupils understand algebraic manipulations, etc.).

v

Use of this book as a text for a formal course could free class time for discussion. The instructor need not repeat the facts and ideas mentioned in the text; instead, the class could use these as a point of departure for independent investigation. Both students and instructor might well disagree with statements here. Disagreement is good. No two people who are actively thinking will find themselves in agreement on all topics; it is often the very issues of disagreement that are most educational for all concerned.

*Contemporary Teaching of Secondary School Mathematics* was written with the reader in mind. The style is informal, to facilitate understanding; the bibliography, rather than being a huge catalogue of titles, is a carefully selected, annotated, representative list of books that are likely to help the teacher and prospective teacher; and the suggested references are aimed at helping the reader to focus his attention on particular and practical problems in mathematical education.

I am indebted to many persons, especially to the students and teachers who read this text in the prepublication version and made many worthwhile contributions. I also wish to thank Dr. Roy Dubisch for his excellent recommendations for improving the manuscript and Dr. Edith Robinson who did most of the research for Chapter 1.

STEPHEN S. WILLOUGHBY

*June 1966*

# CONTENTS

CHAPTER

1   The History of Mathematics Education in The United States   1
2   Modern Mathematics   29
3   Teaching and Learning: Hints for The Classroom   58
4   Arithmetic   91
5   Number Systems and Numeration Systems   113
6   Intuitive Geometry   139
7   Probability for Junior High School   169
8   Language, Logic, and Sets   183
9   Expanding The Number System   231
10  Algebra   262
11  Geometry   297
12  Circular Functions and Trigonometry   323
13  Probability and Statistical Inference   358
14  Calculus   381
15  Teaching Secondary School Mathematics   398

Index   413

# CONTEMPORARY
# TEACHING OF
# SECONDARY SCHOOL
# MATHEMATICS

# THE HISTORY OF MATHEMATICS EDUCATION IN THE UNITED STATES TO 1955

Since 1955, many changes have occurred in the mathematics curricula of United States secondary schools. Even more numerous and more drastic changes have been recommended than have taken place. The recommendations have been accompanied by more publicity and by a greater outpouring of money for new curricula than this or any other country has even seen. One may best understand and evaluate the suggested revisions by viewing them in the context of previous school mathematics curricula and the changes that had occurred or had been recommended before the advent of so-called modern school mathematics.

### Early History of Education in the United States

The early schools in the colonies were founded primarily for the purpose of establishing literacy and educating the clergy. The Puritans promulgated the principle of teaching children their letters so that they could read the Bible and other religious writings themselves. Arithmetic was taught only in schools of towns that had commercial interests.

The first formal education in this country took place in four different types of schools. One was the Dame School, an outgrowth of the idea that each family was responsible for the education of its own children. Families would send their children to a neighborhood lady who would educate several children in her home for a fee. There is clear evidence that at least one Dame School was in existence as early as 1635, and there is reason to believe that several such schools were in existence even prior to that time.[1] A second type of school was the town school. When the idea of a town school was originally imported from England, both writing and arithmetic were taught because the purpose of these schools had been to train clerks. However, the town schools soon concentrated mainly on reading, writing, and religion except in the commercial towns where arithmetic remained a part of the curriculum. A third kind of school was the Latin Grammar School. The earliest of these, the Boston Latin Grammar School, was the first permanent school established in the British colonies in America. Because the purpose of the Latin Grammar School was to prepare pupils to enter college, its curriculum included only classical subjects and religion. Since the purpose of college was to prepare ministers, the Latin schools were, of course, primarily religious institutions. The fourth type of educational institution in the early colonial days was the college. Havard College was the first. The purpose of the colleges was, as noted, to prepare ministers. Puritanism, however, was an intellectual as well as a religious creed, and therefore, the colleges did not neglect such academic topics as natural sciences, mathematics, logic, and ancient history. The language of instruction was Latin.

During the latter half of the eighteenth century, a conflict between the common man and the elite coincided with the conflict between the colonies and England. As a result, a new type of school, the academy, began to find wide acceptance. Benjamin Franklin did not start the first academy, but his name is most commonly associated with the idea since he, one of the nonelite himself, was an outstanding spokesman for the academy. In the academy, such practical subjects as mathematics, mechanical arts, and science were included in the curriculum. The academies were so popular that by 1850 more than 6,000 of them were in existence though they were tuition schools.

The name of Thomas Jefferson is usually associated with the next major change in the schools of this country. Jefferson believed that an educated citizenry was essential to a working democracy. Therefore, he proposed a plan for universal education in his home state of Virginia in 1779 and again in 1817. On both occasions his proposal was defeated, but his dream of universal education contained the essence of what became the American system of education. Actually, there had been earlier attempts to establish universal compulsory education. In 1642

[1] Weiss and Hoover, p. 354.

Massachusetts passed a law requiring a minimum of education for all children; by 1671 all the other New England colonies except Rhode Island had enacted similar legislation. However, these laws had nothing to do with actual schooling (public or private). The assumption was that parents or others responsible for the welfare of children, such as masters to whom children were apprenticed, would see that the young people were taught a trade and how to read. It was up to the selectmen of the town to determine whether the requirement was being met. If the selectmen decided that the requirement was not being met, the parents (or master) could be fined, or the children could be removed from their care.

During the 1820s and 1830s, many of the states passed laws concerning the establishment of public schools, but these schools were neither free nor compulsory. By 1840, however, the free school (sometimes called the common school) was beginning to become an accepted institution. The main objective of these schools was literacy; therefore, the curriculum was limited almost exclusively to reading and writing. Another factor that restricted the curriculum of the common school was the limited education of the teachers. Hence, a teacher of a subject such as arithmetic was dependent on a textbook. Usually there was only one copy of a textbook in a school; the teacher would dictate exercises for the pupils to work according to a rule that the teacher gave for solving that particular type of problem.

One of the most influential textbooks, both for the teaching of arithmetic and for teaching generally, was Warren Colburn's *First Lessons*, originally published in 1821. Colburn's arithmetic text was based on Pestalozzi's object lessons with their appeal to all of the senses and understanding of the child, which made the pupil an active participant rather than a passive recipient. Use of the text probably marked the first time that a pedagogical innovation had been attempted on a national basis and could fairly be described as the beginning of the pedagogical revolution.

The increasing demand for teachers for the common schools was met partially by an increase in the number of the female seminaries but was more directly and more adequately met by a new institution, the normal school. The first normal school was established through the efforts of Horace Mann at Lexington, Massachusetts, in 1839. By 1872 there were more than 100 normal schools in existence in this country. Thus pedagogy, as well as knowledge of subject matter, became an important part of the preparation of teachers.

Meanwhile, free secondary schools were beginning to find acceptance. The first was the Boston English Classical School, established in 1821.

Its name was changed to "high school" in 1824. After the Civil War, high schools became the predominant form of public secondary education, though they still met a good deal of resistance on grounds that the public could not and should not be asked to support them. In 1874, the Michigan Supreme Court upheld the right of public authorities to collect taxes for the support of high schools (in the Kalamazoo case), and thereafter there was no significant legal objection to public high schools.

Curriculum in secondary schools had been determined largely by college entrance requirements; because the secondary schools were neither free nor compulsory until late in the nineteenth century, most of the pupils in these schools were preparing for college. Thus, when more mathematics was added to the school curriculum, it was usually because college entrance requirements had been increased. In the early days, Harvard was the leader in increasing entrance requirements. For example, Harvard did not have a professor of mathematics until 1726, and therefore no mathematics was required before that date for college admission; however, when arithmetic was required by Harvard, it was soon required by other colleges; in 1820 algebra was required by Harvard, and soon thereafter by other colleges. By the middle of the nineteenth century, arithmetic and algebra were commonly taught in the secondary schools since these subjects were required for entrance to most colleges. Harvard was again the leader in the subject of geometry, requiring it for the first time in 1844. By 1875 geometry was commonly taught in secondary schools. It is interesting to note that the order in which the three subjects, arithmetic, algebra, and geometry, are presently taught in this country is the same order in which Harvard and other colleges began requiring them in the eighteenth and nineteenth centuries. Furthermore, other courses that are often taught in the high schools (more advanced algebra, trigonometry, etc.) follow geometry without any obvious logic to the sequence.

Although some similarities existed among the entrance requirements of the various colleges, differences were sufficient to prompt most people to make an early selection of the college for which preparatory study would be undertaken. This disparity in requirements led to a chaotic situation for secondary schools which had to design courses to meet the entrance requirements of particular colleges. Therefore, near the end of the nineteenth century, groups of colleges began working with preparatory schools to set some reasonably uniform standards. The first association of colleges and preparatory schools was founded in New England in 1885. This association created the New England Entrance Certificate Board in 1902, with representatives from the leading colleges and universities of New England. The purpose of this board was to prepare a list of secondary schools whose graduates could be admitted to colleges on certification instead of by examinations. A similar organization, the Association of Colleges and Preparatory Schools of the Middle States and Maryland, was formed in 1892. The College Entrance Examination Board was created by this association in 1900 and shortly thereafter became an independent body. It has had a considerable effect on the teaching and curriculum in secondary schools all over the country during this century.

## Mathematics Education: Committees and Commissions, 1890–1955

Starting in 1890, various committees and commissions have been prominent in making recommendations for changes in the mathematics curriculum and in methods of teaching mathematics. There had been some unrest regarding the way mathematics was taught to children throughout the civilized world, during the latter half of the nineteenth century. In England, J. J. Sylvester, one of the great mathematicians of that country, spoke publicly for the interment of Euclidean geometry, as it was then taught to school boys; John Perry went even further in recommending a much greater emphasis on applied mathematics and the relationship between the physical sciences and mathematics. He thought that more concrete examples should be used, that children should discover many facts (in particular, of geometry) through experimentation rather than deduction, and that there should be a great deal more emphasis on graphic methods. In the United States, E. H. Moore advocated the same general point of view in his presidential address to the American Mathematical Society, December 29, 1902. (This address was printed in the first yearbook of the National Council of Teachers of Mathematics.) In France and Germany, J. Tannery and Felix Klein were advocating similar ideas; Klein was putting somewhat more emphasis on the function concept.

## Committee of Ten

In 1892, The Committee of Ten on Secondary School subjects, led by Charles W. Eliot of Harvard, created subcommittees on various subjects. The Subcommittee on Mathematics under the direction of Simon Newcomb met in 1892. It recommended that some of the arithmetic then taught should be left out of the curriculum—particularly the kind that seemed solely intended to exhaust and perplex the pupil. The subcommittee also suggested that a concrete geometry course be given near the end of grammar school (that is, in the seventh and eighth grades), with plenty of exercises. The committee recommended beginning the formal study of algebra in the ninth grade, and continuing the study of algebra in the tenth grade (two and one-half hours a week) with a parallel course in deductive geometry (also two and one-half hours a week). The parallel courses in algebra and geometry were to continue through the eleventh grade. The parallel courses were proposed so that the teacher could combine algebra and geometry to some extent and could show the relations between these two topics. Thus, the Committee of Ten made a strong appeal for the decompartmentalization of mathematics teaching. Unfortunately, in most schools where the parallel courses were tried, teachers still taught algebra and geometry as though there were no connection between the two; furthermore, many teachers enjoyed one of the subjects more than the other and therefore tended to ignore one while emphasizing the other. Consequently, while many of the other recommendations of the committee were incorporated into the mathematics curriculum of the nation, the parallel courses in algebra and geometry were dropped by most schools where they were tried. The Committee of Ten also suggested that a course in bookkeeping and the technical parts of arithmetic be given after ninth grade algebra for pupils who were not planning to go on to college and that a course in trigonometry and advanced algebra be offered to boys who were going into the natural sciences or technical colleges.

### Committee on College Entrance Requirements

In 1899, the Committee on College Entrance Requirements, formed by the National Education Association to bring about better articulation between colleges and secondary schools, published its report. This committee's recommendations were quite similar to those of the Committee of Ten in many respects, but several subjects had been moved "down" to a grade one year earlier than the levels suggested by the Committee of Ten. This committee proposed concrete geometry and introduction to algebra for grade seven; introduction to demonstrative geometry and more algebra for grade eight; parallel courses in algebra and geometry for grades nine and ten; solid geometry and trigonometry for grade eleven; advanced algebra and review for grade twelve.

### International Commission

At the fourth International Congress of Mathematicians in Rome in 1908, David Eugene Smith made a motion calling for the appointment of an International Commission on Teaching of Mathematics. The motion was carried; Felix Klein (Germany), Sir George Greenhill (England), and Henri Fehr (Switzerland) were named to the committee. Smith was added to the commission in 1912. The International Commission found that some of Perry's ideas were being put into practice all over the world—notably the increased emphasis on graphic techniques and practical applications of mathematics. The United States commissioners (Smith, W. F. Osgood, and J. W. A. Young) found that algebra and geometry were offered for at least one year each in secondary schools in this country. Only about half of the schools offered another semester of algebra, and fewer than 20% offered any more mathematics. The American commissioners also found some changes that were apparently beginning to take place and listed several improvements in curriculum and method which they thought were starting. These included the following: omission of geometric proofs, when either too obvious or too difficult; shift of more difficult parts of algebra from the first to the second year; avoidance of unnecessarily complex algebraic manipulations; giving more prominence to the equation; a great deal more emphasis on practical applications of mathematics to the natural sciences and everyday life; and a modification of teaching goals to conform with recent psychological findings regarding the value of formal discipline. The commissioners cited the need for the better preparation of mathematics teachers.

### Committee of Fifteen

During the same year (1908) as the International Commission was created, a committee was formed for the specific purpose of considering a syllabus for geometry. Actually, two such committees were authorized—one by the National Education Association, the other by the American Federation of Teachers of the Mathematical and Natural Sciences. In the following year the two organizations agreed to make this a joint committee. In this way, the National Committee of Fifteen on Geometry Syllabus was formed. Its report, published in 1911, contained several suggestions; probably the most important of these was that geometry be made more practical and less frightening. The committee suggested that exercises involving abstract originals be replaced by more applications of geometry to architecture, indirect measurement, etc. It suggested that a text, instead of starting with page upon page of definitions, introduce definitions where needed, and that the number of formal definitions be reduced as well. Also, the committee recommended that more informal proofs be accepted and more emphasis be put on (scientific) induction.

### 1923 Report

In 1923, the National Committee on Mathematical Requirements published one of the most important committee reports of the first half of this century. It is often called the 1923 report. Immediately prior to 1916 when this committee was formed by the Mathematical Association of America, a good deal of activity in education, generally, was taking place. In addition to experimentation in educational psychology, trials were proposed, notably by President Eliot of Harvard, for assigning to the seventh and eighth grades some of the work usually reserved for high schools. This proposal combined with the general feeling that the giant step in a child's schooling was taken between the eighth and ninth grades, led several people to advocate a new kind of grade organization for the schools. According to their recommendation, the teaching of secondary subjects should start, perhaps in simplified form, in the seventh grade and preferably in a school other than the elementary or grade school. Thus, 6–3–3 organization of grades was beginning to become popular by 1916 when the National Committee on Mathematical Requirements was formed, and one of its major tasks was to suggest programs that would fit this new type of organization. The magnitude of the new movement was indicated by the following facts. The first junior high schools were created in Berkeley, California, and Columbus, Ohio, in 1909, and another was created in Los Angeles in 1911. By 1917, 9.1% of the nation's high school pupils were enrolled in the reorganized program (that is, in schools with six years of elementary grades and six years of secondary grades, the latter usually divided into junior and senior high schools). By 1925, 41.1% of high school pupils were in reorganized high schools.

The 1923 report set up the following three aims for the teaching of mathematics: (1) the practical purpose of helping the pupil to gain insight into and control over his environment; (2) the cultural purpose of helping him to appreciate the progress of civilization; and (3) the disciplinary purpose of developing habits of thought and action that would make the individual's powers of understanding and analyzing more effective throughout his life. Notice that this last goal is distinct from the philosophy of nineteenth-century educators who felt that the main reason for studying mathematics was its difficulty that would, of itself, develop the mind. The belief underlying the 1923 report was that specific kinds of action and thinking should be encouraged in the hope that these would be influential throughout the individual's life. Although Thorndike's contention that there can be no transfer of learning (unless "identical elements" are present) was having a great effect on education generally and mathematics education in particular, there were still those who thought that some transfer of training was possible if the teacher tried to teach in a way to bring about that transfer.

The 1923 report listed several different plans for junior high school grades and several different plans for the senior high school. These plans emphasized the decompartmentalization, especially in the junior high, of the branches of mathematics as then taught in the schools (arithmetic, algebra, geometry, and trigonometry). The reason for offering several programs (five in junior high and four in senior high) was to allow the teacher latitude for adaptation of the recommendations to particular conditions where he was teaching. This report also advised that all pupils be required to take the mathematics recommended for the junior high school and that those who passed this work successfully be allowed to go on to take the mathematics of the senior high school. For those who were not interested or did not need the more formal work of the senior high school, the report recommended various practical mathematics courses including statistics, shop mathematics, surveying and navigation, and descriptive geometry, wherever sufficient need existed.

## PEA Committee and the Joint Commission

In the early 1930s, two more groups were formed to study the teaching of mathematics. The reports of both groups appeared in 1940. The two groups were the Progressive Education Association Committee on the Function of Mathematics in General Education and the Joint Commission to Study the Place of Mathematics in Secondary Education. The first, set up by the Progressive Education Association, is often referred to as the PEA committee; the second, originally appointed by the Mathematical Association of America, later became a joint commission of the MAA and the National Council of Teachers of Mathematics. The major difference between the two reports was that the Joint Commission outlined a program that its members thought could be offered in schools at the time—in fact, most of the suggestions of this Commission had actually been tried, with some success, in several schools—whereas the PEA Committee produced a profile of a program for the future in terms of general principles of education. Thus, the PEA report was a guide to future experimentation with the mathematics curriculum, rather than a program for immediate incorporation into existing schools.

To allow for flexibility, the Joint Commission proposed two alternative curricula that were supposed to provide continuity in the mathematics program for grades seven through fourteen. It also made suggestions for modification, and discussed acceleration and retardation. The program for grades thirteen and fourteen assumed that mathematics pupils in a junior college would be terminal students rather than continuing mathematics students.

The PEA report was divided into four parts. The first of these set forth the committee's philosophy of teaching mathematics—in summary, that in order to justify its place in the education of our youth, mathematics must contribute to the satisfaction of the needs of the students—and discussed how mathematics could satisfy what the committee felt to be the needs of people. The second and major part of the report dealt with problem solving and how the study of various aspects of mathematics could contribute to students' ability to solve problems in general. The third part discussed the nature of mathematics. The fourth part concentrated on an understanding of the pupils and evaluation of their progress. As mentioned, the PEA report did not spell out a particular curriculum, but rather stated a philosophy of teaching mathematics with its implications for future developmental work in the mathematics curriculum. The committee further assumed that as subsequent experiments produced results, principles that it had enunciated would be reconsidered and perhaps dropped.

**Wartime Committees**

When the United States entered the second World War in 1941, military officials and others began to complain about the poor mathematics preparation of the young men inducted into the service. Several committees were created to study the mathematics curriculum in the light of war needs. The first of these committees, appointed in 1940 as a joint committee of the American Mathematical Society and the Mathematical Association of America, was called the War Preparedness Committee. A second joint committee of the AMS and MAA, the War Policy Committee, was created in 1943. Although these committees had as their primary goal the effective utilization of mathematical manpower to aid the war effort, their reports had some implications for the secondary school mathematics curriculum. Two other committees, more directly associated with the secondary school mathematics curriculum, were the Committee on Pre-Induction Courses in Mathematics and the Committee on Essential Mathematics for Minimum Army Needs; these reported their findings in *The Mathematics Teacher* in 1943. Although the reports were interesting, they had little lasting effect on the mathematics curriculum in the secondary schools aside from indicating that the country was becoming aware of the importance of mathematics to national defense. This awareness apparently lay relatively dormant until the flight of the first Russian Sputnik in October, 1957.

By early 1944 it seemed fairly clear that the Allies were going to win the War. While the need for mathematical competence in the national defense was still vivid in the public mind, the National Council of

Teachers of Mathematics created the Commission on Post-War Plans to draw up a program for secondary school mathematics in the postwar period. This commission published two reports (in the 1944 and 1945 May issues of *The Mathematics Teacher*) and the *Guidance Pamphlet*, an expansion of the second report. The first report, which was preliminary and asked for help from the public to accomplish its goal of making available the best possible mathematics education for all children, made the following five proposals: (1) Schools should provide mathematical literacy to all who can achieve it. (2) The needs of all pupils should be met by appropriate courses. (3) More thought should be given to appropriate work for the slow learners. (4) The teaching of arithmetic should be improved. (5) The regular sequential courses should be improved.

The second report of the Commission on Post-War Plans made many recommendations pertaining to the mathematics curriculum in grades one through fourteen. The first was that the school should provide "functional competence" in mathematics for all pupils who are able to achieve it. The committee followed this nonspecific statement with a list of some 28 items (for example, use of per cents, measurement, vectors, axioms, trigonometry, and dollar-stretching) in which it thought pupils ought to be competent. The list was expanded later when the report was rewritten as the *Guidance Pamphlet*. Other recommendations of the committee included the following: consideration of arithmetic as a content subject as well as a tool subject; wiser use of drill in arithmetic, a two-track program for the ninth grade (with algebra the content of the faster track); a program to satisfy junior college students interested in mathematics for cultural reasons as well as those planning to continue in mathematics and those having prevocational needs; better preparation of mathematics teachers at all levels; and more effective use of multisensory aids in teaching mathematics. After this report, there was no significant committee report until the 1950s and the advent of so-called modern mathematics programs. These will be considered in a later chapter.

## Organizations with an Interest in Mathematics Education

The National Council of Teachers of Mathematics (NCTM) held its first meeting in Cleveland, Ohio, February 24, 1920. The purpose of this organization is to promote interest in mathematics education at both the secondary and elementary levels. In October, 1966, the NCTM's 70,655 members (including institutional subscribers) made it the largest organization in the country with a principal interest in mathematics. In fact, the membership of the NCTM is larger than the combined membership of the other three major mathematical societies, the American Mathematical Society, the Mathematics Association of America, and the Society for Industrial and Applied Mathematics. The National Council holds regular meetings for the presentation and discussion of ideas pertaining to mathematics education. In recent years its annual meetings have been held in April. The NCTM also sponsors various regional meetings each year and usually has a joint meeting with the NEA in early summer. Besides sponsoring meetings, the NCTM publishes three periodicals pertaining to mathematics and mathematics education. *The Mathematics Teacher*, published monthly eight times a year from October through May, contains articles pertaining to mathematics education in the secondary school as well as several departments with short articles on experimental programs, the history of mathematics, international education, and reviews and evaluations of text materials. *The Arithmetic Teacher*, published at the same times as the *Mathematics Teacher*, performs much the same function for the elementary level. *The Mathematics Student Journal*, published four times each school year by the NCTM, includes articles of interest to high school mathematics pupils, contributions by pupils, and a problem department for problems and solutions by pupils. The NCTM also prints yearbooks, available to members at reduced rates, and other materials such as *Computer Oriented Mathematics* and *The Revolution in School Mathematics*, available to members at no charge or at greatly reduced rates. The National Council encourages student memberships by offering special rates. Teachers of mathematics who wish to remain abreast of the latest ideas and research in mathematics education find this organization well worthwhile.

Other organizations with a principal interest in the teaching of mathematics have been formed over the years. Many of these are local groups and have become affiliated with the NCTM. Organizations having a long standing interest in mathematics education include the Mathematical Association of America (organized in 1915 at Columbus, Ohio) and the Central Association of Science and Mathematics Teachers (organized in 1902 and 1903). The Mathematical Association of America is of special interest to college teachers of mathematics, as well as to other mathematicians; its periodical, *The American Mathematical Monthly*, published ten times a year, includes many articles of interest to professors of mathematics education and to teachers of advanced high school subjects. The wide range of the MAA concern with the field of mathematical education is further demonstrated by the great number of committees which it has sponsored over the years with a principal interest in elementary and secondary school mathematics education. Perhaps the most important activity of the MAA, as far as secondary school teachers are concerned, is the publication of the *Mathematics Magazine*. This periodical (published five times yearly) specializes in high quality expository articles on mathematics. Secondary school mathematics teachers should benefit from reading many of these.

The Central Association of Science and Mathematics Teachers (CASMT), although a regional organization in some respects, has had considerable influence on both mathematics and science curricula throughout the country. As its name implies, it is of interest to both mathematics and science teachers, especially at the secondary school level.

### Effect of Psychology on Teaching of Mathematics

To the extent that there was an underlying psychology of mathematics education in the early days of this country, it was a psychology (perhaps more accurately described as philosophy) of mental discipline. Of course, educators hoped that some of the mathematics that was taught to youngsters would be of practical use to them at some time in the future, but the principal purpose in teaching mathematics in the schools was to cultivate and discipline pupil's mental powers so that they would learn to reason correctly. This philosophy has been described, in an oversimplified fashion, as proceeding from the assumption that the mind is a sort of a muscle that becomes stronger with exercise; therefore, one should study the most difficult and often least palatable school subjects, exercising the mind diligently on them. Many educators felt that ancient languages and mathematics were the best of all possible subjects to study in the schools, since these were the most difficult. This viewpoint seems to have been fundamental to a great deal of educational thinking throughout the history of the civilized world. For example, Plato recommended that his philosopher-king study mathematics for twenty years before starting the study of philosophy; the present "Great Books" movement, popularized by Robert M. Hutchins and others, is based on the belief that communication with the great minds of history by study of the classics will help the student to organize his mind and to understand the universe better; and many, if not most, mathematics teachers today will suggest that one of the main reasons for teaching mathematics is to teach children to think logically.

It is difficult to claim that there is no merit whatsoever in the "mental-discipline" philosophy of teaching, but many experiments in the past seventy years challenge the idea that mental discipline acquired in one context is necessarily carried over into another context. Even before the beginning of this century, educators were beginning to revolt against the mental-discipline theory. In this new and developing country, the man on the frontier often had to depend on his own wit and practical knowledge; when it became clear that the study of ancient languages and mathematics did not always help in providing food, constructing a shelter, and acquiring the other necessities of life, some question was raised as to the universal desirability of this kind of education. The academy, mentioned earlier as often associated with that very practical American, Benjamin Franklin, was one such revolt against the classical, mental-discipline approach to education.

Another revolt against the then accepted view of education can be traced to the great Swiss educator, Johann Heinrich Pestalozzi (1746–1827), who held that men were naturally good and that children should, therefore, be allowed to "unfold" and grow naturally with encouragement from sympathetic adults instead of being forced into unnatural situations. The introduction of Pestalozzi's ideas to this country's schools through Warren Colburn's arithmetic textbooks, first published in 1821, has been noted. Colburn believed that the child could learn more by setting up his own rules and making his own generalizations than from memorizing rules given to him by a teacher or textbook. He advocated emphasis on understanding that was built through the inductive study of particular cases rather than heavy emphasis on memory work with little attention to understanding. New concepts could be introduced through practical problems so that the child would proceed from the concrete to the abstract. Colburn later published texts on more advanced arithmetic and on algebra, still using the general principle of working from the concrete to the abstract with as much active participation by the pupils as possible. Although later authors did not accept Colburn's thesis in its entirety many of them tended to place considerably more emphasis on pupil reasoning and less emphasis on memorization of meaningless rules than had been the tradition. Of course, the trend toward more thinking and less memorization on the part of the pupils is not necessarily opposed to the mental-discipline approach and, in fact, could be used to support a variation of that philosophy. The point is that there is some probability that memorization of other people's reasoning may be a less effective way to learn than is figuring out things for oneself with expert guidance.

During the latter half of the nineteenth century, two other educators were having a significant effect on American education. One of these was Friedrich Froebel (1782–1852), a German, whose idea for a kindergarten had spread over the European continent and was introduced into this country shortly before the Civil War. Froebel was a student of Pestalozzi, and many of his ideas were closely akin to those of Pestalozzi. Froebel's work had almost no effect on the teaching of mathematics, but his influence indicated that American education was accepting new ideas and that Pestalozzi's theories were gaining some currency on this side of the Atlantic.

Another German educator, Johann Friedrich Herbart (1776–1841), influenced theories of teaching in this country with his emphases on keeping a child's interest aroused to help him learn effectively and on relating a new concept to previously learned concepts for reinforcement of learning. Herbart believed that the child should become interested in a subject both for its own sake and for its social importance. He proposed the following five formal steps in the offering of subject matter: (1) preparation (2) presentation (3) association (4) systematization, and (5) application. Herbartian philosophy had a great deal of effect on the early teachers' colleges in this country; therefore, presumably, much of the actual teaching in schools was along Herbartian lines. The strong emphasis on lesson plans, still common in this country, can be traced directly to the Herbartian influence in the early teachers' colleges.

In spite of these tendencies to move away from the mental-discipline approach to education, it was not until the turn of the century that experimental psychologists actually delivered the *coup de grace* to this philosophy of teaching. Since this philosophy rested on the theory that the mind is composed of several faculties (reasoning, will, memory, etc.) and that a well-trained faculty would be useful in various contexts, the early experiments tested the hypothesis that training could actually be transferred from one learned task to another task that had not yet been studied but that required the same faculty. William James conducted experiments during the late 1800s, indicating that formal discipline did not seem to improve the memory. Although his experiments were not as carefully controlled as are our contemporary psychological experiments, James's experiments offered evidence that faculty psychology, as accepted prior to his time, should not be accepted in its entirety without further documentation.

In 1901, Thorndike and Woodworth published results of experiments showing that almost no transfer of learning from one task to another existed unless "identical elements" were involved in both tasks and that the more "identical elements" were involved, the more transfer of training would occur between the two tasks. It is a little difficult to determine precisely what was meant by "identical elements"; there is some indication that Thorndike changed and developed his theory as he acquired more evidence. For instance, in his later work, Thorndike used such words as "aspects" and "features" rather than "elements," indicating that what must be identical in the problems could be of a very general nature. At the time of publication of the original experiments, however, the consensus seems to have been that transfer of training was virtually nonexistent beyond problems that were almost identical. Since much of Thorndike's work was associated with arithmetic, his experiments and resulting theories of psychology had a considerable effect on the teaching of mathematics in this country during the first half of this century.

Thorndike's ideas on the teaching of arithmetic (or for that matter, the teaching of any subject) were presented in *The Psychology of Arithmetic*, published in 1922. The general impression one gets from reading this book is that Thorndike did not believe that the mathematics underlying arithmetic was of particular importance in the teaching of arithmetic, but instead he considered each situation from the standpoint of the bonds necessary for learning the particular item. Thorndike's method of teaching consisted of determining what elementary bonds or connectives involved what particular mental functions; the teaching of arithmetic became "in large measure a problem of the choice of the bonds to be formed and of the discovery of the best order in which to form them and the best means of forming each in that order."[2] After making this statement, Thorndike presented recipes for classroom practice in which relationship to mathematics seemed purely coincidental, as for example:

In the case of adding and subtracting fractions, certain specific bonds—between the situation of halves and thirds to be added and the responses of thinking of the numbers as equal to so many sixths, between the situation thirds and fourths to be added and thinking of them as so many twelfths, between fourths and eights to be added and thinking of them as eighths, and the like—should be formed *separately*. The general rule of thinking of fractions as their equivalents with some convenient denominator should come as an organization and extension of such *special habits* not as an edict from the textbook or teacher.[3]

Here Thorndike suggested that specific bonds should be developed through practice, and that the children should then generalize these specific reactions to get general principles. Throndike did the world of mathematics education a great service by debunking faculty psychology, and his objections to such unrealistic problems as finding the perimeter of $\frac{1}{6}$ of a pie $10\frac{1}{2}$ miles in diameter are certainly

[2] Thorndike, *The Psychology of Arithmetic*, p. 70.
[3] Thorndike, p. 78, italics added.

well taken. However, Thorndike seems to proceed from these conclusions to the position that computation is the most important outcome of the teaching of arithmetic, and that reasoning should be an incidental by-product of arithmetic rather than a goal in itself. Similarly, mathematical principles in general would come as incidental byproducts. If Thorndike's pronouncements had not come so near the beginning of an era in which it is easy and cheap to construct a machine that can compute far more efficiently than any man, they probably would have had an even more lasting effect upon the teaching of mathematics and arithmetic in this country.

Thorndike's experiments and resulting psychology of teaching arithmetic and mathematics seem to have had considerable effect upon the textbooks of the time and presumably upon teaching throughout the country. Besides stimulating adherence to his basic psychological principles, Thorndike's work encourages the idea of teaching only what might be immediately useful, because of the doubt that any transfer of training could occur between what was not clearly useful and other situations that would arise in the real world. In an article in the *Elementary School Journal* in 1918, Katherine McLaughlin reviewed then recent arithmetic textbooks; her criteria were the social nature of the problems and the application of Thorndike's psychology. Most of the textbooks reviewed seem to have been making a real attempt to conform to these criteria. She found that *Everyday Arithmetic*, by Hoyt and Peet, was blazing "the trail of the new arithmetic."[4]

It is fair to say that Thorndike's psychology dominated psychological thought for the first half of this century. There have been many variations on it, but the stimulus-response, bond approach to learning is still an important and respected point of view. Three of the important modern psychologists who have espoused a theory based on Thorndike's beliefs are Edwin R. Guthrie, Clark L. Hull, and B. F. Skinner.[5]

In summary of Guthrie's point of view, the stimulus and response ought to occur simultaneously. That is, a combination of stimuli that is accompanied by a movement will tend to be followed by that movement when the combination recurs. The reward, according to this theory, keeps the subject from *unlearning;* thus, if there is no interference (such as might occur if similar stimuli were encountered, for example), practice would not really be necessary. Of course, in everyday life there are so many stimuli that both practice and reward are neces-

[4] McLaughlin, *Elementary School Journal*, 1918, p. 545.
[5] In a work such as this, it is possible only to summarize briefly the work of these men. For a more complete discussion of these topics, the reader should consult a standard work on learning theory such as Hilgard, Ernest R., *Theories of Learning*, second edition, Appleton-Century-Crofts, Inc., New York, 1956, pp. 1–185.

sary for avoidance of unlearning. Guthrie also suggested that it was possible to replace one stimulus (or response) by a similar one and still maintain the bond, a sort of associative shifting.

Hull, on the other hand, centered the essence of learning on what happened between the stimulus and response. His system was carefully worked out in detail, with a sort of axiomatic approach stating a great number of postulates and corollaries. Because of this detailed completeness of his system, errors of incompleteness and inconsistency may easily be found. Although Hulls' mechanistic approach to psychology was of considerable importance between 1930 and 1950, his major contribution was probably the working out in great detail of the quantitative, empirical aspects of his theory. This effort has engendered much experimentation and has encouraged other theorists to create truly systematic and quantitative psychological systems.

Skinner's work with teaching machines pursuant to a stimulus-response psychology is well known, especially in the area of mathematics where much of his work with human beings has been done. He emphasizes that response reinforcement is equivalent to need reduction. In this sense, getting the right answer (and knowing about it) can be thought of as a reward (or reinforcement), and the quicker the reward is forthcoming, the better. Therefore, a teaching machine that gives immediate reinforcement is an ideal method of teaching. Skinner contends that it is possible to get higher and higher orders of conditioning in which body needs are gradually replaced by such things as curiosity. In Skinner's theory of operant conditioning, stimulus follows response—that is, the act of getting the right answer is a stimulus that, in turn, produces a new response, which is a new stimulus, and so on. If it is possible to avoid throwing a wrong answer into the sequence, then it is possible to continue to learn on a higher level. Thus, programming (or teaching) becomes a matter of continuously asking questions that the learner can answer correctly.

Skinner has been very effective in working with pigeons. He is one of the few psychologists who can train a pigeon in front of an audience, using and confirming his basic premises with a certainty of rapid success. He has also been quite effective in training people to react in the "right" way. However, many educators have grave philosophical questions concerning whether people ought to be taught "correct" behavior in the same manner as pigeons.

Edward C. Tolman put forth a theory (or several theories, since his point of view changed as he acquired more information) that might be described as somewhere between Thorndike and others and gestalt psychology. This theory is behavioristic in that it rejects introspection as a method and concentrates on overt behavior. However, it holds that behavior is directed toward a goal and that the particular *movements* in reaching the goal are less important than the general desire to get there. Some experimental evidence (for instance, that mice will *swim* a maze after learning to walk through it) shows that the Tolman theory is correct for mice as well as for men. This theory suggests that the learner does not have to be pushed and prodded through each step of the learning process, and he is learning general meanings rather than specific movements; therefore, he can be taught rather than trained. In a sense, the learner is understanding the territory—reading a map, as it were—and for this reason the theory is sometimes referred to as "sign learning." Although Tolman pointed out many difficulties in the stimulus-response theories, his own theories have not always provided ready solutions to the difficulties. In fact, his theories have remained just a little vague and quite flexible, making for some difficulty in testing and revising them. This difficulty, however, does not mean that his theories are either useless or incorrect.

Gestalt psychology is generally said to have started with Max Wertheimer, although many of the main ideas involved in it were prevalent prior to Wertheimer's work. In essence, gestalt psychology views people as tending to organize data and to look for patterns. Insight is crucial to this theory; helping the learner to acquire insights and look for general principles is more important than leading him through the memorization of apparently unrelated facts. Although some time elapsed between the development of gestalt psychology in Germany and its acceptance in this country, many mathematics educators believe that it is a far more appropriate theory for the human learning of mathematics than are the stimulus-response theories.

Another result of psychological experimentation that affected the schools and the teaching of mathematics was the advent of intelligence tests. Between 1905 and 1911 Binet and Simon produced several such tests, which were quickly revised and translated for use in this country. Although there had been suspicion prior to 1905 that differences existed in the intellectual capacities of children of a given age, the magnitude of those differences was not recognized until a reasonably standard measure for intelligence became available. The establishment of such a measure turned attention increasingly to the need for making some provision for exceptional children at both the lower and upper ends of the intelligence scale.

The new information gained from intelligence tests, combined with rapid growth of the school population, had considerable effect on how certain subjects were taught and on *what* subjects were taught. For an index of the increase in the school population, we may note that in 1890 fewer than 300,000 pupils attended high schools in this country (about one-third of these attended private schools); by 1920, almost 2.5 million students attended high schools in this country (with about one-tenth of these in private schools); and by 1941 nearly seven million students were enrolled in the high schools (still with about one-tenth of them in private schools). This growth was caused at least partially by economic situations and the resulting compulsory school and child labor laws. In any case, the number of students in the high schools increased rapidly at the very time when educators were becoming aware of vast differences in ability among children and were losing faith in the mental-discipline approach to education. Consequently, a great deal more emphasis was placed on the aspects of mathematics that were immediately and obviously practical and useful, and mathematics educators found themselves in the position of having to defend the very idea of teaching mathematics at all except in so-called practical contexts, such as keeping store, paying taxes, mortgaging a house, and so on. In this way the question of *how* to teach mathematics seemed to be going, almost by default, to the psychologists like Thorndike and to philosophers of the progressive movement. Although gestalt psychology was becoming popular in this country in the middle and late 1920s and seemed particularly adaptable to the teaching of mathematics, the other factors mentioned above prevented much application of this psychology to the teaching of mathematics until after the Second World War. Since mathematics is primarily a structure of relationships and not a set of isolated facts, gestalt psychology, which emphasizes the study of the whole and looks for patterns or configurations, certainly seems far more appropriate to the study of mathematics than does a stimulus-response or bond theory in which the isolated facts become of paramount importance.

One theme common to the various psychologies of learnings as applied to the teaching of mathematics concerns transfer of training. Although Thorndike's work was originally interpreted as doing away with the idea of transfer of training, many scholars felt that his position was being overstated. Charles H. Judd was one of the first psychologists to produce evidence that transfer of training could occur under proper circumstances. His contention was that knowledge of a general principle would facilitate transfer. Although his original experiment was not well controlled, it strongly suggested that if children learned a general principle, they would indeed transfer learning gained in one situation to a similar but not identical situation that involved the same general principle. In many respects, Judd's contention resembles that of the gestaltists; it emphasizes general principles and holds that reorganization of the experiences of the individual over a long period of time is important to an understanding of a whole situation. In support of this contention, experiments have shown that drill spaced over long periods of time is more effective than drill concentrated into a small period of time.

In more recent and better controlled experiments, George Katona has carried on the work begun by Judd. He has shown that transfer of training does occur when a method of teaching that promotes understanding is used; a group of children who were taught through the understanding of a general principle performed better with both old and new tasks then did a control group and a group taught by memorization. One of the interesting results of Katona's work was that he found that some children actually demonstrated more than 100% transfer of training. After four weeks, such an individual might achieve about the same results, with a practice task as he had when he learned it, but with a new task he would actually perform better than with the old practice task. Of course, this result is completely inconsistent with any theory of "identical elements," such as Thorndike proposed, since the new task could hardly have more identical elements with the old task than the old task had with itself.

In the *Twenty-First Yearbook* of the NCTM, an excellent article on transfer of training by Myron F. Rosskopf outlines a program that will develop transfer of training effectively. The following steps are suggested: (1) teaching for understanding through discovery and exploration (by the pupil) with no immediate attempt to verbalize the concept; (2) after understanding is achieved, enough practice over a period of time for pupils to reorganize their experiences in light of the basic concept—including, if the concept is important enough in larger problems that will be met regularly thereafter, a stimulus-response type of practice; (3) for those students going on in mathematics, verbalization of the basic principle. For general education courses in mathematics that are not intended for the students who expect to specialize in mathematics, Rosskopf recommends the discovery and exploration of a general principle through many examples and the application of the nonverbalized concept to new problems. Although he does not object to the verbal statement of the principle, he is quite strongly opposed to the requirement of memorizing the basic principle especially when no attempt has first been made to acquire understanding.

As more evidence regarding transfer has been gathered, more complex theories have been developed to describe it. C. E. Osgood, for example, proposed a rather complicated pattern of transfer which allows for both positive and negative transfer. The negative transfer involves what we might call "unlearning." Changes in similarity of stimuli and in similarity of response change the amount (and direction) of transfer, according to Osgood's model.

No commentary on either the history or the psychology of the teaching of mathematics would be complete without some specific mention of problem solving. It is possible to acquire a great deal of information about mathematics and still to have very little idea of how to use it to solve a particular problem; and yet there is some question as to how much all of the knowledge of mathematics is worth without the ability to apply it to problems. Probably the educational movement that has problem solving as its most central theme is the progressive movement. John Dewey, generally considered the founder of the progressive school of education, analyzed reflective thinking in much the same way that most mathematics educators analyze problem solving. Dewey recommended the following five steps in reflective thinking: (1) some inhibition of direct action to produce conscious awareness of a situation that allows for several courses of action; (2) intellectualization of the situation to define the problem; (3) identification of several hypotheses and collection of factual material in the light of these; (4) use of the reason to elaborate each hypothesis and a test of each; (5) action on the basis of the hypothesis chosen in step 4, providing the final test.[6] These steps resemble the terms in which mathematicians and psychologists discuss problem solving. The predilection for problem solving is represented in the report of the Progressive Education Association Committee on the Function of Mathematics in General Education, the last major contribution made to mathematics education by the PEA before it went out of existence.

Mathematics educators usually include facets such as the following in their definition of a problem: (1) an individual's unrealized goal which may be indicated by a vague uneasiness or a specific verbalized question (for instance, "for what value of $x$ is it true that $3x - 7 = 12$?"); (2) some form of blocking that prevents the individual from reaching his goal; (3) consideration by the individual of ways of avoiding the blocking and his trial of certain procedures.[7] It is important to notice that in this definition a problem does not exist without a person. A given question may not be a problem for one person because he knows the answer (such as $6\frac{1}{3}$ for the foregoing question) with almost no thought; it may not be a problem for another person because he has

[6] John Dewey, *How We Think*, pp. 107–116.
[7] See Henderson, Pingry, and the remainder of the *Twenty-First Yearbook* of the NCTM.

no idea of how to go about solving it and therefore cannot consider possible ways of arriving at a solution. By this definition of a problem, its solution should not be "second nature" to its solver, nor should it be impossible for the potential solver.

Once some acceptable definition of "problem" has been established (if the one cited does not appeal to the reader, he can find many others simply by looking through the literature), the question of solving problems becomes of particular importance. If we are limiting our-selves to a discussion of mathematical problems, we may find the best available material on problem solving in the writings of George Polya, professor emiritus of mathematics at Stanford University. Polya's *How to Solve It* was first published in 1945 and is available in paperback form. It is worthy of a place in the library of any teacher of mathematics. Polya believes that to solve a problem is to make a discovery; although the greater the problem, the greater the discover, there is a grain of discovery in the solution of any problem. He feels the triumph of discovery—the enjoyment that comes with the solving of a problem—is important and should not be denied to students of mathematics.

Polya makes many suggestions as to how to go about solving prob-lems and presents many specific examples of problem solving in *How to Solve It.* Some of his hints include the following: similar problems that have already been solved (or are easily solved) can often be found and used to help suggest a solution; the problem may be restated so as to lend itself to easier solution; the problem can actually be changed to a different problem that is easier to solve, perhaps by introduction of some auxiliary element that would be of help, or by use of only part of the given data to see how far toward determining the solution they would take a pupil, or by finding data that would allow him to solve the problem and relate it to the given data, but he must make sure he is not overlooking pertinent data and essential notions in the given problem; when a pupil does solve a problem, he should consider how that problem can be generalized and go back to consider how the prob-lem was solved.

## Summary

The history of mathematics education in this country has been marked by radical changes from its very beginning. In some places and at some times mathematics (including arithmetic) was not taught at all. On some occasions mathematics was taught because it was practical and necessary for life, and sometimes it was taught solely as a method to train the mind. Usually mathematics was taught in such a way as to encourage memorization rather than to bring about understanding. The most notable exceptions to this teaching philosophy were represented by the wide circulation of the Colburn arithmetic and algebra texts in the nineteenth century, and by the efforts of many teachers in the twentieth century to teach for understanding rather than memorization.

Many recommendations have been made to improve the teaching of mathematics in this country over the years. Some of these, notably the recommendations of the Committee of Ten and the 1923 Report, had considerable effect, but most committees did not really have the power or financial resources to assure a wide influence.

Experimental psychology significantly influenced the teaching of mathematics during this century. First, as the century opened, the theory that the mind should be trained in the same way as a muscle is trained by more and harder exercise, was discredited through the work of Thorndike and others. The question of transfer of training then became an important issue, and Thorndike's theory of "identical elements" came into direct conflict with the theory of "understanding a general principle" held by Judd and others. As more evidence accumulated, Thorndike's "identical elements" seem to have become more general so as to include even general principles; and at the same time, it has been seen that transfer of learning sometimes occurs when there is no understanding of a general principle. The strict stimulus-response (or bond) theory of learning proposed by Thorndike, especially in his early work, can also be modified rather easily to include the possibility that a particular stimulus can lead to the recollection of a general principle, and that the general principle can lead to particular activity by the individual. From all this we can conclude that the differences among the various schools of psychology are, perhaps, of more historical interest than practical interest at this time. It is undeniable that Thorndike's bond-theory approach had a large effect (and generally thought to be a poor one by contemporary mathematics educators) on the teaching of mathematics, but at present even the most hardened advocates of teaching machines, programmed learning, and other stimulus-response teaching programs say that they are trying to teach for understanding as well as mechanical facility.

We note with a certain amount of sadness that the great steps in teaching of mathematics seem, like so many other advances, to come only during times of national emergency. It is hard to accept the belief that man is constituted to find the most value in those things that help him to destroy his fellow man—and yet, if we study history, we see that Archimedes was thought by his contemporaries to be a great man largely because he could invent more effective war machines, just as mathematics was thought to be important in this century because it was believed necessary to the winning of the Second World War and later the Cold War.

## Questions for Further Thought and Study

1. Discuss the role of the College Entrance Examinations in United States education.

2. Discuss the pros and cons of a "national curriculum" in mathematics.

3. Compare the positions of Thorndike and Judd on the teaching of mathematics. What does each man visualize as the purpose of mathematics education, and how does the opinion of each compare with opinions held by advocates of "modern mathematics"?

4. Compare the two 1940 reports (PEA and the Joint Commission) as they relate to the recommendations in the Report of the Commission on Mathematics of the College Entrance Examination Board (1959) and the Committee of Ten Report (1894).

5. The dean of a well-known law school once said that the best law students were mathematics majors and that the second best were ancient language majors. Does this support the nineteenth-century "mental discipline" psychology, or is there some other reasonable explanation?

6. Study Colburn's and Thorndike's arithmetic texts and present specific examples showing how each carries out the underlying psychology (Pestalozzi's and Thorndike's, respectively).

7. For whom was the high school curriculum of 1890 designed? For whom should the high school curriculum be designed today? Do you believe that proper provisions are made in today's high school for students who are not college material? If so, explain how present curricula help such youngsters; if not, what should be done?

## REFERENCES

Bigge, Morris L., and Maurice P. Hunt. *Psychological Foundations of Education*, Harper and Bros., New York, 1962. A fairly recent and quite readable account of the various schools of psychology and their relation to learning theory.

Buswell, Guy Thomas, and Charles Hubbard Judd. *Summary of Educational Investigations Relating to Arithmetic*. The University of Chicago Press, Chicago, 1925. As the title implies, this is a summary of the early psychological experiments of such men as Thorndike and Judd. It includes such interesting investigations as J. M. Rice's 1902 report showing that children in schools requiring much time on arithmetic did not necessarily learn more arithmetic than those children in schools requiring far less time for arithmetic.

Cajori, Florian. "The Teaching and History of Mathematics in the United States," *U.S. Bureau of Education, Circular of Information*, no. 3, 1890. Probably the best history of mathematics education in this country up to the time of the Committee of Ten.

Class of 1938, University High School, Ohio State University. *Were We Guinea Pigs?* Holt, Rinehart and Winston, Inc., New York, 1938. Progressive education from the pupil's point of view. Chapters 6 and 7 are of particular interest to mathematics teachers.

Colburn, Warren. *Intellectual Arithmetic upon the Inductive Method of Instruction* (rev. ed.), Houghton Mifflin Co., The Riverside Press, Boston, Cambridge, 1884. This is one of several revised editions of Colburn's First Lessons originally published in 1821. The book is remarkably modern in many respects, including its emphasis on understanding the decimal notation and the use of that understanding to help in the understanding of operations and its emphasis on the discovery method of presentation.

Dewey, John. *How We Think*, D. C. Heath and Co., Boston, 1933. Dewey's admittedly idealized version of how people think is of particular interest to mathematics education because of the emphasis placed upon a problem-solving type of thinking by the leader of the progressive movement.

Eby, Frederich, and Charles Flinn Arrowood. *The Development of Modern Education*, Prentice-Hall, New Jersey, 1946. A comprehensive and scholarly discussion of the educational theories of Locke, Rousseau, Pestalozzi, Froebel, Hall, and Dewey from both a philosophical and psychological point of view with reference to their influence on American education.

Henderson and Pingry (see 21st Yearbook of NCTM).

Katona, George. *Organizing and Memorizing*, Columbia University Press, New York, 1940. An account of Katona's experiments demonstrating the importance of understanding (but not necessarily verbalizing) a general principle in order to achieve transfer of learning.

Judd, Charles H. "The Relation of Special Training to General Intelligence," *Educational Review*, **36,** 1908, 28–42. Here is the beginning of experimental evidence that transfer of training occurs when a general principle is taught. It is one of the first major objections to Thorndike's theory of identical elements.

McLaughlin, Katherine L. "Summary of Current Tendencies in Elementary School Mathematics as Shown by Recent Testbooks," *Elementary School Journal*, **18,** 1918, 543–541, A review of textbooks in light of Thorndike's psychology and the social nature of the problems.

McLellan, James A., and John Dewey. *The Psychology of Number*, D. Appleton and Co., New York, 1895. An early statement of the progressive point of view on the teaching of mathematics. There is a strong defense of teaching mathematics with an equally strong objection to the way it was then being taught. Number is thought of as measurement, and ratio plays an important role in the development.

McMurry, Charles H. *Special Method in Arithmetic,* The Macmillan Co., New York, 1906. The Herbartian point of view is presented both in theory and practice.

Power, Edward J. *Main Currents in the History of Education,* McGraw-Hill Book Co., New York, 1962. An excellent and readable history of education with interesting sections on early American education as well as more recent developments.

Rosskopf (see 21st Yearbook of NCTM).

Seeley, Levi. *Grubé's Method of Teaching Arithmetic,* E. L. Kellogg and Company, New York, 1888. Grubé, a follower of Pestalozzi, had a strong influence both in Germany and in this country. This book is an English summary of Grubé's method and could be described as a systematization of Pestalozzi's method.

Throndike, Edward Lee. *The New Methods in Arithmetic,* Rand McNally and Co., Chicago, 1921. Examples of "improvements" in teaching of arithmetic in light of the "new psychology" are taken from Thorndike's arithmetic series.

Thorndike, Edward Lee. *The Psychology of Arithmetic,* The Macmillan Co., New York, 1922. Thorndike's stimulus-response psychology (sometimes known as "bond" or "neoassociationist" psychology) is applied to arithmetic. Little consideration is given to any underlying mathematical principles.

Weiss, Thomas M., and Kenneth Hoover. *Scientific Foundations of Education,* William C. Brown Co., Dubuque, Iowa, 1960. Chapter 9 on the history of education is interesting and has many pertinent facts about early education in this country.

*Yearbooks of the National Council of Teachers of Mathematics*

Schorling, Raliegh (ed.). *A General Survey of Progress in the Last Twenty-Five Years,* First Yearbook of the NCTM, 1926. Chapter 1 (same title as yearbook) by David Eugene Smith is an excellent review of the teaching of mathematics in this country during the first quarter of the twentieth century written by the most prominent mathematics educator of the time. Chapter 2 is a reprint of E. H. Moore's presidential address. The other chapters, covering topics of interest to mathematics teachers, were contributed by other outstanding men in the field.

Clark, J. R. and W. D. Reeve (eds.). *Selected Topics in the Teaching of Mathematics,* Third Yearbook of the NCTM, 1928. In Chapter 1, C. H. Judd protests the classification of arithmetic as a tool subject, but the rest of the yearbook emphasizes the usefulness of mathematics and its relation to citizenship, life, art, thrift, measurement, etc. The yearbook, apparently indicating the state of mathematics education and the feeling of mathematics educators at the time, makes Judd's voice sound very much alone.

Reeve, W. D. (ed.). *Significant Changes and Trends in the Teaching of Mathematics Throughout the World Since 1910,* Fifth Yearbook of the NCTM, 1930. From the present day point of view, probably the most interesting part of this yearbook is Chapter 8, "A New Approach to Elementary

Geometry," by George Birkhoff and Ralph Beatley. This chapter gives the essence of what is now considered one of the most modern high school geometry textbooks. When Birkhoff and Beatley published their geometry commercially (in 1940) it was a financial failure, but when it was revised by SMSG about 20 years later is was quite successful.

Reeve, W. D. (ed.). *The Teaching of Algebra*, Seventh Yearbook of the NCTM, 1932. Emphasizes the function concept in line with the recommendations of the 1923 report.

Fehr, Howard F. (ed.). *The Learning of Mathematics, Its Theory and Practice*, Twenty-first Yearbook of the NCTM, 1953. An excellent collection of essays on the learning of mathematics in light of developments in experimental psychology. See, in particular, Chapter 7, "Transfer of Training," by Myron F. Rosskopf; Chapter 8, Problem Solving in Mathematics," by Kenneth Henderson and Robert Pingry; Chapter 3, "The Formation of Concepts," by Henry Van Engen; and the introductory chapter by Howard F. Fehr.

*Reports of Important Committees and Commissions* (for comments, see text)

*Report of the Committee of Ten on Secondary School Subjects*, American Book Co., New York, 1894.

Nightingale, A. F. "Report of the Committee on College Entrance Requirements," *Proceedings and Addresses of National Education Association*, 38th Annual Meeting, 1899, 648–651.

Reports of the several committees of the International Commission published as Bulletins by the U.S. Office of Education between 1911 and 1918.

Committee of Fifteen, "Provisional Report on Geometry Syllabus," *School Science and Mathematics*, **11,** 1911, 330.

National Committee on Mathematical Requirements. *The Reorganization of Mathematics in Secondary Education*, Houghton Mifflin Co., Boston, 1923.

Commission on Secondary School Curriculum of the Progressive Education Association. *Mathematics in General Education: Report of the Committee on the Function of Mathematics in General Education*, Appleton-Century-Crofts, New York, 1940.

Joint Commission of the Mathematical Association of America, and the National Council of Teachers of Mathematics. *The Place of Mathematics in Secondary Education*, Fifteenth Yearbook of NCTM, 1940.

Commission on Post-War Plans. Report in *Mathematics Teacher*, **37,** (1944) 262–232; **38,** (1945) 195–221; **40,** (1947) 315–339.

CHAPTER

2

# MODERN MATHEMATICS

During the early 1960s, the term "modern mathematics" was so popular that it became an acceptable part of common discourse. Newspapers have been constantly printing articles on the "new math," mentioning schools that were (or were not) teaching the "new mathematics," listing some of the words of the "new math," and generally cloaking recent developments in the teaching of mathematics with an aura of mysticism.

Many citizens consider modern mathematics (and similar modern programs in the physical sciences) to be the American answer to Sputnik. In actual fact, as described in Chapter I, there has been a continuing development of the mathematics program in secondary schools over many years; on numerous occasions recommendations have been made for the improvement of the teaching of mathematics; and many of these proposals have changed the teaching in the schools. Even such terms as "new mathematics" or "new arithmetic" are not new, since several previous developments were characterized in much the same way; for example, during the 1920s arithmetic texts using Thorndike's methods were called "new arithmetics."

### What is Modern Mathematics?

Any book that discusses the teaching of mathematics in the schools of this country during the latter half of the twentieth century must con-

29

front the question, "what is modern mathematics?" Many people who hold forth most vocally on the topic of modern mathematics seem to have no clear concept of precisely what it is. One person can defend modern mathematics vehemently while another attacks it with equal vehemence, and when the two discuss their respective ideas of how mathematics should be taught and what is important for pupils to learn in mathematics, they may find that they really agree on basic principles and differ chiefly in terminology. It seems ironic that although most modern mathematics programs emphasize precision of vocabulary and clarity of word meaning, the term "modern mathematics" itself is ambiguous.

Well, then, what *is* modern mathematics? One not completely facetious answer to this question is: modern mathematics is that mathematics which is modern. At first glance this answer seems to tell us very little. It is certainly not a satisfactory answer to the question. However, this answer does suggest a fact that is of importance in replying to the question. Many adults have a vague impression that all of the mathematics existing in the world was invented several thousand years ago. The ancient Greeks created geometry at least 2000 years ago; the Arabs (or somebody) created algebra at some unknown time in the past—at least 1,400 years ago. Those who are somewhat more mathematically sophisticated may feel that the last bit of creative mathematics came from Sir Isaac Newton (calculus) about 300 years ago. Very few people in this country are aware that creative mathematics, rather than ending at some time in the distant past, has been constantly advancing and could be said to be in its golden age at present. It has been reliably estimated that more mathematics, and more significant mathematics, has been created in the twentieth century than in all history prior to 1900.

### Acceleration

Many entire new branches of mathematics and major applications of mathematics have been created or largely developed during this century. Just a few of these are linear programming, topology, set theory, functional analysis, modern symbolic logic, various algebras, measure theory, game theory, quality control, and work with computing machines. Such new developments in mathematics have many implications for the teaching of mathematics in the schools. First, the sheer quantity of new mathematics that is being created poses a problem for those who wish to become mathematicians. Because so great an amount of knowledge is now available in mathematics, it is clearly impossible for anyone to know all of it or even any large portion of it.

Before a student can undertake original research in mathematics, he must first learn much that is common mathematical knowledge and then specialize for several years in one particular branch of mathematics. Since most mathematicians do their most significant research while they are still relatively young, many before they are 30, there is strong reason to believe that saving time during the early stages of a potential mathematician's training will help the trainee to produce a greater quantity of creative work. Thus, one effect that the new developments in mathematics are having on school programs is the speeding up of instruction through removal of topics that seem to be of little importance in mathematics now (some of the social arithmetic in junior high school, long calculations with logarithms that can be more efficiently handled in computers, and a full semester of solid geometry, to name but a few), through introduction of some topics at an earlier age (for instance, algebra and geometry in the elementary schools) and through improvements in the organization of a topic to make the presentation quicker and more comprehensible to the pupil (for example, the circular function approach to trigonometry rather than the right-triangle approach).

However, the vast majority of pupils in our schools are not going to be mathematicians. Is it fair to subject all pupils to an accelerated mathematics program just for the benefit of the few who will go on in mathematics? The answer would have to be no, solely in terms of the small minority who will some day be research mathematicians, but our entire society is becoming more mathematical every day. Many fields of endeavor that even recently did not require any mathematical training, or perhaps only the bare essentials of arithmetic and elementary algebra, now place a high priority on a good background in mathematics. For example, it was common for a high school pupil who was interested in science but could not understand mathematics to go into biology; now it is common to require quite a bit of physics and chemistry for an advanced degree in biology, and the physics and chemistry courses are requiring more and more mathematics. Furthermore, an entire new branch of biology (biometrics) in which mathematics plays a central role has recently achieved some prominence. For advancement in the social sciences, a student needed little or no mathematics a few years ago, and now he needs not only statistics but an elementary knowledge of advanced topics of mathematics including calculus, topology, and linear programming to understand the theory of games and other related developments in the social sciences.

Mathematics occupies a much more important place today in many different occupations including medicine, law, teaching, administration, social sciences, and the natural sciences. Before the Second World War, it would have been impossible to predict so wide a use of mathematics in so many different vocations. Although it is impossible today to predict how mathematics will be used and in what fields a quarter century hence, we can be reasonably certain that there will be an even wider use of mathematics by most people, and that those people who do not have any formal training in mathematics beyond the study of arithmetic and simple algebra will have more difficulty in finding jobs than will those who have a substantial background in mathematics. Thus, since it will be desirable for many people to get a substantial exposure to mathematics and also to be better educated in their own fields, the speeding up of mathematics courses offers benefits to the majority of the pupils in our schools and to society as a whole.

The earlier study of various topics in mathematics is an important part of most of the new mathematics programs, but it is neither a particularly new development nor the most important aspect of recent developments in teaching of mathematics. As Chapter 1 pointed out, the algebra that is presently taught in the ninth grade was thought to be a proper subject for college study only about 140 years ago, and geometry was not required for college admission until even later.[1] In fact, there has been a general "moving down" of topics, not only in mathematics, but in many other school subjects throughout the history of education in our country.

### Reorganization and Structure

At least as significant as the earlier introduction of various topics in mathematics are the changing of the topics that are taught and the reorganization of these topics along more logical lines. One of the significant developments in research mathematics in the past century has been greater stress on the study of mathematical structure and the role of axioms and definitions. This has been accompanied by more use of logic and more emphasis on the foundations of mathematics and the interrelations between various branches of mathematics. These changes have had an influence on the teaching of mathematics in both the secondary and the elementary schools since 1955. It is not uncommon today to find elementary school pupils searching for properties inherent to all numbers in their number system. For example, a pupil might note that it does not make any difference in which order he adds two numbers (the commutative law for addition), and at a later time he might

---

[1] This is not an entirely fair argument, because it was not uncommon to find very young children (twelve or thirteen years old) in college 140 years ago. But the general point is still correct.

discover that the distributive law for multiplication over addition apparently applies (for example, $3 \cdot (5 + 8) = 3 \cdot 5 + 3 \cdot 8$) to all the numbers in his number system. After having worked with these and other basic properties, the pupil would begin to use them (which he would take as axioms, or assumptions about his system) to prove in an informal way that other properties also belong to the number system. Thus, the pupil would begin to think of arithmetic and algebra as a basic underlying mathematical structure rather than as a series of unrelated tricks he is expected to memorize and become adept at using. In a modern school mathematics class the pupil looks for general principles and uses them rather than looking for (or being shown) a trick to solve a particular type of exercise which he then practices until he has thoroughly memorized it or perhaps has been mesmerized by it.

### New Topics and Sets

In addition to the new emphasis on structure, contemporary mathematics courses contain many new topics. Some of the more important topics are probability and statistical inference, algebraic inequalities, linear algebra, vectors, and the use of set language. These topics and others will be discussed more fully in later chapters, but a brief comment about sets, set theory, and set language is probably appropriate at this time. Set theory was created during the latter half of the nineteenth century and was developed on a rigorous basis in this century. It is possible to base essentially all of mathematics, from arithmetic to the most advanced topics, on set theory. Thus, in a real sense, set theory is a unifying subject for mathematics. However, set theory is not a subject that is appropriate for secondary school pupils, much less elementary school pupils. Many a college student has floundered on a course called "naive set theory," and graduate students do not find the rigorous study of set theory an easy matter. The "set theory" that is sometimes referred to in school mathematics is merely some of the simpler language and operations of sets applied to elementary mathematics. There is nothing particularly magical about this language, and it would be perfectly possible to create an excellent modern program in mathematics without ever mentioning the word "set." It would be equally possible to use the terminology of sets in creating a very bad program in mathematics.

Although many people have come to believe that "sets" and "modern mathematics" are synonymous, they are quite independent of each other. However, it is so easy to make statements in arithmetic, algebra, geometry, and other branches of mathematics using the language of sets that set language has the advantage of being both a convenience and a unifying influence on school mathematics. Therefore, it is likely that most school textbooks published in the near future will use the language of sets at least to some extent, but their use of that language will not of itself make them modern nor would the lack of such language necessarily make the books not "modern."

## Discovery

Another characteristic of mathematics programs today is emphasis on method. Many new methods are being tried in the teaching of various subjects. These include such widely varied procedures as team teaching and teaching machines and substantial use of visual aids like overhead projectors, television, movies, film strips, and plastic overlays in textbooks.

Appropriate teaching aids are being used by excellent teachers throughout the country. For example, tongue depressors or similar objects in counting are used. Groups of ten such objects are held together with rubber bands to help children understand the base-ten numeration system. An adding machine in the classroom is another effective method of helping children (perhaps at a higher level) to understand the base-ten system. The number line is being used commonly, not only in the secondary schools but even in the early elementary grades. Although teaching aids have been used for many years—in fact, many centuries—the improvements in them in recent years have been significant and have made it possible for good teachers to do an even more effective job of teaching than they did before. The topic of teaching aids will be discussed further in the next chapter and throughout the book.

Probably the most important improvement in method associated with modern mathematics is the discovery method. Actually, a careful reading of Plato will show that Socrates regularly used a discovery method of teaching, so it is hardly appropriate to call the discovery method, itself, modern; but such methods are uniquely appropriate to the teaching of modern mathematics, and have been closely associated with many of the programs described as modern. In many respects, the use of new methods probably is the most important single feature of modern mathematics programs.

Discovery is particularly appropriate to modern mathematics because of the great emphasis on structure and logic in the new programs. It is almost impossible for a pupil to discover, even with expert guidance, all of the unrelated tricks that are so common in the more traditional textbooks. However, with careful and logical development in sequence and timing of questions, it is possible to lead a pupil to discover many facts of mathematics. Furthermore, if the previous development has been good enough, it is possible that even an average pupil will be able to create a proof (on as informal a level as is appropriate for him) of a fact after he has discovered it—or at least to follow somebody else's proof and understand it well enough to make it his own.

Even before the advent of modern mathematics, discovery was used by many fine teachers. The experiments of Judd and Katona, mentioned in Chapter 4, support the contention that when an individual really understands a basic underlying principle, he can use that principle not only in the original task but in other tasks that are somewhat different. We have all had the experience of discovering some fact for ourselves with the accompanying thrill and feeling that here is something that we understand and will always be able to discover again, since it is really almost part of us. A basic human drive seems to be to "want to do it myself" whenever possible; when we do something ourselves, we tend to understand it better and to be able to use the experience more intelligently than we would if we had just been told about it. Hence, there is good reason to believe that when a student discovers a basic principle himself, he understands it better, will remember it longer, and will be able to use it more effectively. Therefore, the procedure of asking many appropriate questions and thus leading a pupil to make his own generalizations has become an important part of most of the good new mathematics programs.

In summary, as the words "modern mathematics" are applied to school mathematics programs, they connote the following elements: (1) a revision of subject matter both in topics covered and in emphasis placed on general structure rather than specific tricks; (2) a simple shifting of subject matter to lower grades so that pupils may learn many things in mathematics earlier than they used to; and (3) a change in method that places more emphasis upon student thought and discovery and less reliance on teacher instruction and student memorization. As we saw in Chapter 1, point (2) is a logical continuation of a process that has been going on in mathematics for many years, and point (3) was recommended and used in the Colburn texts of the 1820s as well as having been the method of Socrates. Therefore, in many respects, point (1) is the only really new aspect of modern mathematics, but the others are certainly an integral part of the improvements and changes that have been recommended.

## Reports Pertaining to Modern Mathematics

During the past decade several significant reports have affected the mathematics curriculum here and abroad. As a rule, these reports did not produce specific text material but stated basic principles and indicated rather generally how the principles might be carried out in practice.

## The Commission on Mathematics of the College Entrance Examination Board

The influence of the College Entrance Examination Board has steadily increased since its creation more than sixty years ago. Many people have feared that the board, through its tests, would actually determine the curriculum for the secondary schools, and in actual fact many secondary schools, especially in the East, have put a fair amount of emphasis on preparation for College Entrance Examinations, in spite of evidence that the only way to get ready for the examinations is to have a sound educational background. Although the board has generally tried to avoid any hint that it might be seeking to set curricula, the mathematics examiners of the CEEB (professors and teachers who make up the examinations) have been concerned over whether the students they were testing had been prepared in curricula appropriate for the second half of the twentieth century. The examiners knew that changes were being made by some teachers in secondary schools and that several colleges were changing their curricula. In light of these and other changes occurring in mathematics and society generally, the examiners thought that perhaps some fairly basic revisions in the mathematics curriculum in the secondary schools were needed.

The examiners referred this problem to the board's Committee on Examinations, which recommended to the board that it establish a commission to study the existing secondary school mathematics curriculum, and make recommendations for its improvement. Because of the nature of its parent body, the Commission on Mathematics of the CEEB considered primarily the college preparatory mathematics curriculum for grades nine through twelve. However, the report affected not only those grades but higher and lower levels and has even had some effect on the curriculum for the noncollege-bound youngster.

The commission was created in 1955 and issued preliminary reports on various subjects before 1959, when it made its major report. The commission was the first body of national stature to propose and defend substantial changes in the mathematics curriculum of the secondary schools along lines now considered to be modern mathematics. The commission, in defending its case, pointed to the drastic changes that were (and are) occurring in mathematics and society and clarified the point that the crisis in mathematics education was not a result of our competition with the Soviet Union but rather a result of the incredible acceleration of our movement into new technology and the augmented need for people who are well prepared in mathematics and the sciences generally.

The major report of the commission was published in two parts: first, the *Report* stating the case for reorganization of school mathematics, presenting a proposed program for grades nine through twelve (plus a short section on prerequisite mathematics), and stressing the necessity for more training for most mathematics teachers in order to carry out the proposed program; second, the *Appendices*, a much longer document written for mathematics teachers, offering materials on sets, relations, irrational numbers, quadratic and linear functions, complex numbers, permutations, a new approach to geometry including coordinate geometry and three-dimensional geometry, and the circular function approach to trigonometry. The materials in the *Appendices* are not intended as classroom teaching units, but they can be used by teachers to familiarize themselves with a new approach to many of the indicated topics. The *Appendices* set up a standard toward which textbook writers could aim and to which teachers of mathematics could look in evaluating new textbooks. While they were waiting for new textbooks, many capable teachers used units from the *Appendices* with a great deal of supplementary material to present modern mathematics to their classes.

Another important book published by the commission is *Introductory Probability and Statistical Inference* (revised preliminary edition). Since the commission suggested that one possible course for the twelfth grade would be probability and statistics but could not find a good high school text presenting these subjects at that time, the members delegated a writing group to produce such a book. This excellent book is now out of print since several textbooks that seem to do the job adequately have come on the market and the commission did not feel that it should be in competition with private book companies.

Although it was the smallest of the three major publications of the commission, the *Report* was undoubtedly the most important and influential. It is impossible to summarize all of the recommendations in a few pages, but the commission itself picked out the following nine points that contained the essence of the *Report* and printed them on its frontispiece:

1. Strong preparation, *both* in concepts *and* in skills, for college mathematics at the level of calculus and analytic geometry.

2. Understanding of the nature and role of deductive reasoning—in algebra, as well as in geometry.

3. Appreciation of mathematical structure ("patterns")—for example, properties of natural, rational, real, and complex numbers.

4. Judicious use of unifying ideas—sets, variables, functions, and relations.

5. Treatment of inequalities along with equations.

6. Incorporation with plane geometry of some coordinate geometry and essentials of solid geometry and space perception.

7. Introduction in grade eleven of fundamental trigonometry—centered on coordinates, vectors, and complex numbers.

8. Emphasis in grade twelve on elementary functions (polynomial, exponential, circular).

9. Recommendation of additional alternative units for grade twelve—*either* introductory probability with statistical applications *or* an introduction to modern algebra.

Although these recommendations were considered rather radical by some people at the time of their original publication, the recommendations of the commission could not now be described by an adjective more colorful than "moderate" in light of succeeding recommendations by others. Many commercial textbooks and virtually all the reports and "experimental programs" produced since the commission published its report have gone further in reorganization and introduction of new materials.

## Secondary-School Curriculum Committee of the National Council of Teachers of Mathematics

In the May 1959 issue of *The Mathematics Teacher* appeared the report of another committee advocating changes in the mathematics curriculum. This committee was created by the National Council of Teachers of Mathematics in 1958 to study the curriculum in this country and in other countries and to make recommendations regarding the mathematics program for all pupils in grades seven through twelve.

The report on European programs indicated that the schools in Europe seemed to be designed primarily for the intellectually elite, a situation that was beginning to cause difficulties because those schools were not producing enough well-trained people to carry on the technical developments of a modern civilization. The report also commented on the earlier specialization in European schools, the integrated courses in mathematics (arithmetic, algebra, and geometry taught for three to four years together), and the substantially more severe training and selection of teachers.

For the seventh and eighth grades, the committee suggested less emphasis on social arithmetic and rote drill, and more work with certain topics from algebra and geometry, and additional topics from arithmetic, such as prime numbers, factors, numeration systems, and properties of our number system.

Other topics recommended by the committee included statistics, probability, and linear algebra. As a general recommendation for teaching of mathematics at all levels, the committee urged more emphasis on concepts and general principles, and less emphasis on recall and skills. Another general recommendation regarding the method of teaching was encouragement of understanding and interest by use of the discovery method of teaching.

Topics that the committee suggested be woven in with the rest of the work (and not taught in isolated units) included sets and set language, inequalities along with equations, general principles (such as distributive law, etc.), logic, vectors, and the geometry of the sphere.

Between them, this committee report and the commission report made a strong plea for revision, modernization, and improvement of the secondary school mathematics curriculum; and the two reports still remain outstanding defenses of major changes in the teaching of mathematics in the schools.

Three pamphlets that also resulted from the work of the committee are: *A Guide to the Use and Procurement of Teaching Aids for Mathematics*, by Emil J. Berger and Donovan A. Johnson; *Mathematics Tests Available in the United States*, by Sheldon S. Myers; and *The Supervisor of Mathematics; His Role in the Improvement of Mathematics Instruction*, by Veryl Schult.

### The Revolution in School Mathematics

By 1960 the activity surrounding the school mathematics curriculum was so great that everybody in the country seemed to be aware that something was going on, but many people in important school positions were not precisely aware either of what modern mathematics was or why there was need for a change. During the fall of 1960, the National Council of Teachers of Mathematics sponsored a series of eight conferences on mathematics in various parts of the United States. The funds for these conferences came from the United States government through the National Science Foundation.

The main purpose of the conferences was to inform school administrators and mathematics supervisors. The conferences presented reasons for changing the curriculum, some insight into what the new programs were attempting to do, descriptions of specific programs, and methods of implementing new mathematics programs. There was ample free discussion. After the eight conferences were over, the presentations and discussions were collected, edited, and published under the title, *The Revolution in School Mathematics: A Challenge for Administrators and Teachers*, by the NCTM.

To some one interested in learning about the new mathematics programs quickly and relatively painlessly, this pamphlet could represent a worthwhile investment of time and energy. However, for people interested in getting a deeper insight into program changes and for teachers who are charged with the responsibility of making decisions regarding the new programs, deeper study is necessary, though even for this group, the *Revolution* is not a bad starting place, since it provides a substantial bibliography.

## O.E.E.C. Report and Synopsis

Meanwhile, European nations were showing considerable interest in the teaching of school mathematics, and the Organization for European Economic Cooperation through its Office for Scientific and Technical Personnel made a survey of the mathematics programs being used in the secondary schools of Europe. After the survey was completed, the O.E.E.C. sponsored a seminar on mathematics education at Royamount (near Paris) from November 23 to December 4, 1959. Each participating country sent three individuals to the conference: one secondary school mathematics teacher, one mathematics educator, and one mathematician. The proceedings of this seminar were later published under the title *New Thinking in School Mathematics* by the O.E.E.C.

This report makes clear that dissatisfaction abounded among the participants concerning the state of mathematics education in the free world. Undoubtedly the most extreme view was that presented by Jean Dieudonne in his now famous "Euclid must go!" speech.[2] Dieudonne suggested that everything interesting or important in Euclid could be taught to an adult in two or three hours and that the time spent on Euclid could more profitably be spent studying matrices, determinants, elementary calculus, complex numbers, polar coordinates, and graphs of functions given in parametric form. Although Dieudonne met a great deal of resistance to his ideas in the seminar, there was general agreement that considerable revision would have to be made in the mathematics curriculum in the secondary schools throughout Europe.

A major recommendation of the seminar was that a synopsis describing several ways in which the secondary school mathematics curriculum could be improved and modernized should be prepared and distributed to the member countries, as an aid in preparing textbooks and manuals.

[2] *New Thinking in School Mathematics*, p. 35 ff.

The O.E.E.C. brought together a group of mathematicians, mathematics educators, and teachers to work on this synopsis during the late summer of 1960. The group worked in Yugoslavia for about four weeks. The report suggested a program aimed at the intellectually gifted (probably about the upper 5%); the report was confined to the subjects of algebra, geometry, and statistics. Since European countries offer mathematics courses in a relatively decompartmentalized fashion, with arithmetic, algebra, and geometry taught together for several years, the organization of this material may be somewhat different from what an American reader would expect. It calls for algebra and geometry to be taught in two cycles: the first cycle would occur early in the education of the youngster and would be reasonably appropriate for a fairly large portion of the population, with the algebra including a considerable amount of work with arithmetic; the second cycle would be aimed at the more advanced and intellectually gifted students and would include a section on probability and statistics. Probably the most radical difference between the recommendations of this group and those of the various groups that have reported in this country is the far greater emphasis on vectors in both algebra and geometry apparent in the recommendations of the O.E.E.C. group. There are also many other differences including the general level toward which the material is directed and the organization of the subject matter.

### Cambridge Conference on School Mathematics

Probably the most radical proposal yet set forth came from the Cambridge Conference on School Mathematics in the report, *Goals for School Mathematics*.[3] At this conference, a group of 29 mathematicians expressed views that were admittedly both tentative and aimed at the future (perhaps thirty or forty years thence). At that time no serious consideration was given to how teachers could be trained to teach the suggested program, but there was a general recognition of the inadequacy of existing teacher training for the task of preparing teachers to educate on the basis of the program outlined in the report. The report of the Cambridge Conference was meant to stir discussion and point the way for developments in the fairly distant future. It has certainly served as the basis for much further discussion.

For elementary school pupils, the proposed program emphasizes the entire real number line (including the negative portion), order properties of the real numbers, functions, simple notions from set theory and

[3] Cambridge Conference on School Mathematics, *Goals for School Mathematics*, published for Educational Services Incorporated by Houghton Mifflin Co., Boston, 1963.

logic, informal algebra along with arithmetic, problem solving (through which a reasonable proficiency in both arithmetic and algebra would be developed), elementary probability and statistics, and much consideration of the relation between mathematics and the physical world. By the end of the twelfth year, the pupils would have studied good solid courses in calculus, linear algebra, and probability. The report suggests a "spiral approach" in which topics are constantly reintroduced, each time with more sophistication and more emphasis on the relationships between a particular topic and other topics in mathematics. In this way, the pupils would see both a good intuitive development of an advanced topic and a more rigorous development of an elementary topic at about the same time and would thus acquire a feeling both for the intuition and the rigor of mathematics. The members of the conference felt that seeing several approaches to the same topic might acquaint the pupils with the idea that mathematics is something that one does rather than something that one absorbs passively (or something that is done to one).

The Cambridge program is clearly ambitious, the very people who created it may have changed some of their ideas long before the program could be put into operation, but it does present some goals for which to aim and some ideas at which to shoot. The purpose of the report was to stir up discussion and make suggestions for the future. It has achieved both purposes.

### Experimental Secondary School Mathematics Programs

Every time a new textbook is produced, whether it is commercial or noncommercial, it is experimental to some extent. During the past ten years many sets of new text materials have been brought out by groups that presumably are not interested in making a profit but rather are only trying to make a contribution to the teaching of mathematics. Many of these have been supported by substantial grants from either the government or private foundations; others have depended largely on devotion of time and energy by dedicated individuals. If we used newness of program as a criteron, we would have to include some of the books from commercial publishers on any list of experimental programs. Even if the criterion were nonprofit publication, several of these same books would still be on the list! The programs about to be discussed include ones that are not primarily commercial and that have been important in the recent development of the teaching of mathematics in this country. For other lists of such experimental material, see *The Revolution in School Mathematics* (mentioned earlier), *An Anal-*

*ysis of New Mathematics Programs* (also published by the NCTM, 1963), and *Studies in Mathematics Education* (Scott, Foresman and Company, 1960).

## University of Illinois Committee on School Mathematics

In December of 1951, professors from the Colleges of Education, Engineering, and Liberal Arts and Sciences at the University of Illinois agreed to investigate the mathematics programs in the high schools; both content and method were to be considered in this investigation. They established the University of Illinois Committee on School Mathematics (UICSM), which has functioned under the direction of Dr. Max Beberman. Since 1956, the project has been supported largely by the Carnegie Corporation. It is interesting to note that this first really new mathematics program was being sponsored in part by the School of Engineering, since engineering schools are so often accused of being quite traditional in matters of this sort.

Professor Beberman and other members of the University of Illinois faculty, most notably Professor Herbert Vaughn of the mathematics department, have written and rewritten text materials for more than fifteen years and have carried on a continuing program of experimentation and reevaluation of these materials in classrooms throughout the country. The work of this group has been so careful and so good that some people in mathematics education feel that the UICSM has *thrown away* more good material than various other experimental groups have had time to create. UICSM materials were tried out for the first time on a broad basis in 1957. At that time twelve pilot schools cooperated in a program involving forty mathematics teachers and about 1700 pupils. Thereafter, the number of experimental schools and classes increased rapidly.

As well as being intellectually and pedagogically sound, the UICSM program has been carefully controlled. At first, the materials were available only to schools and teachers chosen by the staff of the UICSM. Teachers chosen to participate in the program were given special training in the use of the materials and were expected to help the Illinois group in evaluating the materials. Since 1958 the materials have been available to individuals who wished to purchase them, but the Illinois people have not encouraged teachers to use the materials in the classroom unless they first received special training from somebody who had used the materials previously.

In addition to text materials for grades nine through twelve, the UICSM has produced carefully written and detailed commentaries in the teachers' editions of the texts. Also, a Newsletter is published regularly to keep the commentaries current as the committee learns more through its continuing investigations.

Several of the more important aspects of mathematics teaching emphasized by the UICSM since its beginning are mathematical structure, consistency, careful use of language by textbook and teacher, and understanding of general principles through use of the discovery method of teaching. Some new content has been introduced into the program, much of the old content has been rearranged (or removed), and a great deal of work has been done with methods of teaching and teacher training.

As the materials now exist, it would be difficult to use them for a grade or two (say ninth and tenth grades) and then switch to another program; and it would be at least as difficult to switch into the Illinois material after several grades with some other program. Therefore, it is probably fair to say that this is, in effect, one big mathematics course (or textbook) for the entire senior high school program. There are eleven units for the four grades, nine through twelve, which can be completed by an average group of college-capable youngsters in about four years. However, several groups have started the materials as early as the seventh grade, and it has not been at all uncommon for groups to begin the material in the eighth grade. Furthermore, although the first four units are expected to constitute the first year's course (usually ninth grade), it would be perfectly possible to finish either more or less than this in a given year and then continue with the next unit the following year. Since the units are bound separately, it is relatively easy administratively to have groups stop at different places in the texts at the end of a school year. The UICSM materials have recently been turned over to a commercial publisher and are being published in four volumes.

## University of Maryland Mathematics Project

During the 1957–1958 school year, a seminar met weekly at the University of Maryland to discuss and prepare materials for use in junior high school mathematics courses. Units prepared by this group were taught in several schools and the reports were generally favorable. Then, during the following summer, the staff worked on the seventh-grade course in conjunction with a National Science Foundation Institute in which participants studied the materials and helped in the further preparation of the seventh-grade program. The participants in this institute also observed an experimental class of seventh-grade pupils.

During the following year, 1958–1959, the experimental materials were used by 43 teachers in 35 schools. The weekly seminar was continued, and the participants helped with the revision of the seventh-grade materials and also began work on eighth-grade materials to be used the next year. Experimental use of the materials continued to expand, and revisions in light of this experimental use were also continued. In response to a request of the school systems using the materials, the University of Maryland Mathematics Project (UMMaP) tested pupils who were studying traditional materials and also those who were studying UMMaP materials and found that the two groups did about equally well on traditional tests but that the UMMaP pupils did considerably better on tests designed to test the UMMaP materials. Furthermore, there was a great deal of enthusiasm, both on the part of the teachers and the pupils in the UMMaP project, for the new materials.

In these materials, mathematical structure is important, and careful use of language is stressed. There is little emphasis on the so-called social application problems previously found in many seventh- and eighth-grade books; in place of these there is more emphasis on number and numeration systems, logic, some algebra, and such other topics as simple trigonometry, irrational numbers, probability, and statistics.

Besides the other important results of this program, the organization of the writing group had considerable effect on planning of future programs. Here for the first time was a relatively large group of mathematicians (about five) and teachers (about forty) who had used their combined talents to plan and write actual text materials to be used in the classroom. Aided by experts in the fields of psychology and testing and the efforts of many practicing teachers, they evaluated, rewrote, reevaluated, and finally produced good seventh- and eighth-grade mathematics textbooks. This procedure is quite similar to that later employed by the School Mathematics Study Group on a much larger scale. Although the Illinois program had used some procedures similar to this, it had essentially one mathematician (Herbert Vaughn) doing most of the writing and one master teacher (Max Beberman), with many other people also helping. In the Maryland program, although there was a director, Dr. John R. Mayor, the ideas and writing were more of a joint project.

## School Mathematics Study Group

In the spring of 1958, the largest effort ever attempted to improve the school mathematics curriculum was begun. The president of the American Mathematical Society, after consulting with the presidents of the National Council of Teachers of Mathematics and the Mathematical Association of America appointed a small committee of mathematicians and educators to organize a group whose purpose would be to improve the teaching of mathematics in the schools. Professor Edward G. Begle of Yale University (subsequently at Stanford) was appointed director; an advisory committee was formed; the government, through the National Science Foundation, provided large sums of money; and the School Mathematics Study Group (SMSG) started to work.

The SMSG has produced a wide variety of materials, reports, and other publications. SMSG textbooks have been written by teams of mathematicians and teachers (usually, about seven or eight of each on a team) who worked during the summer. Texts were first used on an experimental basis in various sections of the country, and detailed comments were solicited from the teachers who used the material. During the following summer the material was rewritten in light of these comments. The rewrite team was generally comprised of members of the original team but might be smaller. Original work by the SMSG was in secondary school mathematics, but it now includes elementary school work. SMSG now has available at least two choices of textbooks for grades seven through ten, programmed materials that can be used in the ninth grade, materials that emphasize scientific applications for the three junior high school grades, several short texts (elementary functions, matrix algebra, and analytic geometry) for the twelfth grade, one eleventh-grade textbook, and an entire set of texts for the elementary school, kindergarten through grade six.

In the school texts, SMSG emphasizes mathematical structure, the real number system, careful use of language, discovery and experimentation on the part of the pupils, proof, and correct mathematics. Each textbook is accompanied by a teacher's commentary that makes suggestions on how the material can be taught and discusses the underlying mathematics involved. There are also some supplementary classroom materials available through the SMSG for use as separate units, as enrichment for brighter pupils, or as preparation for a specific SMSG course. The SMSG has published several monographs for enrichment of the secondary school program.

Besides the teacher's commentaries, other materials have been prepared for teachers in a series known as "Studies in Mathematics." Most of these were written by practicing mathematicians about subjects pertaining to the high school curriculum; they provide good background material in mathematics for the mathematics teacher.

SMSG has printed newsletters from time to time, assisted in the translation of texts into Spanish and other languages, produced a series of 30-minute films for in-service training of elementary school teachers, and supported several attempts to evaluate work in modern mathematics through widespread testing.

It is not the purpose of the SMSG to produce textbooks competitive with those published by private publishers but to provide concrete examples of good modern mathematics materials prepared for use in schools. As SMSG authorities say:

> These do not form an integrated program, and it is not intended that these texts be regarded as defining the only way of presenting good mathematics to students. They are intended to provide a source of suggestions for the authors of future classroom texts and they provide a stop gap for schools until similar texts become available through the usual channels.[4]

It can be assumed that in the near future the SMSG texts will go out of print as did the Commission's *Probability and Statistical Inference,* since many new textbooks at all levels have been and are being printed having the same general goals and philosophy as the SMSG. Meanwhile, the SMSG has been an invaluable source of ideas and materials for teachers, textbook writers, and others interested in the improvement of the teaching of mathematics. The SMSG has recently begun new programs which can be expected to contribute still more to the improvement of mathematics education.

## Other Programs and Projects

One of the most unusual and exciting of the experimental programs has been carried out at Minnesota under the direction of Paul Rosenbloom. The project, titled "Minnemath," has developed material for children in the early elementary grades and has also produced some material for the upper high school levels. This project combines mathematics with the physical sciences (in much the way that was proposed by the Cambridge Conference) and teaches the children some significant mathematics in a natural and appealing setting. The experiments carried on so far with children have been most encouraging. Although Professor Rosenbloom has moved to Teachers College, Columbia University, there is every reason to suppose that he and his staff will continue to produce interesting and stimulating materials.

Many other programs have been developed by other groups—each with its own particular viewpoint, each different from the others in some respects, but all with the goals of introducing new mathematics into the school curriculum and of improving the presentation to give

---

[4] SMSG Information Memorandum, September, 1963.

the pupil a better understanding of better mathematics. Probably the largest single attempt to evaluate the new materials has been carried on at the Minnesota National Laboratory formerly under Dr. Rosenbloom's direction. So far, most of the work of the Minnesota National Laboratory has tended to show ways of improving testing procedures but there is some evidence (of relatively low statistical significance) that the newer programs have some advantages over the more traditional mathematics programs.

### Experimental Elementary School Mathematics Programs

In American education, it has been customary for the teachers at any level to complain about the sort of education pupils were getting at the lower levels. Thus, college professors complain about the education in the high schools; high school teachers complain about the education in the junior high schools; junior high school teachers complain about the education in the elementary schools, elementary school teachers complain about what the parents do or do not do with the children; and the parents . . . .

Perhaps the most difficult transition is from elementary to secondary school. Most elementary school teachers are generalists—they are expected to teach all (or nearly all) subjects. It is fairly common to have an art supervisor and a physical education teacher to help with those aspects of the curriculum, and even a special music teacher is not unusual; but those elementary schools that have special teachers for mathematics and science and other academic subjects are few. The reason for this situation is the feeling that in elementary school some one person should have complete or almost complete responsibility for the child to give him the security of a sort of home-away-from-home. Because of this arrangement, it is customary to find the same teacher teaching reading, spelling, geography, history, science, music, art (perhaps with some supervision), and mathematics, as well as collecting milk money, settling arguments, wiping noses, taking off snowsuits, etc., during the course of one day. Obviously, a satisfactory elementary school teacher must be a true Nietzschean Superman with the patience and understanding of an angel (probably a contradiction in terms). If such people exist, they are unlikely to be attracted to elementary school teaching by the salaries, working conditions, and prestige accorded this position by our society. Consequently, elementary school teachers are recruited from the ranks of ordinary mortals who have an average college education, a love for children, and a great deal of dedication.

Since there are only four years in the usual college program, and prospective teachers are required to take several professional courses (child psychology, history of education, methods courses, etc.) as well as to become fairly proficient in one field of study, it is quite common for these students to take no more than one college-level course in some of the subjects that they will teach. Furthermore, since any student who can understand mathematics and science well enough to survive several courses in either or both of these subjects is in great demand for other occupations, the vast majority of elementary school teachers are fairly well prepared in the English and social studies fields but have had the minimum of preparation in mathematics and science.

Against this background, it is not surprising that when groups began studying the mathematics curriculum in the public schools, they quickly began to focus attention on the elementary schools as well as the secondary schools. After a quick look at the elementary situation, many of the groups decided that there was little hope of making substantial improvement in it, since it would be difficult to educate and re-educate teachers to carry on a radically different program and since experts in other subject-matter fields would demand that teachers spend equal time learning the latest developments in these. Despite such difficulties, several groups have made interesting and significant recommendations for the improvement of elementary school mathematics.

### Committee on the Undergraduate Program in Mathematics (CUPM)

Although the original purpose of CUPM was to improve college-level education, its recommendations have been meaningful for high school and elementary school education. Fortunately, the members of CUPM have viewed their duties as being broader than the preparation of mathematics majors in colleges and have made specific suggestions as to the sort of program they deem appropriate for secondary school teachers and for elementary school teachers. This committee of the Mathematical Association of America held a series of meetings around the country to which people interested in elementary education were invited. At these meetings, the recommendations of CUPM were discussed, suggestions for modifications were made, and possible ways of implementing a better teacher education program were considered. In this way, a group of people composed largely of pure mathematicians has exerted considerable effect on the mathematics program in the elementary schools through its interest in the preparation of teachers.

CUPM recommends for the education of elementary school teachers a minimum of two years of college-preparatory mathematics (algebra and geometry or a combined course in these) and four courses in college-level mathematics including work with the real number system and its subsystems, basic concepts of algebra, and informal geometry. The material at the college level does not duplicate high school courses but looks at these subjects from a deeper and more mature point of view. CUPM also recommends that at least 20% of the elementary teachers have a considerably stronger background in mathematics than that proposed as a minimum.

As well as general recommendations for improvement in teacher training such as the CUPM recommendations, there have been several projects that have had as their primary objective the demonstration of what can be done with elementary school children by an exceptional teacher with a strong background in mathematics.

### The Madison Project

Professor Robert B. Davis of the Mathematics Department at Syracuse University began preparing materials and teaching children mathematics in the Madison Junior High School (from which the project received its name) at Syracuse, New York, in 1957. Materials from this project have been used (with some success) as early as the second grade and as late as the eighth grade. Professor Davis is presently working from both Syracuse University and Webster College (Missouri). Although much subject matter that is not traditional is included in the Madison Project, the emphasis is on method of teaching rather than new subject matter. Since Davis believes that the child should be exposed to many experiences pertaining to a general principle and should then try to generalize these experiences (with the guidance of a good teacher, of course), a strong emphasis on the discovery approach is central to the Madison Project. New subject matter covered by the project materials includes arithmetic of signed numbers, variables, open sentences, truth sets, functions, one- and two-dimensional coordinate geometry with graphs of conic sections, simple logic, selection of axioms and derivation of theorems, simple work with matrices and vectors, similar triangles, trigonometry, and programming digital computers. Although the project does not go into any of these subjects really deeply at the elementary or junior high school level, the children are obviously being exposed to a rather unusual program.

Probably the best way to learn more about the project is to see some of the films that have been made of sample lessons. These show that the children are active participants and apparently understand rather well some important, and not superficial, mathematics. The question remains whether any large portion of elementary school teachers will eventually be able to handle this sort of material successfully along with their other duties.

## Algebra for Grade Five

Dr. Warwick W. Sawyer of Wesleyan University, the recipient of a British education, is aware that many children in Europe begin the study of algebra and geometry at a somewhat earlier age than do most children in this country. On the assumption that children in the United States are as intelligent as those in other countries, he decided to try an experiment with a group of bright fifth-grade youngsters (the top third in a homogeneous grouping situation) in Middletown Central School, Connecticut. As is done in most other experimental programs, Dr. Sawyer emphasizes discovery and understanding on the part of the pupils. He followed the performance of the same group through successive grades with a continuing program in algebra. Although they were taught the algebra only one day a week, the children seemed to improve in morale and interest more than groups of children who were not challenged by such materials and methods.

## University of Illinois Arithmetic Project

After the considerable success of the UICSM group with high school mathematics, David Page branched off to consider the elementary school program. The University of Illinois Arithmetic Project, working with grades one through six, received a five-year grant from the Carnegie Corporation to study the arithmetic program and improve on it. Like Davis and Sawyer, Page quickly concluded that young children could learn far more mathematics than most educators had supposed and that young children who are not given the opportunity to learn good mathematics early enough might have considerably more difficulty at a later time. Page is continuing his work along these lines under the auspices of Educational Services, Incorporated, and has made a series of films of classroom activities. These films are appropriate for teacher training, and of interest to other people involved in education.

## Geometry for Primary Grades

Professors Newton S. Hawley and Patrick Suppes of Stanford University received a grant from the Carnegie Corporation in the spring of 1958 to teach geometry to first graders at Stanford Elementary School. They then wrote a textbook along the lines of their experiment and received a grant from the government (through the NSF) to try out the materials with a larger group composed of first, second, and third graders. The pupils work with pencils and rulers and later use a compass as well. They are encouraged to try to solve problems and to give reasons for their conclusions. The most significant measurable advantage of this program occurs in the area of reading rather than of arithmetic, but since the program does not in any way depend on arithmetic or try to teach it, this result should not seem surprising. Again, the experimenters concluded that young children easily learned concepts that were once thought too difficult for them.

### Set Theory in First Grade

Professor Suppes has also worked on a program in which elementary "set theory" was taught to first graders, and this material was then correlated with the teaching of arithmetic. A pupil would first learn about union of sets and would then use this concept to help his understanding of addition of numbers. The assumption is that sets are more concrete than are numbers and that it should seem more natural to the child to begin with the study of sets than with the study of numbers. Suppes is presently trying to develop a program in which computers are used to help teachers individualize instruction. So far, the results of this program are most encouraging.

As this account of experimental projects may suggest, there are reasons to believe that young pupils can learn much more than has usually been supposed. In fact after studies of his own, Jerome S. Bruner has gone so far as to suggest that any subject matter can be taught to anybody at any age in some intellectually honest form. Although this statement is patently false (the idea of teaching calculus to a two-day-old Mongolian idiot seems a little ludicrous), the comment does represent the feeling of modern educators that far more can be done with young pupils than has been done in the past, and that probably we should try to teach them considerably more than we now attempt.

Another question is raised by these experiments that show our youngsters' great capabilities for learning. Rather than determining what *can* be learned by pupils, should we now be discussing what they *ought* to learn at any given point in their development? Even though it is probably possible to show that seven-year-olds *can* learn calculus (in some form), there is a very real question whether seven-year-olds *ought* to learn calculus—in any form.

In planning a program, we can assume that almost anything that we wish to teach can be taught in some form. However, there are still important questions to be answered when planning the curriculum.

How does the subject fit into an over-all program for the pupil? Will it lead into other important topics and be important to the student in the long run? Will the learning of this subject improve his appreciation of mathematics, or will it tend to have the opposite effect? Will this topic be more important than other topics in terms of its usefulness, its general education value, and its desirable effects on the pupils? To some extent, these questions must be answered without experimental evidence, since the possible number of topics and the permutations of those topics allow for an astronomical number of experiments. However, there is still much need for continuing experimental evidence regarding the effects of various types of programs on young children. It may turn out that the particular subject matter taught to children is far less important, in the long run, than the way in which they learn it and the feelings this learning produces regarding both the subject and the general process of learning.

## Summary

Acceleration in the activity associated with the teaching of school mathematics, not only in this country but around the world, has been nearly as great in the past ten or fifteen years as the acceleration in activity in mathematics itself. Although many of the suggestions and experiments will continue to be modified, the interest that has been generated in the teaching of mathematics cannot help but be good for mathematics and for society as a whole. Teachers are learning more mathematics and thinking more about how to teach it. Mathematicians are recognizing the importance of school mathematics programs and are making suggestions as to how to improve them. Society as a whole is becoming more aware of the importance of mathematics and the teaching of mathematics. Even if the particular programs that are being suggested were no better than more traditional ones, there is little doubt that the interest and thought that have been generated would be good for mathematics.

None of the programs mentioned in this chapter is claimed by its originator(s) to be *the* answer to problems in teaching of mathematics; rather, each is suggested as a possible way to improve the teaching of mathematics. Thus, the teacher of mathematics would be well-advised to study many of these programs and then give serious thought to pertinent questions. Why do we teach mathematics? How do we expect children to change as a result of having studied mathematics? What sort of program will best achieve the desired goals for the children whom one is teaching?

## Questions for Further Thought and Study

1. Assume that you are teaching mathematics in a high school and a parent asks you why you are (or are not—take your choice) teaching "modern mathematics" rather than traditional mathematics. What would you say to the parent? Cite authorities for your statements when possible.

2. What do you think is the most important good feature of modern mathematics?

3. What do you think is the greatest danger in modern mathematics programs?

4. Compare the Commission Report, the OEEC Report, and the Cambridge Report. What was the purpose of each; what were the major recommendations of each; what do you think of these purposes and recommendations?

5. Study two secondary school mathematics textbooks published after 1960 and two published prior to 1955. Consider each in light of the recommendations of the Commission Report and your own criteria for a good textbook.

## REFERENCES

Adler, Irving. "The Cambridge Conference Report: Blueprint of Fantasy?" *The Mathematics Teacher*, **LIX,** no. 3 (1966), 210–217. An informative and interesting assessment of the controversy surrounding the Cambridge Report during the first three years after its inception.

Allen, Frank B. (editor and director). *The Revolution in School Mathematics, A Report of Regional Orientation Conferences in Mathematics*, National Council of Teachers of Mathematics, Washington, D.C., 1961.*

Allendoerfer, Carl B. "The Second Revolution in Mathematics," *The Mathematics Teacher*, **LVIII,** no. 8 (1965), 640–645. Suggests that there is still much to be done in improving the teaching of mathematics. In particular, we must find out more about how individuals learn and adjust curricula to match individual patterns of learning. Allendoerfer believes we should start with very young children rather than secondary-school age level.

Beberman, Max. *An Emerging Program of Secondary School Mathematics.* Harvard University Press, Cambridge, 1958. A report on the first six years of the University of Illinois Committee on School Mathematics. This project was the first and one of the most exciting experiments with the teaching of modern mathematics in the secondary schools.

Committee on Analysis of Experimental Mathematics Programs of the

* All starred items are discussed in the body of Chapter 2 and thus no comment is necessary here.

National Council of Teachers of Mathematics. *An Analysis of New Mathematics Programs*, National Council of Teachers of Mathematics, Washington, D.C., 1963.*

Commission on Mathematics of the College Entrance Examination Board. *Report of the Commission on Mathematics: Program for College Preparatory Mathematics*, College Entrance Examination Board, New York, 1959.*

————. *Appendices*, College Entrance Examination Board, New York, 1959.*

Committee of Organization for European Economic Cooperation, Office for Scientific and Technical Personnel. *New Thinking in School Mathematics*, O.E.E.C., Paris, 1961.*

————. *Synopses for Modern Secondary School Mathematics*, O.E.E.C., Paris, 1961.*

Committee on the Undergraduate Program in Mathematics (CUPM) of the Mathematical Association of America (MAA). "Recommendations of the Mathematical Association of America for the Training of Teachers of Mathematics," reprinted from the American *Mathematical Monthly*, vol. **67,** no. 10, December 1960, MAA, 1960. Recommended preparation for teachers of mathematics at five different levels (elementary school, junior high school, high school, advanced high school and early college, and college).

————. *Ten Conferences on the Training of Teachers of Elementary School Mathematics*, Report no. 7, Committee on the Undergraduate Program in Mathematics of the Mathematical Association of America, MAA, Buffalo, New York, February, 1963.*

Deans, Edwina. *Elementary School Mathematics: New Directions*, Bulletin no. 13, U.S. Department of Health, Education, and Welfare, Washington, D.C., 1963. Review of many of the newer programs for elementary school mathematics.

DeVault, M. Vere, et al. *Administrative Responsibility For Improving Mathematics Programs*, AASA, ASCD, NASSP, and NCTM, Washington, 1965. Report of the Joint Project on the Administration of Mathematics Programs of the American Association of School Administrators, the Association for Supervision and Curriculum Development, National Association of Secondary-School Principals, and the National Council of Teachers of Mathematics. The report includes suggestions to the administrator for planning, organizing, implementing, and evaluating curricular changes in mathematics. Teachers are likely to find the bibliography helpful, and the reasons given for change may help in discussions with parents and others (fifty cents from any of the organizations listed above).

Fehr, Howard F. (ed.). *Mathematical Education in the Americas*, A Report of the First Inter-American Conference on Mathematical Education, Bogota, Columbia, December 4–9, 1961, Bureau of Publications, Teachers College, Columbia University, New York, 1962. A collection of addresses by outstanding mathematicians and mathematical educators about new developments in mathematics and mathematical education. Also included is a brief summary of a survey of mathematics education in the Americas.

Hilton, Peter. "The Continuing Work of the Cambridge Conference on School Mathematics (CCSM)," *The Arithmetic Teacher*, **13**, no. 2 (1966), 145–149. A summary of the work done by the CCSM up to the time of publication, including a list of some 37 CCSM reports which range in length from one page to two hundred pages.

Kemeny, John G. "Report to the International Congress of Mathematicians," *The Mathematics Teacher*, **LVI**, (February 1963), 66–78. This article was presented at Stockholm, Sweden, August 15, 1962. It summarizes and evaluates the reports from twenty-one nations on attempts to modernize mathematics teaching. In general, although there has been considerable activity, there seem to be two major obstacles to drastic revision of the curriculum in most countries—the shortage of qualified teachers and the lack of suitable text materials.

Kline, Morris. "A Proposal for the High School Mathematics Curriculum," *The Mathematics Teacher*, **LIX**, no. 4 (1966), 322–330. A spirited attack on "modern mathematics" by the most widely known critic of recent trends in the mathematics curriculum. Any teacher of mathematics ought to have considered Professor Kline's point of view, and have examined some of his writing with great care.

Lockard, J. David. *Third Report of the Information Clearing House on New Science and Mathematics Curricula*, American Association for the Advancement of Science and the Science Teaching Center, University of Maryland, College Park, Maryland, 1965. A compilation of answers given by project directors to questionnaires sent out by the AAAS and Science Teaching Center. Includes information of staff, support, objectives, use, and future plans of all the major projects in existence as of March 1965.

National Council of Teachers of Mathematics. *Topics for Elementary School Teachers*, Twenty-ninth Yearbook of the NCTM, Washington, 1964. Published both as a series of pamphlets (30¢ each) and as a yearbook. The topics considered are (1) sets, (2) whole numbers, (3) numeration, (4) algorithms for operations with whole numbers, (5) numbers and their factors, (6) the rational numbers, (7) numeration systems for the rational numbers, and (8) number sentences.

Secondary-School Curriculum Committee of the National Council of Teachers of Mathematics. "The Secondary Mathematics Curriculum: Report of the Secondary-School Curriculum Committee of the National Council of Teachers of Mathematics," *The Mathematics Teacher*, **52** (May 1959), 389–417.*

Schult, Veryl, and Theodore L. Abell. *Promising Practices for Elementary and Secondary School Teachers*, U.S. Office of Education, Washington, D.C., 1964. A report of a conference under the joint auspices of the U.S. Office of Education and the National Council of Teachers of Mathematics. This report of a conference should help in-service teachers become aware of recent developments in mathematics education (fifty cents from U.S. Government Printing Office, Washington, D.C.).

Stone, Marshall H. Review of *Goals for School Mathematics: The Report of the*

*Cambridge Conference on School Mathematics.* The *Mathematics Teacher,* **LVIII**, no. 4 (1965), 353–360. Rejects the CCSM report as being not sufficiently bold and imaginative while at the same time being "over-optimistic and almost completely detached from reality."

Wooten, William. *SMSG—The Making of a Curriculum,* Yale University Press, New Haven, 1965. Describes the origin and activities of one of the most significant of the curricular reform groups. Includes a good chapter on the history of mathematics in this country from 1890 to 1960.

Zant, James H. "A Proposal for the High School Mathematics Curriculum— What Does it Mean?" *The Mathematics Teacher* **LIX,** no. 4 (1966), 331–334. An answer to the article by Morris Kline which appears immediately before it.

# TEACHING AND LEARNING: HINTS FOR THE CLASSROOM

An excellent teacher must know, understand, and love his subject matter; he must know, understand, and love his pupils. If a person does not have the capacity to do both of these, he will never be a truly excellent teacher, and no amount of formal education can alter that fact. On the other hand, if a present or potential teacher has the capacity to love and understand both the subject matter and the pupils, it is entirely possible for formal course work to help him to become a better teacher. The purpose of most education courses is to help a prospective teacher to understand children, and the purpose of mathematics courses is to help the student understand mathematics. The methods courses and student teaching are designed to bring the understanding of subject matter and pupil together in a practical but controlled situation and to help the teacher find better ways to communicate the mathematics to the children.

Beyond these basic understandings, various techniques are learned by a teacher through some experience in teaching. Many of these are almost in the nature of a "sixth sense" and are difficult to describe in words, but some of them can be learned by the beginning teacher who takes the trouble to talk with a successful experienced colleague. The beginning teacher should take advantage of every opportunity to talk about teaching with several different good experienced teachers. He can avoid many mistakes in this way and can save several years in the process of becoming a good teacher himself. Of course, the teacher must still make judgments as to which techniques are appropriate for a given situation.

## Planning

Formal lesson plans have been prominent in American education since the latter part of the nineteenth century when the Herbartian influence was strongest in this country. They have many purposes, one of which is to let a substitute know what to do if the regular teacher should suddenly have to be absent. Since a substitute teacher will probably either have no training or very little training in mathematics, there is some doubt that he will be able to conduct the regular program even with lesson plans; probably the best solution to the substitute problem is for the teacher to devise and describe in detail a particular lesson that could be used at any time during the year by a substitute teacher without much formal training in mathematics. A review test, a puzzle problem, the reading of some history of mathematics, or the reading of some mathematics fiction (for instance, Clifton Fadiman's *Fantasia Mathematics*), might qualify for this purpose. The day-to-day lesson plans of the teacher are an important part of his job, but the particular form the plans take should vary with the situation—certainly a pretty lesson plan does not substitute for inspired teaching.

Before beginning to teach mathematics or any other subject, the teacher should ask himself such questions as: "Why do we teach mathematics?"; "What changes in behavior do we expect to achieve through the teaching of mathematics?"; "How should mathematics be taught in order to attain these goals?"; "Will the goals be different for different pupils, and if so, how shall I teach in order to take care of these individual differences?"

A good teacher will probably go on thinking about these questions and many others like them for as long as he continues to teach without ever reaching a final answer. It is to be hoped that he will continue to revise his answers and try new ways of achieving new goals throughout his career. Hence, nothing presented in this book can be said to answer these basic questions, but perhaps the reader will be encouraged to think about them, and possibly information and ideas presented here will be of help to him in that thinking.

It was mentioned in Chapter 1 that shortly before World War II the major efforts of the leaders in the field of mathematics education seemed to be directed to defending the very idea of teaching mathe-

matics to children. In the atmosphere of the 1960s hardly anyone seriously questions whether mathematics ought to be taught; there seems
to be a general feeling that the more mathematics any child is taught,
the better educated that child will be. High schools commonly make
one or two years of mathematics (after grade eight) a requirement for
graduation. The present high esteem for mathematics has many advantages for the teacher of mathematics, but it is not an unmixed blessing.
When teachers are no longer asked by others, "Why do you teach this
subject?", they often forget to ask it of themselves. And if a teacher
cannot answer that question, at least to his own satisfaction, there is
some doubt whether his teaching is good enough to be worth the time
and effort of the pupils.

There have been many attempts to answer the question, "Why teach
mathematics?" Although the important answers are those that the
teacher (or prospective teacher) provides himself, a brief discussion of
some of the answers that are commonly given and their implications
for the classroom is, perhaps, in order at this time.

"Mathematics is important because it is useful." This answer is often
heard. There are some "pure mathematicians" who feel that "others
can build a better garbage can if they want to, but *I* study mathematics because it's beautiful." However, if mathematics had no useful
application to the real world, it would probably hold no higher place
in our society than do games such as chess and bridge. Even though
the mathematician may not actually know how his mathematics can
be applied to practical situations, if there were no relation at all between his work and the real world, his mathematics would probably be
thought rather insignificant by most of his colleagues and the rest of
the population. Therefore, no matter how "pure" a mathematician or
mathematics teacher may be, he must admit that at least one good
reason for teaching mathematics is that it will be useful to a great
many of those who study it.

In precisely what way will mathematics be useful to an individual
pupil? There is no single way to answer this question for all children.
For those who are going to become engineers, physicists, chemists,
mathematicians, statisticans, computor operators, quality control experts, economists, actuaries, and so on, the answer seems fairly obvious;
but even though we may be confident that these individuals will have
to know quite a bit of mathematics to carry on their chosen occupations, we cannot be absolutely certain precisely what mathematics will
be useful. We know that these professions are constantly changing and
that most of the changes that have occurred in the recent past have
required more, not less, mathematics. We know further that in each

of these professions an individual who understands and can think about mathematics rather than one who has simply memorized formulas or procedures is of greatest value. And, of course, an individual who is able and willing to continue to learn new ideas will be of greater value than one with however good an education who does not continue to learn after completing his formal schooling. Thus, if mathematics is really going to be useful to the individuals who study it in school, perhaps it should be taught so that they understand it, can apply it to various situations, are encouraged to think about it in relation to other situations, enjoy learning it, and are encouraged to try to create new (at least to them) mathematics and apply it in new ways.

But how about the high school pupils who are not planning to go into one of the fields that is obviously dependent, to some extent, on mathematics? Is mathematics going to be useful for them too? In at least some cases, the answer is probably "No." Some individuals now taking mathematics in our schools may never find a use for that mathematics in their vocations. However, there is considerable difficulty in trying to decide in advance which ones these individuals are. Even if we knew for sure what a child would ultimately do for a living (an impossible prediction since even a prince can abdicate or be deposed), we would find it very hard to say for sure that no mathematics would be required in that job twenty years from today.

Many of our best social scientists today have had little or no training in mathematics, but an increasing amount of significant work in the social sciences is being done as noted in Chapter 2, through the use of mathematics both in the use of statistics and computers and in the development of entire new branches of the social sciences. Game theory, which has implications for voting procedures, activities in legislative bodies, individual preferences, and for economics, is dependent on advanced mathematics. The professions of teaching and nursing require a certain minimal amount of mathematics today, and doctors must do considerable work of a mathematical nature. In fact, many mothers and fathers are finding out that it is even difficult to be a good parent without a reasonable background in mathematics—if not to help the children with their homework, at least to be able to discuss it with some semblance of intelligence. Thus, we cannot really say that individual pupils will never need mathematics because we cannot know what they will be doing when they grow up and even if we did, we could not tell for sure what mathematics or how much of it they would need. Again, the implication seems to be that instead of teaching pupils specific techniques, we should strive to teach them understanding, interest in thought, and the desire and ability to learn.

Other reasons that are often given for teaching mathematics include, for example, "Mathematics teaches the pupils to think." Thorndike's work leaves little doubt that students do not automatically learn to think from mere exposure to a course in mathematics. The work of Nunn and Katona indicates rather strongly that pupils who are taught to understand basic principles are able to use these in thinking about other sorts of problems. Thus, again, it seems that if courses in mathematics are really going to help pupils think more clearly, the pupils must first be taught to understand and then be encouraged to use that understanding in thinking about other subjects. There is a good deal of evidence that such understanding can be transferred to problems of a somewhat similar nature, and there is even some reason to believe that with proper encouragement children will transfer basic understandings to considerably different sorts of problems.

Another reason offered for learning mathematics is the sheer beauty and fun of the whole thing. A paradox about this reason is that to anyone who needs to ask why he should study mathematics, this reason obviously would have little meaning, whereas to anyone who understands and believes in the answer, the question would not occur. Teachers who believe that a major reason for teaching mathematics is the beauty of the logic and the enjoyment to be gained may become embarrassed in attempting to explain it to a pupil who only asked the question because he could not see any beauty and enjoyment in the particular course he was taking.

Every teacher of mathematics should continue to think about the question, "Why do we teach mathematics?" and should consider whether in light of his answer he is doing a good job of teaching and whether he could do a better one. Having answered the question, each teacher should, as he begins a particular course, ask similar questions about that particular course. Presumably, he will decide that there are specific objectives for a course in, say, ninth-grade algebra which he did not consider as general objectives in teaching mathematics. One objective of many teachers is preparation for the next course in mathematics. Although this aim is not entirely indefensible, there will be some children in every class for whom it is not appropriate. If, for example, the teachers of grades eight through twelve all took this viewpoint their aim would be to prepare every eighth-grade pupil to take a course in college calculus—certainly an untenable objective. Thus, while teachers should certainly cooperate in their planning to ease the transition from one grade to the next, they should not let the cumulative nature of mathematics compel them to settle for such objectives as "finishing the book" or "getting through quadratic equations because they'll need them next year." Considering the high attrition rate in mathematics courses, the objectives of each course must stand by themselves; it is not fair for an eighth-grade teacher to merely prepare his pupils for the next year, assuming that the teacher of a higher grade is competent and capable of continuing from that point in the student's educational development.

Thinking about general goals for teaching mathematics or a particular mathematics course does not require pencil and paper and can even be done while we are falling asleep at night, shaving in the morning, or driving to school. For a good teacher, it should never come to an end. However, there are other kinds of planning that require much more specific concentration and have a much closer bearing (though not a more important influence) on what happens in the classroom. Obviously, in the specific planning for a particular unit the general conclusions that the teacher has reached must be given consideration. Most teachers will be using a textbook, some sort of outline, or other materials. Before starting to teach a new unit, we should read through the entire unit with a pencil and paper handy. The pencil and paper are not for taking notes but rather for working out proofs, problems, different methods of presentation, etc. The notes will come later.

After the teacher has gone through the whole unit (chapter, section, or whatever) he can come back and make detailed outlines of important points to be covered in any particular lesson. If the teacher knows the material well, he may need to write only four or five key words on a sheet of paper for one day's lesson. On the other hand, if the teacher is not very familiar with the material, he may have to write out the work in much more detail. He may even write several of the more important steps of a proof on the paper. Usually, it is a good idea for the teacher to prepare lessons for several days in advance in this manner so that he knows precisely where he is going; if the class moves through some material faster than he had expected, he is prepared to go on to the next material. Then he should reconsider the material he has outlined, but not covered previously, each day as he continues planning. Thus, each day the teacher might be expected to add about as much to the end of his lesson plans as he took off the previous day by teaching. In this way, each day's lesson will have been considered carefully two to three times before it is actually taught. Of course, any assignment for homework that the teacher believes to be worthwhile and appropriate for the pupils would appear with the plan of each day's lesson.

A teacher with a good background in mathematics should be able to do the general planning for a two- or three-week unit in an hour or two, and the day-to-day planning should probably take no more than ten to fifteen minutes a day. Of course, if more time is spent on planning, the teacher may be able to do a better job of presenting the lessons, but most teachers find that twenty-five hours (or more) of teaching per week plus the various other time-consuming duties that a teacher is expected to perform do not leave much more time for planning. However, any time spent on planning is usually rewarding both in better teaching and in a much more comfortable classroom situation for the teacher.

Every now and then after teaching a lesson, the teacher should reconsider his general goals of teaching mathematics and the course in question and decide whether that particular lesson moved the children closer to the objective. Certainly this consideration should be given after completing each unit and again at the end of a course.

## Grades

A teacher must perform many professional activities other than teaching and planning. For many good teachers, one of the most painful of these is evaluating pupils—the process commonly known as "making up grades." The process is well named. No teacher can ever make up a completely fair way of assigning grades, and, in general, the more certain a teacher is that his method of assigning grades is fair, the more likely it is that the method is highly arbitrary and allows the teacher to assign the grades without considering the characteristics, effort, problems, and welfare of the individual children. A teacher's claim that he has an "objective" means of assigning grades usually means that he has hit on a procedure that does not require him to think or to know very much about the pupils. However, as long as our educational system is set up as it is, teachers will have to continue to give grades, and probably the teachers who have the most difficulty in giving grades will continue to be the ones who do the best job.

In determining grades, the teacher considers several ingredients. The most obvious of these is test grades. How much of the final grade is determined by test grades and how the various test grades are weighted with respect to each other are questions that must be decided in light of specific information available to the teacher, but certain general comments about testing and grading of tests are appropriate here. First, in making up a test, a teacher may find that it is often easy to test for such qualities as rote memorization, ability to repeat the teacher's thoughts, carefulness, speed, and conformity. Are these the qualities for which one is striving in teaching mathematics? If so, then a test that gives those pupils who have these qualities a high grade will give credit where credit is due and will also encourage the development of these traits by all of the other pupils (at least all those who want high grades). On the other hand, perhaps there are other qualities that one considers more important. Perhaps a teacher is interested in "teaching the pupils to think," or would like the pupils to understand and be able to use mathematical generalizations, or perhaps he has other aims in teaching mathematics. Whatever may be one's goals in teaching mathematics, one of the most effective teaching devices at a teacher's disposal is the test. Most pupils try to do well on a test, and are quite observant about the type of test any particular teacher is likely to give. Thus, one of the best ways by which we can realize the teaching goals set for ourselves is to give tests (and grades) that place more weight on the more important goals.

Of course, such traits as speed and accuracy are not to be discouraged, and as for memory, there are certainly many things in mathematics (as in other subjects) that it is desirable to remember. But if a teacher believes that there are more important factors than these for which he would like to test, he can find ways of downgrading the effects of these particular traits on a test. If speed is not meant to be an important factor, he can give a short enough test so that the majority of the pupils will be able to finish (at least *trying* every problem) easily before the end of the alloted time. If accuracy and carefulness are not meant to be the most important items for which one is testing, one may give a wide range of problems from a few very easy ones to a few very difficult ones, and then mark on a "curve" so that a passing grade may be as low as 20 or 30%. Also a teacher can take off only a few points for careless mistakes while giving most of the points for having the right general idea. In this way, he makes it possible for a brilliant student who is a bit careless to get a considerably higher score than a careful but uninspired pupil. On the common grading scale in which any score below 70% is failing, it is necessary to give such easy questions that most of the pupils can solve most of the problems without much difficulty. On such a test the teacher is saying, in effect, "Every pupil in this class should be able to do at least 70% of the problems without any difficulty." In this situation, the only logical reasons for giving that 70% of the test are to see if anybody can be trapped into making silly mistakes and to determine who should fail. Most mathematics teachers would deny that either of these goals is worth so large a portion of the time and energy of either pupils or teacher.

Another factor that commonly affects grades is homework. There is no question that the regular working of problems—both the discovery type of problems and practice problems after a principle has been discovered—helps most students to become better in mathematics. However, there is considerable question whether copying somebody else's homework (no matter how correct it may be), with little application of thought, is a worthwhile procedure. When a teacher spends long hours grading each pupil's homework on the basis of how many problems were solved correctly, the teacher is wasting his own time and also encouraging many of the pupils to copy their work from others. Such a result could better be accomplished by providing the pupils with a mimeograph machine. This is not to say that homework should not be collected nor that the teacher should not look at it. The teacher should collect the homework for the express purpose of checking to see whether the pupils are attempting to do it. If the pupils are mature enough, they should be provided with the correct answers so that they can check the correctness of their work themselves; otherwise, correct answers and methods should be discussed in class before the homework is collected. But homework ought to be counted in the grade only as an indication of the effort that is being put forth by the pupils and not as a kind of examination with marks based on percentage of problems worked correctly.

Other factors that should probably be considered in determining grades include the effort invested by pupils both in class participation and homework, the attitude of pupils (whether an individual thinks for himself or relies on the teacher's answers), and the effect the grade is likely to have on the individual pupil. The last-mentioned factor may seem to be a dubious criterion for determining grades, but if the goal of the teacher is to change the behavior of pupils, then this ought to be accepted as a legitimate use of grades.

One example of the use of grades to affect behavior might be cited. A pupil with an I.Q. score of 80 was in an eighth-grade science class. He gave a report that would have rated a $C$ for any other pupil in the class but was given an $A$ by the teacher who felt that his devotion of effort deserved recognition. The pupil's work improved throughout the rest of the year until by the year end it actually merited an $A$. Interestingly enough, the next time the boy was given an I.Q. test, he scored in the middle 90s. Other examples of a similar nature are not uncommon.

It is often a good idea to grade tests in such a way that an individual pupil's test average is no higher than the grade the teacher expects to give the pupil on the basis of his total performance. Then if a change is to be made for class participation, effort on homework, or for some other reason, the change will be made upward. Generally, the pupils think this method to be fair.

One final comment about grades—after a teacher has taken into consideration all pertinent factors and arrived at a grade he considers just for an individual pupil, he must not change the grade if the pupil complains about it unless he has clearly made a clerical error. There are two obvious reasons for this policy. First, if a teacher changes the grade of one complainer, others will feel (with reason) that they too can get their grades changed, and the teacher will spend many hours arguing with pupils. Second, if a teacher makes a habit of changing grades when pupils complain, he will finally be giving higher grades to the complainers than to the noncomplainers, on the average, and thus will be rewarding complaining.

## Teaching: The Discovery Approach

Of the many excellent teachers in the world, each is different. It is surprising how different the points of view and methods of two excellent teachers can be. This difference might be expected by a person who believes that teaching is an art, whereas one who believes that teaching is a science might be less willing to accept the idea that the methods of two excellent teachers can be radically different. Many educators believe that teaching is both an art and a science.

In spite of the many differences among the methods of excellent teachers, virtually all so-called modern mathematics programs use a discovery approach to teaching. There are several kinds of activity in the classroom that go under the name of "discovery." One of these is the Socratic Method, exemplified in *Socrates and the Slave*, by Plato.[1] In the Socratic approach, the teacher knows in advance that he wants to convince the pupils that a certain fact is true. By asking the right questions, he forces the pupils finally to answer the last question in a sequence by stating the desired fact.

On occasion, a pupil who happens to be a little independent may get to the final question and say "I know the answer, but I don't know how to get it myself. I couldn't go through all that again without you to ask me the right questions." What the pupil is really saying is: "All right, you trapped me, but that doesn't really convince me." Although good demonstrations of the Socratic method are impressive to watch, they really resemble the activities of an excellent lawyer more than the activities of an excellent teacher. We do not really want to trap our pupils. Rather, we want to help them learn and become more independent.

At the other extreme is a radically distorted version of progressive education in which the teacher gives the pupils complete freedom to do

[1] Reprinted in Clifton Fadiman', *Fantasia Mathematics*, Simon and Schuster, New York, 1958, pp. 49–57.

as they wish on the hope that maybe they will learn something. This procedure is highly unfair to the pupils. One of the great advantages human beings have over other living things is the ability to transmit the accumulated wisdom of the ages to each new generation. To deny this advantage to young students in the name of discovery would be a travesty.

Somewhere between the highly structured approach of Socrates and the complete *laissez faire* of radical progressive education is a more appealing approach. In this process, there will be times at which the pupils will simply be told certain things, and times at which they will be given almost complete intellectual freedom. There will be times when the pupil is expected to induce a general principle from several specific instances and times when he is expected to deduce new results from concepts which he already accepts. In general, the procedure used will depend on the particular group of pupils being taught and the subject matter to be learned. Within this context, the "discovery method" will be thought of as any procedure in which the teacher, by posing appropriate problems, encourages pupils to think for themselves and become more independent.

Four of the most commonly mentioned advantages of the discovery approach are these: (1) it helps a pupil understand the material better by showing him that the concepts involved are so reasonable that he can discover them himself (with a little help); (2) it helps a pupil to remember the principle because, having discovered and understood it, he is far less likely to forget it than if he were merely told that it is true; (3) it helps the individual to learn on his own so that he may become increasingly independent of the teacher; (4) it keeps the teacher in touch with his class so that he knows whether the pupils are understanding and following the work or being quiet because they have no grasp of the teacher's meaning.

Several implications of these advantages will occur to the thoughtful reader. One is the importance of using the question approach appropriately. There are teachers who, having heard that the discovery method is good, ask questions just for the sake of asking questions. Recently a ninth-grade teacher was heard to ask "1 + 2 equals what?" She then wrote down "1 + 2 = 3" on the blackboard, since only one of her students seemed to be able to produce the answer. The question had very little to do with the concept that was being developed at the time (inequalities), was clearly insulting to the majority of ninth graders, and certainly did not require thought on their part. If the discovery method is to be used, it should be used only when there is something to be discovered and only when there is some chance that the pupils will discover what they are expected to discover. Definitions and symbolism, in general, do not lend themselves to discovery, since they are matters of convention rather than logic. Of course, there are exceptions. Max Beberman (UICSM) likes to tell the story of the little boy who, having worked with the backward E (∃) as an existential quantifier, suggested that an upside down A (∀) should be used for the universal quantifier. When asked for a reason, the boy replied, "Well, everything in this course is either backward or upside down." In general, however, the discovery approach ought not to be used when there is nothing to discover.

Some teachers who are just beginning to use the discovery approach tend to decide in advance what the answer to a particular question ought to be and to insist that some pupil come up with that answer. But often if the teacher will listen carefully to the answers that the pupils give, he will learn a great deal about the pupils and perhaps something about the question. Once the teacher has asked a question, it is important that he listen carefully to the answer. If the answer is not what he expected, he should start asking himself such questions as these: "Did this pupil understand my question?" "Is his answer correct or reasonably correct, and if so can we develop his answer into a significant fact?" If his answer is incorrect the teacher should ask himself: "What doesn't he understand, and what can I do to help him see what is wrong with the answer he has given?" In general, having asked a question, the teacher should listen to the answer and proceed in light of the answer he gets.

Many beginning teachers enjoy the bright pupils more than they do the slower ones and (especially when an observer is in the room) spend most of their time asking questions of the brightest pupil in the class, ignoring the others. Such a procedure defeats two main purposes of a discovery approach, those of helping the teacher to determine whether the pupils understand and of giving all the pupils the feeling that this is something well within their grasp. If the teacher talks only with the very bright pupils, he will find out only what they know, and the others will quickly get discouraged by the entire process. Thus, questions and answers should be spread among all of the pupils in a class.

One major advantage of the discovery approach is that pupils begin to think and learn on their own and become independent of the teacher. However, if the questions that a teacher asks can always be answered quickly and with relatively little deep thought, the pupils will be quite dependent on the teacher to supply the questions. On the other hand, if questions tend to get increasingly difficult as the pupils progress until they have to go home and think about the questions, experiment, guess, and try to prove their guesses correct, the pupils will tend to do more and more thinking on their own. Furthermore, the pupils should begin to learn to ask their own questions. For example, after solving a particular problem, the pupils should start to wonder whether there is any way to generalize the solution or any implication of this solution for other problems they may face, etc. In general, pupils should be encouraged to ask questions—not because the teacher says "Are there any questions?" but rather because the teacher reacts positively to good questions when they are asked (even if he does not happen to know a good answer). Young pupils love to ask questions—it seems too bad that as they grow older, many stop asking questions, apparently because they get the impression that it is not the thing to do. Julia Adkins has even suggested that perhaps questions that pupils ask are one of the best ways to evaluate the excellence of the teacher.[2]

Many examples of the discovery approach are available, such as the films and tape recordings made in connection with several of the experimental programs (for instance, the Madison Project), and demonstration lessons are often given at conventions of mathematics teachers. As an illustration of a simple, short discovery lesson with a group of average ninth-grade pupils who had not previously been exposed to "modern mathematics," we reproduce the following: [3]

The teacher was not the regular teacher, and he had been given as his assignment the problem of developing the commutative and associative laws of addition. The corresponding laws for multiplication were to be presented the next day, and the distributive law was to be presented on a third day.

The teacher began by asking: "What do you know that is true about all numbers?" The shocked silence lasted only about half a minute and then one boy said: "They're all either even or odd."

"Is $\frac{1}{2}$ even or odd?"

"That's not the kind of number I was talking about."

"Do you think we ought to specify what kind of number we are talking about?"

"Yes."

"What kind of number would you like us to talk about?"

"The numbers 1, 2, 3, and so on."

"All right . . . "

[2] Julia Adkins, "Are Students' Questions a Valid Criterion for Evaluating Creative Teaching?" *The Mathematics Teacher*, vol. 55, pp. 177–178, March, 1962.
[3] Stephen S. Willoughby, Gene Tornow, and M. Vere DeVault, *The Mathematics In-Service Education Program in Watertown Public Schools*, Department of Education, University of Wisconsin, Madison, Wisconsin, 1963.

Some discussion of universe, even and odd numbers, natural numbers, and other possible true statements followed, but nobody seemed particularly close to the commutative or associative laws. Then the teacher changed the question slightly and said: "Suppose I add a couple of natural numbers, say 3 and 5" (*writing* "3 + 5" *on the board*), "what can you say about this?"

A boy who had been quiet previously raised his hand and said: "You'll always get a number." This response provoked laughter from the class, and a couple of derisive comments about the boy's intelligence were heard. The teacher then asked one of the laughers: "Is that true about subtraction? For example, is 3 − 5 a number in our set?"

"No."

"Then, does the fact that we always get a number in our set when we add two numbers in the set seem to be an important fact about addition and the set of numbers we're discussing?"

"I guess so."

"Can anybody else think of anything that is true about all the numbers in our set?"

Another boy: "If you multiply two of them, you always get another number in the set."

"Good. We sometimes describe these two facts by saying that the set of natural numbers in closed under addition and multiplication; that is, we can always find the answer to an addition or multiplication problem, involving members of the set, in the set itself—without going outside the set."

A pupil put up her hand without being asked any further questions and said: "It doesn't make any difference in what order you add."

"Can you give us an example?"

"3 + 5 = 5 + 3."

"Good, we could write that as a general statement this way" (*writing on the board*) "for all natural numbers, a and b, $a + b = b + a$."

About half the hands in the room were now waving in the air, and the information that order is not important in multiplication was immediately forthcoming. The pupil who volunteered this information was prevailed upon to write this on the board as a general statement in a manner similar to the one used by the teacher for addition. The teacher then said: "These are sometimes called the commutative properties for addition and mutiplication."

A discussion of the meaning of the word "commute" and the connection between that and the commutative property ensued.

With a little more help involving the binary nature of addition and multiplication and a question about what happens when you add three numbers, the associative properties of addition and multiplication were discovered, written in general form, labeled, and discussed.

Without further comment the teacher next worked out several examples such as

$$3 \times (5 + 7) = 3 \times 12 = 36$$
$$(3 \times 5) + (3 \times 7) = 15 + 21 = 36$$
$$4 \times (2 + 8) = 4 \times 10 = 40$$
$$(4 \times 2) + (4 \times 8) = 8 + 32 = 40$$
$$7 \times (12 + 15) = 7 \times 27 = 189$$
$$(7 \times 12) + (7 \times 15) = 84 + 105 = 189$$

The children noticed a pattern and were able to provide further examples of the same phenomenon, but they had difficulties putting their ideas into words. However, one girl did volunteer to write this new principle on the board in a manner similar to the way the other four principles had been written. She wrote:

For all natural numbers, $a$, $b$, and $c$, $a \times (b + c) = (a \times b) + (a \times c)$.

Several more examples of this principle were produced and then the instructor suggested that there had always been two laws, one for addition and one for multiplication for the previous properties developed, and perhaps we could find another law by interchanging the "+" and the "×" in this new principle. The pupils told the instructor how to write this: "For all natural numbers, $a$, $b$, and $c$, $a + (b \times c) = (a + b) \times (a + c)$." Although there was general agreement that this new principle was reasonable, checking it with an example or two seemed desirable. Needless to say, this seemingly reasonable rule was cast out after only one example. After several summarizing comments about rules and number systems in general, the pupils started on their homework.

Several observations about the foregoing example are appropriate. First, the pupils were able to discover for themselves many facts that a teacher might ordinarily relate. Second, they showed a great deal of enthusiasm that did not usually occur with this particular class. Third, the pupils, on occasion, gave answers that the teacher was not expecting but instead of saying "No, you're wrong," or "No, that's not what I meant," he incorporated those answers into aspects of the discussion that he had not originally expected to develop but that were significant and related to the intended topic. For example, the "odd or even" answer led to a discussion of universe, and the principle of closure was discussed in some detail after it was suggested by one of the pupils. Fourth, it is necessary for the teacher to know considerably more about mathematics than appears in the textbook, if he is going to do a good job of teaching by the discovery method; otherwise, he will be unable to develop ideas other than those he had planned to discuss. Fifth, it is possible for children to make conjectures that are incorrect (for instance, conjecturing the wrong distributive law), and they should get into the habit of trying to check conjectures as best they can. In this particular case, the children could not prove the principles (in the sense that we usually think of proof), but they were able to convince themselves one way or another of the validity of most of their discoveries.

One major factor that was missing from this example of the discovery method was development of pupil self-reliance. Since the teacher in question had that class for only one day, it was difficult for him to encourage much self-reliance and self-motivation on the part of the pupils, but there are examples of student controlled discovery lessons in the literature, which the interested reader may wish to consider.[4] Of course, such lessons last over a longer period of time.

## Discipline

Rewards for the teacher of young pupils include their enthusiasm, their willingness (in fact, desire) to learn new concepts, the brightening of a small face as the mind behind it suddenly "sees," etc. These rewards are not, however, gained at a low price. Although there are many attractions in the teaching profession, there are some hazards, such as the problem of maintaining discipline. A person could be the best of all possible teachers in all other respects and still be a complete failure as a teacher if he could not handle this problem. Of course, discipline problems are worse at some levels than others. The college teacher almost never has a discipline problem, and teachers of small children usually find that the children are so anxious to please the teacher that discipline difficulties are often not a major concern in the elementary school. Probably the most difficult discipline problems occur in the junior high schools and in classes of pupils who are waiting until they are old enough to leave school. Perhaps the best and most direct solution to the latter problem is to let the children go to work (if they can find a job) and come back to school later if they decide to continue their education. Unfortunately, as our society is presently constructed, this may not be a practical solution for many youngsters. Most of the comments on discipline that follow are aimed at situations involving pupils

[4] See, for example, Stephen S. Willoughby, "Discovery," *The Mathematics Teacher,* vol. 56, pp. 22–25, January, 1963.

who, presumably, really belong in school, though many of the comments may apply, more or less, to all situations involving discipline.

It is a primary rule for maintaining good order in a classroom that a teacher always acts as though he expects the pupils to behave themselves and is genuinely surprised when they do not. The teacher should get down to business right away at the beginning of the period so that pupils expect their attention to be demanded from the moment the bell rings. If the school requires an attendance slip at the beginning of each period, have a pupil fill it out—the pupil will enjoy being given the responsibility, the attendance records will probably be more accurate, and the teacher should have more important things to do. We must try constantly to maintain the interest of the pupils. If a teacher gives the pupils something to think about, they will not have time to think about getting into trouble; if he does not give them something to think about, they will find something. One of the advantages of the discovery approach is the two-way communication that not only helps the teacher to know whether the children understand and are interested but also allows the teacher to handle some potential problems without directly referring to them. For example, if one pupil turns around to talk to the pupil behind him, the teacher should ask the turner a question—preferably a simple question so as not to embarrass him, since all the teacher wants is to let him know that he is being observed. If he uses this technique, it is important that he know the name of each pupil in the class; the effect will be lost if the teacher says, "Will the boy in the third row who is not paying attention please answer the following question?" At the beginning of the year and for as long as needed, the teacher should keep a seating chart handy at all times so that a quick glance at it will give him any name he wants.

Some special classroom situations of which the beginning teacher ought to be aware include the matter of turning one's back to the students. When a teacher is writing on the board, he should always glance back at the class at intervals of about every five seconds (time enough to write about four words or one short equation). There are two reasons for this. First, a pupil may have a question or not be able to see or have some other problem of which you ought to be aware. Second, it is obvious that a teacher with his back to the class is in no position to stop potential discipline problems. There are still schools where the teacher dare not show the back of his head to a class lest it be hit by a flying object (though not recommended as ideal places in which to teach, even these schools harbor rewards for the truly dedicated teacher). When a pupil is working at the board, it is desirable for the teacher to move to the back of the room (assuming the board is in the front) so that the class is between him and the pupil. Reasons for this are: first, the teacher will not obscure the view of members of the class; second, he will be able to tell if the pupil at the board is writing clearly enough and talking loudly enough to communicate with the pupils in the back of the room; and third, it is not necessary for him to turn his back to the class when reading something on the board or talking with the pupil at the board.

A different sort of situation sometimes occurs near the end of a period when the pupils are given a few minutes to start on the next day's homework. Presumably, the reason for such an interval is to enable the teacher to make sure that the pupils understand the assignment and are getting off on the right track. Therefore, the teacher should wander around the class checking to see that everybody is properly started and helping those who are having a little trouble. However, one should not spend a long time working with a particular pupil and ignoring the rest. If one pupil seems to be having a lot of trouble, the teacher should ask him to come in for a few minutes during a free period or after school— the reasons are obvious both in terms of fairness to all of the pupils and in terms of maintaining good discipline.

So far the discussion has centered on trying to avert disciplinary problems. This is certainly the generally preferably procedure. But there are times when unpleasant situations seem unavoidable. Take the pupil upon whom questions, hints, and glaring looks have apparently no effect. What does a teacher do? The first thing *not* to do is to threaten him. The teacher might make a general announcement, facing the transgressor at the time, that pupils are expected to behave in a reasonably civilized manner. The challenge presented by telling a class what one plans to do if it fails to behave as expected is much too great for the children to resist.

If a general announcement does not succeed, the teacher had better approach the recalcitrant pupil quietly and invite him to remain a few minutes after class is over, after school, or whenever it might be convenient. The important thing is not to embarrass him in front of other pupils; an individual challenged in front of the class has to maintain face among his peers and will never change his behavior or back down before an audience. When the pupil turns up for the private talk, the teacher can ask him why he seems uninterested in the class work or why he behaves as he does, or some other question bearing on the main point: "Don't you think you can do better?" This may hold for a while, and the simple reminders outlined earlier may be used, this time with some impact. The teacher, of course, must never leave an impression that he dislikes the child or is out to get him. Sympathy and understanding often solve disciplinary crises.

If the child fails to show up at the designated time, the teacher faces another kind of problem. He might be given another appointment, again made out of earshot of fellow pupils, and reminded to keep it. If he forgets again, the matter should be referred to the principal or appropriate administrative officer.

On rare occasions, a problem may become so acute that one feels it necessary to get a pupil out of the classroom immediately. In such a situation, it is usually advisable to find out in advance from some experienced teacher what to do. If there is a mathematics office manned by a teacher or a teacher in a nearby room who is free, perhaps the problem child can be sent to either place. Otherwise, he should be sent to the school office, and the office administrator should be fully informed of the action. The teacher should call, send a message, or even accompany the child. Under no circumstance should a problem pupil be permitted to wander unattended during class.

Crucial to the handling of discipline problems are advance planning so that the teacher is not caught unprepared; consistent self-control (a teacher should be sorry that he has to discipline a pupil and should show compassion rather than temper); the courage to handle discipline problems oneself; avoidance of bribes or threats; consideration of physical matters such as ventilation, lighting, heating, seating arrangements, etc., which affect the comfort of the pupils and their ability to pay attention; recognition of the distinction between acceptable and nonacceptable noise; generosity with praise and constructive attitudes the provisions for emergencies, such as appointment of someone to take over if the teacher must leave; and the like. Attention to these points will increase the children's respect for the teacher and reduce disciplinary problems.

**Teaching Aids**

Since World War II educators have been putting a great deal of emphasis on teaching aids. Films, filmstrips, educational radio and television, teaching machines, programmed learning, field trips, physical models, and many other teaching aids have been tried and recommended. Among all of the teaching aids that are available today, the two most commonly used by teachers are those least commonly mentioned in lists of teaching aids. One of these is the book; the other is the blackboard and chalk (of which a small model known as pencil and paper is frequently in the hands of the pupil).

## Textbooks

At one time in American education there was likely to be only one book in a classroom, if, indeed, there was any book at all. Any written material that the pupil took home had been written by himself. The many advantages of having a textbook for each pupil have prompted most schools all over the country to provide textbooks for the pupils or to require the pupils to purchase textbooks for themselves. The textbook has certain significant advantages over some of the newer aids, and even though we need not choose a single aid to the exclusion of all others, we might consider some of the advantages of the often underestimated textbook.

Good textbooks help the teacher to plan his work but are still flexible enough to permit the teacher to rearrange some topics, use different methods, and generally fit a program to the needs of the particular class that he is teaching. A textbook is small enough and inexpensive enough so that each pupil can have one to study individually, to review, to help him move ahead more rapidly, or to enable him to make up work missed because of absence. A good index makes it easy for a pupil to refer to anything he wished to recall during the course and after the course is finished. There is a wide variety of excellent textbooks available for all grade levels, giving the teacher great freedom of choice.

Of course, various other aids also have advantages, but a new device is not necessarily good just because it is new any more than an old device is necessarily poor simply because it has been used for many years. At the present time, there seems to be no serious probability that the textbook will be replaced as a major aid to the teaching of mathematics by any of the new aids that have come on the market. Therefore, it is still important for a teacher to know how to use and choose this important teaching aid.

Even though most textbooks are already in use, rather than subject to selection, when a beginning teacher starts work, it is logical to consider the choosing before the using.

Before a teacher or committee of teachers starts to select a textbook, he or it should decide what sort of program is desired. This sort of decision should not be made independently at each grade level but ought to be a schoolwide or systemwide decision involving an organized program from kindergarten through grade twelve (or fourteen, if that exists in the system). Obviously, this is a difficult task, but a great deal of help in making the decision can be found in various reports and model texts for all grade levels. In determining a program, the mathematics teachers will want to make provisions for individual differences so that a good student of mathematics can progress with more speed and depth than a student who has less aptitude for mathematics, so that the "late bloomer" can continue with a good program in mathematics, and so that errors in grouping can be corrected when they are discovered. Some sort of flexible homogeneous grouping will probably be an integral part of any program in mathematics.

Having outlined a program in mathematics that seems appropriate for the school system concerned, the planners' next step is selection of a book or series of books well suited to carrying out that program. If the program is well organized, the choice of one series (with an "overlap" of authorship from one grade to the next) will probably be more appropriate than selections of books from various series, although a fast group might be using an entirely different sort of book from that used by a slower group in the same grade.

In choosing a book or a series of books, teachers should look for several things beyond the question of whether the material fits the particular program. It is desirable—and not as obvious as it sounds—that the mathematics be correct. In actual fact, there is probably no high school textbook in which all of the mathematics is completely correct, and any author who tries to give the reader the impression that all of his mathematics is completely correct ought to be suspect. However, there are many books in which a serious attempt is clearly being made to be correct and in which the authors have succeeded, at least to some extent. Such books will be more useful to good teachers than will books full of mathematical errors. One of the facts of life, which all teachers must face, is that people are more likely to believe the printed word (when they read it) than the spoken word. It is not always easy for a good teacher to correct the misconceptions that are received from a textbook. More important, however, than the question of trivial mathematical errors are questions of whether the book has an organization that clarifies and emphasizes mathematical structure. Is the book organized around some important mathematical ideas? Have the chapters just been brought together in random order with special tricks for each chapter? The ideas considered in a textbook ought to be important and should be organized in a logical manner. These ideas should also fit into the mainstream of mathematical thought and should probably not involve definitions that are radically different from those that are commonly accepted in mathematics.

Another factor in the choice of a textbook is the question of method. Although the teachers will to a large extent determine the method of teaching used, some books lend themselves well to certain methods, while other lend themselves to other methods. For example, if a book is made up largely of pages with a rule at the top and fifty exercises below (with perhaps one or two worked-out examples between), it will be difficult to use a discovery approach, since the pupils will quickly find that the best way to make a discovery is to turn to the top of the page and read the rule. Some newer textbooks are using a discovery approach. These books will usually lend themselves to a discovery approach in the classroom and also have the advantage that they can make a reasonably adequate teacher out of the (very bad) teacher who does nothing but read the book to the pupils and then assign homework. When looking for the method used (or usable) in a textbook, the teacher should remember that one great advantage of textbooks is their provision of large quantities of practice material for the pupils. No matter how good its mathematics and approach, a book loses much of its usefulness if it lacks exercises for children to take home and do by themselves (after appropriate development in class); such a book may compel the teacher to mimeograph large quantities of practice material.

Other factors that enter into the choice of a textbook are the reputation of the authors (usually a fairly reliable criterion as to method and material) and the layout and clarity of type; most books printed in this country are reasonably good on both counts. The convenience of teaching materials can be important in determining the use that can be made of the book. The strength of the binding and paper will determine how long the book will last and should probably be considered, along with price, in deciding between two books that are approximately equal in other respects.

Once a textbook has been chosen, the way in which it is used will be of utmost importance. To a large extent, the question of using the textbook has already been considered in the section on planning, but some specific comments may be helpful. If a book is well written, it is usually desirable to follow the outline it presents unless there is good reason for doing otherwise. If the outline is not followed and a teacher does not plan ahead very carefully, he may find himself needing material he has not covered. It helps the pupil for the teacher to follow the work in the textbook reasonably closely, explaining it as he goes, so that the pupil can refer in the book to what happened in class. Of course, the teacher has a great advantage over the textbook in being able to see and talk to the pupils and he therefore should not hesitate to explain more fully, go more deeply into some topic of interest, try a different sort of proof that may seem simpler to the pupils, and, in general, tailor the lessons to the individuals in the class.

In assigning homework from a book, the teacher should not make a habit of assigning work just because it is there or just because the end of the period has come and the children need something to keep them busy. In general, the homework assigned should fit into the class work and should have some reason for being done—either in the nature of discovering new concepts or practicing old ones.

## Programmed Learning

Since the work of Thorndike and Pavlov near the beginning of this century, there have been many who felt that children could and should learn in much the same way as did the experimental animals used by these men. Probably many people do learn many things in about that way. In very simple form, the stimulus-response or modern associationist psychology advocated by Thorndike and others suggests that people learn in small steps, that correct behavior should be rewarded as quickly as possible, and that general principles come to the mind as the sum of many concrete facts. There can be little doubt that this psychology is largely responsible for the advent of teaching machines in this country even though many contemporary writers of programs accept relatively little of its philosophy.[5]

Aside from the underlying psychology or philosophy, the use of teaching machines and programmed learning has been surprisingly successful in teaching certain things to certain individuals in numerous experiments. Many teachers of mathematics have been disturbed because a large portion of the experiments with teaching machines have been conducted in the area of mathematics. More disturbing is the willingness of even those educators who reject teaching machines in general to accept the idea that mathematics can be taught with machines.[6] The reason for the close association between teaching machines and mathematics is the common notion that mathematics is a collection of unrelated facts that have to be committed to memory. Many textbooks and teachers have taught mathematics on that basis in the past, and it is just possible that some of these books and teachers can and should be replaced by machines. However, educators who are closely associated with the new developments in the teaching of mathematics are not happy to see their emphasis on understanding of general principles and on ways of thought thrown aside by a new technique in teaching. We have the peculiar spectacle of a group of mathematics teachers calling the advocates of programmed learning "reactionaries" because the programmers emphasize traditional sorts of mathematics tasks, while the advocates of the machines are calling the teachers

---

[5] See, for example, Jack E. Forbes, "Programmed Instructional Materials—Past, Present, and Future," *The Mathematics Teacher*, vol. 56, pp. 224–227, April, 1963.
[6] See, for example, Margaret S. Matchett, "Teaching Machines or What?" *The Mathematics Teacher*, vol. 55, pp. 351–355, May, 1962.

"reactionaries" because the teachers are reluctant to accept new methods of teaching.

As one might suppose, things are not quite as bad as either group believes. Many of the writers of programs are good mathematics teachers who are simply writing, in program form, a development of basic concepts of mathematics in about the same way as they would develop them in a classroom, while many teachers of mathematics have been very willing to try programmed materials with their classes.

Many experiments of a more or less controlled nature have been carried on with programmed learning of various sorts. It is difficult to draw clear conclusions from the results, but there seems to be some evidence that bright students can learn the facts of a course in mathematics very rapidly from certain programs, but that a program written to be useful to a slow student will soon bore a fast student. Programmed materials have been tried on slow learners who usually lost interest in a relatively short time. Programmed materials have been tried on pupils who have a special interest in some topic and want to pursue it further, with reasonably good results, but perhaps similar results would have been obtained if the pupils were just given a book. Programmed materials that do not require an expensive machine seem to be about as effective as those that do require a machine (after the novelty of the machine wears off); and programs that provide the answer in close proximity to the question seem to be about as effective as those that hide the answer by some means. If we consider the implications of the last sentence, we see that the only important distinction between a well-written program and a well-written textbook could easily be that the program is two to three times as long and incorporates many small steps that the text omits.

From a practical point of view, the teacher is likely to find that programmed materials will be of little substantial use to him except, perhaps, in very special situations with students who wish to make up some work or move ahead in a particular subject, and even to these students some special human attention should probably be given on occasion. However, such materials are certainly worth trying (once a teacher has established that the mathematics in the program is reasonably good) in any situation where he believes they might be of help. Usually, any novel experiment has some good effects just because people like to do things differently now and then.

## Visual Aids

The visual aid used most often in mathematics classes is the blackboard. An experienced teacher can give many hints on how to use a blackboard. However, most of the important techniques of working with a blackboard will occur naturally if he remembers that the chalk and board are to help him to communicate with the class. A teacher should write clearly and in an orgainized fashion so that his audience can figure out what he is doing. He should concentrate on the pupils (not the blackboard) so that everybody in the room can see and read what he writes. A pupil should not have to copy it so fast that he cannot think about what is being written. If the object is to get the words from a notebook into the notebooks of the pupils as quickly as possible (without necessarily going through either his own mind or the children's minds), he should mimeograph his notes and save everybody a lot of effort. Pictures drawn on the board often help a pupil to visualize a situation (no matter how poor an artist a teacher may be) and should be used freely. Many children (especially young ones) like to go to the board to do some work, and this is often a good way to let them work off excess energy. Other comments on the use of blackboards, made in the section on discipline, will be worth remembering.

A visual aid with many of the advantages of the blackboard and some distinct advantages of its own is the overhead projector. This equipment allows the teacher to write on a sheet of plastic in front of him; the writing is immediately projected onto a screen behind him. The teacher can thus look at the pupils while he writes material for them to see. He can also prepare complicated pictures and tables in advance and simply place them on the projector. The major difficulty that some teachers have found with the overhead projector is lack of room for all the material that the pupils should be able to see on the screen simultaneously. Also, some teachers find that looking at the projecting light for four or five periods a day is somewhat of a strain for the first few days, but most seem to get used to it after some time. The overhead projector has obvious advantages for a large audience because the image can be made as large as desired.

Since the federal government has made funds available for purchase of laboratory materials, many mathematics teachers have bought large quantities of models and other devices for teaching mathematics. Some of these can be used to clarify certain concepts, but many seem to be more for show than for meaningful teaching. Furthermore, there is considerable evidence that pupils learn more when they themselves make models and other devices than when these are bought ready made. An entire yearbook of the National Council of Teachers of Mathematics is devoted to multisensory aids, and about half of it concentrates on models and devices. Anybody who wishes to learn more about the use or construction of such objects is referred to that source.[7]

[7] NCTM, *Eighteenth Yearbook: Multi-Sensory Aids in the Teaching of Mathematics*, 1945.

Films and filmstrips are commonly used visual (or audiovisual) aids. Before using films or filmstrips, the teacher should preview the material to determine whether it is of good enough quality to show and to be able to call the pupils' attention to particular features of the presentation as the film is run. The pressures of time may sometimes make it necessary to show a film without prior viewing, but a teacher so pressed should be sure to have a strong recommendation for the film from a colleague whose opinion is valued.

In reviewing a film, a teacher should consider whether the film does anything that he could not do at least as well without the film. If it does not, there is a serious question as to whether the fuss of setting up a projector and darkening the room is worth the results. There was a time when seeing a film in school was a real treat for children, but in many schools children are now shown so many films that they really prefer not to see one unless it is particularly entertaining.

Of course, if the mathematics in a film or filmstrip is not correct, it should not be shown. Many films credit a mathematics consultant at the beginning, but unfortunately there is no guarantee that he had the final verdict on what mathematics went into the film; the mathematics may still be quite bad, even when a good consultant is listed.

In recent years so many films and filmstrips have been produced that it is quite difficult for any individual teacher to review all of them. He can limit his problem by considering only films that are related to the particular subject(s) he is teaching and that seem, from the description of the distributor, to demonstrate something he could not do himself. However, there are still many more films than any individual can conveniently review. Fortunately, the National Council of Teachers of Mathematics has set up a committee (actually, a group of committees) to review and report on these. Their first report appeared in *The Mathematics Teacher* in December, 1963. This and subsequent reports should be of considerable help to the teacher who wishes to use films in his classroom.

## People

Pupils are not the only people with whom a teacher must deal in carrying out his duties. Although the pupils are, or course, the most important, it is necessary that the teacher work with and get help from other people if he is to do his most effective job.

One large and important group with a legitimate interest in the process of education is composed of the parents. Although some teachers have been known to wish that they could get a job teaching in an orphanage (especially at the end of a particularly trying parents' night or PTA meeting), teachers and parents have common interests and goals and can be of great help to each other when they work together. In order to work together effectively, each should have some idea of what the other is trying to do. When a teacher is attempting something that is different from what the parents are probably expecting, he should take every opportunity (or make one) to explain to the parents what he is doing and why. For example, if the mathematics teacher has decided to use a more "modern" approach, he should explain in terms a layman can understand what modern mathematics is, how it is different from what the parents probably studied when they were in school, and why the teacher believes this approach to be an improvement. After such an explanation, the parents are usually delighted that their children have such a fine teacher and are ready to do everything they can to help him achieve his goals.

Some parents are a trial to the teacher. There is, for example, the father who failed mathematics when he was a boy "because the teaching wasn't any good" but is now an expert on the teaching of mathematics and eager to share his knowledge with the poor uneducated teacher. There are the parents of a child with no aptitude for or interest in mathematics who are convinced that the child can get an "A" in mathematics if he only applies himself: "We make him study mathematics for an hour every day, and we don't let him go out to play for a month after he receives a grade below an A in mathematics, but for some reason he still doesn't seem to like mathematics—now what more can we do for him?" (This is quoted from a real conversation.) There are many types of parents who may not appeal to the teacher, but it is particularly important that the teacher meet them in order to understand the behavior of the children. In general, however, teachers find that parents are interested in doing what they can to provide the best possible education for their children and will expend considerable effort to help teachers do a more effective job. The good teacher usually looks forward to opportunities to meet parents, even though he may join some of his colleagues in good-natured complaints about it.

A teacher's colleagues form another important group that can be quite important in determining what sort of a job he does. Among his fellow teachers, he is likely to find at least one who retired (at least mentally) shortly after beginning his teaching career. Such an individual may be getting credit for thirty years of teaching experience on a salary schedule but probably has had only one year of experience—thirty times. He goes through the motions of putting in about a five-hour day and spends the rest of his time sitting around the teachers' room complaining about how hard a life he leads and how he hates children and how he despises all these new-fangled notions about teaching. The best that can be said for him is that he serves as a bad example. To avoid becoming as bitter, anti-intellectual, and antisocial as he is, a teacher must keep on learning about both people and his subject matter; and if he comes to feel that he dislikes either, he must do something else to be happier.

Most teachers are dedicated people who are constantly trying to learn more about their subject and their pupils. They are proud when "one of my children" does well and feel a sense of failure when one of them does not live up to his potential. Almost all teachers get discouraged at times and complain on occasion, but most love children and get a great deal of satisfaction from teaching them. An experienced and dedicated teacher has much to impart to a beginning teacher, and a young man starting his career will often find that the best part of his education will come after he has finished his formal schooling, and that his best teachers will be his pupils and his colleagues. Of course, the new teacher, like any other human being, must make his own decisions and be responsible for them, but he should not fear to learn from experience even if the voice of experience does not always agree with the latest theories in professional books and magazines.

Perhaps the most maligned individuals associated with the public schools are the administrators. Some administrators seem to lose track of their principal purpose of life, the improvement of education. They get wrapped up in gimmicks that will make for good publicity; they refuse to take steps to improve the educational process if such steps will make for a more difficult administrative job (or will not have sufficient public relations advantages). Administrators have many pressures on them from such groups as teachers, parents, pupils, their school boards, elected officials in various departments, and sundry organizations which have an axe to grind with respect to the public schools. A good administrator finds it difficult, sometimes, to satisfy all these different groups and still perform his primary function of seeing that the quality of education is high. However, each of these groups has (or should have) as its primary objective the improvement of the schools; if the administrator can keep them all informed, he can often manage to satisfy them, at least to some extent, while doing the job he is supposed to be doing. With this in mind, the teacher should keep the administrator informed of his activities so that the administrator can avoid the embarrassing position of not knowing what is going on in his own school or school system. New projects, different methods of teaching, new subject matter, and similar plans should usually be discussed in advance with the principal for the purpose of keeping him informed and of getting ideas about how such projects might be improved. Although the principal may not know very much about the teaching of your particular subject, he is usually a former and presumably successful teacher who should be able to make valuable suggestions regarding teaching.

If teachers think of administrators as allies in the general war on ignorance, they should be able to get along well with them and to use them effectively in improving their own teaching. Instead of waiting for the administrator to visit and supervise, a teacher might go out of his way to invite him to watch some particularly interesting project under development. When the administrator does appear in his class room (invited or not), the teacher should continue to do the best job of teaching he can without trying to hide any problem from the principal (such as the pupil who does not do his work or the discipline problem). He can seek the administrator's aid later in solving the problem. If there are problems of a schoolwide nature (such as a need for homogeneous grouping of mathematics classes), he should present the administration with all the evidence he can collect showing that a problem exists and how it should be solved, and then ask for help. Usually when there is good evidence that a change should be made and that the teacher can use that change to improve education, an administrator will go out of his way to see that the appropriate change is made.

Of course, there are administrators who should not be allowed to administer *anything*. If a teacher happens to have the misfortune of getting one of them and knows that there is no real chance of changing him, that teacher should probably leave the school and look for work elsewhere. Of all the things that can interfere with the proper functioning of a good teacher, a poor administrator is one of the worst and one of the hardest to avoid.

There are other people in the school system who will be able to help a teacher carry out his duties. Often one of the most helpful members of any school staff is the guidance counselor. When a child is having troubles, the guidance department frequently can furnish facts and records that are of great help in determining a course of action. In severe cases, the child should probably have an appointment with the counselor (after the counselor has been given the background). If necessary, the counselor should be able to refer the case to any other source of aid that seems appropriate.

### Question for Further Thought and Study

1. Think about the teacher who was your favorite when you were in high school. What were the qualities that made you like him? Was he

an excellent teacher or was he only popular? What do you think are the qualities that make for excellence in a teacher?

2. Think of the worst teacher you had in high school. What were the qualities that made him a poor teacher?

3. What is the goal of a well-taught mathematics course? How do you think such a course should change the behavior of the pupils? Answer with respect to pupils of differing abilities and interest.

4. Prepare lesson plans for a topic of your choice and present a lesson to your class or other interested individuals.

5. Pick a topic from secondary school mathematics and prepare a test on that topic. What sort of part credit (if any) would you give for various types of wrong answers to each of your questions? What do you think should be a passing grade on your test? What score would be good enough for an A? How much time would you allow the pupils to take the test?

6. What do you believe is the best way to maintain order in the classroom?

7. Pick two teaching aids other than textbooks and blackboard and chalk and tell how you might use them in order to present some particular topic in mathematics more effectively.

8. Pick a textbook for high school mathematics and evaluate it on all points that you believe are important for such textbooks.

9. Read through one set of programmed instruction materials for high school mathematics and evaluate it as to its mathematical content and its effectiveness as a teaching device.

10. Review a film that you think might be of some value to you in teaching high school mathematics. Does the film do something which you could not do better by other means? If so, what and how? Evaluate the film's over-all effectiveness as an aid to teaching.

## REFERENCES

Adkins, Julia. "Are Students' Questions a Valid Criterion for Evaluating Creative Teachers?," *The Mathematics Teacher*, **LV** (March 1962), 177–178. Suggests that perhaps a good criterion for evaluating teacher effectiveness is the originality and spontaneity of pupils' questions. Do pupils ask only how to solve the problem at hand or do they try to open up new paths for investigation?

Ausubel, David P. "Learning by Discovery: Rationale and Mystique," *National Association of Secondary School Principals, Bulletin*, **45**, no. 269, (Dec., 1961). One of the most persistent critics of the discovery approach to teaching accepts the concept at early levels when children are relatively unsophisticated, and the time-cost factor is not important, but rejects the idea of using discovery methods in the upper high school grades.

Bartnick, Lawrence P. *Designing the Mathematics Classroom*, National Council of Teachers of Mathematics, Washington, D.C., 1957. Considers physical facilities, equipment, floor plans, etc.

Berger, Emil J., and Donovan A. Johnson. *A Guide to the Use and Procurement of Teaching Aids for Mathematics*, National Council of Teachers of Mathematics, Washington, D.C., 1959. Discusses how to use and where to acquire various aids to the teaching of mathematics. Bibliographies, reference materials, prices, and sources of materials are also included.

Committee on Aids for Evaluation of Textbooks of NCTM. "Aids for Evaluators of Mathematics Textbooks," *The Mathematics Teacher*, **LVII** (May 1965), 467–473. A brief description of what the six committee members thought was important in choosing a textbook or series of textbooks. (Available for 40¢ as a separate reprint. Write to the NCTM.)

*Computopics*, February 1965. Association for Computing Machinery, 211 E. 43rd St. New York. This special issue of the ACM's monthly news magazine includes a career guidance bibliography, which will be of interest to pupils considering any branch of mathematics, and a set of short reviews of motion pictures related to computers and the computer sciences. (May be obtained for 50¢ from the ACM.)

Council of Chief State School Officials and National Science Foundation. *Purchase Guide for Programs in Science and Mathematics*, Ginn and Co., Boston, 1965. An updated list of recommended items for elementary and secondary schools. Includes new guidelines for the purchase of such things as laboratory furniture and considers the role of the computer.

Fadiman, Clifton (ed.). *Fantasia Mathematica*, Simon and Schuster, New York, 1958. A collection of interesting, easily read essays, stories and poems about mathematics. Can be used for motivation or to give a substitute teacher something interesting and worthwhile to do.

———. *The Mathematical Magpie*, Simon and Schuster, New York, 1962. More of the sort of thing found in *Fantasia Mathematica*.

Forbes, Jack E. "Programmed Instructional Materials—Past, Present, and Future," *The Mathematics Teacher*, **LVI** (April 1963), 224–227. A good discussion of the underlying psychology of programmed learning and the place of programmed learning in the future of education.

Hoffman, Walter, et al. "Computers for School Mathematics," *The Mathematics Teacher*, **LVIII** (May 1965), 393–401. A practical discussion of ways to use a digital computer in the education of high school pupils and for other purposes in a school. Suggests various different methods of operation (courier service to a computer center, acquisition by school, etc.) and lists the pros and cons of each. Should be helpful to anybody considering a computer program for high school. (Now available free as a reprint. Write to NCTM.)

McDonald, Blanche, and Leslie Nelson. *Successful Classroom Control*, William C. Brown Co., Dubuque, Iowa. Includes many good practical hints on general classroom control in the elementary school and in secondary school.

Matchett, Margaret S. "Teaching Machines or What?" *The Mathematics Teacher,* **LV** (May 1962), 351–355.

Mathematical Association of America. *Guidebook to Departments in the Mathematical Sciences,* MAA, 1965. A survey of mathematics departments in the United States and Canada. This survey provides information on the faculty and facilities for teaching mathematics in colleges throughout North America. It should be of great value to teachers and guidance counselors who are advising pupils with substantial interest and ability in mathematics. (Can be obtained for 50¢ from the Mathematical Association of America, SUNY, at Buffalo, New York.)

May, Kenneth O. *Programed Learning and Mathematical Education,* Mathematical Association of America, Buffalo, 1965. A review of programed learning and programs in mathematics at the college level. May concludes that there is a need for better programs that encourage more independent work by the students. However, he believes that teacher and textbook will and should remain the most important factors in college mathematics classes. He also calls for more experimentation with all forms of auxiliary materials. (Single copies may be obtained free from the Executive Director, Committee on Educational Media, P.O. Box 2310, San Francisco, California.)

Myers, Sheldon S. *Mathematics Tests Available in the United States,* National Council of Teachers of Mathematics, Washington, D.C., 1959. Provides pertinent information about standardized tests including references in which reviews of specific tests can be found.

National Education Association. *A Manual on Certification Requirements for School Personnel in the United States,* NEA, Washington, D.C., 1965. Covers such topics as certification practices and trends among the states, a state-by-state listing of certificates and requirements, securing a teaching job in the United States or abroad, etc. (Available for $4.00 from the National Education Association, 1201 Sixteenth St., N.W., Washington, D.C.)

National Education Association, Department of Instruction. "The New Mathematics," *Audiovisual Instruction,* **VII** (March 1962), 136–186. Entire issue considers the use of audiovisual aids in teaching current mathematics programs. Also includes articles on programed materials.

Schaaf, William M. *The High School Mathematics Library,* National Council of Teachers of Mathematics, Washington, D.C., 1960. Annotated bibliography of mathematics books which are appropriate for a high school library.

Willoughby, Stephen S. "Discovery," *The Mathematics Teacher,* **LVI** (January 1963), 22–25. A description of an extended discovery lesson in which pupils had great freedom and responsibility in determining what was to be discussed.

Willoughby, Stephen S., Gene Tornow, and M. Vere DeVault. *The Mathematics In-Service Education Program in Watertown Public Schools.* Department of Education, University of Wisconsin, Madison, 1963. Report on an in-service mathematics program for teachers. See quotations in chapter.

*Enrichment Mathematics for High School.* Twenty-eighth Yearbook of the National Council of Teachers of Mathematics, Washington, D.C., NCTM, 1961. Discussion of many topics of mathematics which, though not essential for the usual high school curriculum, may be of great interest mathematically to the talented pupil.

*Evaluation in Mathematics.* Twenty-sixth Yearbook of the National Council of Teachers of Mathematics, NCTM, Washington, D.C., 1961. Considers the general theory of measurement as it applies to achievement in mathematics. Many topics which are of interest to the classroom teacher are discussed and a list of published tests in mathematics is provided with some comments.

"Reviews of Films, A Report of Some Reviewing Committees," *The Mathematics Teacher*, **LVI** (December 1963), 578–605. Reviews of more than 150 mathematics films.

# ARITHMETIC

If a school has a strong mathematics program for kindergarten through twelfth grade, not only arithmetic, but also a good deal of simple algebra and intuitive geometry will be studied by the pupils before they reach the seventh grade. If no such program exists, the secondary school teacher should, as a minimum, find out what is being taught in the elementary schools so as to plan an intelligent course on that base.

Some of the newer programs for elementary school include work with factoring and prime numbers, sets, numeration systems, properties of operations (commutative, associative, and distributive laws), simple exponents, the number line (both positive and negative ), lines, planes, congruence, angle measure, coordinate systems, circles, and volumes as well as more emphasis on understanding arithmetic than has been common in the elementary schools. Clearly, such a program in the elementary school would have considerable effect on what can, and should, be done in the secondary school. Some of the work presented in this and later chapters may have already been completed in the elementary schools, but should be familiar to a secondary school teacher so that he will be able to continue the program intelligently, review adequately, and plan an appropriate program including those topics that have not been covered previously.

One important new development in the teaching of mathematics at all levels is the increased emphasis on understanding. Since carrying out most of the fundamental operations of arithmetic depends on the numeration system used, it is important that children understand the decimal system. One way to attain a better understanding of the decimal system is to study another, similar, numeration system and note the similarities and differences. For this reason, there has been some emphasis on other numeration systems in many of the newer junior high school programs and in some of the elementary school materials.

## Multiplication

Perhaps the best way for individuals who have already learned the algorithms[1] of arithmetic to study the decimal system is to attempt to explain why some of them work. Ask any normal adult to multiply 347 by 862, and he will probably write down the following work, in about the following way:

$$
\begin{array}{r}
347 \\
\times\,862 \\
\hline
694 \\
2082 \\
2776 \\
\hline
299114
\end{array}
$$

If we ask the individual why he takes these particular steps, he will be unable to explain clearly. If the reader will consider this same question, he may be surprised at his own lack of understanding of this basic arithmetic procedure. For example, since we are accustomed to reading from left to right, why do we start at the wrong end? Why, in multiplying the 7 by 2, do we not just write down the 14 somewhere instead of "putting down the 4 and carrying the 1"? Why do we break up the 862, multiplying first by the 2, next by the 6, and finally by the 8, and than add the products obtained? Is there any reason to suppose that this really works, other than that we were told that it does when we were too young to protest? Other questions that can be asked about the algorithm of multiplication call attention to some of the more obvious difficulties a young pupil might face if he were to try to understand the multiplication process.

---

[1] An algorithm (sometimes spelled "algorism," and pronounced appropriately) is any procedure for carrying out a specific operation in arithmetic. Thus, the procedure commonly used for long division is an algorithm, as is any procedure for finding a square root. Although newspaper articles sometimes refer to this as one of the new words in modern mathematics, it has been with us for some time as shown by the fact that it is derived from the name of a ninth-century Arab mathematician.

The answers to all these questions are inherent in our numeration system and in certain basic facts about addition and multiplication. First, let us consider the numeration system. What does the numeral "347" mean? Does the "3" in "347" really stand for three, or does it stand for three hundreds, or 300? Similarly, does the "4" actually stand for four tens, or 40? Then, the numeral "347" could be written "300 + 40 + 7," or even, "3 × 100 + 4 × 10 + 7." In a similar way, "862" can be written "800 + 60 + 2" or "8 × 100 + 6 × 10 + 2." Now, with knowledge of the multiplication table through nine times nine, and certain facts about products of powers of ten, the following calculations can be carried out (without discussing at this juncture whether the procedure of "breaking up the 862 and then adding the partial products" is legitimate):

$$
\begin{array}{r}
300 + 40 + 7 \\
800 + 60 + 2 \\
\hline
14 \\
80 \\
600 \\
420 \\
2400 \\
18000 \\
5600 \\
32000 \\
240000 \\
\hline
299114
\end{array}
$$

Although this procedure takes more space than the commonly used method presented earlier, it has distinct advantages for the pupil just learning to multiply. The most obvious is that the beginning pupil does not have to "carry numbers in his head" while doing the multiplications. Another advantage is that this procedure is easier to explain. Before continuing with the explanation, a couple of comments should be made. First, it does not make any difference in which order we work. We could start by multiplying 300 by 800, getting 240,000. Done as it was it seems more similar to the usual procedure and thus more familiar to the reader. It probably should be done this way in school in order to make the shortcut which may be introduced later seem more reasonable. There is probably no truth to the rumor that we write our numerals the way we do—backwards—because the Arabs wrote backwards; many changes have occurred in the Arabic numeration system since it was introduced into Europe. More likely, the system has remained this way because the bigger numbers are usually more important, and we do not like to be kept in suspense. It is also worth noting that in this book we assume the reader is familiar with the arithmetic of powers of ten and their simple multiples, but an elementary school teacher would have to spend considerable time developing these ideas prior to considering multiplications of the sort under discussion.

There is still the matter of why the algorithm works. In order to explain this, certain basic facts of arithmetic, which in no way depend on the numeration system used, must be considered. These were presented in Chapter 3 (in the discovery lesson) but we shall state them again, explicitly. First, addition and multiplication can be carried on in either order without changing the results (the commutative laws). Second, when adding (or multiplying) three numbers, the results will be the same if the third is added to (multiplied by) the sum (or product) of the first two, or if the sum (product) of the last two is added to (multiplied by) the first (the associative laws). The difficulty in stating clearly these and the following facts in the English language suggests one advantage of algebraic notation. The third fact, which is not as intuitively obvious as the other two, is called the *distributive law*. It says that the product of a number and the sum of two others is equal to the sum of the products obtained by multiplying the first by each of the others. These five laws can be stated using algebraic notation in the following manner:

Commutative law (addition):   For all numbers, $a, b, a + b = b + a$.

Commutative law (multiplication):   For all numbers, $a, b, a \times b = b \times a$.

Associative law (addition):   For all numbers, $a, b, c, a + (b + c) = (a + b) + c$.

Associative law (multiplication):   For all numbers, $a, b, c, a \times (b \times c) = (a \times b) \times c$.

Distributive law (multiplication over addition):   For all numbers, $a, b, c, a \times (b + c) = (a \times b) + (a \times c)$.

These five laws are basic properties of our number system, and ought to be well known to any student of mathematics. Furthermore, they are fundamental to an understanding of the basic algorithms of arithmetic, and therefore, they are commonly taught in the elementary schools.

Using the distributive law (twice), we can rewrite the product $(800 + 60 + 2) \times (300 + 40 + 7)$ as $(800 + 60 + 2) \times 300 + (800 + 60 + 2) \times 40 + (800 + 60 + 2) \times 7$, and then, by using the distributive law in conjunction with the commutative law for multiplication, we can rewrite this as $800 \times 300 + 60 \times 300 + 2 \times 300 + 800 \times 40 + 60 \times 40 + 2 \times 40 + 800 \times 7 + 60 \times 7 + 2 \times 7$. Therefore, the product of 862 and 347 can be written as the sum of the foregoing products. If these products are written in the usual column form, the procedure on p. 93 is justified.

Once pupils have understood and practiced an algorithm, they may start looking for shortcuts, or their teacher may help them to find some. For example,

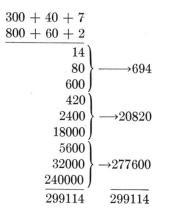

$$
\begin{array}{r}
300 + 40 + 7 \\
800 + 60 + 2 \\
\hline
\left.\begin{array}{r} 14 \\ 80 \\ 600 \end{array}\right\} \longrightarrow 694 \\
\left.\begin{array}{r} 420 \\ 2400 \\ 18000 \end{array}\right\} \longrightarrow 20820 \\
\left.\begin{array}{r} 5600 \\ 32000 \\ 240000 \end{array}\right\} \longrightarrow 277600 \\
\hline
299114 \qquad 299114
\end{array}
$$

The partial products found by multiplying by 2 can be added easily. Thus 14 and 80 are added to get 94 and then the 600 is added to get the partial product of 694. In a similar way, the number 20,820 can be seen to be the sum of the partial products found by using 60 as the multiplier, etc. Are there other shortcuts? One common answer is, "Yes, we can leave off the zeros from the partial products (and the multipliers) if we are careful to put the partial products in the right place.[2]" This is indeed correct, but let us see if we can find a more significant short cut.

Notice that in the multiplication procedure, only one of the partial products contributes anything to the units column of the final answer, namely, $2 \times 7$, or 14. Customarily, we "put down the 4 and carry the 1," since we know that the 1 stands for one 10, and therefore should be added in the tens column. How many of the partial products contribute to the tens column (ignoring, for the moment, the 1 which we

[2] Technically, the partial product is a number, and cannot be written or put anywhere. One of the trends in newer mathematics courses is to be very careful about the distinction between a number and a numeral. However, a great deal of care makes for awkward language and a great deal of difficulty as concepts become more abstract. Therefore, when no possible confusion could occur, we will follow the common custom of abbreviating a phrase such as "put the numeral for the partial product" with the phrase "put the partial product."

are carrying from the previous partial product)? Is the sum of 80 and 420, 500? This can be thought of as 50 tens. Recalling that we are to add the one 10 which was "carried" from the units column, we have 51 tens and can put down the 1 in the tens column and carry the 5 into the hundreds column. Three products will contribute to the hundreds column. The reader should be able to see what these are simply by looking at the original problem.

Will $2 \times 300$ result in some number of 100s? Will six 10s times four 10s result in some number (24) of 100s? Will 800 times 7 result in 56 100s? Then, by adding $6 \times 100$, $24 \times 100$, and $56 \times 100$ to the $5 \times 100$ which was left from the tens column will we find the correct number of 100s? Using the distributive law, we find $91 \times 100$ as the answer. Then we put the 1 in the hundreds column and carry the 9 into the thousands column, since 90 hundreds equals 9 thousands. The products that contribute to the thousands column are $60 \times 300$ and $800 \times 40$, resulting in 18,000 and 32,000 respectively. The sum of these is 50,000, added to the 9,000 carried from the hundreds column, is 59 thousands; we put down the 9 and carry the 5. Finally, the only product that contributes to the 10,000 column is $300 \times 800$ which produces a product of 24 ten thousands, or 240,000. If we add the 5 ten thousands which were carried from the thousands column, the result is 29 ten thousands. Since there are no products that contribute to any column to the left of the 10,000 column, we write the 9 in the ten-thousands column and the 2 in the hundred-thousands column, and the problem is finished.

If this procedure were written in standard form, the steps would look as follows:

347

862

4 (carry 1)                $2 \times 7 = 14$, put down 4 and carry 1.

347

862

14 (carry 5)               $2 \times 4 = 8$, $6 \times 7 = 42$, $8 + 42 + 1 = 51$, put down 1 and carry 5.

347

862

114 (carry 9)              $2 \times 3 = 6$, $6 \times 4 = 24$, $8 \times 7 = 56$, $6 + 24 + 56 + 5 = 91$, put down 1 and carry the 9.

347

862

9114 (carry 5)             $6 \times 3 = 18$,   $8 \times 4 = 32$,   $18 + 32 + 9 = 59$, put down 9 and carry the 5.

  347

  862

299114                     $8 \times 3 = 24$, $24 + 5 = 29$.

The only thing that would appear on paper would be the multiplicand, the multiplier, and the product, as in the last step. This is clearly a shortcut, at least in terms of the amount of paper used. It has the same relation to the usual procedure as that procedure has to writing down every partial product without attempting to add until all partial products have been written. Therefore, this method should be as easy for the reader to learn as the usual procedure is for the elementary school youngster. Does this mean that the method should be taught to all schoolchildren? Probably not. Remembering all the sums that are required without using paper while doing the multiplication necessitates some concentration, and there is reason to believe that young pupils should be dwelling on the important steps of the multiplication algorithm rather than the shortcuts which require much concentration in themselves. By the same reasoning, the common algorithm should probably not be taught until the children have understood and become adept at finding a product by writing down each partial product and computing the sum. In other words, the moral is not that there is a shorter way to do multiplication, but that short cuts are fine in their place, though understanding is far more important, especially, when learning a procedure.

The procedure described above, for multiplying multidigit numbers, is commonly advocated by present-day mathematics educators, and is found in many textbooks. However, there is some reason to suppose that young pupils who are learning the algorithm for the first time do not follow and fully appreciate the several uses of the distributive law required to justify the procedure.

In light of this, perhaps the following procedure would be more appropriate when introducing multiplication of multidigit numbers for the first time. If the pupil understands multiplication, he will agree that the answer to the question "37 $\times$ 24 equals what?" can be found by adding 24 to itself 37 times, or by counting the number of objects in the following array:

At first glance, the prospect of counting all of the objects in the array may dismay the fainthearted. However, one of the beauties of mathematics is that it can be used to make difficult and complicated problems easy. In this case, it will be noticed that the objects were grouped in groups of ten. This is standard procedure in a numeration system based on ten. Now, the pupil can be encouraged to discover that there are several rectangles (or "boxes"), each of which is a ten by ten array. From his knowledge of the numeration system, he will immediately conclude that there are 100 objects in each of these. How many groups of 100 objects are there? Six (if he does not notice the relation between this number and $3 \times 2$, that can wait for the time when he has done more problems and more complicated problems).

There are also three groups of ten fours, or three groups of four tens, depending on whether horizontal or vertical groups are considered—in this case, the latter procedure is more helpful. So far, 600 plus $3 \times 4 \times 10$, or $600 + 120$, objects have been counted. There are two groups of seven tens, or 140 objects. And, finally, there are seven groups of four objects, or 28. Thus, the answer to the problem can be found by adding: $600 + 120 + 140 + 28$.

The relationship between this procedure and the usual algorithm should be obvious to the reader. With more practice, and perhaps a little encouragement, the children will move quickly to the point of finding the partial products and adding without benefit of the picture.

It is worth noting that there was no long train of reasoning to follow, and no use of principles that may still seem rather vague to the pupils. It is also worth noting that from such procedures, the distributive law and similar laws can be discovered quite easily by the pupils—if the teacher believes such laws are worth having at this time.

## Division

The procedures in a standard long-division problem are every bit as mysterious to the average adult as those used in multiplication. For example,

$$
\begin{array}{r}
1996 \ R \ 10 \\
37)\overline{73862} \\
37 \\
\overline{368} \\
333 \\
\overline{356} \\
333 \\
\overline{232} \\
222 \\
\overline{10}
\end{array}
$$

Why do we divide the 37 only into the 73 on the first step rather than into the whole number? Why do we bring down precisely one digit at the beginning of each step? What is the division process all about anyway—that is, what sort of answer do we seek?

In a division problem such as this one, we are looking for a number $Q$ and a number $R$ such that $37 \times Q = 73,862$ or $37 \times Q + R = 73,862$, where $R$ is a positive integer less than 37. An alternate way of saying this is that if we subtract 37 from 73,862 as often as possible without getting a negative result, the number of times that we subtract 37 will be the quotient (Q), and any positive integer (less than 37) that remains will be the remainder (R). This last sentence can be used to explain the division algorithm and to write it in a form that will make more sense to the child who is beginning to learn long division.

Suppose one wished to find out how many times he could subtract 37 from 73,862 and still get a nonnegative result. One way he could do this would be to start subtracting and count. There must be a faster way. Suppose, instead of subtracting only one 37 at a time, we subtract one-hundred 37s or even one-thousand 37s, the process will be much faster. Could we subtract two-thousand 37s from 73,862? The answer is no, but it is not really necessary to make that decision at this time. If it is possible to subtract 2000 37s, we can find that out by first subtracting one-thousand of them and then seeing whether we can subtract another thousand of them. Here the division process is reduced to a sequence of successive subtractions. In order to keep track of the number of 37s that have been subtracted, we will write them in a column to the right of our work and add this column when we are finished.

$$
\begin{array}{r|r}
37)\overline{73862} & \\
37000 & 1000 \\
\hline
36862 & \\
18500 & 500 \\
\hline
18362 & \\
11100 & 300 \\
\hline
7262 & \\
3700 & 100 \\
\hline
3562 & \\
2960 & 80 \\
\hline
602 & \\
370 & 10 \\
\hline
232 & \\
185 & 5 \\
\hline
47 & \\
37 & 1 \\
\hline
10 & 1996 \\
\end{array}
$$

This procedure requires more paper, and it looks less efficient than the customary procedure. But notice some of the advantages of this method over the one that is commonly used. One of the most difficult problems in the long-division algorithm, for a child who is just learning, is the choice of the right trial divisor. If the wrong divisor is chosen, the pupil must erase his work (making quite a mess, usually) and try again. The trial and error method can be discouraging. In the process shown, if the pupil guesses a number that is too small, he can make it up on the next step. In the example, we have gone out of the way to guess an unusually small number on the second step (500) in order to show that no matter how low the guess, no irreversible error is involved. In actual practice, pupils will generally round the divisor (37) off to the next higher number for which only the first digit is something other than zero (40) and use this as a trial divisor. Thus 900 would have been the second partial quotient (since 40 goes into 36,862 900 times—with room to spare), and the others would be 80, 10, 5, and 1 as indicated.

As pupils get better at this, they learn to make more accurate guesses until they can guess the correct digit for each column rather well on the first try, without extra motion. By this time, they may start omitting superfluous zeros and adding the numbers "in their heads," so that they simply write down the quotient beside the dividend without having to add a column of figures. Also, the zeros in the subtrahends may be omitted, and the resulting calculation will look very much like the one commonly used. Finally, in order to keep track of the place in which each digit of the quotient belongs, they may find it convenient to write the quotient above the dividend, in the customary way. However, it is important for the pupil's learning that the short cuts come *after* his basic understanding instead of coming at the very beginning of his exposure to the concepts of division. "Short division" should probably not be taught to a pupil until after he has acquired an understanding of long division—by then it should be easy for him to learn and understand.

If many members of a seventh or eighth grade class lack understanding of long division (or multiplication) one might well spend a day or two on a discussion of this sort to help them understand these processes better; but in general it is better to teach through understanding the first time than to teach by rote and then say "Now would you like to know what you've been doing all of this time?"

## Square Roots

Undoubtedly, the arithmetic algorithm with the most mystery for most people is the square-root algorithm. One national television show pictured a group of adults who were attempting, one after another, to find the square root of a simple number. Each adult used a somewhat different procedure, and each got an entirely different answer (when an answer was forthcoming at all). Finally, a small child walked into the store where the program was being televised and did the problem with no trouble at all. The child had undoubtedly just learned the algorithm and therefore had no difficulty with it. However, had that same individual been offered the same problem several years later, he would probably have reacted in about the same way as did the adults. At least 99 % of the adults in this country who are not actively using the square-root algorithm (most of those who are using it are undoubtedly those who are teaching it) cannot remember how to do it—they remember that there is such a procedure and that it is very important, but if they were marooned on an island with no way to get off until they had found the square root of 87,654 to the nearest hundredth, they would spend the rest of their lives on the island.

Square roots are really quite easy to find to any degree of accuracy, and any normal adult can find the square root of any number as accurately as desired after only a few seconds of instruction. Any person who can answer the question, "What is a square root?" and who knows how to multiply can find a square root. The square root of 87,654 is the number that when multiplied by itself, produces a product of 87,654. You can find the square root of 87,654 if you multiply numbers by themselves until you get a product of 87,654 (or something reasonably close to 87,654). The following procedure is about what would be expected:

$200 \times 200$ or $200^2 = 40000$
$300^2 = 90000$

87654 is between 40000 and 90000 but much closer to 90000; therefore, the next reasonable guess is 290.

$290^2 = 84100$

87654 is between 84100 and 90000, perhaps a little closer to 90000 but not much; therefore, a next reasonable guess is 295 or 296.

$295^2 = 87025$
$296^2 = 87616$
$297^2 = 88209$

The square root of 87654 must be greater than 296 but less than 297. Since the difference between 88209 and 87654 is 555, and the difference between 87654 and 87616 is only 38, the answer must be much closer to 296 than to 297. Try 296.1. $296.1^2 = 87674.21$; 87674.21 is too large (by 20.21), and therefore the answer is between 296 and 296.1, probably about $\frac{2}{3}$ of the way from 296 to 296.1. The answer is probably between 296.06 and 296.07. If each of these is tried, it can be seen that the answer *is* in fact between 296.06 and 296.07 and slightly closer to 296.06.

The reader's reaction may be that this is an inefficient method of finding a square root, and indeed it is. With no use of computing devices, this procedure will probably take about twice as long as the standard algorithm. However, is it not more important that people understand what a square root is and know at least *some* method of finding one than that they memorize a procedure that is quick but easily forgotten?

Notice that a person has almost nothing to remember when he seeks square roots by this process. If he remembers the definition of square root and knows how to multiply, the rest is obvious. Some people have decided that this is the modern way to teach square root but that we should try to make it more efficient. These people insist that the pupils memorize the square and square root tables up to 100 so that the first guess will be very accurate. They teach several other tricks that allow the pupils to carry out the squaring process quickly. This "efficiency" misses the point because speed gained at the cost of understanding is not worth the price. If the object is to create something that will perform a calculation quickly and accurately without thinking, it is cheaper and more efficient to make machines than to educate people.

Once the pupils have a complete understanding of the square-root procedure that was described, they can be shown shortcuts that they should be able to understand. For example, let us suppose we guess that 300 is the square root of 87654. If we divide 300 into 87654 and it really is the square root of 87654, what would the quotient be? If 300 is too small, would the quotient be greater than 300 and also greater than the desired answer? If 300 is too great, would the quotient be less than 300 and also less than the desired answer? Then, if 300 is divided into 87654 and the average of 300 and that quotient is found, should that average be approximately the desired square root? The following calculations show how the square root of 87654 would be obtained by this means:

$$\frac{292.18}{300)\overline{87654}}$$    The average of 292 and 300 is 296, so we use that as

the next guess.

$$\frac{296.12}{296)\overline{87654.00}}$$    The average of 296 and 296.12 is 296.06, which is

correct to the nearest hundredth. If it is desired to find the square root more accurately, 296.06 can be used as a divisor:

$$\frac{296.0683^{+}}{296.06)\overline{87654.0000000}}$$    The average of 296.06 and 296.0683 is ap-

proximately 296.0642, which is the correct answer to the nearest ten thousandth.

Several comments should be made about this procedure. First, it is fast—probably faster than the standard method for most square roots, and certainly faster than the guess-and-multiply method, though not as intuitively obvious (the author spent about two minutes getting the answer 296.06 in contrast to two and one-half minutes by the standard algorithm and four minutes by the guess-and-multiply method. Second, this procedure makes good sense to most junior high school children when it is explained to them, and they remember it much better than the standard algorithm. Third, this method and the guess-and-multiply method both have built-in correcting procedures. If a pupil makes a mistake in either method, he will find out at the next step that his new guess is not as accurate as it should be. If the mistake is not very significant, he can ignore the error and will still tend to get closer to the square root with each successive step. But with the standard algorithm, he will usually find a mistake only by checking over all the work he has done or by recomputing the square root by some means; either of these procedures requires about double (or more) the original effort expended. The method described of dividing and averaging is often called Newton's method, since it is similar to (in fact, is a special case of) a procedure used by Newton to approximate the zeros of a function. It is also an iterative technique. This is one of the few cases in school mathematics where an iterative process is appropriate. Considering the great importance of iteration in more advanced mathematics and applications, this is another reason for using this procedure rather than the traditional one.

No discussion of square roots would be complete without consideration of the standard algorithm. The strength of tradition in our society is demonstrated by the young children who, when taught one of the foregoing methods of taking square roots, will come to school and tell the teacher that they would now like to learn *the* method for taking square roots. The teacher says, "But you've just learned a method for taking square roots." "But there's another method that's better," the children insist. "Oh, how do you know?" the teacher asks. "My father (mother, sister, brother, or uncle) told me so." The teacher suggests, "Well, then, why don't you ask your father how to do it?" And the answer is, "I did—he's forgotten how—but it's the best method of doing it, he told me so!" "Do you think you'll ever forget the method you've just learned?" "No, how could anybody forget anything as simple as that?" "But you still believe this method that your father remembers but has forgotten how to do is better?" "Well, yes, I guess so,—anyway, I want to learn how to do it." It is not the place of the teacher to withhold knowledge, however useless or transitory, from pupils, or to shake their faith in tradition or relatives; if a pupil is insistent, a teacher should teach him the traditional algorithm but be sure to explain to him why it works, too.

The traditional algorithm is used below to approximate the square root of 87654 to the nearest ten-thousandth with no explanation. An explanation follows.

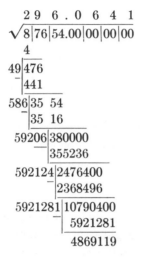

From the size of the remainder, it is clear that the next digit would be about 8, and therefore the answer, correct to the nearest ten thousandth, 296.0642. The reader is presumably familiar enough with the algorithm to follow the steps that were taken; if not, the following explanation should make clear both how and why the steps were taken.

First, the reason for dividing the digits of the given number into groups of two starting from the decimal point and working in both directions is that the square of any number has either twice as many digits as the number or one less than twice as many. Further, in the procedure that is shown, one new digit is acquired at a time, and two additional digits of the given number are sufficient to produce the next digit of the answer accurately. Actually, once the first step has been taken correctly (finding the largest perfect square in which only the first digit is nonzero), it makes no difference how many digits are "brought down" as long as at least two new ones are available each time.

Now, imagine a large square with an area of precisely 87654 square units (Fig. 4.1). The problem is to find the length of one side of this square. Because 300 is too large, we take 200 as a first guess. A square with a side 200 units in length will have an area of 40000 square units, and therefore the remaining area must be 87654 minus 40000 or 47654.

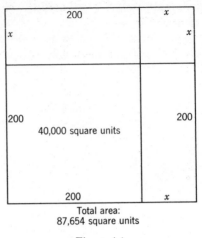

Total area:
87,654 square units

Figure 4.1

But the remaining area is made up of two rectangles, each 200 units in length and $x$ units in height ($x$ is the number that must be added to 200 to get the desired square root), and one square that has a side $x$ units in length. If the rectangles and the square are placed together as in Fig 4.2, the length of the resulting rectangle is $200 + 200 + x$ and the height is $x$.

Thus, in order to find the desired square root, the number $x$ must be determined. It is clear that the number $x$ is such that $(400 + x)$ times $x$ is 47654, and therefore a good approximation of $x$ can be found by dividing 47654 by $400 + x$. Since $x$ is unknown, this does not look particularly easy, but in practice it is not as difficult as it may seem. Here 90 is the greatest integer having the desired properties, with the only nonzero digit the first one.

From Fig. 4.2, it is clear that if 90 is taken as the approximate height

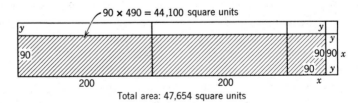

Total area: 47,654 square units

Figure 4.2

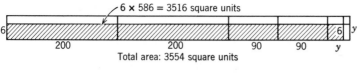

6 × 586 = 3516 square units

Total area: 3554 square units

Figure 4.3

of the rectangle, the area of the new rectangle shaded is 90 times 490 or 44100 square units. Since the desired rectangle should have an area of 47654 square units, there is a difference in area of 3554 square units. Thus, the number $x$ must be equal to $90 + y$ where $y$ is the height of the small rectangles at the top of the figure. Rearranging the rectangles as before (Fig. 4.3), we see that the new rectangle has a height of $y$ and a length of $200 + 200 + 90 + 90 + y$ or $580 + y$ (twice the approximate square root, 290, plus $y$), and the area of the rectangle is $47654 - 44100$ or 3554. Thus, the next trial divisor will be $580 + y$, the next best approximation (for $y$) is 6, and the process can be continued in a similar fashion as long as desired. Omitting zeros and decimal points and "bringing down" just the right digits at any given time are simply trivial ways to speed up the procedure but are not fundamental to it. One might get a better estimate on any particular step by trying to guess more than one digit at a time. For example, on the first step 290 could have been used instead of 200, or on the second step 96 could have been used instead of 90. But the time that would be saved by this action would not be enough to justify the extra effort and higher probability of mistakes. In fact, the entire algorithm has very little to recommend it except historical interest.

### Fractions

Although the concepts involved in addition and subtraction of fractions are not particularly simple, the treatment of these operations in the elementary schools has been surprisingly good. In general, children are introduced to fractions in connection with parts of objects or parts of sets of objects. Most people who have gone through an elementary arithmetic program are accustomed to thinking of $\frac{3}{4}$ as a pie or some similar object that has been cut into four pieces of the same size with one piece removed (or not counted). Similarly, $\frac{1}{3}$ is familiar as one of three equal-sized pieces of a whole pie. If a pupil has reason to add these two fractions, he can simply think of each pie as cut into 12 pieces of equal size, with the quarters cut into thirds and thirds into quarters (see Fig. 4.4). The $\frac{3}{4}$ can be seen to represent the same amount of pie as

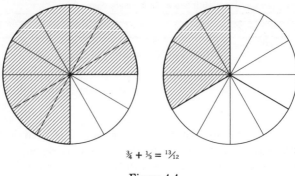

$$\tfrac{3}{4} + \tfrac{1}{3} = {}^{13}\!/_{12}$$

Figure 4.4

$\tfrac{9}{12}$, while the $\tfrac{1}{3}$ represents the same amount of pie as $\tfrac{4}{12}$. Thus, the amount of pie represented by $\tfrac{3}{4} + \tfrac{1}{3}$ is the same as the amount represented by $\tfrac{9}{12} + \tfrac{4}{12}$. Now the total amount of pie can be represented by $\tfrac{13}{12}$. Subtraction can be approached by using a large number of physical examples that can be actual physical objects in the hands of the pupils. Even multiplication is usually considered in a way that makes it seem reasonable; at least in part because of the naturalness of the process itself, few pupils get to high school without being able to multiply fractions.

However, division of fractions causes an amazing amount of difficulty among secondary school mathematics students as well as among many adults. This difficulty apparently results from the teaching of the division of fractions as a procedure that must be committed to memory rather than as a procedure to be explained and understood.

There are many ways to explain the division algorithm with fractions, and any one of these that the children really understand should help them to remember the procedure and use it more effectively. A good teacher of mathematics can, with a little thought, present at least one method that children can readily understand. Several ideas are offered for consideration.

Consider $\tfrac{3}{7} \div \tfrac{5}{8}$. From previous work they have done, the pupils should see no difficulty in rewriting this problem as: $\tfrac{3}{7}/\tfrac{5}{8}$. The pupils must know that when a number is multiplied by 1, the product is equal to the original number. They should also have seen different names for 1, such as $\tfrac{3}{3}$, $\tfrac{11}{11}$, and $\tfrac{2}{3}/\tfrac{2}{3}$. Is there any name of 1 that would be particularly convenient to use when multiplying $\tfrac{3}{7}/\tfrac{5}{8}$ by 1? At this point, pupils may have a little difficulty, but a teacher might help with a hint about finding a fraction in which the denominator is 1. Then the following calculations should not seem very strange:

$$\frac{3}{7} \div \frac{5}{8} = \frac{\frac{3}{7}}{\frac{5}{8}} = \left(\frac{\frac{3}{7}}{\frac{5}{8}}\right) \times \left(\frac{\frac{8}{5}}{\frac{8}{5}}\right) = \frac{\frac{3}{7} \times \frac{8}{5}}{\frac{5}{8} \times \frac{8}{5}} = \frac{\frac{24}{35}}{\frac{40}{40}} = \frac{\frac{24}{35}}{1} = \frac{24}{35}$$

Of course, this calculation is drawn out almost to the extreme, but every step should make good sense to a pupil who has a good background in arithmetic up to, but not including, division of fractions. After going through this complete calculation a few times, many pupils begin to abbreviate it themselves; it would be surprising if most of them did not come up with a method equivalent to the "invert and multiply" system (without those words) in a fairly short time.

Another explanation depends upon the definition of division. In using this explanation, one may employ the convention of omitting the "$\times$" or "times" sign between variables, numerals and variables, and expressions within parentheses. A raised dot will be used to designate multiplication, when convenient. From the definition of division, $\frac{3}{7} \div \frac{5}{8} = x$ if and only if $\frac{3}{7} = \frac{5}{8} x$. So the problem boils down to one of finding a number, $x$, such that $\frac{5}{8}$ times the number is $\frac{3}{7}$. We know that $\frac{3}{7}$ times 1 is $\frac{3}{7}$, so if we could find a number that, when multiplied by $\frac{5}{8}$, would yield 1, the answer would follow immediately. Now $\frac{5}{8} \cdot \frac{8}{5} = 1$. So $(\frac{5}{8} \cdot \frac{8}{5}) \cdot \frac{3}{7} = \frac{3}{7}$ or $\frac{5}{8} \cdot (\frac{8}{5} \cdot \frac{3}{7}) = \frac{3}{7}$. But the number in parentheses must be precisely the number for which we were looking, since $\frac{5}{8} x = \frac{3}{7}$ where $x = \frac{3}{7} \div \frac{5}{8}$. Therefore, $\frac{3}{7} \div \frac{5}{8} = \frac{3}{7} \cdot \frac{8}{5}$.

There are other ways of finding out how to divide fractions, but the important thing is for children to learn processes such as this through understanding rather than by rote. Otherwise, they will grow up with some vague notion such as, "You invert one of them and multiply, but I don't know why, nor do I know which one to invert—but at least I have a 50–50 chance of getting the right answer."

One more comment is necessary before we leave the topic of fractions. Many people are under the false impression that fractions and ratios are essentially the same. The very way in which the two are commonly written encourages this thought. The multiplication of fractions, on occasion, by ratios lends even more credence to this misconception. Actually, a ratio is an entirely different animal from a fraction. This difference can be seen in their relation to the real world—they communicate different kinds of information. A ratio expresses a comparison between two numbers; for example, "I bought three apples for eight cents" can be expressed by the ratio $\frac{3}{8}$, or "We have won two out of three games" can be expressed by the ratio $\frac{2}{3}$. Although the ideas expressed by these ratios are closely related to ideas that can be expressed by use of fractions (for example, "We have won two-thirds of our games" or "I bought apples at the rate of $\frac{3}{8}$ of an apple per penny"), the use of fractions in these instances is a little artifical and does not provide the same information. However, it is very clear that ratios and fractions are different when one tries to define simple operations for them.

The definitions of the operations for fractions are well-known ($a/b + c/d = (ad + bd)/bd$ and $a/b \cdot c/d = ac/bd$), but what about the operations for ratios? Actually, for these operations to be defined so as to represent the corresponding physical situation, they must be defined in the same way as the corresponding operations for vectors. Thus, if we wish to add the ratios $\frac{3}{8}$ and $\frac{5}{7}$, we do not get $\frac{61}{56}$ as we would if they were fractions; instead, the answer is $\frac{8}{15}$. This can be illustrated by two simple examples: first, if we should buy three apples for eight cents and then get a bargain and buy five apples for seven cents, we would have bought a total of eight apples for 15 cents; second, if a team should win three out of its first eight games and then win five of its next seven games, the team will have won eight out of 15 games and not 61 out of 56 games. For addition, at least, it is clear that ratios do not behave in the same way as fractions. Ratios are not fractions and should not be confused with them. Usually, addition and multiplication of ratios are not defined in elementary mathematics.

### Summary

This chapter considers only a few of the aspects of arithmetic that will arise in the secondary schools. If the general emphasis on understanding that has been adopted here is carried on into the other topics, the pupils will understand, remember, and use their arithmetic more effectively. One benefit of the study of algebra ought to be a better understanding of arithmetic.

### Questions for Further Thought and Study

1. Study two arithmetic textbooks published prior to 1955 and two published since 1960, and describe the major differences. Which do you believe would be easier for the pupils to understand? With which program do you believe the pupils would be better able to perform the usual numerical calculations quickly and accurately? Which seems to do the best job with problem solving?

2. What is the place of such physical aids as an abacus, Cuisenair rods, an adding machine, play money, etc., in the teaching of arithmetic?

### Exercises

1. Multiply 891 by 743 in each of the following ways:
(a) Write down nine partial products and add.

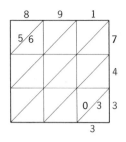

(b) Write down three partial products and add (the usual way).

(c) Write down no partial products (do all additions "in your head" as described in the chapter).

(d) Using the box above (or a similar one drawn on your paper), write each product in the appropriate square with the tens digit above the diagonal (as has been done for 7 times 8 and 3 times 1). Add "down" the diagonals to the left, starting with the bottom right diagonal (getting 3). You should be able to read the product down the left side and across the bottom.

2. Explain, using the commutative, associative, and distributive laws, why $26 \times 39 = 1014$.

3. Explain, using appropriate laws, why $36 + 893 + 77 + 2359 = 3365$.

4. Divide 89374 by 56 two times. First, use the algorithm discussed in the chapter (successive subtractions) and then use the regular algorithm.

5. Find the square root of 87932 to two significant figures in three different ways. (You might be interested in timing yourself for each method—if you do, try not to remember the results of one procedure when using another.)

6. Give an algebraic explanation of why the traditional square root algorithm works.

7. Devise an algorithm for taking the cube root of a number.

8. Explain how to divide $\frac{3}{7}$ by $\frac{4}{5}$ as though you were talking to a seventh-grade pupil who had forgotten how to divide fractions.

## REFERENCES

Crouch, Ralph, and George Baldwin. *Mathematics for Elementary Teachers*, John Wiley and Sons, New York, 1964. A study of the mathematical concepts underlying the elementary school mathematics program. Written for elementary school teachers. Includes number systems from the natural numbers to the reals, and work with simple concepts of geometry.

Deans, Edwina. *Elementary School Mathematics: New Directions*, U.S. Office of Education, Washington, D.C., 1963. See comments in Chapter 2.

National Council of Teachers of Mathematics. *Enrichment Mathematics for the Grades*, Twenty-seventh Yearbook, NCTM, Washington, D.C., 1963.

Considers material which is not included in the usual elementary school program. The material can be used with groups or for individual study. The bibliographies should be of considerable help. Some of the material might be helpful for under-achievers in junior and senior high schools.

National Council of Teachers of Mathematics. *Topics for Elementary School Teachers,* Twenty-ninth Yearbook of the NCTM, Washington, D.C., 1964. See comments in Chapter 2.

Smith, David Eugene. *A Source Book in Mathematics,* 2 vols., Dover Publications, New York, 1959. Excerpts from the works of mathematicians who were active in creating various branches of elementary mathematics from the middle of the fifteenth century to the beginning of the twentieth. The first 200 pages (on arithmetic) include excerpts from the first arithmetic text ever printed (translated from the Italian by Smith), some of Robert Recorde's discussion of arithmetic algorithms, and the first attempts to make a calculating machine.

Van Engen, Henry. *Twentieth Century Mathematics for the Elementary School,* National Council of Teachers of Mathematics, 1959, Washington, D.C., 1959 (reprinted from the *Arithmetic Teacher*). An excellent discussion of new concepts of mathematics and of mathematics teaching.

Wagner, John. *Mathematics Text Materials for the Undergraduate Preparation of Elementary School Teachers,* Committee on the Undergraduate Program in Mathematics of the Mathematical Association of America, Pontiac, Michigan, 1963. Reviews all books which various publishers thought would be appropriate for a mathematics course for elementary school teachers.

CHAPTER

5

# NUMBER SYSTEMS AND
# NUMERATION SYSTEMS

An important feature of many new mathematics programs is emphasis on careful use of language. It is generally desirable to use language (in mathematics) in such a way that there is no doubt as to the meaning of any statement. School boys have long known such tricky questions as "How can you take half of twelve and get seven?" The answer is "Take the top half of 'XII' and get 'VII'." A slight variation on this trick was used in UICSM ninth-grade questions such as, "Which is greater, 5 or 3?" It is clear that if we are talking about numbers, 5 > 3, it is also clear that the numeral (the written mark designating three) "3" is considerably larger than is the numeral "5". Undoubtedly the distinction between objects and their names is important, and confusion would occur in the students' minds should their teachers and books be constantly confusing names and objects for which the names stand. But there is reason to believe that there was less confusion about these distinctions *before* this new emphasis occurred than there is now. When people are so concerned over how they say something that they no longer worry about what they are saying, the emphasis is in the wrong place. Surely any student of the foundations of mathematics must distinguish carefully between objects and their names, and teachers should not bewilder their pupils by confusing the two; but certainly

113

we should not emphasize these distinctions to the exclusion of more fundamental ideas. In this book there is some attempt to distinguish between objects and their names when no great complications will result from such distinctions, but there is no compulsion to be completely consistent in this regard. For a further discussion of the distinction between objects and names, see Chapter 8 or any good logic book.[1]

The distinction between numbers and numerals leads to a corresponding distinction between number systems and numeration systems. Thus, numeration systems differ in the way in which numbers are named, whereas number systems differ from one another in the actual behavior of the objects under discussion. This distinction should become clearer as these ideas are discussed more fully.

### Numeration Systems

In the numeration system with which most adults are familiar, the number ten plays a particularly important role. Ten is said to be the base of this system, which is called the *decimal system*. There is every reason to suppose that we use a decimal system of numeration because we have ten fingers. It is not entirely unreasonable to suggest that some civilizations developed number systems that were at least partially based on the number twenty because the people in those climates did not wear shoes. Let us suppose, however, that we had each started out life with only one hand (instead of two hands) on which were five fingers. Then, it would be natural to count in the following way: one, two, three, four, one hand; one hand and one, one hand and two, one hand and three, one hand and four, two hands; two hands and one, and so on. If the numerals "0, 1, 2, 3, 4" were used with their usual meanings, the numeration system that would go with this situation would look something like this: "1, 2, 3, 4, 10, 11, 12, 13, 14, 20, 21, 22, 23, 24, 30, 31, 32, 33, 34, 40, 41, 42, 43, 44," and so on. Here the numeral "10" stands for one hand and no units or five. Similarly, "20" stands for two hands or ten. What numeral would come after "44", since "44" means that the number counted so far is four hands and four, and one more would mean that we have another full hand? If another hand is to be counted in this system (which has no numeral for five), we must have a hand of hands; using this notation, we have 10 hands or 10 × 10 or 100. Continuing, the next numeral would be 101 (a hand of hands and one), and then 102, etc. The reader might find it entertaining to write several

[1] See Robert M. Exner, and Myron F. Rosskopf, *Logic in Elementary Mathematics*, McGraw-Hill Book Co., New York, 1959. Pp. 9–16.

more numerals from this system on a piece of paper. Remember, the numerals 5, 6, 7, 8, and 9 cannot be used.

With young children, a teacher can sometimes add fun to discussing such a system by making up names that seem appropriate for the various numerals. Thus, "13" might be read "handy-three," while "22" would be read "two-hands-and-two" or, perhaps shortened to "twandy-two." In a similar way, "30" might be read "trandy"; "40" would come out "frandy"; "100" would be read "one handred"; and "1000" would undoubtedly be read "one thoushand."

After suitable names have been established, a child might be asked, "Is handy-three (13) even or odd?" If the pupil were to answer quickly, he would probably say "odd." Of course, he would be wrong, since "13" (in this system) stands for one hand and three or five plus three or eight, which is an even number. In other words, the customary way of checking to see whether a number is odd or even (by looking at the last digit—if it is odd, the number is odd and if it is even, the number is even) does not work for a numeration system with base 5. Why not? Answers to this question and to many others like it should help pupils to understand their own (decimal) numeration system better.

Consider any whole number[2] that is represented by a numeral in the decimal system—for example, 3456. The "6" stands for six units, the "5" stands for five tens, and so on. Thus, the number 3456 can be represented in the following way:

$$6 + 5 \cdot 10 + 4 \cdot 100 + 3 \cdot 1000$$

Since 10 is divisible by 2, $5 \cdot 10$ must also be divisible by 2. Since any power of 10 is divisible by 2, $4 \cdot 100$ and $3 \cdot 1000$ must also be divisible by 2. By the distributive law, if $5 \cdot 10$, $4 \cdot 100$, and $3 \cdot 1000$ are divisible by 2, then $5 \cdot 10 + 4 \cdot 100 + 3 \cdot 1000$ has a factor of 2; the entire number, 3456, is divisible by 2 if 6 is divisible by 2 and is not divisible by 2 if 6 is not divisible by 2. This argument can be used for any number expressed in the decimal system; therefore, any number expressed in decimal notation is even if (and only if) the last digit of the numeral stands for an even number. It can be seen from this argument that the property in question depends on whether the base (10) of the numeration system is an even number or has a factor of 2. Does 5 have a factor of 2? Then, is there any reason to suppose that this same property would hold for a numeration system to the base 5? As a matter of fact, it is easy to show that this property cannot hold for any numeration system with a base that is not even.

[2] In this section "number" will refer to the nonnegative integers, 0, 1, 2, 3, . . . unless otherwise specified.

Is there any number, $n$, other than 2 for which it is possible to determine whether a number is divisible by $n$ if the last digit (in the decimal representation of the number) is divisible by $n$? From the foregoing argument, it should be apparent that this property would hold for any number that is a factor of 10. Are there any factors of 10 other than 2? Then, should this property work for both 5 and 10? Can one tell by just looking at the last digit of any numeral in the decimal system whether the number it represents is divisible by 5 and by 10? The reader may find it profitable to go through the earlier verification replacing 2 by 5 (or by 10).

Considering the numeration system to the base 5 again, does 5 have any factor other than itself and 1? Then, looking at the last digit of a numeral in the base 5 system would not help in determining divisibility (except by 5).

Is there any other way of determining whether a number expressed in the base 5 system is divisible by 2? Let us look at numerals in the base 5. The following is a table of how one would count in base 5:

|   |   |   |   |   |
|---|---|---|---|---|
| 1 | 2 | 3 | 4 | 10 |
| 11 | 12 | 13 | 14 | 20 |
| 21 | 22 | 23 | 24 | 30 |
| 31 | 32 | 33 | 34 | 40 |
| 41 | 42 | 43 | 44 | 100 |
| 101 | 102 | 103 | 104 | 110 |
| 111 | 112 | 113 | 114 | 120 |
| 121 | 122 | 123 | 124 | 130 |
| 131 | 132 | 133 | 134 | 140 |
| 141 | 142 | 143 | 144 | 200 |
| 201 | 202 | 203 | 204 | 210 |
|   |   | . . . |   |   |
| 441 | 442 | 443 | 444 | 1000 |
|   |   | . . . |   |   |

Which numbers are divisible by 4? (List the base 5 numerals for at least thirteen numbers that are divisible by 4.) The reader should actually write these out before proceeding. Now, add the digits of each of these numerals. Is there anything interesting? Are the sums of the digits (in base 5) the following: 4, 4, 4, 4, 4, 13, 4, 4, 4, 4, 13, 13, 4? Is the sum of the digits of the first thirteen numbers that are divisible by 4 either 4 or a number divisible by 4 if a numeration system to the base 5 is used? Does it seem reasonable to suppose that this pattern continues? Is there a similar phenomenon in the decimal system? What is it? That is, for what number, $n$, is any given number, $N$, divisible by

$n$ if and only if the sum of the digits of $N$ expressed in the decimal system, is divisible by $n$?

The careful reader will actually find two numbers that have the property mentioned in the last paragraph—they are 3 and 9. For the time being, we will concentrate on the number 9. Consider the number 3762 (base 10). This number can be expressed: $2 + 6 \cdot 10 + 7 \cdot 100 + 3 \cdot 1000$. The sum of the digits is $3 + 7 + 6 + 2$. Therefore, the difference $(D)$ between the number $(N = 3762)$ and the sum of its digits $(S)$ is $(2 + 6 \cdot 10 + 7 \cdot 100 + 3 \cdot 1000) - (3 + 7 + 6 + 2) = (2 - 2) + (6 \cdot 10 - 6) + (7 \cdot 100 - 7) + (3 \cdot 1000 - 3) = 9 \cdot 6 + 99 \cdot 7 + 999 \cdot 3$. Is $9 \cdot 6$ divisible by 9? Is $99 \cdot 7$ divisible by 9? Is $999 \cdot 3$ divisible by 9? In general, is any number that can be expressed in the form

$$\text{``9999} \cdots 9d\text{''}$$

where $d$ is a digit, divisible by 9? Then, for any number, $N$ (expressed in decimal notation), is the difference $(D)$ between the number $(N)$ and the sum of its digits $(S)$ always divisible by 9? From the equation $D = N - S$ and the knowledge that $D$ is always divisible 9, we should see that $N$ is divisible by 9 if and only if $S$ is divisible by 9. This fact can, perhaps, be made even clearer if we add $S$ to both members of the equation, getting $D + S = N$. Now, if $S$ is divisible by 9, then by the distributive law $D + S$ is divisible by 9 and, therefore, $N$ is divisible by 9 (since it is the same number as $D + S$). In a similar way, we can show that if $N$ is divisible by 9, then $S$ must also be divisible by 9. Therefore, any number is divisible by 9 if and only if the sum of its digits is divisible by 9. It is reasonably clear that if one considers the sum of the digits of a number and finds the sum of the digits of *that* sum, and then finds the sum of the digits of this last sum, and so on, sooner or later we will find a sum that can be represented by a single digit. If this happens and the original number was divisible by 9, what will the single digit be? Could it be 1, 2, 3, 4, 5, 6, 7, or 8 (remembering that it must be divisible by 9)? It cannot very well be zero, since it will always be the sum of positive numbers; therefore, it must be 9. Hence, if the sum of the digits of a number is found and then the sum of the digits of that sum is found, and so on until only a single digit remains, the original number is divisible by 9 if and only if the final remaining digit is 9.

A precisely similar argument can be used to show that 4 has the same property in a numeration system to the base 5 as has 9 in a numeration system to the base 10. In any numeration system, the number that is one less than the base always has this property.

Three is another number of interest in a numeration system with base

10. Any number that is divisible by 3 is either divisible by 9 or is 3 less than a number divisible by 9 or is 6 less than a number divisible by 9. If the digits of such a number are added, the resulting sum will have the same relation to a number divisible by 9 as had the original number. This fact can be easily proved by using a number system modulo 9, and the reader may wish to consider such a proof after such number systems have been considered later in the chapter. At this time we will simply assume this fact. We can see that if the sum of the digits of a number are continually added until a single digit number results, the original number was divisible by 3 if and only if the final sum was 3, 6, or 9.

Finally, returning to a question that was asked earlier, how can it be easily determined whether a number expressed to the base 5 is divisible by 2 (even) or not? From the foregoing discussion, the reader should see that if the sum of the digits of a number expressed in base 5 is even, then the original number was even. If the summing process is continued until only one digit remains in the base 5 representation of the number, then the final number would be 2 or 4 if and only if the original number was even.

A process for checking operations in arithmetic is called "casting out nines." This process, which can be explained with the material just discussed, is worth considering for a moment. Let us suppose that we wish to find the product of 372 and 566. We multiply and obtain 210552. Is this answer correct? A simple way of checking is addition of the digits of each of the original numbers until only a single digit remains. The digit corresponding to 372 is 3, and the digit corresponding to 566 is 8. The product of these two numbers ($3 \times 8$) is 24, and the sum of the digits of 24 is 6. If the multiplication has been carried out correctly, the sum of the digits of 210552 should also be 6 (after a sufficient number of additions). Let us see: $2 + 1 + 0 + 5 + 5 + 2 = 15$, and $1 + 5 = 6$. Does this mean that the answer 210552 is correct? Of course not. But it does indicate a probability that the answer may be correct. If we make no mistake in the check, we can catch an incorrect answer with this procedure approximately eight out of nine times. The same sort of check can be used for other operations with whole numbers. The reason why this works should be fairly clear already, but the reader will not be asked to prove it until after the section on modular number systems.

Other interesting techniques are easily explained in terms of the base of a numeration system. For example, an extension of the system for determining whether a number is divisible by 2 can be used to determine whether a number (expressed in base 10) is divisible by 4, 8, or any power of 2. To determine whether the number 37,496 is divisible by 4, we need to check only the number represented by the last two digits.

The reason for this follows: 37,400 is equal to $374 \times 100$ or $374 \cdot 10^2$; since 10 has a factor of 2, $10^2$ must have a factor of $2^2$ or 4, and thus 37,400 is divisible by 4; by the distributive law, if 96 is divisible by 4, then $37,400 + 96$ or 37,496 is also divisible by 4; 96 is divisible by 4, and therefore 37,496 must be divisible by 4. Is 37,496 divisible by 8? Can this be checked by checking only the last three digits? Since 10 has a factor of 2, must $10^3$ have a factor of $2^3$ or 8? Then, will the product of 1000 and any number have a factor of 8? Therefore, must 37,000 have a factor of 8? Then, 37,496, or $37,000 + 496$ is divisible by 8 if and only if 496 is divisible by 8. Clearly, the expression of 37,496 as $3 \cdot 10^4 + 7 \cdot 10^3 + 4 \cdot 10^2 + 9 \cdot 10 + 6$ is the important element in an argument such as this. The reader should be able to suggest a check to see whether a number is divisible by 16, 32, etc. He should also be able to suggest a corresponding check to determine whether a number is divisible by 25 ($5^2$), 125 ($5^3$), etc.

We have now found simple checks for divisibility by 2, 3, 4, 5, and 9, assuming the number is expressed in the usual decimal notation. Divisibility by 6 can, of course, be checked by checking for divisibility both by 2 and by 3. However, the important feature of this discussion is not so much that these simple procedures exist as that they can be demonstrated easily to anybody with a good understanding of the numeration system that is being used. Actually, it is possible to create a check for divisibility by any number (even 7) if the creator has a good knowledge of the base 10 system and a fair amount of imagination and motivation, but most of the other checks are considerably more difficult to use, in practice, than is dividing by the number and observing whether the division "comes out even."

Besides base 10 and base 5, a numeration system that is of considerable interest is base 2. The principal reason why this system is of great interest is that it is the system used in most computors. An electric current can be made to represent different digits (from 0 to 9, for example), but if something goes slightly wrong with the machine, a very small difference in current could change the indicated number. It is much simpler and safer to construct a computor in which the current is either on or off; therefore, it is convenient to have a numeration system in which only two different digits are used. Such a system is the binary (or base 2) system that uses only the two digits "0" (for off) and "1" (for on). In this system, a person would count as follows: one unit, one two (and no units), one two and one unit, one two-twos (no twos and no units), one two-twos and one unit, and so on. Or, using only the digits "0" and "1," one would write these: 1, 10 (meaning 1 two and no units), 11 (meaning 1 two and 1 unit), 100 (meaning 1 two times two or 1 two squared or 1 two-twos), 101, and so on. In this system, facts of the sort derived for systems to the base 5 and 10 are true but rather trivial. For example, a number is divisible by 1 if only if the sum of its digits is divisible by 1; a number is even if and only if the last digit is 0.

One other numeration system is commonly studied and is of interest primarily because its base is divisible by many numbers and therefore many divisibility checks are quite simple. This is the duodecimal system or the base 12 system. There are vestiges of the duodecimal system in out measurments in this country and elsewhere—for example, 12 inches in a foot, 12 hours in each half day, and 360° (12 × 30) in a complete revolution. Twelve is certainly a convenient number to use for the base of a numeration system since it is divisible by 2, 3, 4, and 6. In fact, there is a group of people who believe that our numeration system should be changed to base 12 because of the conveniences that would result. This group is called the "Duodecimal Society" and publishes a periodical at regular intervals.

If a number system to the base 12 were to be used, it would be necessary to have twelve digits. Since we only have ten digits in common use (0, 1, 2, 3, 4, 5, 6, 7, 8, and 9), two more digits would be needed. We will use "T" to stand for ten, and "E" to stand for eleven. Thus, we would count: one, two, three, four, five, six, seven, eight, nine, ten, eleven, one twelve (10), one twelve and one (11), one twelve and two (12), and so on. These numerals would be written: 1, 2, 3, 4, 5, 6, 7, 8, 9, T, E, 10, 11, 12, and so on.

Any person who understands the discussion so far should have no trouble writing a table that shows how to write the numeral for any particular number in a given numeration system, but we shall produce a short table of numerals for base 2, 5, 10, and 12 for convenience. Base 10 is listed first because it is the one with which the reader is presumably most familiar.

There are several ways to construct a table such as this one. The most obvious way is simply to start counting in a given system, keeping the numerals in their proper order, and pairing them with corresponding numerals in other systems. However, if it is desired to convert a particular numeral from base 10 to the corresponding numeral in the base 5 system, the process is a little more complicated. In discussing this further, we follow the usual custom of writing out the base below and to the right of a numeral when the base is other than base 10. For example, $110 = 420_{\text{five}} = 92_{\text{twelve}}$, etc. Now, to convert 110 to a numeral in base 5, we start by noticing that $5^3$ (or 125) and all greater powers of 5 are greater than 110; therefore, the first question to answer is now many

| Base Ten | Base Two | Base Five | Base Twelve |
|---|---|---|---|
| 1 | 1 | 1 | 1 |
| 2 | 10 | 2 | 2 |
| 3 | 11 | 3 | 3 |
| 4 | 100 | 4 | 4 |
| 5 | 101 | 10 | 5 |
| 6 | 110 | 11 | 6 |
| 7 | 111 | 12 | 7 |
| 8 | 1000 | 13 | 8 |
| 9 | 1001 | 14 | 9 |
| 10 | 1010 | 20 | T |
| 11 | 1011 | 21 | E |
| 12 | 1100 | 22 | 10 |
| 13 | 1101 | 23 | 11 |
| 14 | 1110 | 24 | 12 |
| 15 | 1111 | 30 | 13 |
| 16 | 10000 | 31 | 14 |
| 17 | 10001 | 32 | 15 |
| 18 | 10010 | 33 | 16 |
| 19 | 10011 | 34 | 17 |
| 20 | 10100 | 40 | 18 |
| 21 | 10101 | 41 | 19 |
| 22 | 10110 | 42 | 1T |
| 23 | 10111 | 43 | 1E |
| 24 | 11000 | 44 | 20 |
| 25 | 11001 | 100 | 21 |
| 36 | 100100 | 121 | 30 |
| 100 | 1100100 | 400 | 84 |
| 110 | 1101110 | 420 | 92 |
| 140 | 10001100 | 1030 | E8 |
| 141 | 10001101 | 1031 | E9 |
| 142 | 10001110 | 1032 | ET |
| 143 | 10001111 | 1033 | EE |
| 144 | 10010000 | 1034 | 100 |

25s ($5^2$s) there are in 110. After subtracting the four 25s, we still have two 5s left, but after these 5s are removed, there are no units left. Thus, 110 can be rewritten as four 25s + two 5s plus no units, or $420_{\text{five}}$.

Similarly, to convert 110 to a numeral in the base 12, we notice that 110 is less than 144 ($12^2$) and all greater powers of 12, and therefore, we start by finding how many 12s there are in 110. When the nine 12s are removed, there are still two 1s left over, so $110 = 92_{\text{twelve}}$.

If a more formal method is desired, we can convert the procedure into a relatively mechanical process. In converting the numer 110 to base 5, we could start by subtracting 5 from 110 as many times as possible. The number of times we subtracted would be the number of 5s in 110; the number that remained after the subtractions had been completed would be the number of units left when all possible groups of 5 had been removed. This procedure can be speeded up by using division. If 110 is divided by 5, the quotient is the number of 5s in 110, and the remainder is the number of units left over (in this case, 0). Thus, the remainder will be the digit (base 5) that should be put into the units column. Now, if the quotient is divided by 5 again, the new quotient will be the number of 25s in the original number while the remainder will be the number of groups of 5 left after all groups of 25 are removed, and so on. This procedure is carried on formally in a manner similar to the following:

$$
\begin{array}{lll}
\dfrac{22 \text{ R } 0}{5)\,110} & \dfrac{4 \text{ R } 2}{5)\,22} & \dfrac{0 \text{ R } 4}{5)\,4}
\end{array}
$$

Taking the remainders in reverse order, $110 = 420_{\text{five}}$. A similar method will work to convert any number (expressed to any base) to any base. For example, to convert 100 to base 2,

$$
\begin{array}{llll}
\dfrac{50 \text{ R } 0}{2)\,100} & \dfrac{25 \text{ R } 0}{2)\,50} & \dfrac{12 \text{ R } 1}{2)\,25} & \dfrac{6 \text{ R } 0}{2)\,12}
\end{array}
$$

$$
\begin{array}{lll}
\dfrac{3 \text{ R } 0}{2)\,6} & \dfrac{1 \text{ R } 1}{2)\,3} & \dfrac{0 \text{ R } 1}{2)\,1}
\end{array}
$$

Taking the remainders in reverse order, $100 = 1100100_{\text{two}}$.

Conversions of this sort can be made without using a numeral to the base 10. For example, to convert $1030_{\text{five}}$ to base 12, divide $1030_{\text{five}}$ by 12 to the base 5, or $22_{\text{five}}$. Since division in base 5 may not be familiar to the reader, it will probably be easier to use the subtractive form than the conventional long-division form (all numerals are base 5):

$$
\begin{array}{r}
0 \text{ R } 21 \\
22_{\text{five}})\overline{21} \\
\end{array}
$$

$$
\begin{array}{r}
20 \\
22_{\text{five}})\overline{1030_{\text{five}}} \\
440 \\
\hline
40 \quad\quad 1 \\
22 \\
\hline
\text{R } 13 \quad\quad 21 \\
\end{array}
$$

$13_{\text{five}} = 8_{\text{twelve}}$, and $21_{\text{five}} = E_{\text{twelve}}$, therefore, $1030_{\text{five}} = E8_{\text{twelve}}$.

A good way for a teacher or a pupil to get a deeper insight into algorithms in the decimal numeration system is to carry on corresponding calculations in another numeration system. An example of the division algorithm in base 5 was presented previously. Just for reference, we present below a simple case of taking square roots by the traditional algorithm in base 5.

$$
\begin{array}{cc}
\begin{array}{r}
2\ 3 \\
\sqrt{1134} \\
4 \\
\hline
43\overline{)234} \\
234 \\
\hline
\end{array}
&
\begin{array}{r}
\text{check:} \quad 23 \\
23 \\
\hline
124 \\
101 \\
\hline
1134 \\
\end{array}
\end{array}
$$

Converting to base 10, $23_{\text{five}} = 13$, and $1134_{\text{five}} = 169$, so the calculations can also be checked in base 10, if desired.

All of the numeration systems discussed so far in this chapter have been what are usually called place-value numeration systems. The reason for this name is that the particular place in which a symbol appears affects the meaning, or value, of the symbol. Thus, in the decimal system, the symbol "3" can mean three, three tens, three hundreds, three thousands, three ten thousands, or many other things. Which of these it means depends on where the 3 is placed with respect to other symbols. Various other systems have been used in the past, but the place-value system has distinct advantages over the others.

One other system is the tally system. In the tally system, a single mark $\left(\,|\,\right)$ is used to indicate a unit; to indicate two units, two marks are used $\left(\,|\,|\,\right)$, and so on. In this system, the number 12 would be written: $|\,|\,|\,|\,|\,|\,|\,|\,|\,|\,|\,|$ . In variations of the tally system, the tallies may be grouped in some way that makes reading easier. Thus, the number 12 might be written $|\,|\,|\,|\,|\ \ |\,|\,|\,|\,|\ \ |\,|$ , or each fifth tally might be run diagonally across the previous four: $\cancel{||||}\ \cancel{||||}\ |\,|$ . The Roman numeral system with which most school children are familiar is a refinement of the tally system, with new symbols introduced to take the place of certain groups of symbols. Thus, V takes the place of $|\,|\,|\,|\,|$, X takes the place of VV or $|\,|\,|\,|\,|\,|\,|\,|\,|\,|$, and so on. The convention of placing a symbol "out of order" or before the symbol for a greater number to indicate subtraction is not a place-value system but is rather just a simple abbreviation. The Romans and others who performed calculations with Roman numerals did *not* use this abbreviation while making computations. It is instructive to carry out a simple multiplication in both Arabic and Roman numerals to show the difference in amount of work required. Assuming relatively few shortcuts in each system, forty-seven is multiplied by sixty-four in each of the following:

| | | | |
|---|---|---|---|
| 47 | XXXXVII | IIII | II s = VIII |
| 64 | LXIIII | IIII | V s = XX |
| 28 | MMCCCCCCCCLLLXXXXXVIII | IIII | XXXX s = CLX |
| 160 | | | |
| 420 | D     C     L | X | II s = XX |
| 2400 | C | X | V s = L |
| 3008 | D | X | XXXX s = CCCC |
| | M | | |
| | and the final result is: | L | II s = C |
| | MMMVIII | L | V s = CCL |
| | | L | XXXX s = DDDD = MM |

The products indicated at the far right with Roman numerals would presumably be known by anybody who would work with this numeration system regularly. Therefore, the symbols

MMCCCCCCCCLLLXXXXXVIII

could presumably be written down immediately, perhaps in a different order, and the simplification would require one more step. Multiplication with Roman numerals is not a great deal more complicated than with Arabic numerals, but as numbers became larger, complications increased, and more was required of the arithmetician's memory (or ingenuity) to determine, for example, the product of L and D quickly. In any case, the simple writing of Roman numerals for large numbers requires a good deal of space as well as symbolism, and most arithmetical computations were carried out on the abacus in countries where Roman numerals were used. It is interesting to notice the close connection between the abacus and the place-value system that we use. For example, the number 3072 is written "MMMLXXII" in Roman numerals, but on an abacus it would look like this

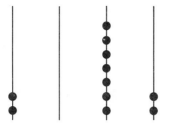

Notice the close similarity between the abacus (3 beads, 0 beads, 7 beads, 2 beads) and the Arabic numeral 3072. It is not surprising that the Arabic numeral system replaced Roman numerals as quickly as it did, considering this similarity to the abacus—rather, what is surprising is the resistance to Arabic numerals by some Europeans who knew how to calculate with an abacus.

Various other kinds of numeration systems could be (and have been) used. For example, we could simply have a different symbol for each number. This would be a code system. However, the difficulty of remembering the code for all numbers up to 100, for example, would be so great that few people would be able to get much use out of such a numeration system.

While studying different numeration systems, the teacher should keep in mind the reasons for doing so. The most important reason for studying these systems is to help the pupils understand their own system better and make better use of it. Becoming adept at calculations in another system or at converting from one system to another, etc., should not become aims in themselves; rather, the goal of understanding should be uppermost in the thinking and planning of the teacher. There are, of course, other reasons for studying other numeration systems. Their connection with computors, their historical aspects, and other general educational values ought not to be forgotten, but for these purposes it is not necessary to become proficient in trivial computations. A good understanding is the principal objective.

## Modular Number Systems

Although numeration systems may differ in their usefulness, the objects under consideration are essentially the same no matter what they are called. The Arabic numerals name the same things that the Roman numerals name. If the operation 73 + 54 is carried out with Arabic numerals, the result (127) will correspond with the answer to the analogous problem (LXXIII + LIIII = CXXVII) carried out with Roman numerals. There are, however, number systems that differ essentially from each other. The system of rational numbers, for example, is quite different from the system of integers. In a later chapter the commonly used infinite number systems will be discussed in some detail, but in this chapter we shall consider some finite systems that resemble familiar number systems in enough aspects to justify their being called number systems.

First, let us present the following definition.

DEFINITION.    If $n$ is an integer greater than 1, and $a$ and $b$ are integers such that $a - b$ is divisible by $n$, we say that $a$ is congruent to $b$ modulo $n$. This is usually abbreviated: $a \equiv b \pmod{n}$.

For example, since $7 - 2$ is divisible by 5, $7 \equiv 2 \pmod 5$. It is also true that $2 - 7$ is divisible by 5 (the set of integers includes negative numbers such as $-1$), and therefore, $2 \equiv 7 \pmod 5$. Since $3 - (-2) = 5$ is divisible by 5, $3 \equiv -2 \pmod 5$. Is it true that $18 \equiv -2 \pmod 5$? Since 0 is divisible by any number (for any number $q$, $q \cdot 0 = 0$, so $0 = 0 \div q$) any number is congruent to itself modulo $n$.

There are several simple theorems which can be proved about integers modulo $n$. The fact that was just mentioned, for example, can be stated as follows.

THEOREM 1.    Any integer ($q$) is congruent to itself, modulo $n$ ($q \equiv q \pmod{n}$). In general, we shall not restate the restriction on $n$ that it be greater than 1; this will simply be assumed because of the definition of "mod $n$."

THEOREM 2.    For any two integers $p$ and $q$, if $p \equiv q \pmod n$, then $q \equiv p \pmod n$.

*Proof.*    If $p \equiv q \pmod n$, then there is some integer, $r$, such that $(p - q) \div n = r$ or $nr = p - q$. But if $r$ is an integer (for example, $r = -2$), then $-r$ is also an integer (in this case, $-r = -(-2) = 2$). So, $n(-r) = -(nr) = -(p - q) = -p + q = q - p$. Therefore, if $p - q$ is divisible by $n$ (with quotient $r$), then so is $q - p$ (with quotient $- r$), and the theorem is proved.

THEOREM 3.    For any three integers, $p$, $q$, and $r$, if $p \equiv q \pmod n$, and $q \equiv r \pmod n$, then $p \equiv r \pmod n$.

*Proof.*    By hypothesis, there exist two integers, $s$ and $t$, such that $p - q = ns$, and $q - r = nt$. Adding corresponding members of these equations $(p - q) + (q - r) = ns + nt$. Using the associative law and the fact that $-q + q = 0$, we see that the left member can be simplified to $p - r$. By use of the distributive law, the right member can be rewritten: $n(s + t)$. Since the sum of two integers is always an integer, $s + t$ is an integer (call it $u$) and we have an integer $u$ such that $p - r = nu$, so $p - r$ is divisible by $n$.

The three properties considered in theorems 1–3 are called the reflexive, symmetric, and transitive properties, respectively, and any relation that has all of these properties is called an equivalence relation. The properties can be stated for any relation, $\sim$.

Reflexive property:     For all $a$, $a \sim a$.
Symmetric property:     For all $a$ and $b$, if $a \sim b$, then $b \sim a$.
Transitive property:     For all $a$, $b$, and $c$, if $a \sim b$ and $b \sim c$, then $a \sim c$.

There are many relations that have these three ρroperties. For example, equality is an equivalence relation, as are similarity and congruence among geometric figures. The reader can undoubtedly think of many more—having the same weight or having the same parents would illustrate equivalence relations.

Suppose we consider the set of all integers that are congruent to 0 modulo 5. Is 0 itself a member of the set? Is 5 a member of the set? Is it true that $-15 \equiv 0 \pmod{5}$? Then, is $-15$ a member of the set of all integers that are congruent to 0 modulo 5? Would every multiple of 5 (positive, negative, or zero) be a member of the set? Since congruence modulo 5 is an equivalence relation, a set such as this is sometimes called an equivalence class.

In defining an equivalence class formally, we find it is convenient to use some notation for sets. We shall usually use curly brackets "{     }" to enclose the names of members of the set. Thus, to designate the set of all men who were President of the United States during the eighteenth century, we might write {George Washington, John Adams}. If it were not convenient to write out all the names of members of a set, a descriptive phrase might be used with a variable. For example, the previous set could be described this way: $\{x | x$ was President of the United States during the eighteenth century}, to mean "the set of all $x$ such that $x$ was President of the United States during the eighteenth century." Notice that the vertical bar, "$|$", is read "such that" when it is written in conjunction with the set brackets. The set of all integers that are congruent to 0 modulo 5 might be written: $\{x | x$ is an integer and $x \equiv 0 \pmod{5}\}$. On occasion when there are many elements of a set, we shall write the names of several members, assume that the pattern is obvious, and write three dots to indicate that the pattern continues. Thus, $\{x | x$ is an integer and $x \equiv 0 \pmod{5}\}$ could also be written: $\{\ldots, -15, -10, -5, 0, 5, 10, 15, \ldots\}$. If there is a first member of the set (following the given pattern) or a last member, its name will generally be written in the appropriate place; for example, the set of integers from one to one hundred would be indicated {1, 2, 3, 4, . . . , 100}.

With this notation, an equivalence class can be defined as follows.

DEFINITION.    If $\sim$ is an equivalence relation, then $\{x \mid x \sim a\}$ is said to be an equivalence class and will be designated $[a]$.

From this definition and theorems 1–3, it can be shown that there are exactly $n$ equivalence classes for the relation congruence modulo $n$. This can be seen by noting that if any integer $a$ is divided by $n$, a quotient ($q$) and a remainder ($r$) will result, and the remainder will be less than $n$ (but not negative).[3] This can be written: $a/n = q + r/n$ or, multiplying by $n$, $a = qn + r$ (where $r$ is $0, 1, 2, \ldots,$ or $n - 1$).

Now, subtracting $r$ from both members, $a - r = qn$, and $a \equiv r$ (mod $n$). Thus, for any integer $a$, there exists a nonnegative integer $r$, less than $n$, such that   $a \equiv r$ (mod $n$). Therefore, for congruence modulo $n$, the $n$ equivalence classes can be designated: $[0], [1], [2], [3], \ldots, [n - 2], [n - 1]$. Or, in the particular case of congruence modulo 5, the equivalence classes are

$$[0] = \{\ldots, -10, -5, 0, 5, 10, 15, \ldots\}$$
$$[1] = \{\ldots, -9, -4, 1, 6, 11, 16, \ldots\}$$
$$[2] = \{\ldots, -8, -3, 2, 7, 12, 17, \ldots\}$$
$$[3] = \{\ldots, -7, -2, 3, 8, 13, 18, \ldots\}$$
$$[4] = \{\ldots, -6, -1, 4, 9, 14, 19, \ldots\}$$

Of course, there are other names for each of these equivalence classes; for example, $[0] = [5] = [1395] = [-4325]$, etc.; however, we shall usually use the names used above for convenience and uniformity.

Operations that are similar to addition and multiplication can now be defined on the set of elements $\{[0], [1], [2], [3], [4]\}$. Since the operations are not identical to the corresponding operations for integers, we shall use different symbols to designate them, though many authors do not bother with this distinction when the context makes the meaning clear.

[3] This will be true even if $a$ is a negative integer, as can be seen by considering a number line with all multiples of $n$ (both positive and negative) marked. Then,

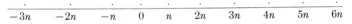

the integer $a$ must have its graph either on the graph of one of the multiples of $n$ or between the graphs of two of them. If $a$ is a multiple of $n$, then $r = 0$, and if it is between two such multiples of $n$ (e.g., $-3n$ and $-2n$) then $q$ can be taken as the smaller of the two multiples (in this case, $-3$) and $r$ is clearly a positive number less than $n$. A more rigorous proof of this fact can be found in most books on modern algebra under the topic of "division algorithm."

DEFINITION.    $[a] \oplus [b] = [c]$ if and only if $(a + b) \equiv c \pmod{5}$.

DEFINITION.    $[a] \odot [b] = [c]$ if and only if $(ab) \equiv c \pmod{5}$.

Corresponding definitions can, of course, be made for operations modulo $n$, where $n$ is an integer greater than 1.

Before continuing the discussion, one should notice that the operations $\oplus$ and $\odot$ are well defined—in other words, for any integers $a$ and $b$, $[a] \oplus [b]$ is always a unique member of the set. It is clear from the fact that $a + b$ and $ab$ are always integers when $a$ and $b$ are, that there will be at least one element $[c]$, which satisfies the above definitions. The only possible difficulty would occur if different notation could produce different results. For example, could $[2] \oplus [3]$ possibly be a different element from $[-8] + [23]$? In order to show that this could not happen, it is necessary to show that if $a \equiv b \pmod{n}$ and $c \equiv d \pmod{n}$, then $a + c \equiv b + d \pmod{n}$, and $ac \equiv bd \pmod{n}$.

THEOREM 4.    If $a \equiv b \pmod{n}$ and $c \equiv d \pmod{n}$, then $a + c \equiv b + d \pmod{n}$ and $ac \equiv bd \pmod{n}$.

*Proof.*    If $a \equiv b \pmod{n}$, then there exists an integer $p$, such that (1) $a - b = np$; and if $c \equiv d \pmod{n}$, then there exists an integer $q$, such that (2) $c - d = nq$. Adding corresponding members, $(a - b) + (c - d) = np + nq$ or $(a + c) - (b + d) = n(p + q)$ and $a + c$ is congruent to $b + d$, modulo $n$.

For the second part, rewrite (1) and (2) $a = np + b$ and $c = nq + d$ and multiply corresponding members getting: $ac = n^2pq + npd + nqb + bd$, or subtracting $bd$, $ac - bd = n^2pq + npd + nqb = n(npq + pd + qd)$. Since the quantity in parentheses represents an integer, $ac \equiv bd \pmod{n}$.

Often, the circle around the "+" and "·" and the square brackets indicating an equivalence class are omitted when there can be no confusion. Thus, in a number system for modulo 5, we might say: $3 + 2 = 0$ or $4 + 3 = 2$, etc. Tables for addition and multiplication, modulo 5, appear below. It is interesting to notice that since the universe in ques-

| + | 0 | 1 | 2 | 3 | 4 |   |   | 0 | 1 | 2 | 3 | 4 |
|---|---|---|---|---|---|---|---|---|---|---|---|---|
| 0 | 0 | 1 | 2 | 3 | 4 |   | 0 | 0 | 0 | 0 | 0 | 0 |
| 1 | 1 | 2 | 3 | 4 | 0 |   | 1 | 0 | 1 | 2 | 3 | 4 |
| 2 | 2 | 3 | 4 | 0 | 1 |   | 2 | 0 | 2 | 4 | 1 | 3 |
| 3 | 3 | 4 | 0 | 1 | 2 |   | 3 | 0 | 3 | 1 | 4 | 2 |
| 4 | 4 | 0 | 1 | 2 | 3 |   | 4 | 0 | 4 | 3 | 2 | 1 |

tion is finite (there are only five members), it is possible to write down the entire addition and multiplication tables rather than a small part of them as with the usual number systems.

When discussing modular arithmetic in junior high school, a teacher often refers to the dial of a clock (or some similar mechanism) to justify the addition and multiplication tables. If a dial has the numerals 0, 1, 2, 3, and 4 at equal intervals around it (Fig. 5–1) and the pointer can only move in a clockwise direction, one can see that moving the pointer two units from the numeral 3 will place it on the numeral 0 and moving it three units from the numeral 4 will place it on the numeral 2.

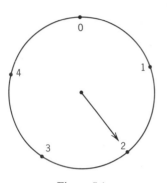

Figure 5.1

Although this is a convenient physical model for such a system, certain difficulties are inherent in this procedure. The objects being added (or multiplied) are not really the same. One of the addends (and the sum) is a position on the face of the dial or a numeral, while the other addend is a positive integer (the number of units to be moved). Since one of the things we wish to illustrate with such a system is closure, we question whether the physical model clarifies the situation. In this book we shall use equivalence classes, modulo $n$, and thus avoid this potential difficulty, but the reader may wish to consider the dial as a concrete example.

Many of the properties that ordinary number systems have are found in a modular arithmetic system. In fact, a modular arithmetic has some properties that the systems of natural numbers and of integers do not have but that are important in the larger systems of rational numbers and of real numbers. The properties that we shall now discuss in relation to a modulo 5 number system will be considered whenever we are talking about number systems; and some of them have already been mentioned in previous developments of thought.

As we have seen (in Theorem 4 and the discussion preceding it), the operations for modular arithmetic are well defined. An operation is said to be well defined if it has the properties of closure and uniqueness. Operations lacking one or both of these properties occur in certain number systems. For example, in the system of natural numbers subtraction is not closed because, for example, $5 - 8$ is not a natural number. Similarly, in the set of real numbers the operation of taking square roots is not uniquely defined, unless a special convention is accepted, because 4, for instance, has two square roots, 2 and $-2$. The operations of addition and multiplication, however, are closed and unique for all commonly accepted number systems as well as for the modular 5 arithmetic.

The commutative laws have been discussed previously, but it is worth repeating that an operation, *, is commutative if and only if, for all elements, $a$, $b$, of the system, $a*b = b*a$. It is easy to show that addition modulo 5 is commutative in the following way: Since $a + b \equiv a + b$ (mod 5) $[a] + [b] = [a + b]$ by definition of $\oplus$. By the commutative law for *integers*, $a + b = b + a$, and therefore $[a + b] = [b + a]$. $[b] + [a] = [b + a]$ by reasoning similar to that of the first sentence of this proof; therefore $[a] + [b] = [b] + [a]$. It is important to notice that although a commutative law for addition (modulo 5) was being proved and a commutative law for addition (for integers) was used in the proof, the two laws are different from each other, and therefore there is no reason why we cannot use one in the proof of the other.[4] The commutative law for multiplication, modulo 5, can be proved in much the same manner as was the commutative law for addition modulo 5. A trivial change will also make it possible to prove the commutative laws for addition and multiplication modulo $n$ where $n$ is any integer greater than 1.

Associative properties have also been discussed previously but will be restated here for emphasis and convenience. An operation, *, is associative if for any three elements of the system, $a$, $b$, $c$, $(a*b)*c = a*(b*c)$. Since the usual operations of addition and multiplication are binary (that is, are defined for pairs of elements only), it is necessary to have some special convention for combining more than two elements in a given operation. When parentheses are used, the operations inside the parentheses are to be carried out first. Thus, $(3 + 7) + 8 = 10 + 8 = 18$. The associative law for addition says that this result is the same as it would have been if the 7 and 8 had been added together first and then that sum had been added to 3. It is interesting to note that some operations are not associative. For example, it is not true that $(3 - 7) - 8 = 3 - (7 - 8)$ because the left member is equal to $-4 - 8$ or $-12$ while the right member is equal to $3 - (-1)$ or 4. Using reasoning similar to that used in proving the commutative law for addition, we can take the following steps to show that multiplication modulo 5 is associative: $([a] \odot [b]) \odot [c] = [ab] \odot [c] = [(ab)c] = [a(bc)] = [a] \odot [bc] = [a] \odot ([b] \odot [c])$. The reader should be able to supply the reasons for all of these steps. The changes that must be

---

[4] Of course, we must be careful not to use the second law to prove the first at a later time—this would be a clear case of circular reasoning. At present, we are assuming the usual laws for integers, though these can be proved using more fundamental assumptions if desired.

made for addition modulo 5 or for either addition or multiplication modulo $n$ are obvious.

A useful law from elementary arithmetic combines multiplication and addition. It is called the distributive law for multiplication over addition. In general, the operation $\circ$ is distributive over the operation $*$ if for any three elements of the system, $a$, $b$, $c$, $a\circ(b*c) = (a\circ b)*(a\circ c)$. Although multiplication is distributive over addition in the widely known number systems, addition is not distributive over multiplication. For a simple example, $3 + (5 \times 7) = 3 + 35 = 38$, but $(3 + 5) \times (3 + 7) = 8 \times 10 = 80$. The distributive law for multiplication over addition modulo 5 (or modulo $n$) can be proved by the distributive law for integers and the same sort of reasoning used in the preceeding two paragraphs.

In the set of integers, the integers 0 and 1 have special properties with respect to the operations of addition and multiplication. The integer 0 has the property that for any integer, $a$, $a + 0 = 0 + a = a$; and the integer 1 has the property that for any integer, $a$, $a \cdot 1 = 1 \cdot a = a$. These are called *identity elements* because they leave other elements unchanged under the appropriate operations. In general, an element, $z$, is said to be an identity element for the operation $*$ if, for any element of the system, $a$, $a*z = z*a = a$. It can be seen that $z$ is unique by assuming $z'$ is an identity element and showing that $z*z' = z'*z$ is equal to both $z$ and $z'$. If the operation is also commutative, part of the above requirement can be omitted with no loss. Using reasoning quite similar to that used previously, one can show that [0] is the identity element for $\oplus$, and [1] is the identity element for $\odot$. Here is the proof for [0]: Since $0 + a$ is congruent to itself, modulo $n$, $[0] \oplus [a] = [0 + a]$ by definition of $\oplus$, and $0 + a = a$ because 0 is the identity element for addition of integers; therefore, $[0] \oplus [a] = [0 + a] = [a]$. Similarly, it can be shown that $[a] \oplus [0] = [a]$ and that $[1] \odot [a] = [a] \odot [1] = [a]$.

In the set of integers, every number has a corresponding number such that the sum of the two numbers is zero, the identity element for addition. These two numbers are called additive inverses of each other. In general, a system is said to have inverses with respect to the operation $*$ if there is an identity element, $z$, for $*$, and for any element of the system, $a$, there is an element of the system, $a'$, such that $a*a' = a'*a = z$. Again, if the commutative law holds for $*$ in the system, part of this restriction can be omitted. For the system modulo 5, it is clear by inspection that the additive inverse of [0] is [0], that [1] and [4] are additive inverses, and that [2] and [3] are additive inverses; therefore, every element has an additive inverse. In general for a modulo $n$ system, [0] is its own additive inverse, and the other inverses come in pairs as follows: [1] and [n − 1], [2] and [n − 2], . . . [b] and [n − b]. If n is even, [n/2] is its own additive inverse, but if n is odd, [0] is the only element that is its own inverse.

In multiplication, the inverse situation is slightly different. For integers, of course, only two elements have multiplicative[5] inverses; these are 1 and −1. Every rational number but zero has a multiplicative inverse. By simply looking at the multiplication table (p. 129), we can see that every element of the modulo 5 system except [0] has a multiplicative inverse; [1] and [4] are their own multiplicative inverses, and [2] and [3] are each other's multiplicative inverses. We might jump to the conclusion that in any modular system every element but [0] has a multiplicative inverse, but this would be a mistake. For example, the modular 4 system does not have a multiplicative inverse for every nonzero element. The reader can find the one nonzero element in the modular 4 system that does not have a multiplicative inverse by creating a multiplication table modulo 4 and inspecting it to see which row (or column) does not have a 1 as a product. In general, only if n is a prime number will the system modular n have multiplicative inverses for all nonzero elements. Whenever a number, r, is a factor of n, then r will have no multiplicative inverse.

The properties discussed previously belong to an important type of of mathematical system called a *field*.

DEFINITION.    A *field* is a set of at least two distinct elements over which two operations, + and ·, are well defined (closed and unique) and satisfy the following conditions:

1. (+ commutative):    For all $a, b, a + b = b + a$.
2. ( · commutative):    For all $a, b, a \cdot b = b \cdot a$.
3. (+ associative):    For all $a, b, c, (a + b) + c = a + (b + c)$.
4. ( · associative):    For all $a, b, c, (a \cdot b) \cdot c = a \cdot (b \cdot c)$.
5. (distributive, · over +):    For all $a, b, c, a \cdot (b + c) = (a \cdot b) + (a \cdot c)$.
6. (+ identity):    There is an element, 0, such that for any element, $a$, $a + 0 = a$.
7. ( · identity):    There is an element, 1, such that for any element, $a$, $a \cdot 1 = a$.
8. (+ inverses):    For each element, $a$, there is an element, $-a$, such that $a + (-a) = 0$.
9. ( · inverses):    For each element, $a$, if $a \neq 0$, then there is an element $a^{-1}$ such that $a \cdot a^{-1} = 1$.

---

[5] According to dictionaries, this word is pronounced mŭl′ tĭ plĭ kā′ tĭv; however, most mathematicians pronounce it mŭl tĭ plĭ′ kă tĭv, and even though this is not an acceptable pronounciation according to the dictionary, it should probably be used in mathematics classes so that the pupils will know what professors are talking about when they get to college.

The rational, real, and complex number systems are all fields, and therefore it seems reasonable that children should spend some time studying these basic concepts. Using the aforementioned properties we can prove many other facts about a field, including the following two theorems.

THEOREM 5.    If 0 is the additive identity for a field, then for any element, $n$, of the field, $0 \cdot n = 0$.

*Proof.*    By the definition of 0, $n + 0 = n$. Since multiplication is well defined, $n \cdot (n + 0) = n \cdot n$.[6] By the distributive law, $n \cdot n + n \cdot 0 = n \cdot n$. Since every element has an additive inverse and $n \cdot n$ is an element of the system (because multiplication is closed), $n \cdot n$ has an additive inverse. We can call it $-(n \cdot n)$. By adding $-(n \cdot n)$ to both members and simplifying, we get $n \cdot 0 = 0$; and $0 \cdot n = 0$ by the commutative law.

THEOREM 6.    In a field, 0 cannot have a multiplicative inverse.

*Proof.*    Let us suppose that 0 has a multiplicative inverse and call it $q$. Then $0 \cdot q = 1$. But $q$ is an element of the system and by Theorem 5, $0 \cdot q = 0$. Therefore, $1 = 0$. But if $1 = 0$, then for all elements, $n$, of the field, $n = 1 \cdot n = 0 \cdot n = 0$, and there is only one element of the field, namely, 0. By the definition of a field, there are at least two distinct elements of a field, and therefore $1 \neq 0$ and 0 does not have a multiplicative inverse.

Although modular arithmetic is useful in some higher mathematics (for example, in number theory), the principal reason why pupils study such systems is to obtain a better idea of what a mathematical system is and to learn about various properties that are important in the number systems used in everyday life. Although the system of integers and the system of natural numbers are not fields, they have many of the properties of a field; it is partially because of their lack of certain properties that we expand them to create richer number systems. If the system of natural numbers has the elements 1, 2, 3, . . . , it is clear that addition and multiplication are well defined, commutative, associative, and that multiplication is distributive over addition. Only one of the other properties of a field belongs to this system. What is it? Some authors refer to the set of numbers {0, 1, 2, 3, . . . } as the natural numbers, but we shall refer to this set as the set of cardinal

---

[6] Equality, in elementary mathematics, means we have two names for the same object. Therefore, if $a = b$, $a$ and $b$ are two names for the same number. If both $a$ and $b$ are multiplied by some number $c$, the results must be the same because multiplication is uniquely defined so that there can be only one product of two given numbers. Thus, the rule that equals multiplied by equals produce equal products is explained by the fact that multiplication is uniquely defined. In a similar way, the fact that sums of equals are equal can be explained.

numbers. What property of a field does the system of cardinal numbers have that the system of natural numbers lacks?

Questions of the sort asked in the foregoing paragraph are important in the creation of new number systems and in the understanding of number systems. They will be considered again in the chapter on expanding our number system, and they should be considered fairly early in the mathematical education of a child. A study of modular arithmetic provides a good motivation for this broader study of number systems generally.

## Teaching Hints[7]

The principal reason for teaching a unit on numeration systems is to help the pupils understand their own (base 10) numeration system. With this in mind, the teacher should plan a short unit and discuss thoroughly the relation of other numeration systems to the base 10 system. Furthermore, he should not place great emphasis on converting efficiently from one numeration system to another because the reason for converting from one system to another is increased understanding of the base 10 system. Thus, an algorithm for converting from base 7 to base 5 (etc.) is of relatively little value in the whole scheme of things.

For studying a base 5 system (for example) the teacher may find that an abacus is a great help. An abacus that has five (or four) beads in the lower half and two (or one) in the upper half can be used effectively. For class demonstrations, the teacher may want a larger abacus. Seventh and eighth grade pupils can make excellent ones (or the teacher can make them). If paper beads are used in making a large demonstration abacus, the beads will tend to stay in place when the abacus is held in a vertical position (assuming they are fit tightly to the string). For studying base 10, a regular abacus (or better yet, one with 10 beads) is very helpful.

Excellent examples of measuring in base 12 and base 16 systems can be discovered by the children if they are asked to think about it. A tape measure will do for base 12 (if the thing to be measured is more than 12 feet long, some explanation will be necessary). In similar ways, pounds and ounces can be considered. This discussion will lead naturally into consideration of the metric system.

Young children are fascinated by different numeration systems that other civilizations have used, and some may want to write research papers on such systems as the Mayan, the Roman, the Greek, and

---

[7] Although the reader will find many teaching suggestions throughout each chapter, several suggestions that do not fit conveniently into the main text will be found at the end of chapters in sections labeled as above.

others. It will also be both instructive and interesting to the children to learn how to compute in, for example, the Roman numeration system. The procedures are not difficult to understand but are messy. The organization required and the review of number facts will be helpful, and the lack of place value will be revealing. Of course, the children must remember that numerals should not be written in the "subtractive" form, or confusion will result—that is, four should be written "IIII" not "IV," nine should be written "VIIII" not "IX," etc. The subtractive forms were not used in computations.

Before beginning a unit on modular number systems, the teacher should determine whether the pupils have studied them before, and if so, just what they studied (more reliable information may come from previous teachers than from the pupils on this matter). Many "modern" programs introduce such things at a very early level, and there is no point in continually repeating the same thing; the same idea may apply, to a lesser extent, to the study of numeration systems.

Again, the reason for studying number systems is to get a better understanding of the number system most commonly used. Modular number systems and other similar systems tend not to add a great deal of knowledge about the real number system, and they should not be overemphasized.

Undoubtedly, use of a clock face or like device is one of the most effective pedagogical methods of introducing modular number systems in the early grades (seven or eight). The presence of the device in class, where the children can see it, helps many pupils. If the question of closure arises (and it probably will not), the elements of the system can be defined as motions in the clockwise direction. For example, in base 5, the pointer is assumed to have started at 0. Then, $3 + 4$ is represented as a motion of 3 followed by a motion of 4. The question is what single motion would have resulted in the pointer's being at the same place.

Symbolism (such as that for sets) ought to be introduced when it is needed and appropriate, and it should be organized later, if necessary. Thus, a chapter or unit on sets should come after a clear need for using sets has been established. This pacing will give the children better motivation and will help them to remember the ideas. Of course, appropriate definitions are necessary when a symbol is introduced, but an entire theory is not necessary at first.

### Exercises

1. Write the following numbers (base 10) in base 2, 5, 7, and 12: 2, 5, 7, 12, 16, 26, 48, 57, 64, 75, 97, 98, 125, 126, 127, 128, 129, 130, 131, 132, 624, 1727, 2048.

2. Show that if the base of a numeration system is not even, some even number will be expressed with a unit's digit that represents an odd number, by writing at least one such number (using $b$ as the base that is odd).

3. Show that any number with a decimal representation that ends in 5 or 0 is divisible by 5.

4. Show that any number is divisible by 4 if and only if the sum of the digits of its base 5 representation is divisible by 4.

5. Generalize the argument in Exercise 4 for base $b$ and the number $b - 1$.

6. Prove that in the standard decimal notation the sum of the digits of any number is congruent to the number modulo 9, thus demonstrating why a check by "casting out nines" works.

7. How could you check to see whether a twelve-digit number, expressed in base 10, is divisible by 16 without doing the entire division?

8. Do Exercise 7 replacing 16 by 25; by 125; by 625.

9. List at least five members of each of the following equivalence classes using set braces and three dots (before and after the numerals). For example,

$$\{x|x \equiv 3 \ (\mathrm{mod} \ 5)\} = \{. \ . \ . \ , \ -7, \ -2, \ 3, \ 8, \ 13, \ . \ . \ .\}$$

(a) $\{x|x \equiv 4 \ (\mathrm{mod} \ 5)\}$     (b) $\{x|x \equiv 2 \ (\mathrm{mod} \ 7)\}$
(c) $\{x|x \equiv 5 \ (\mathrm{mod} \ 2)\}$     (d) $\{x|x \equiv -6 \ (\mathrm{mod} \ 4)\}$

10. Name each of the following equivalence classes using the form "$\{x|x \equiv p \ (\mathrm{mod} \ n)\}$" where $p$ is a nonnegative integer less than $n$. For example:

$$\{. \ . \ . \ , \ -9, \ -4, \ 1, \ 6, \ 11, \ . \ . \ .\} = \{x|x \equiv 1 \ )\mathrm{mod} \ 5)\}$$

(a) $\{. \ . \ . \ , \ -7, \ -4, \ -1, \ 2, \ 5, \ . \ . \ .\}$
(b) $\{. \ . \ . \ , \ 18, \ 27, \ 36, \ 45, \ 54, \ . \ . \ .\}$
(c) $\{. \ . \ . \ , \ -37, \ -31, \ -25, \ -19, \ . \ . \ .\}$
(d) $\{. \ . \ . \ , \ -900, \ -450, \ 0, \ 450, \ 900, \ . \ . \ .\}$

11. Describe a relation that is transitive but is neither reflexive nor symmetric.

12. Describe a relation that is reflexive and transitive but is not symmetric.

13. Describe a relation that is symmetric but not reflexive or transitive.

14. Describe a relation that is symmetric and reflexive but is not transitive.

15. If $+$ and $\cdot$ modulo 5 had been defined by use of a clock face instead of equivalence classes, the table on p. 129 would look the same, but the various proofs in the text would not be appropriate. The same facts could be demonstrated by simply trying every possibility. For example, to show that the commutative law is true, replace $a$ and $b$ by each element of the system in the equation $a + b = b + a$ and see if a true statement results in every case. The cases involving 0 are trivial; try the cases that do not involve 0. For instance, $3 + 4 = 2$, and $4 + 3 = 2$ is one case, and so on.

16. Show that multiplication modulo $n$ is commutative.

17. Show that addition modulo $n$ is associative (do not omit the reasons).

18. Show that multiplication modulo $n$ is distributive over addition modulo $n$.

19. Show that $[1] \cdot [a] = [a] \cdot [1] = [a]$ for all $[a]$ in the modulo $n$ system.

20. Make an addition and multiplication table, modulo 6, and decide which of the field properties do not hold for this system. For which elements does any such property not hold?

21. Which properties of a field apply to the system of natural numbers (1, 2, 3, 4, . . .)?

22. Which properties of a field apply to the system of cardinal numbers (0, 1, 2, 3, 4, . . .)?

23. Which properties of a field apply to the system of integers $(-3, -2, -1, 0, 1, 2, 3, . . .)$?

24. Which properties of a field apply to the system of nonnegative rational numbers $(0, \frac{1}{2}, \frac{2}{3}, \frac{4}{7}, \frac{83}{17}, 12,$ etc.)?

25. Which properties of a field apply to the system of rational numbers (positive, negative, and zero)?

## REFERENCES

Crouch, Ralph, and George Baldwin. *Mathematics for Elementary Teachers*, John Wiley and Sons, New York, 1964. See Reference 1 in Chapter 4.

Dubisch, Roy. *The Nature of Number*, The Ronald Press, New York, 1952. An interesting and readable account of number systems.

Freitag, Herta T., and Arthur H. Freitag. *The Number Story*, NCTM, Washington, D.C., 1960. History of the growth of number notions from prehistoric time to the present.

Smith, David Eugene. *Number Stories of Long Ago*, NCTM, Washington, D.C., 1919. A fanciful but instructive history of numbers. Very readable and interesting for children or adults.

———*A Source Book in Mathematics*, 2 vols., Dover Publications, New York, 1959. See reference 5 in Chapter IV. As well as the topics mentioned in the earlier reference, the section on arithmetic includes work with real numbers, primes, and logarithms. In the last section (pp. 677–683) Hamilton's work with Quaternions is considered.

*Concepts of Algebra*. School Mathematics Study Group, Studies in Mathematics, Vol. VIII, Yale University Press, New Haven, 1961. A voluminous discussion of elementary algebra with emphasis on structure. Appropriate for junior high or elementary school teachers.

See also References for Chapters 9 and 10.

# INTUITIVE GEOMETRY

Before Euclid wrote his *Elements of Geometry*, people knew most of the facts that are now taught in high school geometry classes. Therefore, there is some historical reason to suppose that the informal study of geometry ought to be started before the formal, deductive study of the subject. Furthermore, if high school classes are to place as much emphasis on logic, proof, structure, coordinate geometry, non-Euclidean geometry, and space geometry as modern planners propose, the pupils must know most of the facts of geometry before they undertake formal study of the subject. Although the informal study of geometry probably should begin at a very early age, at least in the early elementary school, a large portion of the work will come in the junior high school.

In this chapter we shall discuss briefly a few of the geometric facts that can be considered in the junior high school and how they can be studied.

## Geometry Without Measurements

The word "nonmetric" may seem strange to an individual who has never heard it before, and perhaps it is even frightening to a person who studied some advanced geometry in college where the word "non-

139

metric" appeared in connection with difficult concepts. All it means, when used as an adjective with "geometry," is "without measuring." Thus, nonmetric geometry is the geometry that does not depend on an ability to measure. Since there are many facts of geometry that can be studied without measuring and they are often fairly simple facts, we shall first consider some ideas from nonmetric geometry.

When a pupil enters the seventh grade, he usually has some idea of what a line or a point is, and he may well have a good notion of planes, space, angles, triangles, curves, circles, and so on. However, it is desirable that he get a good intuitive sense of what these words mean to the mathematician as well as what they mean in everyday language. The relations among these various objects are important, simple, and can be considered at an early age.

"Point," "line," "plane," and "space" are usually taken as undefined words in geometry. Although it is possible to define them, their definitions would almost certainly be in terms of concepts that are less obvious, intuitively, and there would still have to be *some* undefined words or symbols in the system. With this in mind, we should probably not try to define any of the four words, but rather should offer examples of physical models with properties that remind us of the mathematical objects. For example, a line can be represented by a ray of light, a wire stretched very tightly, etc. A plane might be thought of as an extension of the blackboard, the floor, or some other flat surface. A point might be described as the intersection of two lines (neglecting for the moment the question of what "intersect" means) or the head of pin made ever so much smaller, etc.

Probably these examples can be elicited from the children in a class rather than given by the teacher. There are several advantages to letting the children suggest the examples. One of these is that the teacher can question the pupil whether the example really has all of the properties the pupil would like it to have. If a pupil suggests that a line can be represented by a wire that is stretched tightly, the teacher might ask, "Does a wire always have two end points?" And, "Do you think that lines should have two end points or should go on forever without end points?" If the child thinks that lines ought to have end points, the teacher would have to suggest that perhaps we want two different sorts of objects—some having two end points, which we will call line segments, and some having no end points, which we will call lines. Perhaps a bright pupil will ask what happens if the object has only one end point. If no pupil asks this question, the teacher could encourage it by asking whether a beam of light from a flashlight would be a line or a line segment (lasar rays might be discussed in this context). If the beam of light continued forever, it would have only one end point, its point of origin. It should seem natural to pupils to call this a ray considering their familiarity with the sun's rays.

It is convenient to think of most geometric objects as sets of points. For example, a line is a set of points; a line segment is the set of all points of a line between two given points and includes the two given points. An angle is the set of all points on two rays that have a common end point, etc.

Children can discover many of the basic relationships between points, lines, planes, etc., without much difficulty. For example, ask an average 12-year-old, "How many different lines can go through two distinct points?" He will probably conclude, perhaps after considering several physical models, that only one line can go through the two points. Similarly, he is pretty certain to conclude that only one plane can exist through three points that are not on one line. As physical examples for this, he might use three fingers and a book, a tripod turned upside down with different lengths for legs, etc. Other facts of a similar nature can be discovered by pupils if enough physical models are considered. The walls of a classroom can often be used as good examples of planes, and the edges of the classroom are good examples of lines in various positions. Of course, the pupil must remember that the mathematical objects would continue forever rather than ending where the classroom ends.

With appropriate examples, children discover such facts as these: (1) if two points of a line are in a plane, the entire line is in the plane; (2) if two planes have a point in common, they have at least an entire line in common (and if they have more than an entire line in common, then they are identical); (3) through one point, any number (an infinite number) of lines can be drawn; (4) through one line, any number of planes can be drawn; (5) a point separates a line into two half-lines; (6) a line separates a plane into two half-planes; (7) a plane separates a space into two half-spaces, etc. With a little help, they may even be able to find out that there are as many points on a one-inch line segment as on a two-inch line segment.

In Figure 6.1, let $\overline{PQ}$ be the one-inch segment and $\overline{P'Q'}$ be the two-inch segment. Then $\overleftrightarrow{PP'}$ and $\overleftrightarrow{QQ'}$ intersect in a point, $O$ (neglecting the possibility that they are parallel). For any point $X$ of $\overline{PQ}$ there will be a line $\overleftrightarrow{OX}$ through $O$ and $X$. Since $\overleftrightarrow{OX}$ will intersect $\overline{P'Q'}$ in only one point, for any point, $X$ of $\overline{PQ}$, there is a corresponding point, $X'$ of $\overline{P'Q'}$. If two lines are distinct they can have no more than one point in common;

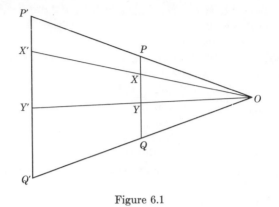

Figure 6.1

hence only one point of $\overline{P'Q'}$ will correspond to $X$. Similarly, for any point $Y'$ of $\overline{P'Q'}$, there is one line $\overleftrightarrow{OY'}$ and only one point, $Y$ of $\overline{PQ}$, corresponding to $Y'$. Thus, we see a one-to-one correspondence between the points of $\overline{PQ}$ and the points of $\overline{P'Q'}$, and there must be the same number of points on one as on the other.

Of course, this "proof" contains several weaknesses concerning whether certain lines and line segments really intersect, but relatively little teacher effort can eliminate these deficiencies when the pupils are mature enough to recognize their existence. During junior high a teacher can begin to remove some of the weaknesses by discussing *intersection* and *betweenness*— for example, by asking the children, "How would you define '$A$ is between $B$ and $C$'?" If a pupil does not insist that the three points be on the same line, he might agree that $A$ is between $B$ and $C$ (Figure 6.2), but then he would logically have to concede that another point $A'$, slightly more distant from $\overline{BC}$, also lies between $B$ and $C$. Another point $A''$ would also line between $B$ and $C$, and if the process is continued, a point can be found that will clearly not be between $B$ and $C$. Therefore, the clearest way to consider betweenness would be to require that all three points be on the same line.

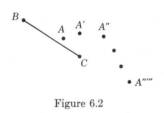

Figure 6.2

Most traditional textbooks do not distinguish line, ray, line segment, and length of a line segment. Clearly these are four distinct objects, and if two of them are confused, a pupil would tend to have difficulty under-standing the concepts being considered. Therefore, it is desirable to distinguish these objects, both with words and the notation used. The School Mathematics Study Group has chosen appropriate notation to distinguish these objects, which most authors have accepted. Newer textbooks commonly use the following notation: $\overleftrightarrow{AB}$ is the line through points A and B; $\overrightarrow{AB}$ is the ray with vertex $A$ which includes $B$ as an element; $\overline{AB}$ is the line segment which has $A$ and $B$ as endpoints; and $AB$ is the length of line segment $\overline{AB}$. The simplicity and logic of this notation is apparent, and needs no further comment.

### Measurement and Formulas

Probably one of the best ways for pupils to learn to measure is for them to measure something. For example, each pupil in the class might be asked to use a ruler and measure the three dimensions of his text-book. Even if their textbooks have approximately the same dimensions and their rulers are calibrated the same way (assume in 16ths of an inch), the measurements will vary considerably. If each pupil is asked to write down his answer before hearing someone else's, the variation will tend to be greater than if he is allowed to compare results with others beforehand. Many pupils may come up with an answer of, say, $9\frac{1}{4}$ inches for length, while others will report $9\frac{5}{16}$ or $9\frac{3}{8}$ inches, and still others $9\frac{3}{16}$ or $9\frac{1}{8}$ inches. Which answer is correct? Some bright pupil might suggest that the average of all measurements is probably the correct one, while another, equally bright, might insist that *his* answer is correct because he measured more carefully than his classmates. In all probability, none of the answers is correct, and a *very* careful measurement, perhaps with more sophisticated instruments, might show the length of the book to be somewhere between $9\frac{17}{64}$ and $9\frac{19}{64}$ inches.

The matter of the correct answer is less important than the question of how anybody might find out the exact length of the book. If pupils pursue the discussion far enough, they will come to the conclusion that no matter how good an instrument they use and how careful they are, there will probably be some error in any measurement. We say "prob-ably" because it is indeed possible that the length of the book is some simple length such as $9\frac{1}{4}$ inches (neglecting questions from atomic physics which cast doubt on the existence of any unique length). Of course, the probability that 30 books would all be exactly $9\frac{1}{4}$ inches is low (in fact, the probability that either all 30 books, or one particular book would be precisely $9\frac{1}{4}$ inches long is essentially zero).

Any measurement, no matter how carefully taken, is likely to be in error, and it is important to approximate the magnitude of the error. Only the person who makes the original measurement, or someone who is watching the activity closely, can judge the size of the error. After the measurement, unless the measurer supplies some information with his answer, nobody can tell from the simple number (and accompanying unit) whether $9\frac{1}{4}$ inches is likely to be $\frac{1}{4}$ inch, $\frac{1}{8}$ inch, or a whole inch off. It is therefore customary when reporting measurements also to report the potential limits of error. Thus, a person measuring the aforementioned book might write his answer "$9\frac{9}{32}$ inches $\pm \frac{1}{64}$ inch," thereby indicating his confidence that the correct answer is somewhere between $9\frac{17}{64}$ inches and $9\frac{19}{64}$ inches.

In attempting to simplify the reporting of such information, some people have suggested that the manner in which the answer is written will furnish the required information. Thus, an answer of $9\frac{1}{4}$ inches would suggest that the measurer believes his answer to be correct to the nearest $\frac{1}{4}$ of an inch—in other words, the correct answer is closer to $9\frac{1}{4}$ inches than it is to either 9 inches of $9\frac{1}{2}$ inches, or no more than $\frac{1}{8}$ of an inch from $9\frac{1}{4}$ inches. An answer of $9\frac{2}{8}$ inches, on the other hand, would indicate that the measurer is claiming that his answer is correct to the nearest $\frac{1}{8}$ of an inch, or no more than $\frac{1}{16}$ of an inch off. Thus, it would not be desirable to reduce all fractions, since a fraction such as $\frac{2}{8}$ would have a different meaning from the fraction $\frac{1}{4}$.

There has also been a suggestion that the calibration on the measuring instrument should determine the potential measurement error. Of course, the fineness of the calibration *would* affect potential answers, but it would not necessarily produce results that are easily predictable in a textbook. For example, one school of thought suggests that if the smallest unit on the ruler is an inch, then the answer should be in inches. Here the greatest possible error must be taken as $\frac{1}{2}$ inch. In fact, a careful and reasonably experienced individual can estimate more accurately. On the textbook measuring problem, for instance, most pupils could be quite certain with a ruler calibrated in inches that the correct answer lies between 9 and $9\frac{1}{2}$ inches, assuming the correct answer is between $9\frac{1}{4}$ and $9\frac{17}{64}$ inches. But with a ruler marked off in $\frac{1}{128}$'s of an inch, most would make considerably greater errors than $\frac{1}{256}$ inch. Certainly, there is more to the question of precision in measurement than the calibration on the measuring instrument.

Nevertheless, pupils should become aware of the probably error in any measurement and should proceed accordingly, both when making measurements and using them. Calculating with measurements is a difficult problem. When we add or subtract measurements, the ranges of possible errors must be added. For example, if 5 inches $\pm \frac{1}{4}$ inch is subtracted from 7 inches $\pm \frac{1}{8}$ inch, the answer must be between 2 inches $- \frac{3}{8}$ inch and 2 inches $+ \frac{3}{8}$ inch, since the original numbers might have been $5\frac{1}{4}$ and $6\frac{7}{8}$; or they might have been $4\frac{3}{4}$, and $7\frac{1}{8}$, or anything between the extremes. Multiplication is considerably more complicated. However, if the possible errors are carried through the computations, there is no reason to believe that the largest possible error in the result cannot be determined. For junior high school children, no doubt the lesson to be learned from all this is that if two numbers that are likely to be in error are put together by means of some arithmetic operation the answer cannot be assumed to be more precise than the known information. Therefore, carrying out a division, for example, to six decimal places when neither the divisor nor the dividend is beyond two places, is generally a waste of effort.

One more comment about measurements is needed. Measures are actually numbers and can be treated like numbers, but there seems to be no mathematical reason for carrying along the units. However, if the units were not indicated by the numeral, utter chaos would result. Therefore, it is appropriate to indicate the units in the usual ways.

## Area

Children should become acquainted with area and volume measure as well as with linear measure. In order to carry out two- and three-dimensional measuring procedures, children have to learn several formulas. However, it is not necessary for these formulas simply to be stated for children to summarize. Almost every desirable formula for area or volume can be discovered if children are given the proper encouragement.

To begin with, it is necessary to decide on a unit. For area, the natural unit seems to be the square. Suppose we wished to determine the area of a rectangle that has a length of seven centimeters and a height of four centimeters. What we must do is to count the number of square centimeters in the rectangle (Fig. 6.3). One way to do this is to start counting. A reasonably clever pupil will decide quickly that there is a better way to do it. Since there are seven squares in each of the four rows, it will suffice to add seven to itself four times, or multiply seven by four. The area of the rectangle in Fig. 6.3 is thus 28 square centimeters.

The same procedure would obviously work for any rectangle in which the length and height were given as a whole number of units. But suppose that the height were $3\frac{1}{2}$ inches and the length, $2\frac{2}{3}$ inches. It is difficult to count the number of square inches in this case. After count-

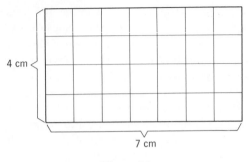

Figure 6.3

ing the six square inches in the bottom left-hand part of the rectangle (in Fig. 6.4a) there are several areas left over. It would be possible to figure out the area in each of the small rectangles and add these to obtain the total area, but it is simpler to change the unit for the time being. Rather than using a unit that is one inch on a side (one square inch), let us substitute a unit of $\frac{1}{6}$ of an inch on a side, as in Fig. 6.4a. How many of these are there in the original unit? It is clear that there would have to be 6 × 6 or 36 of the new units in each old unit. In $3\frac{1}{2}$ inches, there are $\frac{21}{6}$ of an inch and in $2\frac{2}{3}$ inches there are $\frac{16}{6}$ of an inch. Therefore, there must be 21 rows of 16 square units each or 21 × 16 = 336 of the new units. Since there are 36 of the new units in each of the old units (square inches), there are $\frac{336}{36}$ square inches in the rectangle, or $9\frac{1}{3}$ square inches.

If we consider the process used to arrive at this answer, it becomes clear that we would achieve the same result by multiplying $\frac{16}{6}$ by $\frac{21}{6}$, or alternately, $\frac{8}{3}$ by $\frac{7}{2}$. This means, or course, that the area is found by multiplying the length by the height. The procedure is perfectly general and can be used with any rectangle if the measurements are given in rational numbers of units. Junior high pupils are not likely to think of incommensurable cases, nor would the effort expended in trying to solve such problems be well spent.

Having spent some time discovering the formula for finding the area of a rectangle, the pupils would be ready to approach more complicated figures. In working on these, information already discovered may be used. By using such information, the children would improve their acquaintance with it. Therefore, it would be perfectly natural to apply the formula for the area of a rectangle to finding the area of a triangle. However, unless junior high pupils have learned previous formulas with understanding, it would be appropriate to review them in such a way that the children themselves become able to figure out the formulas. There are two reasons for this. First, pupils will understand the formulas better because of having gone over them again, and second, some of the methods used in simple figures such as rectangles and triangles can also be applied to more complicated figures, such as parallelograms and trapezoids.

Let us start with a right-angled triangle, usually called a right triangle. Suppose the triangle has a height of four centimeters and a length

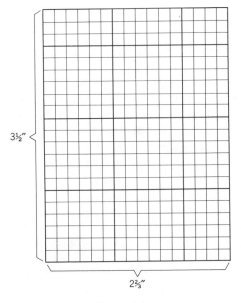

3½″  ⟨

2⅔″

Figure 6.4a

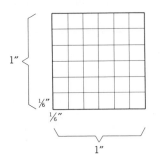

1″  ⟨

⅙″
⅙″

1″

Figure 6.4b

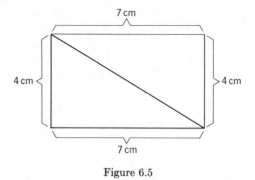

Figure 6.5

of seven centimeters. A rectangle can be drawn with the two sides (not the hypotenuse) of the triangle as sides of the rectangle (Fig. 6.5). We can see that the area of the rectangle is 4 × 7 or 28 square centimeters. Figure 6.5 shows the rectangle divided into two triangles of the same size and shape; the triangles are congruent. Therefore, if the area of the rectangle is 28 square centimeters, the area of the triangle must be half that much, or 14 square centimeters.

In general, the same procedure could be carried out with any right triangle; therefore, the area of a right triangle is one-half the base times the height in square units. Quite likely, if the teacher asks the proper questions, the previous procedure can be carried out entirely by the pupils. For example, the teacher can start by drawing the right triangle on the board and giving the pupils the appropriate measurements. Then he may inquire if they see any relationship between this problem and the area of a rectangle: is there any way they could change this problem so that it involves finding the area of a rectangle?

Once the pupils have discovered that the area of a right triangle is one-half the base times the height, they are ready to try other kinds of triangles. Consider a triangle similar to that in Fig. 6.6. The children

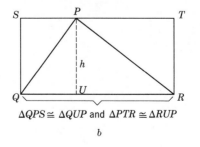

$\triangle QPS \cong \triangle QUP$ and $\triangle PTR \cong \triangle RUP$

$b$

Figure 6.6

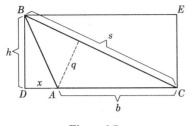

Figure 6.7

should have little trouble completing the figure and showing that the area of *this* kind of triangle is also equal to $\frac{1}{2}$ the base times the height.

Now the pupils are ready for an interesting problem. Take Figure 6.7. We have already shown that the area of this triangle is $\frac{1}{2}\,sq$ if the triangle is turned over so that $\overline{BC}$ is the base and $q$ is the height. But we have not shown that it is equal to $\frac{1}{2}bh$. Perhaps the best thing is to discuss the problem for several minutes to avoid mistakes such as showing the area equals $\frac{1}{2}sq$ and then let the pupils work on it for homework. They will know the answer, of course, but showing that $\frac{1}{2}bh$ is correct is fairly difficult. The easiest solution to this problem involves completing rectangle $BECD$, finding the area of triangles $BDA$ and $CBE$, and subtracting them from the area of the rectangle. The algebra involved may be challenging to young pupils, but if they have mastered the commutative, associative, and distributive laws, they should be able to work out this problem using variables for the various measures.

In discovering area formulas it is common to consider parallelograms before triangles and thus reduce each of the foregoing problems to a relatively trivial exercise of completing a parallelogram. However, if this procedure is used, all kinds of parallelograms must be considered. Seldom does this happen, and when it does, there is some reason for approaching problems in the opposite order (triangles before parallelograms) because this sequence presents more challenge to the pupils and also gives them greater understanding of the problems of working with parallelograms. (Since a triangle is a two-dimensional simplex, it is basic to all area problems.)

An ordinary parallelogram is handled in the obvious way (see Fig. 6.8) by "cutting off a piece from one end and putting it on the other end," or, more formally, showing that triangle $ABE$ is congruent to triangle $DCF$ and therefore the area of the parallelogram $ABCD$ is the same as the area of rectangle $BCFE$. However, if the parallelogram happens to look like the one in Fig. 6.9, no triangle can be cut off quite

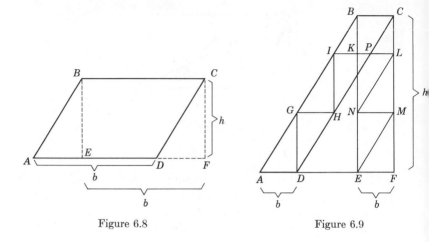

Figure 6.8                    Figure 6.9

so easily, and the problem becomes much more interesting. It is not correct to take the length $AB$ as the base of the parallelogram, since that is clearly not the same length as $AD$ (nor is either $AB$ or the new height equal to $h$). There are several ways to handle this problem. One of these is similar to the way in which the two previous triangle problems were solved—namely, completion of a rectangle and application of some algebra. Another, which usually appeals more to junior high pupils, but which can be messy unless carried out with a great deal of care, is to "cut up the parallelogram into right triangles and make a rectangle out of the triangles." This requires showing that $\triangle ADG \cong \triangle EFM$, $\triangle DGH \cong \triangle ENM$, $\triangle GHI \cong \triangle NML$, $\triangle HIP \cong \triangle NKL$, and $\triangle IKB \cong \triangle PLC$, and therefore the area of the parallelogram is equal to the area of rectangle $BCFE$ which has an area of $bh$. It is often surprising to see what a group of clever seventh or eighth graders can do with a problem such as this if left to their own devices. If the problem is assigned for homework, every pupil who has a method of solving it should be given an opportunity to show his method (if it is different from those shown by others, of course), both for the sake of his ego and for the education of his fellow pupils. The teacher may also learn a new method of attacking the problem.

If a class has discovered the formulas for Figs. 6.8 and 6.9, a reasonable homework assignment is to ask them to determine the area of a trapezoid given the height ($h$) and the lengths of the two bases ($B$ and $b$). Pupils can arrive at the correct answer by assuming that the trapezoid is isosceles; but it is important that they realize that this would be a special case. They must *not* assume that $AB = CD$. The two best-known methods of determining the area of a trapezoid, such as the one in Fig. 6.10, are (1) to construct a congruent trapezoid, upside-down and adjacent to $ABCD$ ($A'CDB'$), thus forming a parallelogram ($AB'A'B$) which has double the area of the original trapezoid; and (2) to cut the trapezoid along the line through the midpoints of $\overline{AB}$ and $\overline{DC}$ rotating the top piece around $M$ to form parallelogram $CD'M''M'$ (trapezoid $BD'M''M$ is constructed congruent to $ADM'M$) which has the same area as the original trapezoid.

If, rather than hinting at how to work the problem, the teacher simply presents the assignment, he will find several more interesting solutions to the problem. In some cases, a small amount of algebraic help from the teacher may be needed to complete a derivation. For example, in one eighth-grade class, a pupil extended the two nonparallel sides until they met in point $P$, called the height of triangle $PAD$ $x$ (Fig. 6.11), and found the area of the trapezoid to be $\frac{1}{2}B(h + x) - \frac{1}{2}bx$. Since he knew that the answer was not supposed to involve $x$, he looked for a way to "get rid of the $x$" and came up with the proportion: $x/b = (x + h)/B$ but then got discouraged by the apparent algebraic difficulties. The teacher was impressed with the work and helped the pupil to finish the small amount of algebra necessary to achieve the usual formula for the area of a trapezoid.

Another method of solving the problem involves dropping perpendiculars from A and D, putting the two right triangles together, and adding the area of the resulting triangle to the area of rectangle $ADFE$ (Fig. 6.12). Notice that it is not legitimate to assume that $\triangle ABE$ and $\triangle DCF$ are the same size, since this is equivalent to assuming the given

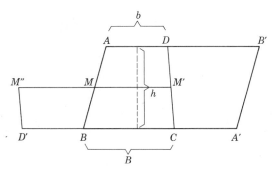

Figure 6.10

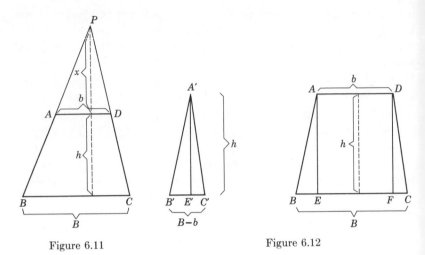

Figure 6.11

Figure 6.12

trapezoid is isosceles. If either $\angle B$ or $\angle C$ has a measure greater than 90°, the problem is complicated slightly—the special case should probably be solved separately.

There are other methods of finding the area of a trapezoid, and encouraging pupils to find these is good for them. This will probably tell the teacher a good deal about the ingenuity of his class. Probably the methods that ought to be taken most seriously are the first two, since

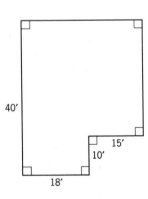

Figure 6.13

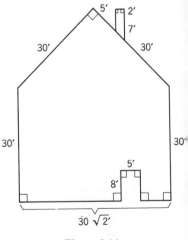

Figure 6.14

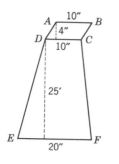

ABCD is a
parallelogram
DC ‖ EF

Figure 6.15

they make the final formula seem intuitively clear, while the others are circuitous enough to obscure their relation to the final formula.

Having gone through the work described, pupils should be permitted to practice their formulas and methods on other interesting problems. For example, they can be given figures such as 6.13, 6.14, and 6.15 (with the measurements) and asked to find the areas.

## Volumes

Having discussed one-and two-dimensional measurements, we should naturally proceed to three-dimensional measurements. Indeed, it might even seem appropriate to go on to four, five, or $n$-dimensional measurements, but for the fact that we happen to live in a three-dimensional world. For a charming story, which encourages $n$-dimensional thinking, the reader should see *Flatland*, by Edwin A. Abbott.[1]

The procedures used to discover formulas for areas of two-dimensional figures help to find formulas for volumes of three-dimensional objects. The counting of cubic units in three dimension is analogous to the counting of square units in two dimensions. Thus, the volume of a right-rectangular prism (a box) is represented by the formula $V = lwh$ (where $l$, $w$, and $h$ are linear measures: length, width and height, respectively). In a manner quite similar to the derivation of the area formula for a parallelogram, the formula for the volume of any prism (box with polygon for a base and with the lateral edge not necessarily perpendicular to the bases) can be found to be the area of the base multiplied by the height.

[1] Edwin A. Abbott, *Flatland: A Romance of Many Dimensions*, Dover Publications, Inc., New York, 1952. The second (revised) edition of this book was published in 1884, and it was written by a nonmathematician, yet the basic idea is significant to twentieth century mathematics. It is not beyond the comprehension of a bright junior high school pupil.

It may be convenient to determine the formula for a right-triangular prism prior to the more general formula for any prism. With some intuitive work with limits, it is then an easy step to the belief that the volume of a cylinder must be the product of the area of the base and the height.

Models can be obtained or constructed that show a prism being separated into three pyramids, all with heights and bases equal to the original prism. Moreover, a room may be considered as being divided into pyramids in such a way that two pyramids are formed, one with the ceiling as base and the other with the floor as base, with a substantial volume left over. A pupil with a sharp insight may note that the remaining volume is, in fact, equal to the volume of one of the pyramids. Perhaps the best way to see the relation between the volume of a prism and a corresponding pyramid (or a cylinder and the corresponding cone) is to have the children obtain physical models, fill the pyramid (or cone) three times with some harmless material, and pour the contents into the prism (or cylinder) each time. After the final pouring, the prism (or cylinder) will be filled to the top. Students are entirely capable of making the models in question, and many of them who are not otherwise outstanding mathematics students may find that this is their chance to shine in class. In general, the demonstration is enhanced if the model to be filled is transparent, or at least transluscent.

In addition to the volume formulas for three-dimensional objects, the children should be able to calculate surface areas. For the right cylinder, for example, a child should see that the two bases are circles, and that each has an area of $\pi r^2$, while the lateral surface can be cut along a line in a way that transforms it into a rectangle when flattened out. In fact, when making models, the children will have to employ this knowledge, or something like it, to fit the models together. Since the circumference of the original circle would be $2\pi r$, the width of the rectangle would also be $2\pi r$ and the area of the laterial surface, $2\pi rh$. The total area is $2\pi rh + 2\pi r^2 = 2\pi r(h + r)$.

Other exercises will fascinate pupils while helping them to develop conceptions of space. For example, imagine that a cube is painted and then divided into 27 cubes, all with equal volume. How many of the new cubes will be painted on all six sides? How many on five? Four? Three? Two? One? None? What if the original cube is divided into eight cubes? Into 64 cubes? Into 125 cubes? The student might attempt to work out a general pattern and see if he can prove that his pattern (or formula) will always work.

Since the pupils will mostly see two-dimensional pictures of three-

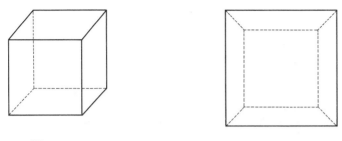

Figure 6.16                          Figure 6.17

dimensional models, they should spend some time learning to draw pictures of three-dimensional objects and to interpret other people's pictures. Also, having learned how to draw a cube using two squares and four parallelograms or two squares (one bigger than the other) and four trapezoids, as in Figs. 6.16 and 6.17, they might try to discover how one might draw a three-dimensional picture of a four-dimensional object. A pupil with a good imagination should have no trouble with this problem. Of course, the pupil with a well-developed imagination will notice that he can draw a two-dimensional picture of the three-dimensional figure of a four-dimensional object and will begin to wonder how he might draw a three-dimensional picture of a four-dimensional picture of a five-dimensional object, and so forth. Much work has been done with this sort of thing in many schools, and the interested reader should readily find more material on models of fourth-, fifth-, and sixth-dimensional objects.[2]

## Angles and Triangles

Before undertaking the study of angles and triangles, let us briefly dwell on the terminology of sets. The term "union" as applied to sets is used much as in everyday language—"bringing together." Thus, the *union* of sets $A$ and $B$ is the set that contains the elements of both set $A$ and set $B$ but no elements that are not in either set. The symbol "$\cup$" indicates union. Thus it is correct to write:

$$A \cup B = \{x | x \in A \quad \text{or} \quad x \in B\}$$

[2] See, for example, Harriet B. Herbert, "Balsa and Clay as Teaching Aids in High School Mathematics," pp. 245–252, *Multi-Sensory Aids in the Teaching of Mathematics*, Eighteenth Yearbook of the National Council of Teachers of Mathematics, Bureau of Publications, Teachers College, Columbia University, New York, 1945. There are also many other articles in this yearbook which will be useful to the teacher who wishes to help his pupils make models that will be helpful in teaching geometric concepts.

This can be read, "$A$ union $B$ is equal to the set of all $x$ such that $x$ is an element of $A$ or $x$ is an element of $B$."

In a similar way, the *intersection* of two sets is the set of all elements in both of the original sets. Thus,

$$A \cap B = \{x | x \in A \quad \text{and} \quad x \in B\},$$

where "$\cap$" is read "intersection" or "intersect." The expression can be read "$A$ intersect $B$ is equal to the set of all $x$ such that $x$ is an element of both $A$ and $B$."

A *subset* of a set contains only elements of the original set. Thus $A \subseteq B$ (read $A$ is a subset of $B$) means that for all $x$, $x \in A$ implies $x \in B$.

Two sets are *disjoint* if they have no elements in common. Thus if $A \cap B = \emptyset$ (the null set) then $A$ and $B$ are disjoint.

Using these conventions, we shall define certain concepts from geometry. We shall assume the concept of "betweenness" as applied to three points on a line.

DEFINITION.    The *ray* $\overrightarrow{PQ}$ is the union of $(P)$ (the set whose only element is $P$) with the half-line of $\overline{PQ}$ which contains $Q$. $P$ is called the endpoint of ray $\overrightarrow{PQ}$.

DEFINITION.    An angle is the union of two rays with a common endpoint.

The definitions of half-line and ray should seem obvious to the reader, but the definition of angle may appear peculiar. Many people believe that the interior of an angle should be part of the angle. It is certainly possible to define angle to include this, but most mathematicians do not define it that way at present. Thus, geometric figures generally consist of the outline of the figure and do not include the inside. This will also be true of the definition of a triangle.

DEFINITION.    The segment $\overline{AB}$ is the union of $\{A, B\}$ with the set of all points between $A$ and $B$.

Since betweeness pertains only to points on a line, segment $\overline{AB}$ is the subset of line $\overleftrightarrow{AB}$ which is made up of all the points between $A$ and $B$ including the points $A$ and $B$ themselves.

DEFINITION.    Triangle $ABC$ is the union of the four sets: $\{A, B, C\}$, $\overline{AB}$, $\overline{BC}$, $\overline{CA}$.

If two persons agree on the meaning of such basic words as "between," "line," and "point," and understand the definitions presented previously, they can hardly disagree on the meaning of the words defined. This does not necessarily mean that these definitions should be presented to young pupils in the way they are written here. In fact, probably the best way to arrive at these definitions (or similar ones) is to discuss the intuitive meaning attached to the concepts to be defined, and then try to reach a general agreement as to how to define the object in question. (Do we want the interior of the triangle included? If the pupils answer yes, let them define it. The definition will probably be complicated enough to encourage the other definition. Then, of course, the teacher must tell them the usual agreement.) It is surprising how similar will be the definitions arrived at in this way, assuming, of course, that the pupils have an elementary knowledge of set language and are thinking of a line and a plane as sets of points.

### Using Devices to Discover Geometric Facts

Pupils studying geometry in the junior high school should have several pieces of equipment with them in class. Each pupil should have a ruler which has both a centimeter and an inch scale (the inch scale will be more useful if there are two, one divided into tenths and the other divided into sixteenths), and a protractor. It is possible to have all three rulers and the protractor combined on the same piece of material. Each pupil should also have a compass (sometimes pluralized, but the singular form of the word will be used in this book), a piece of cardboard or a pad of paper to put under his work so that the compass will not make holes in the furniture, and plenty of paper and sharp pencils. With this equipment and proper guidance, pupils can discover a great deal of geometry.

For example, given the measures of two angles and the side between them of a triangle, pupils can be asked to construct a triangle with these measurements. They may be asked if all triangles having these measures must be congruent (that is, must have all corresponding measures the same). If there is doubt, scissors can be provided, and the triangles cut out to see whether they fit on top of one another. The same thing might be attempted with a side, a given angle opposite it, and a second angle. Or again with two sides and the angle between them. It might also be tried with three angles (at the beginning, it is probably desirable to have the sum of the angles be 180°), but the pupils should see that these triangles are not congruent, though of "the same shape" or similar. Or this may be tried with two sides and an angle not between them. If the pupils miss the exception, its existence might be hinted to see if some of them can come up with the so-called ambiguous case. For example, if the angle has a measure of 40°, the adjacent side is 5 centimeters long, and the opposite side 4 centimeters long, the two triangles (obviously not congruent) in Fig. 6.18 can be constructed. We

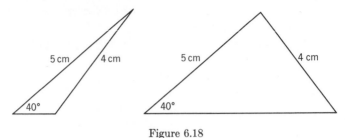

Figure 6.18

must make sure that there is more than one triangle having the required measurements. The ambiguous case is considered further later. The pupils should be able to guess which case is left to try and establish, at least to their own satisfaction, that given three sides of a triangle, the triangle is determined. They should now be able to state the standard congruency theorems for triangles.

When the class is given the three measures of the angles of a triangle, the pupils may notice that the sum is always 180°. If not, the teacher might give them three more measures whose sum is not 180° and see what happens. The class should agree with reasonably rapidity that the information given does not fit any triangle. They should find, by measuring, that the sum of the angles of every triangle measured is reasonably close to 180°. If they are honest, they will probably suggest figures slightly different from 180° fairly often, because of accumulated errors. If there is time, and the pupils enjoy cutting things out, the teacher can have them cut out triangles and then *tear*, not cut, the three angles off the triangle (if they cut, they will be confused by all the extra angles). Putting the angles together, they can see if they seem to make a straight line. The results will be remarkably close in all cases.

This experimentation, will probably convince the pupils that the sum of the (measures of the) angles of a triangle is 180°. Yet it may be interesting to relate this idea to certain basic concepts about parallel lines in order to begin giving the pupils an idea of proof. First, we need some definition of parallel lines. If the teacher asks the class for such a definition, or at least some idea of what parallel lines are, the pupils will probably supply at least two different answers. If they have had no previous formal experience with parallel lines, the most common answer is likely to be "parallel lines are lines that go in the same direction." The fact that the lines have no points in common will seem less obvious to the average twelve year old, but will probably be acceptable to him. Let us agree that both facts are true of parallel lines. Next we need some working information about what it means for two lines to

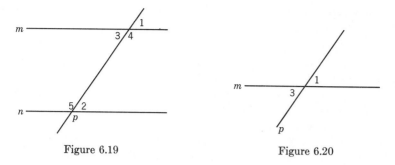

Figure 6.19                               Figure 6.20

"go in the same direction." If the two lines, $m$ and $n$ cross a third line $p$, the angles that correspond to each other, for example, ($\angle 1$ and $\angle 2$)— called corresponding angles have the same measure. They are usually written $\angle 1 \cong \angle 2$ and read "angle 1 is congruent to angle 2".

If $\angle 1 \cong \angle 2$, are $m$ and $n$ parallel? One more fact is needed to proceed with the proof. If two lines, $m$ and $p$ intersect, angles 1 and 3 are vertical angles. Do these angles look as though they have any special relationship to each other? In general, youngsters are more likely to be willing to accept the fact that vertical angles are congruent than the proof using supplementary angles, but either method is probably acceptable. In Fig. 6.19, angles 2 and 3 are called "alternate interior angles." Since $\angle 2 \cong \angle 1$ (if $m \parallel n$), and $\angle 3 \cong \angle 1$, what is true about $\angle 2$ and $\angle 3$? Are angles 4 and 5 also alternate interior angles? Are they also congruent to each other if $m \parallel n$?

In Fig. 6.21, what is the sum of the measures of $\angle 1$, $\angle 2$, and $\angle 3$? Draw line $m$ parallel to $AB$ through point $C$. What is true about $\angle 1$ and $\angle 5$? What is true about $\angle 2$ and $\angle 4$? Then is the sum of the measures of $\angle 1$, $\angle 2$, and $\angle 3$, the same as the sum of the measures of $\angle 5$, $\angle 4$, and $\angle 3$? But, what is the sum of the measures of angles 5, 3, and 4? Since $\triangle ABC$ could have been any triangle, does it seem that the sum of the measures of the angles of any triangle is 180°?

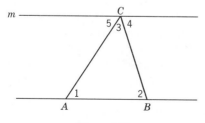

Figure 6.21

It will be fairly clear to the careful reader that the proof is based on Euclid's parallel postulate, or an equivalent assumption. However, such an assumption will not seem unreasonable to young pupils, whereas they would be less likely to believe, without performing a great many measurements, that the sum of the measures of a triangle is 180°. This is the kind of proof pupils should see early in their mathematical training. It will then seem to them that they have accomplished something with the proof. Later, they can begin to acquire an idea of mathematical structure, the relation between assumptions and theorems, and so on. Of course, going back and discussing the assumptions used in the foregoing proof would not be harmful to the pupils, and actually might be a worthwhile experience for many of them, but the important point is that we have deduced a fact that is not at all apparent from a group of statements that seem quite reasonable to the average twelve year old. Such informal proofs will smooth the path to more formal proofs in later mathematics courses.

Many other interesting facts can be discovered by children who have the use of the various mathematical instruments previously mentioned. There are many books which may be helpful to the teacher interested in pursuing this topic further. Several of the recently published, better commercial textbooks for the junior high have a considerable amount of this material. Both the School Mathematics Study Group and the Maryland Project materials provide good material on intuitive geometry; and there is an excellent little book, originally published in England (W. H. E. Bentley and E. W. Maynard Potts, *Geometry, Part One: Discovery by Drawing and Measurement*, Ginn and Company, Ltd., London, 1937), which is a fine guide to discovery and intuitive proof through experimentation with mathematical instruments.

## Circles

Many facts about circles can be discovered without much difficulty by junior high school pupils. Most likely, the pupils cannot estimate $\pi$ very accurately but it may be surprising how close they can come to this number by making precise drawings and performing simple calculations. For example, if they draw a circle with 10-centimeter radius (using a compass, with the radius carefully measured by a ruler) on a standard 8-inch-wide sheet of paper and measure the circumference as accurately as possible, the result should fall between 62 and 64 centimeters. A careful job ought to produce an answer of about 62.8 centermeters. Then, dividing this figure by the diameter (20 cm), the value of $\pi$ can be estimated as approximately 3.14. Measuring the circumference is difficult. A quick way to do so is to mark a point on the circle and turn the ruler slowly around the circle always keeping it tangent to the circumference. (By placing a fingernail on the circle and turning around it, and then moving the finger slightly, this can be accomplished.) A more time-consuming procedure which should prove a little more accurate is to place a large number of pins (or tacks) in the circle, then wrap a string around these, and measure the string. Neither procedure will give an accurate estimate of $\pi$, but both will give the pupils some idea of how they might go about evaluating $\pi$ and what this number is (the quotient of the circumference of a circle and the diameter).

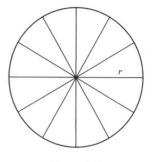

Figure 6.22

Once the formula $C = 2\pi r$ has been established (by definition of "$\pi$"), it is easy for pupils to compute the area of a circle. Assume the circle is cut into a large number of equal sized segments as in Fig. 6.22. Imagine that each segment is cut out and all are placed alternately with the point up and then the point down as in Fig. 6.23. As the number of segments is increased indefinitely, the resulting figure seems to come closer to being a rectangle. The length of this rectangle would be half of the circumference of the circle (or $\pi r$) and the height would be the radius of the circle (or $r$). Therefore, the area of the circle[3] must be about the same as the area of the rectangle, or $(r)(\pi r)$ or $\pi r^2$. Although this derivation is dependent upon limits, there is no reason why pupils cannot understand it and agree that each step seems reasonable. A rigorous discussion of the limit process would be out of place at this level.

Many other facts about circles can be discovered in the junior high

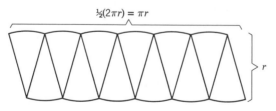

Figure 6.23

[3] By "area of the circle" we mean the area enclosed within the circle, since the circle itself (the curved line) has no area—similar comments apply to triangles, rectangles, and so on, in this proof and elsewhere.

mathematics classes. For example, the relationship between a circle and various angles which can be drawn is interesting, important, and not difficult to comprehend. Once there is agreement that the measure of a central angle and its intercepted arc are equal, most standard facts about angles and circles are easily derived. For example, what is the measure of $\angle 1$ in Fig. 6.24? Since $\triangle ABO$ is isosceles ($\overline{OA}$ and $\overline{OB}$ are radii of the circle), $\angle 1 = \angle 3$. But the sum of the measures of angles 1, 3, and 4 is 180°, as is the sum of the measures of angles 4 and 2. By simple arithmetic, angle 1 has a measure one-half as great as angle 2. When the center of the circle does not lie on a side of the angle, a ray can be drawn from the vertex of the angle through the center of the circle; the rest will be obvious. The other theorems associating angles and circles are similarly not particularly difficult and are worthwhile to present in junior high school classes.

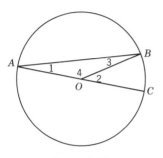

Figure 6.24

## Pythagorean Relationship

In many schools, there are tiles on the floors or ceilings of the classrooms which are squares divided into four congruent right triangles by their diagonals. These offer fine motivation for the important Pythagorean Theorem. Consider any particular right triangle (for example, $\triangle ABC$ in Fig. 6.25 and notice that side $\overline{AC}$ is also the side of one square tile, notice that $\overline{BC}$ is also both a side of the right triangle and a side of a square tile. $\overline{AB}$ is the side of the right triangle which is opposite the right angle (the fact that this side is called the hypotenuse might be mentioned). Now what is the relationship between the square which has the hypotenuse as a side ($ABDE$) and the squares which have the other two legs as sides? For this case, the square on the hypotenuse is equal to the sum of the squares on the other two sides. Is this fact true in general, or does this work only for isosceles right triangles? One way for the children to find out whether this applies to all triangles or only this particular kind of triangle is for them to draw several different right triangles, measuring the sides carefully, multiplying each length by itself (squaring it) to find the area of its square, and adding to see if the theorem holds for the given triangle (within the limits of measuring errors). If these computations and

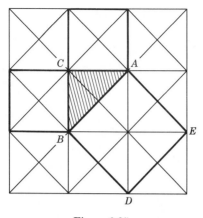

Figure 6.25

measurements are carried out with caution and accuracy, the results will be satisfactory.

No matter how many special cases are tried, it would be more convincing if a general proof could be produced which would be comprehensible to the pupils. The Pythagorean Theorem is one of the best-known theorems of geometry and has probably been proved in more different ways by more different people (including a President of the United States) than any other theorem in existence. From this large number of proofs, surely one that is understandable to junior high school pupils can be found. One proof the teacher might consider is based on the picture in Fig. 6.26. It is reported that the first person to find this proof simply drew the figure and presented as his entire proof the word "Behold!" The reader might try providing the more mundane aspects of this proof without reading further, if he is interested in such exercises.

Given right triangle $ABC$ with the right angle at $C$, complete the figure with one square and four congruent right triangles inside another square. The area of the large square is clearly $(a + b)^2$ and the area of the small square, $c^2$ (where $a$, $b$, and $c$ are the lengths of the sides opposite $A$, $B$, and $C$, respectively). The area of each of the right triangles is $\frac{1}{2}ab$, and the area of the four right triangles, $2ab$. Any pupil who knows the distributive law can multiply $(a + b)(a + b)$ getting $(a + b)a + (a + b)b$. Using the distributive law again in conjunction with the commutative law for multiplication he will find this equal to

$$a^2 + ab + ab + b^2 = a^2 + 2ab + b^2$$

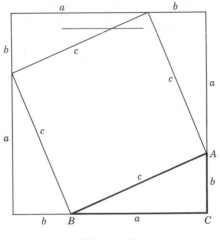

Figure 6.26

We now know that the area of the large square is $a^2 + 2ab + b^2$ and that the area of the four triangles is $2ab$. Hence, what is the area of the small square? We also knew that the area of the small square was $c^2$. Therefore, $c^2 = a^2 + b^2$, and the theorem is proved for the general case.

There are many other proofs of this theorem, and it may be worthwhile for the teacher to spend some time on several of these. Certainly it seems that with the many proofs of this theorem available, at least one ought to be used on an informal level when the theorem is first discussed.

As well as the topics discussed in this chapter, there are many facts of plane and solid geometry which can be discovered by junior high school pupils. Furthermore, there is no reason why pupils should not be introduced to simple informal proofs of some of the theorems. The amount of formalism should be kept, of course, to a minimum in the junior high, and the proofs should be aimed at convincing the pupils through the use of logic rather than through having them learn formal methods.

**Teaching Hints**

Pupils begin to learn geometry informally long before they enter school, and continue to learn throughout their formal schooling. In beginning the study of informal geometry in junior high school, this knowledge should be used. One of the best ways to start such a unit is to begin by asking, "What geometric figures can you name?" (If the question is not clear, give some examples.) If there is a tendency to name only plane figures, the teacher should call attention to the fact that we live in a three-dimensional world. After a large number of figures have been named (one student or the teacher should make a list where it can be seen by all), the next question is, "what do you know about each of these figures?" These two questions, and the answers ought to consume at least one class period, and probably more, if time is taken to convince all the pupils that the facts listed are indeed correct.

By using leading questions and physical models, a great many more facts can probably be discovered by the children. These facts include not only areas unknown to the pupils, and incidence relations (such as given two points, how many lines do you think can be drawn through the two points?), but volumes, numerical relations from similar and right triangles, etc. The important points to remember here are that physical models may be helpful (but can be misleading) and that the best physical models for educational purposes are the ones the children make themselves. Funds from the NDEA can be used for acquiring models or materials for the pupils to make such models. (Your principal will be familiar with the National Defense Education Act.)

A great deal of good material for a measurement unit can be found by sending each child home with the assignment to collect at least ten measurements which have been made by others and published somewhere; such measurements can come from the newspapers, almanacs, encyclopedias, etc. Once the list of measurements is available, it will be interesting to discuss how the measurements were acquired in the first place, what kind of error there is likely to be in each measurement, how one might get a more accurate measurement, etc. This will lead naturally into a discussion of how to handle measurements, which are approximations, when performing calculations. Questions such as "how can they tell how far it is to the moon?" can be answered in such a way as to show the power of mathematics, and the children are entirely capable of following an argument involving similar triangles.

The definitions of geometric figures in terms of sets should not be overstressed in the junior high school grades. A few examples of this will, however, begin to acquaint the pupils with sets and formal definitions, and will not do any harm if not overdone.

In geometry, as in all mathematics, it is desirable to relate the mathematical knowledge to the real world where possible. For example, pupils can find examples of symmetry in nature, listing as many objects as possible which have the form of a pentagon (from a building in Washington to a fire-hydrant wrench), discussing the properties of a three-legged stool as opposed to those of a four-legged stool (and the relation of three points to a plane), etc. Pupils can also learn a considerable amount of geometry from paper folding and using mirrors to try to make one pattern from another.

Studying the various possible positions of a triangle cut out of cardboard can also be instructive. If careful records are kept as to what motions are compositions of what other motions, the pupils will see an example of a noncommutative group.

### Exercises

1. Without "moving" the line segments, show that there are as many points on $\overline{PQ}$ as there are on $\overline{P'Q'}$ in Figure 6.27. Assume that $\overleftrightarrow{P'P} \| \overleftrightarrow{Q'Q}$.

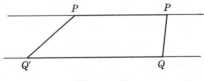

Figure 6.27

2. Show that there are at least as many points on a 1-inch line segment as there are on an entire line. *Hint:* Figure 6.28 may be of some help.

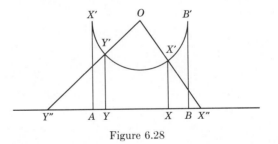

Figure 6.28

3. Given the measurements $6 \pm 1$ inch, and $7 \pm \frac{1}{2}$ inch as the length and width of a rectangle, what is the area of the rectangle—that is, between what two numbers must the area be (in square inches)?

4. Find the area of obtuse triangle $ABC$ (p. 149) in at least two different ways. *Hint:* Besides the method discussed in the text, you could use the area of right triangles $BDA$ and $BDC$.

5. Show another method of doing exercise 4 assuming you know the formula for the area of a parallelogram.

6. Show at least two methods of finding the area of a parallelogram in which no point of the "top" base is directly "over" a point of the "bottom" base (that is, no line $\perp$ to the bases intersects both).

7. Show how to derive the area of a trapezoid in at least four different ways.

8. Find the area of Figs. 6.13 6.14, and 6.15 on pp. 152 and 153.

9. Show how to derive the formula for the volume of a right-triangular prism given the area of the base.

10. Show how to derive the formula for the volume of any right prism given the area of the base (a polygon).

11. Compute the total area of a right circular cone which has radius $r$, height $h$, and slant height $s$. *Hint:* If cut in the obvious way, a cone can be spread out to be a sector of a circle with radius $s$. Then a proportion can be set up using the required area, the area of the circle with radius $s$, the length of the arc of the segment $(2\pi r)$, and the circumference of the circle $(2\pi s)$.

12. Solve the problem in the text (p. 154) about painting a cube and dividing it into smaller cubes. *Hint:* Let $n^3$ be the number of cubes into which the large cube is divided. The fact that a cube has eight vertices, twelve edges, and six faces may be of some help. You can check your answer by adding up your results—have you counted $n^3$ cubes altogether?

13. Draw a two-dimensional picture of a three dimensional model of a four-dimensional equivalent of a cube.

14. Given sets $A = \{a, b, c, d\}$ and $B = \{a, c, e\}$, list the elements of each of the following within set braces.

(a) $A \cap B$.

(b) $A \cup B$.

(c) Each of the subsets of $B$ (there are eight).

(d) At least three pairs of disjoint subsets of $B$.

15. State a definition for the interior of a triangle. *Hint:* The concept of betweeness can be used and may be helpful.

16. Under what conditions will the measures of the following parts of a triangle determine precisely one triangle? (This may be difficult without a good knowledge of trigonometry—it is discussed further in Chapter 12.)

(a) Three sides (*Hint:* Does 3, 4, 8 work?).

(b) Two sides and an included angle.

(c) Two angles and an included side.

(d) Two sides and a nonincluded angle.

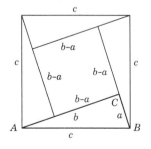

Figure 6.29

(e) Two angles and a nonincluded side.

(f) Three angles.

17. Prove that the measure of an angle inscribed in a circle has one-half the measure of its intercepted arc.

18. What is the measure of an angle whose sides are tangent to a circle (with vertex outside the circle, of course)?

19. Using Fig. 6.29 on p. 167 as a guide, construct a proof of the Pythagorean Theorem for right-triangle $ABC$ with angle $C$ as the right angle.

## REFERENCES

Abbott, Edwin A. *Flatland,* Dover Publications, New York, 1952. See comments in text.

Bentley, W. H. E., and E. W. Maynard Potts. *Geometry,* Part One: *Discovery by Drawing and Measurement,* Ginn and Co., London, 1937. See comments in text.

School Mathematics Study Group, Studies in Mathematics, *Intuitive Geometry,* **VII,** Stanford University, Palo Alto, Calif., 1961. A mature discussion of intuitive geometry of the type found in many of the newer seventh and eighth grade textbooks.

*Multi-Sensory Aids in the Teaching of Mathematics.* Eighteenth Yearbook of the National Council of Teachers of Mathematics, Bureau of Publications, Teachers College, Columbia University, New York, 1945. In the yearbook there are many articles which will give the teacher ideas on how to use various materials and aids to help pupils understand various geometric concepts. The material is particularly appropriate for the teacher of young children or for the teacher of slower mathematics pupils.

# PROBABILITY FOR
# JUNIOR HIGH SCHOOL

"What is the probability that I'll get an $A$ in math this term?" "There is a 50–50 chance that it will rain today." "I'll bet you two-to-one that we'll win the game." "What are the chances that Mike will ask me to the dance on Saturday?"

In each of these cases, the person speaking is attempting to predict some future occurrence. In each, he does not know what is going to happen, but would like to make a reasonably intelligent guess, and have some idea of the likelihood of its coming true.

The subject of probability has considerable significance in the world today. It is of interest to people of all ages, including junior high school pupils. One of the best ways to arouse interest in mathematics is to present some topic which arrests the attention of the pupils. Probability is such a topic. Of course, the teacher wants to be reasonably sure that his course is not being misused, but the interest generated in mathematics is undoubtedly worth the slight risk involved in presenting material which can be used for rather questionable purposes.[1]

[1] The material in this chapter is based on material taught by the author in 1955— at that time, one of the brighter pupils in the class won rather large sums of money from several pupils who were not in the class by playing games that seemed to be games of chance but that were clearly favorable to the boy in question. Of course, if all of the pupils learn the same thing, they will have good enough judgment to avoid such contests. Thus, keeping the children in ignorance is not the solution; rather, educating all of the children is the answer to this problem.

Probability was first used by gamblers who wanted to be able to predict, with some certainty, that particular results would occur more often than others in games of chance. In spite of this profligate infancy, probability has grown to be one of the most respected and useful branches of mathematics. It is the basis of all insurance and much of modern science.

Probability is most easily determined when there are a certain number of (presumably) equally likely possibilities of which only some are favorable. For example, suppose someone draws a card at random from an ordinary deck of 52 cards. We would like to know the probability of its being a seven. We know there are 52 equally likely chances and that the deck contains four sevens. Therefore, there are four chances out of 52 of his drawing a seven; the probability is $\frac{4}{52} = \frac{1}{13}$ that a seven will be drawn. If, however, somebody had removed all of the sevens and replaced them with jokers, the probability of drawing a seven would be $\frac{0}{52}$ or 0. If the deck were a trick deck in which all 52 cards were sevens, this probability would be $\frac{52}{52}$ or 1. The lowest probability an event can have is 0, in which case there is no chance at all of getting the desired result; the greatest probability an event can have is 1, in which case there is no chance of not getting the desired result—that is, the desired result will certainly occur.

If the entire set of possible outcomes has $n$ elements, all assumed to be equally likely, and the subset of favorable outcomes has $f$ elements, then the probability of a favorable outcome is $f/n$. Clearly 0 is less than or equal to $f$, and $f$ is less than or equal to $n$ (written $0 \leq f \leq n$). Therefore, the probability, $p = f/n$, of a favorable outcome lies between 0 and 1, inclusive ($0 \leq p \leq 1$).

With this preliminary knowledge, children can figure out many simple probabilities, and should be given the opportunity to do so. For example, what is the probability that a normal coin will come up "heads" when tossed? What is the probability of drawing a heart from a well-shuffled, regular deck of cards? What is the probability of drawing a card that is not a heart? What is the probability of throwing a three with a single die (note that the singular of "dice" is "die")?

What is the probability of rolling a seven with two dice? Since the set of possible outcomes (possible total spots showing on both dice) has eleven members: {2, 3, 4, 5, 6, 7, 8, 9, 10, 11, 12}, a reasonable guess would seem to be $\frac{1}{11}$, but this is not correct. The events listed do not happen to be equally likely. If we assume that the dice are independent of each other, and each die is equally likely to fall with one of the following numbers facing up—1, 2, 3, 4, 5, 6—there are more than eleven possible outcomes, more than one of which is a seven.

From several concrete cases, students will learn that in order to find the total number of possibilities in two events it is necessary to multiply the number of possibilities in the first by the number in the second. For example, with two dice, the first die may come up in any one of six different ways. With each of these six ways, the second die can also come up in six different ways. Thus, the set of all equally likely possibilities is:

$$\{(1, 1), (1, 2), (1, 3), (1, 4), (1, 5), (1, 6)$$
$$(2, 1), (2, 2), (2, 3), (2, 4), (2, 5), (2, 6)$$
$$(3, 1), (3, 2), (3, 3), (3, 4), (3, 5), (3, 6)$$
$$(4, 1), (4, 2), (4, 3), (4, 4), (4, 5), (4, 6)$$
$$(5, 1), (5, 2), (5, 3), (5, 4), (5, 5), (5, 6)$$
$$(6, 1), (6, 2), (6, 3), (6, 4), (6, 5), (6, 6)\}$$

If we are going to find the probability of rolling a seven with two dice, we must count the number of favorable cases and divide by the total number of possibilities, 36. There are six cases in which the total number of spots up is 7. Therefore, the probability of getting a seven with two dice is $\frac{6}{36}$ or $\frac{1}{6}$.

In the case of two coins, there are $2 \times 2$ or four possibilities: $\{(H, H), (H, T), (T, H), (T, T)\}$. With a third coin, we would have two more possibilities to associate with each of these four or $(2 \times 2 \times 2 = 8)$ eight possibilities: $\{(H, H, H), (H, H, T), (H, T, H), (H, T, T), (T, H, H), (T, H, T), (T, T, H), (T, T, T)\}$.

Having understood the discussion thus far, the student is ready to attempt a large number of probability problems. He will not do them by the most efficient method possible, but he will be able to do them. Exercises which might be used include:

1. What is the probability of rolling a five with two dice?

2. What is the probability of rolling a seventeen with three dice?

3. What is the probability of throwing two heads and one tail with three coins?

4. If a penny and a nickel are tossed, what is the probability that the penny shows heads and the nickel tails? (Notice that this is not the same problem as getting one head and one tail with two coins.)

5. If we throw two dice, what is the probability that *at least* one shows a six?

6. Take three coins. Flip each one and record the results. Do this at least 20 times and record the number of times all are heads, two are heads and one is a tail, two are tails and one is a head, and three are tails. Compare these numbers with the theoretical probabilities. (If an entire class performs this experiment and all results are put together, the results should be within 1 or 2% of the theoretical answer.)

7. Given a pair of eight-sided regular dice, what is the probability of throwing a nine with the pair? (In the geometry section, the five regular solids can be discussed and constructed by the pupils.)

8. What is the probability of throwing a 13 with two 12-sided dice?

9. With one 20-sided die, what is the probability of rolling a 10?

10. With one six-sided die, what is the probability of rolling a seven?

11. What is the probability of rolling a twelve with five four-sided dice? (This one may be hard to solve with the understandings developed so far, but it is possible. Its point would be to encourage the pupils to start thinking of better ways of counting, which is the next topic for consideration.)

## Permutations

When the lady of the house expects 13 guests for dinner, and is worried about the seating arrangement, the mathematician cannot give her much comfort in regard to the social amenities of the situation, but he can tell her the exact magnitude of her problem. In choosing the occupant of the first seat, she has 13 possibilities. For each of these 13 first choices, she has a choice of 12 people to sit to the right of the first person. Thus, there are (13 × 12 = 156) 156 different ways to fill the first two chairs. These 156 cases can be indicated by letting the first 13 letters of the alphabet stand for the people as follows:

| ab | ac | ad | ae | af | ag | ah | ai | aj | ak | al | am |
|----|----|----|----|----|----|----|----|----|----|----|----|
| ba | bc | bd | be | bf | bg | bh | bi | bj | bk | bl | bm |
| ca | cb | cd | ce | cf | cg | ch | ci | cj | ck | cl | cm |
| da | db | dc | de | df | dg | dh | di | dj | dk | dl | dm |
| ea | eb | ec | ed | ef | eg | eh | ei | ej | ek | el | em |
| fa | fb | fc | fd | fe | fg | fh | fi | fj | fk | fl | fm |
| ga | gb | gc | gd | ge | gf | gh | gi | gj | gk | gl | gm |
| ha | hb | hc | hd | he | hf | hg | hi | hj | hk | hl | hm |
| ia | ib | ic | id | ie | if | ig | ih | ij | ik | il | im |
| ja | jb | jc | jd | je | jf | jg | jh | ji | jk | jl | jm |
| ka | kb | kc | kd | ke | kf | kg | kh | ki | kj | kl | km |
| la | lb | lc | ld | le | lf | lg | lh | li | lj | lk | lm |
| ma | mb | mc | md | me | mf | mg | mh | mi | mj | mk | ml |

Notice that the arrangements listed in the first row all have *a* as the first choice, and each of the other twelve is considered as a possible second choice. In the second row, *b* is the first choice, and so on. Thus, there are 13 rows, with 12 pairs in each row, for a total of 156 pairs. With each of these 156 ways of filling the first two seats, there are 11 ways to fill the third seat. For example, if *e* and *j* are chosen, in that order, to fill the first two, there is a choice of *a, b, c, d, f, g, h, i, k, l,* and

$m$ for the third spot, and so on. Thus, the hostess has a choice of 156 $\times$ 11 or 1716 ways to fill the first three seats. This product could also have been written "13 $\times$ 12 $\times$ 11" to remind us of how it was acquired.

If we follow this type of reasoning to the end, we find that there are

$$13 \times 12 \times 11 \times 10 \times 9 \times 8 \times 7 \times 6 \times 5 \times 4 \times 3 \times 2 \times 1$$

or 6,227,020,800 (six billion, two hundred and twenty-seven million, twenty thousand, and eight hundred) ways in which the hostess can arrange her 13 guests at the dinner table. There is a tale, certainly apocryphal, that when mathematicians first saw this sort of calculation, they exclaimed at the size of the resulting number, and therefore decided to write such a number as a "13" with an exclamation point after it: "13!" This is read "thirteen factorial."

If it should happen that the hostess has a perfectly round table, the position in which she puts the first guest would make no difference, since all places at an empty round table look the same. Now there would be 13 times fewer, or only 479,001,600, ways to arrange the guests. This can be seen more easily with a smaller number of people.

If we wish to seat three people on a bench, there are 3 $\times$ 2 $\times$ 1 or six different arrangements possible:

| | | |
|---|---|---|
| (1) *abc* | (2) *bca* | (3) *cab* |
| (4) *acb* | (5) *cba* | (6) *bac* |

However, if the same three people are seated at a perfectly round table, cases 1, 2, and 3 are identical to one another; and cases 4, 5, and 6 are also identical to one another. Here there are only two distinct cases, or (3 $\times$ 2 $\times$ 1)/3 cases. In general, with groups of identical arrangements, we must divide by the number of identical arrangements per group that we wish to count—assuming, of course, that there are the same number of identical arrangements in each group. For example, if we were arranging Alan, Bill, Carol, and Doris along a bench, we would find that there are 4 $\times$ 3 $\times$ 2 $\times$ 1 or 24 ways of arranging them, but if we arrange them only according to whether a girl or a boy occupies a particular position, we would find only $\dfrac{4 \times 3 \times 2 \times 1}{2 \times 1 \times 2 \times 1}$ or six possible arrangements. The four arrangements

| Boy | Boy | Girl | Girl |
|-----|-----|------|------|
| *A* | *B* | *C* | *D* |
| *B* | *A* | *C* | *D* |
| *A* | *B* | *D* | *C* |
| *B* | *A* | *D* | *C* |

all of which would be counted in the first case, would be counted only once in the second case. Similarly, for each arrangement of boys and girls, there would be four different arrangements of Alan, Bill, Carol, and Doris. Therefore, the number 24 must be divided by four to get the answer to the boy-girl problem.

Arrangements of this type are called permutations. There is no particular reason for using this word in the junior high school classes, but on the other hand, there is no good reason for not using it, if convenient. Applying essentially the same principles, we can figure out how many subsets of a particular size a given set has. For example, if the given set has 20 elements, and we wish to find out how many three-element subsets it has, we can choose the first element in any of 20 ways. Having done this, we find 19 remaining elements to choose for the second. With each of these $20 \times 19$ ways of choosing the first two, there are 18 ways to choose a third element. Thus, there are $20 \times 19 \times 18$ ways of choosing the members of a subset containing three elements, if the order in which they are chosen makes a difference. In counting these, however, we would have treated $\{a, b, c\}$, $\{a, c, b\}$, $\{b, a, c\}$, $\{b, c, a\}$, $\{c, a, b\}$, and $\{c, b, a\}$ as different subsets. However, each of these sets has the same elements, even though they are listed in different order. In a similar way, for each subset we wished to count, we would count six subsets ($3 \times 2 \times 1$ being the number of rearrangements of a set with three elements), and therefore, to get the desired answer, we must divide $20 \times 19 \times 18$ by $3 \times 2 \times 1$. The number of subsets containing three elements of a set containing 20 elements is thus $(20 \times 19 \times 18)/(3 \times 2 \times 1) = 1140$. This might also be referred to as the number of combinations of 20 things taken three at a time.

Notice that in the foregoing dicussion, there is no attempt to develop a formula, and certainly none to have the pupil memorize one. At this level, it is more important for the children to understand a basic principle which they can apply to any situation of the sort than to learn a formula in a hurry which they can then apply to many problems without thinking about the basic underlying ideas. One of the nice things about probability is the virtual impossibility of developing general formulas which will work for all similar cases. For the case we have considered, formulas can be derived, but it is better to defer this until a later time.

After working out several permutation and combination problems (such as how many ways are there to rearrange the letters of MISSISSIPPI, counting all I's as identical, and so on? How many ways can a president, a vice president, and a secretary be chosen from a class of 30 pupils? How many ways can the teacher choose three pupils to carry books from a class of 30 pupils?) the class is ready to return to the question of getting a 12 with five four-sided dice (p. 172, number 11). Almost certainly, anyone who attempted this problem before and solved it (or was even close to being correct) spent a great deal of time on it. Now, let us consider how it can be done more efficiently.

First, n, the number of possible cases is $4 \times 4 \times 4 \times 4 \times 4$ or 1024 since each of the five dice can produce one of four results. Next, there are many ways of getting 12. Starting with the largest number of spots on the far left-hand die, we can work toward the right always making the next number less than or equal to its predecessor. Then, when we have listed all such ways of attaining 12, all that remains is to determine the number of different arrangements of each case. The reader will find this easier to follow if he goes through the work himself rather than just reading about it. Any logical pattern will suffice. It is only necessary that he follow *some* pattern to avoid skipping a case:

4, 4, 2, 1, 1    possible rearrangements: $\dfrac{5 \times 4 \times 3 \times 2 \times 1}{2 \times 1 \times 1 \times 2 \times 1} = 30$

4, 3, 3, 1, 1    possible rearrangements: $\dfrac{5 \times 4 \times 3 \times 2 \times 1}{1 \times 2 \times 1 \times 2 \times 1} = 30$

4, 3, 2, 2, 1    possible rearrangements: $\dfrac{5 \times 4 \times 3 \times 2 \times 1}{1 \times 1 \times 2 \times 1 \times 1} = 60$

4, 2, 2, 2, 2    possible rearrangements: $\dfrac{5 \times 4 \times 3 \times 2 \times 1}{1 \times 4 \times 3 \times 2 \times 1} = 5$

3, 3, 3, 2, 1    possible rearrangements: $\dfrac{5 \times 4 \times 3 \times 2 \times 1}{3 \times 2 \times 1 \times 1 \times 1} = 20$

3, 3, 2, 2, 2    possible rearrangements: $\dfrac{5 \times 4 \times 3 \times 2 \times 1}{2 \times 1 \times 3 \times 2 \times 1} = 10$

Total number of ways to get twelve spots:                      155

The number of favorable cases is 155, and the probability of getting a 12 with five four-sided dice is 1024. Similar problems can now be presented without the pupils' being required to do a large number of relatively pointless manipulations even though there are still a few computations left for them to tackle.

## Insurance Problems

As noted earlier, probability is important in calculating insurance rates and payments. Some companies will insure almost anything—

even the weather. In order to do this, an insurance company must have an idea of how much it is likely to have to pay in claims. For example, suppose a company insures against rainy weather in the Virgin Islands (that is, they promise to pay the hotel bill of anyone who is there on a day when it rains). The company must find out, first, how many days it is likely to rain in a season and second, how much it is likely to have to pay for each of these times. It would compile an experience table of the number of days it has rained each year for several years. The company would assume that for the next few years it would rain, on the average, about the same number of days per year. The company would also try to find out how many people are likely to be staying in the islands' hotels on any given day. After gathering this information, the company would set rates high enough so that it could expect to break even (or better) on the venture after paying all expenses.

Suppose we were going to go into the business of insuring the lives of turtles. The first thing we would do is to acquire a large number of baby turtles which we thought to be average and keep them under normal conditions. After a certain length of time, we would be able to make an experience table similar to Table 7.1. There are shortcuts which would allow us to make this table in a shorter time than 260 years.

### Table 7.1
### Experience Table for Turtles

| Age of Turtles (X) | Number of Turtles Surviving to Age X |
|---|---|
| 0 | 10,000 |
| 20 | 9,200 |
| 40 | 9,000 |
| 60 | 8,900 |
| 80 | 8,700 |
| 100 | 8,300 |
| 120 | 7,800 |
| 140 | 7,000 |
| 160 | 6,100 |
| 180 | 5,100 |
| 200 | 3,900 |
| 220 | 800 |
| 240 | 40 |
| 260 | 3 |

If we wished to determine the probability that a 60-year-old turtle would live for another 60 years, we would note that of 8900 turtles alive at age 60, only 7800 would survive to the age of 120. There are, therefore, 7800 chances out of 8900 for an individual 60-year-old turtle to live to the age of 120. The probability is $\frac{7800}{8900}$, or approximately .88, that a 60-year-old turtle will live to the age of 120.

If we wished to find the probability of a 33-year-old turtle's living to the age of 133, we would first have to find out how many turtles we expected to be alive at these ages. To do this, we must assume that turtles die at a constant rate between the ages of 20 and 40 and also between the ages of 120 and 140. This probably is not a correct assumption, but it will give us a good approximation of the answer.

1. From Table 7.1:
    Age 20    9200 turtles survive
    Age 40    9000 turtles survive

2. Therefore, in 20 years, 200 turtles died with an average of $\frac{200}{20}$, or ten per year.

3. In 13 years, we would then expect 13 × 10 or 130 turtles to die.

4. If 130 turtles died between the ages of 20 and 33, there must be 9200 − 130 or 9070 turtles surviving at 33.

By a similar process, the pupils could find that 7280 turtles would be expected to survive to the age of 133. Therefore, the probability that a 33-year-old turtle will survive for another 100 years is $\frac{7280}{9070}$ or about .80.

A similar problem is to determine the age to which a 20-year-old turtle has an even chance of living. Of course, the probability is $\frac{1}{2}$ that a 20-year-old turtle will live till the time when there are exactly half as many turtles as at the age of 20, or until there are 9200/2 or 4600 turtles left. We can determine the approximate age by noting that an average of (5100 − 3900)/20 or 60 turtles die per year in this interval. For 5100 − 4600, or 500 turtles to die, it would take $\frac{500}{60}$ or $8\frac{1}{3}$ years beyond the age of 180. Rounding off to the nearest year, the probability is $\frac{1}{2}$ that a 20-year-old turtle will survive to the age of about 188.

Several comments ought to be made about this section on insurance. First, most of the facts are purely imaginary, but the procedures are important (though hardly sufficient to let us begin working for an insurance company without more training). Second, the idea of collecting data from which to derive probabilities is important and fits into a branch of mathematics known as statistics. Third, the first problem (probability of turtle age 60 surviving to age 120) is essentially the same sort of problem as already worked, with the only new aspect being the reading of some figures from a table. The problem of the 33-year-old turtle's living another 100 years requires a new insight which will be used many other times as long as pupils continue to work with mathematics or with tables that are not as complete as they would like them to be. This is the process of interpolation. Notice that we attacked this problem in a purely intuitive way. There is no attempt whatsoever to develop a formula, or even to insist upon a particular method of pursuing the problem. We simply take apparently reasonable steps as they occur, noting the assumptions, probably false, we make in the process. All these steps will occur fairly naturally to a good group of seventh- or eighth-grade pupils. The problem of the 20-year-old turtle's life expectancy requires a sort of reverse interpolation, but should seem quite natural to the children

Having grasped these ideas, the pupils would be ready to undertake a large number of exercises based on this material. For example:

1. What is the probability that a newborn turtle (age 0) will live to the age of 200?

2. What is the probability that a 120-year-old turtle will live for another 100 years?

3. What is the probability that a newborn turtle will live to the age of 70?

4. What is the probability that a newborn turtle will live to the age of 223 years?

5. What is the probability that a 43-year-old turtle will live to be 187?

6. The probability is $\frac{1}{2}$ that a newborn turtle will live to what age?

7. The probability is $\frac{1}{2}$ that a 57-year-old turtle will live to what age?

8. The probability is $\frac{1}{2}$ that a 223-year-old turtle will live to what age?

9. The probability is $\frac{1}{3}$ that a 180-year-old turtle will live to what age?

10. How old would a turtle have to be in order to have an even chance to live to the age of 200?

11. How old would a turtle have to be in order to have an even chance of living to the age of 190?

12. What is the probability that a newborn turtle will live to the age of 260 (give the answer to the nearest thousandth)?

Notice that the problems start out requiring relatively little difficult arithmetic and only a small amount of thought about concepts. Then they get progressively more difficult until the pupils actually have to figure out some fairly challenging concepts for themselves. Of course, there would be several problems of each type in an ordinary classroom situation. Some of the arithmetic becomes fairly difficult (that is time consuming and requiring some care) in later problems, but there is no reason to apologize for this fact since junior high pupils are still in need of some practice in arithmetic, and this is probably one of the most palatable ways for them to get it.

There are other topics from probability and statistics which can be studied with some profit in the junior high school. Collecting information; graphs of all sorts (bar graphs, circle graphs, line graphs, etc.); measures of the "middle" of a distribution (mean, mode, median, or 50th percentile) and the distribution's spread (percentiles, standard deviation); probabilities of compound events (conjunctions, disjunctions, and conditional probabilities); trick problems—any of these can be pursued if there is enough time. The teacher should be careful, however, not to overformalize such studies and also not to spend so much time on trick problems that he overlooks important concepts. Tricky problems sometimes presented in probability classes are the following:

1. If there are five white socks and seven black socks in a drawer, and I must remove them without first seeing them (the room is dark), what is the probability that I will get a pair if I take three socks (by "pair" is meant either at least two white socks or at least two black socks)?

2. I have two cards, one of which is black on both sides while the other has one black side and one white side. One of these is chosen at random and placed on a table so that only one side can be seen (the side which is up is also picked at random). If the side that can be seen is black, what is the probability that the other side will be white?

Problem 2 is an example of a conditional probability problem. If there are pupils who insist that the answer is either $\frac{1}{2}$ or $\frac{1}{4}$, an experiment can be performed (choose cards and side at random, being careful to point out that when a white side happens to be up we do not count that case as either a success or a failure) to show them that the answer is neither. Usually about 30 trials will be necessary to get a good approximation of the correct answer, but the method used should clarify the problem sooner so that the pupils will recognize their mistake.

Another problem, which involves the probability of a disjunction, is:

3. Our football team has a probability of .2 of winning the conference championship and our basketball team a probability of .3. Assuming the two events are entirely independent of each other, what is the probability that we will win at least one of the two championships this year?

If the children answer .5 the teacher might try changing the numbers to .6 and .9 and challenge the answering pupils to use their method on *this* problem, and defend the answer they get. (It will be 1.5.)

Probability is an important branch of mathematics. It is easily studied in the junior high school and provides a large amount of interesting practice material. If teachers can restrain their inclination to formalize the procedures used, a great deal of good mathematics can be understood through the study of probability—furthermore, the topic is naturally interesting to young children (or for that matter, to most people of all ages) and provides a substantial amount of practice material for children. Certainly probability (and statistics) is a proper subject for study in the junior high school mathematics classes—*especially* for those pupils who are not likely to go far enough in mathematics to be exposed to the techniques of probability and statistical inference at a later time.

## Teaching Hints

From their past experience, pupils in a junior high school class will have various ideas about probability. One of these ideas may be that the subject is a little shady. It is tempting to try to avoid this assumption by emphasizing the nongambling aspects of probability, but, on the other hand, this notion on the part of the pupils can be utilized, to some extent, in attracting their interest. Pupils always seem to be more interested in topics that are not altogether above the suspicion of being less than respectable. In view of this, it is probably not desirable to play down completely the gambling aspects of probability. On the other hand, these should not be over-emphasized.

In beginning a class, it is desirable to ask some questions to find out how much the pupils know and to arouse their interest. In this case, one might start by asking, what is the probability that a coin will fall "heads" when it is tossed? There may be disagreement on this, but everybody will have the same answer in mind. Some may reply in terms of odds ("even," or "1 to 1"), while others will say "$\frac{1}{2}$." In this case, it will be necessary to reach agreement as to the meaning of terms. Using the coin problem, the teacher should easily convince the pupils that a probability cannot be greater than 1, and also cannot be less than 0. His questions can become progressively more difficult until there is substantial disagreement on the answer; this should happen with two or more dice or with several coins. Then, the children will see the need for developing a theory.

As we develop a theory, we should also bring the pupils back to reality on occasion. For example, when the teacher decides that the probability of getting a "seven" with two dice is $\frac{1}{6}$, it is worth trying a number of (maybe 600—have the class do it for homework, and combine the results) throws of the dice to see if the results are at all close to the expected value. This should help the pupils to accept the theory as a good description of reality, while reminding them that the object of the course is to describe reality reasonably. It is worth recalling that there are problems in physics which appear to be analogous to the two-dice problem but turn out to have the alternate answer (analogous to $\frac{1}{18}$).

The study of permutations can be motivated by solution of a difficult propability problem. For example, if the pupils try to solve number 11 (p. 172), they will spend a long time and almost certainly get the wrong answer. If they then see the exercise done correctly in about two minutes, they will be curious to know how it was managed. They are now ready to learn about permutations. The teacher can point out that it is easy for anyone to list the ways of getting 12 with five four-sided dice if the numbers are ordered and become smaller (or stay constant) from left to right. Having listed these (this process will take about a minute if no explanation is required), their only remaining problem is to find out how many different ways each set of numbers can be rearranged. Thus, it is desirable to study arrangements, or permutations.

It is possible to do the insurance problem in conjunction with a science class and actually collect one's own data. Of course, short-lived animals (for example, various kinds of insects) would have to be used and the possible effects of breeding be eliminated in some fashion, such as removing larvae at regular intervals. Having created the table, the children might then wish to check to see how well it predicts the activities of other individuals of the same species.

Two purposes of this chapter are to help the pupils to learn how to interpolate from a table and to consider the theory behind such interpolations through a concrete physical situation (if the class makes up its own table from a group of animals, it can compare interpolated figures with the true figures for given times). It might be wise to plan another unit involving tables shortly after this one so that the technique is not forgotten. Such a unit might include squares and square roots, or numerical trigonometry.

In order to get a feeling for the long-term stability of the fraction of successes in N trials, even when the answer is not theoretically obvious, thumbtacks or other irregular objects can be thrown a large number of times. One interesting experiment of this sort involves spinning pennies on a hard, flat surface. If a relatively new penny is used, the probability is NOT at all close to $\frac{1}{2}$ that it lands heads. While developing a feeling for the long-range stability of the ratio of successes to trials, for a given experiment, the teacher should also emphasize the unpredictability of individual trials. The "law of probability" does not say that a coin that lands "heads" ten times will land tails on the eleventh time—or even that it will land tails more often than heads in the future. The "law of probability" depends upon a swamping effect, not upon the memory of the coin.

If experiments with the "law of probability" are tried early in a discussion of probability, the probability of success for a given experiment can be defined as the limit of quotient of the number of successes divided by the number of trials as the number of trials gets large without bound. At present, this is the widely accepted definition, but does not have particularly great advantage from a purely utilitarian point of view.

Colored corks in a malted milk cup can be used in many ways to develop probability and statistical concepts (see 1965 report of the Cambridge Conference).

### Exercises

1. Do Exercises 1–11   (p 172).
2. (a) What is the probability of rolling a 15 with five four-sided dice?
   (b) What is the probability of rolling a 10 with four four-sided dice?
   (c) What is the probability of rolling an 8 with five four-sided dice?
   (d) What is the probability of rolling a 10 with five four-sided dice?

   (e) How many different ways are there of rearranging the letters of "ABRACADABRA"? Interchanging an "A" with another "A" is not considered a new arrangement, but changing an "A" with a "B" is.

   (f) How many ways are there to rearrange the letters of "STATISTICS"?

   (g) How many ways are there to rearrange the letters of "MISSISSIPPI"?

3. Do Exercises 1–12 (p. 178).
4. Do Exercises 1, 2, and 3 (p. 179).
5. Prove that there are exactly five regular solids.

### REFERENCES

Meserve, Bruce E., and Max A. Sobel. *Mathematics for Secondary School Teachers*, Prentice Hall, Englewood Cliffs, N.J., 1962, pp. 55–76. One of the few discussions of probability designed for junior high school teachers as opposed to high school or college teachers. Includes bibliographical references to experimental programs with junior high units on probability.
See chapters in several recent commercial seventh and eighth grade textbooks as well as SMSG and Maryland materials for junior high school.
See references for Chapter 13.

# LANGUAGE, LOGIC, AND SETS

"Words! Words! Words! . . . Show me!" So sings Eliza Doolittle in *My Fair Lady*. This might be an appropriate refrain for some "modern mathematics" classes in which there seems to be a great deal of emphasis on language and very little on understanding basic concepts. The purpose of language is to communicate; if there is nothing to communicate, there is no need for the language. Most languages in common use today are quite ambiguous. This not only makes them more interesting, but also makes it possible for people to live with themselves and with other people. In mathematics, in contrast, the objective is precision. We seek to communicate clearly, concisely, and without possible misinterpretation. This need for clarity places a great deal of emphasis on language in modern school mathematics programs.

Unfortunately, some teachers have become so concerned about being careful with language that they no longer worry about what they are saying, as long as they say it correctly. Certainly it is more important for pupils to have correct intuitive concepts than to be able to verbalize them in a correct form. We should never become so preoccupied with form that we encourage its memorization rather than understanding the underlying idea.

With this much caution against overzealous care in the use of language, let us consider some of the background for its careful use in mathematics. Let us explore the ways in which care has been used in school mathematics, and some ways in which it has been misused.

During the latter part of the nineteenth century a group of mathematicians began to investigate the foundations of mathematics. Perhaps the best known among them was Berstrand Russell. Probably the most significant single contribution to the foundations of mathematics came years later from Kurt Gödel, who in 1931, published a paper entitled "Über formal unentscheidbare Sätze der Principia Mathematica und verwandter System."[1] Gödel showed that it was impossible to prove the consistency of arithmetic (or any system rich enough so that arithmetic could be derived from it) without relying on a system that was at least as likely to be inconsistent as arithmetic itself. He also showed that any system from which arithmetic could be derived was essentially incomplete. In other words, there are statements in arithmetic that cannot be proved to be either true or false, as well as a possibility that there are arithmetic statements that actually contradict each other.

Although the results of Gödel's proof were astonishing, his method probably had as much significance, both for mathematics generally and for school mathematics in particular. Gödel's work had for its inspiration the reasoning used by a French mathematician, Jules Richard, in "proving" a mathematical contradiction known as the "Richard Paradox." The paradox is quite similar to Russell's Paradox (about the set of all sets which are not elements of themselves), the important point is that Richard had not really proved his conclusion because he had made the mistake of confusing properties of the objects under consideration with properties of the notational system.

Although somewhat similar to Richard's proof in many respects, Gödel's carefully distinguished between objects and their names. In general, when working with the foundations of mathematics, it is important to take care in determining the objects under consideration. Since the foundations are, in a real sense, central to all of mathematics, such considerations are likely to be important to all of mathematics. Certainly, theorems that are thought to be about mathematical objects must not turn out to be true only for the particular notational system being used. Thus, in revising the school mathematics program,

---

[1] For an excellent and readable account of Gödel's proof, the reader is referred to Ernest Nagal, and James R. Newman, "Gödel's Proof," published in James R. Newman (editor), *The World of Mathematics*, Simon and Schuster, New York, 1956, pp. 1668–1695.

many mathematicians and teachers have distinguished names of objects from the objects themselves.

To appreciate how a failure to distinguish objects from their names might cause difficulty, consider the following two examples:

1. Which is greater, 7 or 3? Which is greater, "7" or "3"? The answer to the first question is that 7 is greater than 3 since we are using numerals to talk about numbers and the particular numerals used are not really pertinent to the discussion. In the second case, the quotation marks indicate that we are actually talking about the numerals in question and not the numbers. Therefore, it could be correct to say that "3" is greater than "7" in this case. In a similar way, if Jonathan were a small boy and Joe a large boy, it could be correct to say that "Jonathan" is bigger than "Joe" but Joe is bigger than Jonathan. The use of the quotation marks is simply correct English usage. It has no particular mathematical significance, except to provide one way for mathematicians to distinguish the use of symbols to talk about objects and their use (with quotation marks) to talk about the symbols themselves.

2. What is wrong with the following proof?

$$\tfrac{2}{3} = \tfrac{4}{6}$$

The denominator of $\tfrac{2}{3}$ is odd. Therefore, by substitution, the denominator of $\tfrac{4}{6}$ is odd.

Again, the difficulty lies in the confusion of symbols and objects. The number $\tfrac{2}{3}$ has neither a numerator nor a denominator. One way of expressing the number, for example, is ".6666 . . ." or ".$\overline{6}$" where the bar over the 6 indicates that it is to be repeated indefinitely. The second statement should therefore be revised to read: "The denominator of $\tfrac{2}{3}$ stands for an odd number." The substitution in the third statement is clearly incorrect, since "$\tfrac{2}{3}$" is not equal to "$\tfrac{4}{6}$". These are different numerals for the same number, but are not the same numeral.

Virtually any of the newer mathematics textbooks makes some attempt to distinguish names from objects being named. This distinction is emphasized with numerals and numbers, and is often carried on into more advanced topics. However, it is safe to say that no series of books from grade 1 through grade 12 has been entirely consistent in distinguishing objects from names of objects while remaining appropriate for the children who are learning the mathematics. Although this sort of distinction may be central to mathematics, as the hole is to the doughnut, it is neither of great significance nor particularly appetizing to young children. Furthermore, if such distinctions are carefully made throughout a school mathematics program, the effort required to say relatively simple things in a way that makes them understandable will be out of proportion to the advantage gained from making the distinction.

To reduce the possibility of confusion, the following procedures might be appropriate. First, whenever there can be any doubt, authors of textbooks should make it clear whether they are talking about an object or a name for it. When there is no chance of confusion or a distinction obscures more important concepts, the distinctions should be skipped. Many authors point out in a footnote or a note in the teachers edition that they have deliberately not made the distinction because they thought it pedagogically unsound to do so.

In general, teachers should follow about the same sort of criteria set forth for authors. However, teachers can usually be a little less careful about the language used since a good teacher will be communicating with the pupils and presumably finding out if they have misunderstood any abbreviations or simplifications of the language used.

Finally, young pupils ought not to be required to make careful distinctions between numbers and numerals, but should be encouraged to use language correctly through the example set by teachers and textbooks. Of course, at a later time when distinctions are of great importance, students should be held responsible for making them, but that time probably ought not to occur in the mathematical training of the average high school mathematics pupil. In other words, it is desirable that ideas be expressed clearly and concisely so that children can understand them without confusion. It is further desirable that the children learn by example to make statements carefully and correctly, but it is not desirable to expend great effort to get them to verbalize every concept with great care and correctness. It is far more important for them to understand and be able to use the concept in question.

In addition to the distinction between objects and names, there has been considerable emphasis of late on using words correctly. If a word is defined in a certain way, it ought to be used in that way, rather than taking on some other meaning at a later time. An example of this is the word "cancel." This word has been used to mean several different things at one time or another in the past. For example, if $3 + x = 3 + 7$, there is a law called the "cancellation law for addition" that says that $x = 7$. There is a similar law for multiplication ($ab = ac$ implies that $b = c$ if $a \neq 0$). The word "cancel" is also used with fractions in the following way:

$$\frac{\overset{1}{\cancel{2}}}{\underset{1}{\cancel{3}}} \times \frac{\overset{3}{\cancel{9}}}{\underset{2}{\cancel{4}}} = \tfrac{3}{2}$$

The 2's and 3's are said to cancel here. Actually there is a perfectly good justification for this last procedure. It involves multiplying $2 \times 9$ and $3 \times 4$, looking for common factors, and then noting that $\tfrac{6}{6}$ is equal to 1 (or, alternately, "dividing numerator and denominator by 6").[2]

If the number system in question contains additive and multiplicative inverses, the cancellation laws for addition and multiplication are quite simple to justify. The question is, how should the word "cancel" be used? From the mathematical point of view, it makes no difference. Because of the low probability that the uses may be confused, there is no particular reason for not using the word in both senses. However, the word has been misused and misunderstood by many pupils and some teachers in the past, especially in connection with fractions. Some pupils have acquired the impression that whenever there is a "3" in the denominator of one fraction and also a "3" in the numerator of another fraction, and the two fractions are being multiplied, the "3's should cancel." This sort of reasoning results in the following sort of computations:

1. $\dfrac{3+7}{5} \times \dfrac{9}{3} = \dfrac{7}{5} \times 9 = \dfrac{63}{5}.$

Besides the obvious incorrectness of the computation, the pupil is also probably thinking that both "3's" have been replaced by "0's," which makes the calculation even more ludicrous.

2. $\dfrac{\overset{1}{\cancel{3}}}{\underset{3}{\cancel{6}}} \times \dfrac{2}{7} = \dfrac{3}{21}.$

The difficulty here is that the pupil has learned that cancellation is done when two fractions are being multiplied, but it is not fair to do

---

[2] The careful reader is presumably rephrasing this as "dividing the number for which the numerator stands and the number for which the denominator stands by 6." Any reader who continues to make such corrections throughout the rest of the book will see why this author does not feel such distinctions are worth making unless some clear difficulty is likely to arise.

in the same fraction. This is a misconception which could not occur if the pupil really understood the basis for this type of cancellation, though the answer is really not incorrect.

Owing to misconceptions of this sort, it has become common for teachers, writers, professors, and others to treat the word "cancel" as though it were a bad word. There is really nothing wrong with the word itself. Words are neither good nor bad in themselves. It is only the way we use them that can be helpful or not helpful in communicating. It is far more important to emphasize understanding the basic concepts behind any of these forms of "cancellation" than to change the word while continuing to teach the procedure without understanding it.

Another case of changing a word mistakenly was observed in a ninth-grade classroom. The teacher had heard that "−3" should be read "negative three" rather than "minus three" but had apparently made no effort to find out why. To be up to date, whenever he read such a sentence as "5 − 3 = 2" he would say "five negative three equals two," insisting that his pupils do likewise. The teacher assured an observer that the pupils understood better than they had when he had used the "old" system of reading the sentence "five minus three equals two."

In elementary algebra the symbol "−" is used in three different ways, but this multiplicity of meanings tends to confuse some beginning students. Some educators have suggested that different names be used to indicate each of the three uses, and further, that as teachers start to talk about negative numbers, they should employ a different symbol, such as a raised minus sign, to show that it does not stand for subtraction. The three ways in which "−" is used in elementary algebra are:

1. To indicate the operation of subtraction (5 − 3 = 2).
2. As a part of the numeral for a new kind of number (−3).
3. To indicate the additive inverse of a number (−x is the number which can be added to x to produce a sum of 0; the additive inverse of −3 is 3, and thus, −(−3) = 3).

Through long usage, it has become customary to employ the word "minus" for the first meaning of the "−" symbol. Both "minus" and "negative" commonly designate the second meaning of the "−" symbol. And "minus," "negative," and "additive inverse" all indicate the third meaning. However, many good teachers of ninth-grade algebra use "minus" in the first case, "negative" in the second, and "additive inverse" in the third. Some mathematicians prefer to use "minus" in all three instances since, in general, no serious confusions can occur once the student has acquired a clear understanding of the distinctions. Thus, the disinclination to use "minus" in certain contexts is primarily pedagogical (but based on mathematical considerations). In no way does this indicate anything inherently bad in the word itself. Indeed, if one is going to get along with only one word for all three meanings, "minus" is undoubtedly the best one to use, simply because it is customary to do so.

Many other words have been discussed in great detail in so-called modern mathematics programs, but cannot all be considered here. Three important points should be remembered about the use of words. First, words are neither good nor bad in their own right; second, words may be used in any manner as long as they help teachers to communicate clear understanding to their pupils; and third (a sort of restriction on two), where possible, words should be used in the same way as in the mathematical world in general to avoid making pupils learn and unlearn a vocabulary without good reason. Although the pure mathematician may agree with Humpty Dumpty when he says "When I use a word, it means just what I choose it to mean—neither more nor less," the teacher of mathematics is expected to be somewhat less cavalier in his diction.

Teachers of mathematics should also exercise care in their use of language in many other ways. Take the use of negations. For instance, what does the statement "All rational numbers are not integers." mean? It does not mean the same thing as "Not all rational numbers are integers." The first sentence says that no rational numbers are integers, whereas the second says that some rational numbers (at least one) are not integers. It has become common to use these sentences interchangeably. One well-known television commercial says something to the effect that "ALL girls who use our shampoo are not beautiful . . ." If this statement is interpreted literally, a girl would have to be either antisocial or illogical to use the shampoo. Unfortunately, many teachers misplace the negation in much this same way in talking about mathematics, and at times this can lead to much confusion. In general, it is preferable to say what you mean, and not assume that pupils will interpret your misstatement the same way you do. The important point is to communicate important ideas in a way that pupils understand, but this goal is usually achieved more readily by the correct than the incorrect use of language.

## Formalism

Intuition has been responsible for many of the great advances in mathematics, but it has also failed in some cases. Some examples of intuition's failures can be found in almost every branch of mathematics. For example, one of the great achievements of Euclid was the assumption of the parallel postulate. Yet for more than 2000 years after Euclid's time, many mathematicians thought it was intuitively obvious that the parallel postulate could be proved from other Euclidean assumptions. Not until the early part of the nineteenth century did mathematicians show that a geometry could be created in which all of the axioms[3] of Euclid, except the parallel postulate, were true, and that these new geometries were just as "good" from a logical point of view as Euclid's geometry. In fact, there is reason to suppose, in light of twentieth century developments in physics, that one of these other geometries may be a better approximation of the real world than is Euclidean geometry. Thus, Euclid was correct when he decided that the parallel postulate had to be assumed and could not be proved, but a great number of other mathematicians who felt that this statement's provability was intuitively obvious were not.

Figure 8.1

Another example of intuition's leading people astray occurs in analysis and geometry. This concerns whether a curve has a tangent line at a given point. On some curves there are points at which there is no tangent. For example, in the curve in Fig. 8.1 there is no tangent line at the "corner." Furthermore, other curves exist which do not have such clear "corners" and also do not have tangent lines at certain points. For instance, the curve illustrated in Fig. 8.2. This is a wave

[3] In general, we shall take the words "axiom," "postulate," and "assumption" to be synonymous in this book.

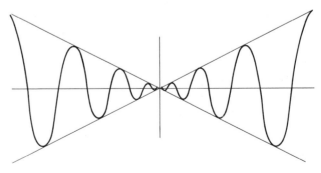

Figure 8.2

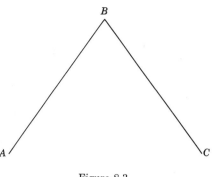

Figure 8.3

curve in which both the amplitude and the wave length approach zero as the curve nears the origin. Although such a curve will be continuous, it does not have a tangent line at the origin. However, to most people it seems intuitively obvious that any curve that is continuous everywhere will have a tangent line at most points.

In spite of the apparent intuitive obviousness of this fact, during the last century Karl Theodor Weierstrass created a curve that was continuous everywhere but had a tangent line at no point. Weierstrass' calculations are beyond the scope of this text, but some feeling for the curve in question can be gained by considering the following sequence of curves. The curve[4] $ABC$ in Fig. 8.3 can be replaced by the curve of Fig. 8.4, which also goes through the points $A$, $B$, and $C$. In Fig. 8.5 each of the small curves ($ADE$, $DEF$, $FGH$, etc., with some overlap) has been replaced in the same way as $ABC$ was replaced to get Fig. 8.4.

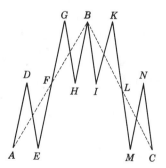

Figure 8.4

This process can be imagined to continue until there is a curve that is continuous everywhere but also has a corner at every point. In other words, there would apparently be a curve that was continuous at every point but had a tangent line at none. If this is not intuitively obvious, the reader should recall that we are discussing the actual failure of intuition in this case. Weierstrass did show quite convincingly that

[4] "Curve" applies to figures involving straight-line segments as well as figures which are actually "curved."

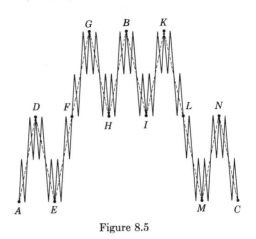

Figure 8.5

there are curves that have the property of being continuous every-where with tangents at no point, but his proof was considerably more difficult and much more rigorous than ours.

The point of all of this is that during the last century mathematicians began finding more and more reasons for distrusting intuition. Further-more, the advent of non-Euclidean geometries encouraged greater emphasis on abstractions than on intuitive physical models. As a result, mathematical publications have become much more abstract and rigorous. It had been the custom for mathematicians, when pub-lishing results, to print only the final proof without giving any indica-tion of how they had decided the outcome was true or how they had hit upon the particular proof. With greater emphasis on rigor and abstraction, mathematical papers became increasingly austere.

Now the same rigor and abstraction is making inroads among secondary (and even elementary school) mathematics programs. Of course, some feeling for abstraction and rigor is important for good high school mathematics students, but emphasis on these aspects should come only after important ideas have been understood through con-crete examples. In most mathematical work, intuitive understanding precedes rigorous proof and abstraction. This should also be true in mathematics education. Thus, before starting the formal proof of a theorem, the teacher should help the children "discover" the fact to be proved, and then ask why they believe it is true. After some practice, the pupils should be able to produce a satisfactory informal proof of the theorem without reference to the book. Then, the process of formal-izing the proof becomes a relatively simple matter. On the other hand, if the pupils' first acquaintance with a theorem includes a formal proof which they do not understand, they can hardly be blamed for memorizing the proof and theorem rather than trying to understand them. Thus, although formalism has a place in mathematics and mathematics education, it should not be allowed to usurp the place of understanding and intuition.

## Logic

Perhaps the most common answer teachers give to the question "why teach mathematics?" is "to teach the pupils to reason or think logically." However, it is uncommon for a mathematics teacher to spend many of his class periods actually talking specifically about logic. Logic is usually thought of as the construction of acceptable arguments or proofs. In this sense, it certainly seems desirable for children to learn to construct and recognize reasonable arguments.

Before discussing the construction of proofs, perhaps we should consider what a proof is. Some people believe that a proof is anything that convinces. In many respects, this is a good description of a proof. In a more formal sense, a proof is supposed to show that if certain assumptions are accepted, certain conclusions must follow. Opponents of a well-known Senator sometimes described him as a man who could start with false assumptions and reason, using impeccable logic, to false conclusions. If this were true of the Senator, he would be able to lay some claim to being a good mathematician, for mathematicians are primarily interested in the correctness of their reasoning rather than the physical truth of their assumptions. Thus, a proof in mathematics does not really give us any information about the real world; rather it tells us that if certain things are true in the real world, certain other things must also be true. In general, a mathematician hopes that his assumptions are applicable to the real world, and his work would not be of much importance if there were no connection between it and the physical universe; but the correctness of a mathematician's work is not dependent upon its relation to reality.

## Rules of Inference

In writing a proof, there is generally some attempt to present it in such a way that if we know that one step is true, we are assured that the next step is true, and so on. The rules by which we determine whether this criterion has been met are called *rules of inference*. The most often used inference rule is undoubtedly the one usually known as *modus ponens*, but sometimes called "the rule of detachment," or some other name. According to this rule, if we know that a certain statement, say $P$, implies another statement, say $Q$, and also that $P$ is true, we can conclude that $Q$ must be true. To take a specific example, let the statement $P$ mean "John passes the final examination," and the statement $Q$, "John passes the course." Thus the statement $P$ implies $Q$ can be interpreted "John passes the final examination implies that John passes the course," or, in more common English usage, "If John passes the final examination, then John will pass the course." If the teacher has made this statement and we have inside information to the effect that John has passed the final examination, we can conclude that John will also pass the course.

Another inference rule which is often useful is *modus tollens* or contrapositive inference. In this scheme, we know that $P$ implies $Q$, but this time $Q$ is not true. From this we conclude that $P$ is not true. Using the example of the previous paragraph,

If John passes the final examination, then he passes the course.
John does not pass the course.

From these two statements, we can conclude that John must not have passed the examination; if he had, he would have passed the course.

There are other inference rules which are useful in formal logic. These include conjunctive inference (putting two true statements together with the conjunctive "and" to get a new true statement), hypothetical syllogism (if $P$ implies $Q$, and $Q$ implies $R$, then $P$ implies $R$), and others. Most of these will seem quite natural to children and it would probably seem like overformalization to discuss all of them when beginning to talk about proofs. However, *modus ponens* is used so regularly, and is so important to what is generally thought of as a proof that it should certainly be discussed in some high school mathematics class without necessarily using that name. Contrapositive inference is also important in certain types of proofs (notably in indirect proofs, and pseudo-indirect proofs which are referred to in the next section as contrapositive proofs), and should probably be discussed shortly after pupils have acquired a good understanding of *modus ponens*.

*Proof.*    The most common kind of proof in mathematics as well as in other fields of human discussion is the direct proof. In such a proof, the person presenting the argument will start with a certain assumption or hypothesis (or perhaps several) and show that if the hypothesis is accepted, a certain conclusion must follow. A symbolic description of this might resemble the following.

HYPOTHESES:    $A$
CONCLUSION:    $K$

*Proof.* *A* is true by hypothesis. *A* implies *B* (because of a previously proved theorem, or an axiom, or a definition), therefore, *B* is true (*modus ponens*). *B* implies *C* (theorem, axiom, or definition), and therefore *C* is true.

This sort of process would continue until in the last statement the proponent would conclude that *K* was true. Most proofs, mathematical and other, would end when *K* had been shown to be "true."

In actual practice, it is not *K* that is to be proved, but rather the theorem "*A* implies *K*." For example, if we are proving that the base angles of an isosceles triangle are congruent, we are likely to end the proof with a statement such as "therefore angle *ABC* is congruent to angle *ACB*," when what we are actually trying to prove is that if *AB* = *AC* in triangle *ABC*, then angle *ABC* is congruent to angle *ACB*. The difference between the conclusion and the theorem that was to be proved is worth noting since it could easily be the explanation for some of the difficulties that some children have with proofs.

It is probably worth mentioning explicitly that if we can take any triangle (*ABC*) and show that by assuming two of its sides to be equal (*AB* = *AC*) the angles opposite them are congruent ($\angle ABC \cong \angle ACB$), we can say that the same proof would work for any particular triangle, and that we have proved the theorem true for all triangles. Thus, the final statement of our proof should be the theorem itself. The reason for this last statement is usually called the "deduction principle" in logic. This principle says that if we take the hypothesis of a theorem as an assumption (along with all of the axioms of the system under consideration) and deduce the conclusion by use of the usual inference patterns, we can assert that the hypothesis implies the conclusion in the system under consideration.

Another form of proof is called an indirect proof to distinguish it from the type of proof (called direct proof) just described. Indirect proof begins by assuming that the theorem to be proved is false. Using the usual inference schemes, we find that assumption leads to a contradiction (or statement known to be false). Thus, the negation of our theorem implies a false statement. By *modus tollens* or contrapositive inference, we conclude that the *negation* of our theorem is *not* true and that the theorem itself must therefore be true. This form of proof is based on the assumption of a bivalued logic—that is, a statement must be either true or false. Some well-known mathematicians, known as intuitionists, have raised serious questions about the validity of this sort of reasoning when applied to infinite sets in which it seems entirely possible that we cannot show that a statement or its negation is necessarily true, but we will allow indirect proof here with no further comment.

Another type of proof often called indirect is more correctly a contrapositive proof. In this kind of proof, we start by assuming the conclusion to be false (as opposed to assuming the entire theorem false) and then deduce the negation of the hypothesis, rather than a contradiction. Thus, if the theorem we are trying to prove is $P$ implies $Q$, we would assume that $Q$ is not true and show that this means that $P$ is not true. Using formal logic, we can show that the statement "$Q$ is false implies $P$ is false" is equivalent to the statement "$P$ implies $Q$." Thus, in a contrapositive proof, we are actually proving an alternate form of the theorem. The equivalence of an implication and its contrapositive form will be discussed in more detail later, but an example may help the reader to see that the two statements say the same thing. Let $P$ be the statement "I hit the billiard ball," and $Q$ the statement "The billiard ball moves." Then, $P$ implies $Q$ becomes

If I hit the billiard ball then it will move.
and "$Q$ is false implies $P$ is false" becomes
If the billiard ball doesn't move, then I didn't hit it.

A brief consideration of the situation should convince the reader that the two implications really mean the same thing even though the second seems to put more emphasis on its negative aspects. Notice that neither statement says anything about what will happen if I do not happen to hit the billiard ball. It may be that someone else will hit the ball, or tip the table, or perhaps an earthquake or some other natural phenomenon will make the ball move. But both statements make it clear that if I do hit the ball it will move and that if it does not move we can conclude that I did not hit it.

## Statement Calculus

Words such as "not," "and," "or," "implies," and "is equivalent to" are often used in mathematics and logic, but do not always have the same meaning that is attributed to them in everyday language. Therefore, a discussion of these words is certainly appropriate in a mathematics class where they are being used in their technical rather than their conversational sense. It is also common in logic courses to use special symbols for these words and then construct a system using variables for statements and symbols for the various operations indicated by the words. Although such a development would be as out of place in this book as in a typical high school classroom, we shall discuss the beginnings of such a system because of the interest in the system itself as well as the information about logical usage which will emerge.

Negation is one of the simplest of logical operations. In the English language, it is usually accomplished by simply putting a "not" in the appropriate place. Almost any English sentence can be negated by writing "it is not the case that" in front of it. For example, the sentence, "John is a good swimmer," can be negated in either of the following ways:

John is not a good swimmer.
It is not the case that John is a good swimmer.

Ordinarily, the first of these two methods is more appropriate because it results in smoother writing and reading; however, there are times when some people have difficulty determining how to negate a sentence correctly so that it reads easily. For example, the sentence, "All girls are smart," might be negated correctly in either of the following ways:

It is not the case that all girls are smart.
Not all girls are smart.

However, it would be incorrect to negate this sentence: All girls are not smart.

The first two statements could be interpreted to mean that there is at least one girl who is not smart, but the third statement says that there are not any girls who are smart. Presumably, most nonbiased observers would agree that the statement "All girls are smart," is false, and that its negation must therefore be true. The same observers would probably agree that the statement, "All girls are not smart," is equally false, but that the statement, "Not all girls are smart," is indeed true since it is the negation of "All girls are smart." Actually, the difficulty with this example occurs as much because of the quantifier (all) as because of the negation. Most of the other difficulties with negations occur because of a lack of understanding of the original statement. If a student really understands the original statement, he should have no difficulty determining its negation.

Other than negation, the commonly used operations of logic are all binary. This means that they involve two elements of the universe in question—in this case, a universe of statements. The conjunction "and" is used in logic and mathematics in much the same way as in everyday language. Thus, if two statements are connected with "and" the new statement formed is true when both component statements are true, but it is false in all other cases. Examples of statements formed by using "and" are:

1. Washington was President and Lincoln was President.
2. Washington was President and Jones was President.
3. Smith was President and Lincoln was President.
4. Smith was President and Jones was President.

Assuming the obvious interpretations, the first statement is true because both Washington and Lincoln were President of the United States at various times. On the other hand, statement (2) is false because Jones was never President, whereas (3) is false because Smith was never President. Of course, (4) is false because neither of the component statements is true.

A second binary operation in logic does not mean precisely the same thing in English as the more technical word does in logic. The disjunction "or" is usually interpreted in everyday usage to mean that one of the two component statements is true, but not both of them are true. For example, "Adams or Jefferson was Washington's Vice-President." The usual dictionary definition of "or" indicates that this interpretation is the accepted one: "A coordinating particle that marks an alternative; as, you may telephone *or* you may write."[5]

However, it is quite common to use "or" in the inclusive sense, too. For example:

If you drive too fast or drive through a stop sign without stopping, you will get a ticket.

It is perfectly clear that performance of both acts will win a ticket just as certainly as performance of either. In legal documents, the inclusive "or" is usually indicated by "and/or." In some languages, there are two separate words for the two different meanings. For example, in Latin, *aut* was used to indicate the exclusive "or," whereas *vel* was used to indicate the inclusive. The symbol most commonly used to indicate the logical operation of disjunction is a " $\vee$ " which is the first letter of *vel* and indicates that the logical "or" is always inclusive rather than exclusive. Whenever the word "or" is used in mathematics or logic, it is assumed that it is inclusive unless otherwise specified. Consider the following sentences.

1. Washington was President or Lincoln was President.
2. Washington was President or Jones was President.
3. Smith was President or Lincoln was President.
4. Smith was President or Jones was President.

In logic, all but the fourth statement are true. In everyday English, we might agree that statement number 1 is true, but ordinarily we would not make it. We would feel that it gave the impression that only one of the men was President when in fact we know that both were.

[5] *Webster's New Collegiate Dictionary*, G. & C. Merriam Co., Springfield, Mass., 1953.

Probably the most common form for a sentence in mathematical arguments (or any kind of arguments, for that matter) is

If _____, then _____.

This is sometimes referred to as implication or a conditional. The symbol most commonly used to indicate the conditional is a small arrow, "→" between the two statements. Thus, we might write the sentence "if it rains you will get wet."

It rains → you get wet,

which could be read: "It rains implies you get wet."

Often, time is indicated by the English statement, but this is not the case in a logical statement. Thus, in the foregoing example, the speaker is apparently assuming that the object of the discussion will be out in the rain and get wet shortly after it starts to rain. On the other hand, a mathematician would say the sentence is true even if it happens that the object under discussion takes a bath when it rains—even if he takes it before the rain actually starts. Thus, cause and effect, in the physical sense, have nothing to do with logical implication. The important question for the logician is whether or not he can be assured that the individual under discussion will always be wet whenever it rains. The sentence could be restated, "it can't rain unless you get wet." The only other commonly used binary operation in logic is the biconditional or equivalence relation. A doubleheaded arrow ("↔") is usually used to indicate this relation. As indicated by the word "biconditional" and the doubleheaded arrow the two statements in a biconditional imply each other. Thus, if a student has high enough grades so that if he passes the final examination he will pass the course, but low enough so that if he passes the course he must have passed the examination, we would say that passing the exam and passing the course are logically equivalent for him. Another way of putting this is

He will pass the course if and only if he passes the examination. Or, using the doubleheaded arrow
He passes the course ↔ he passes the examination.

Thus, a sentence created by placing a doubleheaded arrow between two statements is a true statement when the component statements are both true or both false, but is a false statement when one component statement is true while the other is false.

Since many theorems and most definitions involve the phrase "if and only if" (sometimes abbreviated "iff") we shall discuss the biconditional, or if and only if, relationship a little more fully. The statement

He will pass the course if he passes the examination.

means that if the student passes the examination he will pass the course, or using symbols,

He passes the examination → he passes the course.

But the statement

He will pass the course only if he passes the examination

actually says that if one knows the student has passed the course one also knows that he must have passed the examination. Notice that in the English language, the time element is likely to confuse many pupils. Since the examination is presumably taken before determination of the grade, it hardly seems appropriate to suggest that passing the course is the cause and passing the test the effect. The logician is not interested in cause and effect in the physical sense; all that is important here is whether we can be sure that one statement is true whenever another is true. In this case, if we know that the statement:

He will pass the course only if he passes the examination

is true and we also know that he has passed the course, we can conclude, therefore, that he must have passed the examination. Thus, this statement can be rephrased

If he passes the course, then he passed the examination.

Or, using the arrow for implication

He passes the course → he passes the examination.

Thus, the statement

He will pass the course if and only if he passes the examination

is equivalent to the conjunction of the two statements:

He passes the examination → he passes the course

and

He passes the course → he passes the examination.

The "if and only if" phrase can then be translated into two implications or conditionals, thus making the term "biconditional" seem quite reasonable as well as using the doubleheaded arrow to translate such sentences.

The discussion can be summarized through use of a neat device known as a truth table. Two symbols which were not defined in the text must first be defined. We shall use the symbol "∼" to indicate "not" or negation and the ampersand "&" to indicate the conjunction "and." "$P$" and "$Q$" will be thought of as statement variables or symbols which can be replaced by statements and the "$T$" and "$F$" symbols will stand for the truth value of a given statement (that is, whether it is true or false). Thus, in reading across the first line in Table 8.1, we see that when $P$ and $Q$ are both true, $\sim P$ is false, $\sim Q$ is false, $P \& Q$ is true, $P \vee Q$ is true, $P \to Q$ is true, and $P \leftrightarrow Q$ is true.

The table for $P \to Q$ usually causes more difficulty among students than any of the others. The first two lines seem quite reasonable, but the last two seem to cause a great deal of confusion. Of course, the truth table can simply be thought of as a definition, but this does not really solve the underlying problem. The difficulty that seems to bother most pupils is how the first component ($P$, sometimes called the premise) can be false and still have the statement considered true. An example will sometimes help in clarifying this point. One such example might be the following. Replace $P$ by the statement

He passes the examination;

and $Q$ by the statement:

He passes the course.

Then, the statement $P \to Q$ becomes

If he passes the examination, then he will pass the course.

Now, if somebody had made this statement and the student passed the examination and the course, we would all be inclined to believe that the person who made the statement had told the truth. On the other hand, if the student passed the examination but not the course, we would be inclined to believe that the person who made the statement had told a lie (or at least, was mistaken). Therefore, the first two cases seem quite reasonable. Let us now skip to the fourth case. Suppose the student failed the examination and also failed the course. In actual fact, we have no information as to what would have happened if he had passed the examination, but we would tend to believe that the person who made the statement was telling the truth because there is no evidence to the contrary. Ordinarily, students will have some reservation about the form of the last statement ($F \to F$) but will accept it as being true after having seen one or two examples like the

### Table 8.1

| $P$ | $Q$ | $\sim P$ | $\sim Q$ | $P \& Q$ | $P \vee Q$ | $P \to Q$ | $P \leftrightarrow Q$ |
|---|---|---|---|---|---|---|---|
| $T$ | $T$ | $F$ | $F$ | $T$ | $T$ | $T$ | $T$ |
| $T$ | $F$ | $F$ | $T$ | $F$ | $T$ | $F$ | $F$ |
| $F$ | $T$ | $T$ | $F$ | $F$ | $T$ | $T$ | $F$ |
| $F$ | $F$ | $T$ | $T$ | $F$ | $F$ | $T$ | $T$ |

foregoing one. Once this has been accepted, precisely the same reasoning can be used for the third case, which is almost always the most difficult for pupils to accept.

If the student does not pass the examination but does pass the course, we really do not have any information as to what would have happened if he had passed the examination. We would generally be inclined to assume that he would probably have passed the course in that case also and therefore the person who made the statement was probably telling the truth. The difficulty here is again the cause and effect relationship which most people attach to an "if _____ then _____" statement. In the case of the examination, if the student fails the examination and passes the course, it is clear that passing the examination would not have been the cause of his passing the course. However, the speaker did not say anything about cause and effect. What he said was that in the event that the student did happen to pass the examination he would also pass the course. There is no suggestion (except, perhaps, one that may be inferred by the listener) that not passing the examination will automatically result in not passing the course.

While on the topic of the conditional, it is appropriate to discuss the various rearrangements of the symbols in $P \to Q$. The converse of $P \to Q$ is $Q \to P$ which does not have the same truth value as $P \to Q$, as can be seen from Table 8.2. The statements $P \to Q$ and $Q \to P$ differ in their truth values in the second and third lines of the table. An example illustrates the point in question. Let $P$ be the statement "It is a dog (in good condition)" and $Q$ the statement "It has a head." Now, it seems clear that $P$ implies $Q$, but equally clear that $Q$ does not imply $P$, since it is possible for an animal to have a head without necessarily being a dog.

It is now possible to talk about a logical system in which the elements are statements assumed to be either true or false (which will be represented by capital letters $P$, $Q$, $R$, $S$, etc.) and in which the oper-

**Table 8.2**

| $P$ | $Q$ | $P \to Q$ | $Q \to P$ |
|-----|-----|-----------|-----------|
| $T$ | $T$ | $T$ | $T$ |
| $T$ | $F$ | $F$ | $T$ |
| $F$ | $T$ | $T$ | $F$ |
| $F$ | $F$ | $T$ | $T$ |

ations are $\sim$, &, $\vee$, $\rightarrow$, and $\leftrightarrow$. From the definitions of the operations, we know that if $P$ is a statement, then $\sim P$ is also a statement and has the opposite truth value of $P$; if $P$ and $Q$ are statements, then $P \vee Q$ is a statement which is true except when both $P$ and $Q$ are false but false in that case; etc.

Although we have defined all operations except $\sim$ for two elements, we may wish to create statements involving more than one operation and more than two statements. What, for example, does "$P$ & $Q$ & $R$" signify? In general, we shall use parentheses in much the same way they are used in algebra to group symbols. Thus, $P$ & $(Q$ & $R)$ is the conjunction of the statement $P$ with the statement $Q$ & $R$, etc. Usually, certain conventions are created regarding which operations are to be carried out first, but for the time being, we shall rely upon parentheses to determine this.

With this much notational convention, we can define several operations in terms of others. For example, $P \rightarrow Q$ can be defined as $(\sim P) \vee Q$. Relying on our knowledge of English, we should find this reasonable, since the second statement says that $P$ is not true or $Q$ is true, which might be rephrased as "whenever $P$ is true, $Q$ must also be true." This, of course, sounds as though it says the same thing as "$P$ implies $Q$." It is dangerous to conclude that because two statements sound alike they really say the same thing, but such considerations will often furnish a clue as to what sort of statements might say the same thing. It is generally safer to use a truth table or some other relatively formal device to be sure about the equivalence of such statements (see Table 8.3). Since the truth table is the same for $(\sim P) \vee Q$ as for $P \rightarrow Q$, the two are equivalent. Similarly, we can define each of the binary operations in terms of several other operations. In this development, we shall use all of the operations, for simplicity's sake, even though it would be possible to get along without several of them.

Since we have referred to the set of statements involving certain operations as a system, it may seem natural to inquire whether the

**Table 8.3**

| $P$ | $Q$ | $\sim P$ | $Q$ | $(\sim P) \vee Q$ | $P \rightarrow Q$ |
|-----|-----|----------|-----|-------------------|-------------------|
| $T$ | $T$ | $F$ | $T$ | $T$ | $T$ |
| $T$ | $F$ | $F$ | $F$ | $F$ | $F$ |
| $F$ | $T$ | $T$ | $T$ | $T$ | $T$ |
| $F$ | $F$ | $T$ | $F$ | $T$ | $T$ |

system has various properties of other mathematical systems. In particular, we have discovered that in mathematical systems, certain operations are sometimes commutative or associative; one operation may be distributed over another; there may be identity elements for certain operations; and so on. Let us consider some of these properties as they relate to the system of formal logic.

First, since negation ($\sim$) is unary rather than binary, it makes little sense to inquire whether it is commutative, etc. Let us then turn to the operation of disjunction, $\vee$. Is it true that $P \vee Q$ is equivalent to $Q \vee P$? That is, do the two statements have the same truth values for various values of $P$ and $Q$? If the reader has trouble answering this question, he may wish to write out a truth table for this situation. Next, is $\vee$ associative? That is, does $P \vee (Q \vee S)$ have the same truth values as $(P \vee Q) \vee S$ for various values of $P$, $Q$, and $S$? Again, a truth table may be of some help. Even if the answer is obvious to the reader, the question of how many rows there should be in the truth table in this case may be of some interest. A slight knowledge of permutations and combinations will lead to the conclusion that since there are two possible values for $P$, and for each of these there are two choices for $Q$, and for each of these four choices, there are two choices for $S$, there must be a total of $2^3$ or 8 ways of arranging the $T$'s and $F$'s.

These 8 cases will be easier to produce if some particular procedure is followed. In this book we shall follow the procedure of determining the number of rows needed, then under the first variable writing $T$ in the top half of the table and $F$ in the bottom half. For the second variable, the top quarter will be $T$'s, the next quarter $F$'s, the third quarter $T$'s, and the final quarter $F$'s. For the third variable, the top eighth of the rows will have $T$'s, and then the $T$'s and $F$'s will alter-

**Table 8.4**

| P | Q | S |
|---|---|---|
| T | T | T |
| T | T | F |
| T | F | T |
| T | F | F |
| F | T | T |
| F | T | F |
| F | F | T |
| F | F | F |

nate, etc. Thus, for three variables, the truth table would look like Table 8.4.

The reader should now recognize that ∨ and & are both commutative and associative. It may be more interesting to determine whether → and ↔ are commutative or associative. We shall leave this to the exercises.

## Exercises

1. Using a truth table, show that $P \to Q$ is equivalent to $(\sim Q) \to (\sim P)$.

2. Using only & and →, give an equivalent statement for $P \leftrightarrow Q$. Show by using a truth table that the two are really equivalent. (Parentheses may be used, of course.)

3. Using only $\sim$ and ∨, give an equivalent statement for $P$ & $Q$. (*Hint:* Try to construct a statement that has exactly opposite values from $P$ & $Q$ and then negate the whole thing.)

4. Using only $\sim$ and &, give an equivalent statement for $P \vee Q$.

5. Using only $\sim$ and &, give an equivalent statement for $P \to Q$.

6. State whether each of the following operations is commutative: ∨, &, →, ↔. Show that your answer for the last two operations is correct by using truth tables.

7. State whether each of the following operations is associative: ∨, &, →, ↔. Show that your answer for the last two operations is correct by using truth tables.

8. Is ∨ distributive over &? Substantiate your answer with a truth table.

9. Is & distributive over ∨? Substantiate your answer with a truth table.

10. Is ∨ distributive over ↔? Substantiate your answer with a truth table.

11. Is & distributive over ↔?

12. Is ↔ distributive over ∨?

13. Is ↔ distributive over &?

14. Among the set of all possible statements, can you find at least one identity element for the operation ∨? Will any statement with truth value $T$ do?

15. Give an example of an identity element for &.

16. Can you find an identity element for ↔? What is it?

17. Prove that for some elements of the system, there are not inverses with respect to ∨.

18. Prove that for some elements of the system, there are not inverses with respect to &.

19. What is the inverse of $T$ with respect to ↔? What is the inverse of $F$ with respect to ↔?

The biconditional (↔) is usually thought of as a relation rather than as an operation. That is, two statement formulas will produce the same truth table if and only if they are equivalent to each other (that is, when they are connected with the biconditional ↔, the truth table produces nothing but $T$'s). However, if $\leftrightarrow$ is thought of as an operation, the results of the previous exercises lead to the conclusion that in the usual axioms of a field, if $\times$ is replaced by $\vee$, and $+$ is replaced by $\leftrightarrow$, a surprising number of the field properties is true. The only one that fails is the "multiplicative" inverse property. Perhaps the reader may wish to study such a system further in light of what he knows about fields to see if more interesting properties can be discovered about the system.

It is more common to study the system involving the two operations $\vee$ and &, using $\leftrightarrow$ as the equality relation. Here two distributive laws provide an extra bonus, but several other properties of a field are not true.

Operations and relations can be confused in logic because the values in the universe under consideration are True and False. Although a relation is ordinarily a set of ordered pairs, one may also consider all possible ordered pairs, putting a $T$ after those that belong to the relation and an $F$ after those that do not. Thus, when the universe of a relation contains the elements True and False, the relation gives rise to an ordered triple (or a binary operation, in this case).

Certain statement formulas are of particular interest because no matter what truth values are assigned to the components, the resulting statement is always true. Such statement formulas are usually called valid statement formulas or tautologies.

There are many valid statement formulas which are quite useful in logic; the reader can undoubtedly list many of these from his experience in the previous set of exercises.   We shall list a few of the more common ones.

|  |  |
|---|---|
| 1. $P \vee (\sim P)$ | Excluded Middle |
| 2. $\sim(P \,\&\, (\sim P))$ | Negation of a Contradiction |
| 3. $P \,\&\, Q \leftrightarrow Q \,\&\, P$ | Commutative Law (&) |
| 4. $P \vee Q \leftrightarrow Q \vee P$ | Commutative Law ($\vee$) |
| 5. $[P \,\&\, (Q \,\&\, R)] \leftrightarrow [(P \,\&\, Q) \,\&\, R]$ | Associative Law (&) |
| 6. $[P \vee (Q \vee R)] \leftrightarrow [(P \vee Q) \vee R]$ | Associative Law ($\vee$) |
| 7. $[P \vee (Q \,\&\, R)] \leftrightarrow [(P \vee Q) \,\&\, (P \vee R)]$ | Distributive Law ($\vee$ over &) |
| 8. $[P \,\&\, (Q \vee R)] \leftrightarrow [(P \,\&\, Q) \vee (P \,\&\, R)]$ | Distributive Law (& over $\vee$) |
| 9. $(P \rightarrow Q) \leftrightarrow [(\sim Q) \rightarrow (\sim P)]$ | Contrapositive |
| 10. $(P \leftrightarrow Q) \leftrightarrow [(P \rightarrow Q) \,\&\, (Q \rightarrow P)]$ | |
| 11. $[\sim(P \,\&\, Q)] \leftrightarrow [(\sim P) \vee (\sim Q)]$ | De Morgan's Law |
| 12. $[\sim(P \vee Q)] \leftrightarrow [(\sim P) \,\&\, (\sim Q)]$ | De Morgan's Law |
| 13. $(P \rightarrow Q) \leftrightarrow [(\sim P) \vee Q]$ | |
| 14. $(P \rightarrow Q) \leftrightarrow [\sim(P \,\&\, (\sim Q))]$ | |
| 15. $[\sim(\sim P)] \leftrightarrow P$ | Double Negative |

Although there are many other valid statement formulas, the ones listed are of particular interest. The reader will recognize most of them as being either answers to exercises or variations on these. In general, the names attached to the valid statement formulas have an obvious derivation. De Morgan's Laws are named after a nineteenth century logician.

## Quantification

Many statements in mathematics do not really fit into the form of statement formulas. Rather, they are statements about all members of a particular set, or perhaps statements to the effect that at least one element of a given set has a certain property. For example, in elementary algebra, we may make a statement such as

For all real numbers, $x$ and $y$, $(x + y)^2 = x^2 + 2xy + y^2$.

It is worth noticing that the two statements are quite different from such sentences as $xy > 4$ and $2x + 3y = 5$. These last two sentences are not really statements, since we cannot tell whether they are true or false without more information about $x$ and $y$. In fact, these would ordinarily be thought of as problems to be solved rather than as statements, if appearing without further context. On the other hand, it is possible to make statements out of the last two sentences by indicating something about the replacement set of the variables. For example, "for all real numbers, $x$ and $y$, $xy > 4$" is a statement—a false statement, to be sure, but a statement nonetheless. A true statement can be created in the following way:

There exists at least one pair of real numbers, $x,y$, such that $xy > 4$. In a similar way, a true statement can be made using the sentence $2x + 3y = 5$.

The phrases "for all" and "there exists at least one" are commonly used (or assumed) in mathematics. Many times there is no doubt about these assumptions, but on occasions a great deal of confusion results because the teacher understands one of these phrases to apply, whereas the pupil does not. For example, in proving trigonometric identities, we ordinarily wish to show a statement to be true for all values of a variable. Hence, we must be careful not to use a step that might not be true for some values of the variable. On the other hand, when solving a trigonometric equation, all we must do is to make sure that the final answer really satisfied the original equation. (Of course, it is also necessary to be reasonably careful not to eliminate roots.) Thus, a great deal more care must be exercised in proving identities than in solving equations. Unfortunately, many pupils do not realize why the extra effort is necessary with the identities. They would probably recognize this more readily if they were to write "for all" in front of such sentences as $\sin^2 \theta + \cos^2 \theta = 1$; then perhaps it would be clear that multiplying both sides of the equation by an expression involving a variable (such as $\tan \theta$) might have the effect of either multiplying or dividing both sides by zero. Either way, there would be a serious question as to whether the next step would be equivalent to its predecessor.

Because of the fact that the phrases "for all" and "there exists at least one" occur so often in any careful development of mathematics or logic, it is common to represent them by symbols. "For all $x$" is usually abbreviated either $\forall(x)$ or simply $(x)$, and "there exists at least one $x$" is generally abbreviated $(\exists x)$. The symbols are called quantifiers. It is probably inappropriate to use quantifiers in the earlier elementary mathematics classes since this would only add to the symbolism and formalism. On the other hand, whenever there could be any confusion as to what is being said, it is certainly appropriate to say in words that the sentence under consideration is supposed to be true of all members of a given set, or for at least one member of the set, or whatever the case may be.

In carrying on arguments in mathematics or logic, it is often important to be able to deduce unquantified statements from quantified ones, and vice versa. For example, in the proof that the base angles of an isosceles triangle have equal measure, we actually carry on the proof without quantification, starting with a triangle that is isosceles and then when finished we conclude that what we have done applies for all isosceles triangles. Similarly, in the well-known syllogism from Aristotelian Logic:

All men are mortal.
Socrates is a man.
Therefore, Socrates is mortal.

It is necessary, somehow, to get from the statement that all men are mortal to the statement that a particular man (Socrates) is mortal. In general, the following kinds of inference involving quantified and unquantified statements are allowable:

1. Whenever a statement is true for all members of a set, we can assume it to be true for any particular element of the set.

2. Whenever a statement is known to be true for some element of a set, it is legitimate to let a variable stand for that element as long as no other restrictions are imposed on the variable.

3. Whenever a statement involving a variable has been derived we may assume it to be true of all elements of the set if no restrictions have been placed on the variable.

4. Whenever a statement involving a variable has been derived it is legitimate to assume that there is at least one element of the set for which the statement is true.

In a formal logic, it is necessary to state the restrictions on (2) and (3) with utmost care so as not to confuse several variables and quantifiers, but for ordinary use, common sense should be sufficient. In fact, we use (3) rather regularly in most mathematical proofs, usually without formal reference to it.

## Proof and Mathematical Structure

The foregoing informal discussion of logic and proof is meant to give the teacher some feeling for the sort of thing a person might do if he were going to try to formalize mathematical proofs. There are many good books on the subject of logic and its application to elementary mathematics,[6] but the important thing is for the teacher to have some fairly clear concept of what a proof is and then to give the pupils a good informal feeling for proof. As the pupil matures, his concept of proof can become more formal. Thus, we would start with very simple short arguments of the "if $A$ then $B$; $A$ is true; therefore $B$ is true" type. These gradually become more complicated and more formal, with the pupil acquiring more information about what sort of steps are allowed. Generally, any previously accepted "fact" would be allowed along with statements in the form of valid statement formulas, or statements that can be derived from previous steps through the use of one of the inference rules for quantified or unquantified statements. Contrapositive proofs and indirect proofs should probably be reserved until pupils acquire an understanding of direct proofs and have had some experience with the contrapositive form of an implication.

After some experience with proofs, it might be interesting for pupils to start trying to trace the subject under discussion to its foundations. For example, in talking about numbers, we might agree that the sum of two even numbers is always even. Yet some pupils might feel that they can prove this statement true. Having proven the statement from other statements, they might face the question: Can we prove all the statements used in the proof? If we can, which is a little unlikely,

[3] For example, Robert M. Exner, and Myron F. Rosskopf, *Logic in Elementary Mathematics*, McGraw-Hill Book Co., New York, 1959.

can we then prove the statements used to prove THESE statements? And so on. It is reasonably clear that we cannot really prove all statements about arithmetic, since we always need some that are assumed to be true in order to prove any other statement. Thus, we would have to begin by assuming that some statements were true and then use those to prove other statements.

Similarly, it seems impossible to define every word of a mathematical system, since we must always use other words in order to define any given word. Pupils are usually quite disturbed when they look a word up in a dictionary and find that it is defined in terms of a second one they do not know, which is defined in terms of a third word they do not know, which is defined in terms of the first word. Yet, if we consider the way in which definitions are made, this seems entirely appropriate, otherwise, it would be possible to learn an entire foreign language simply by looking up words in the dictionary of that language. Clearly, then, we must have some statements that are assumed to be true in any mathematical system, and some words that are not defined. From a pedagogical point of view, it is desirable for the assumed statements to seem fairly reasonable to the pupils and for the undefined words to have some meaning to the pupils, at least in the first one or two mathematical structures which they study. As mathematical structure and proof become more familiar to them, these criteria become less important.

Once having agreed on undefined words and axioms (or assumed statements), we are ready to start proving things again. This time, however, the pupils should have a different idea of what "proof" means. When they begin the study of mathematics, most pupils believe that if a statement is proved, then the statement is known to be true in some absolute sense. Now it should be clear that when a theorem has been proved, all we have really shown is that if certain basic assumptions are made about certain undefined objects, then certain other things must also be true about those objects. The mathematician officially does not care whether the original assumptions have any basis in the physical world with respect to particular physical objects.

A mathematical system will begin with several axioms about certain undefined terms. Then, various theorems will be proved. In the process of proving theorems, it may be convenient to define certain other terms. For example, in geometry, the mathematician may over and over again find himself using the phrase "the union of a set of three noncollinear points with the sets of points between them," and may decide that he would like a single word to stand for such a set of points. He might decide to call the set a triangle in order to simplify his exposition.

## Sets

"Modern mathematics" and "sets" have become synonyms in the minds of many people who have only a passing acquaintance with the improvements being made in the teaching of mathematics. Needless to say, this vast oversimplification is not accurate. On the other hand, one of the many steps which is being taken to unify and simplify the teaching of mathematics involves the use of the language of sets when discussing concepts from various branches of mathematics. Set theory, in and of itself, has no place in the ordinary high school classroom; but if the language of sets can be used to clarify concepts from elementary mathematics and unify these in the minds of the students, it is certainly appropriate to use that language. It should be emphasized, however, that many teachers of mathematics have done an excellent job of teaching without ever using the word "set," whereas many poor courses in mathematics involve a great deal of use of the term. In other words, although the use of set language and simple concepts about sets may help teachers to do a better job of teaching mathematics, their use does not indicate whether the teacher is doing a good job. Certainly any teacher who uses sets only in order to be able to say that he is teaching modern mathematics (probably synonymous with "good mathematics" in the eyes of his administrator) is probably doing a poor job of teaching, and might do a better one if he ignored sets entirely.

As mentioned, we can teach an excellent course in mathematics without using the word "set." However, there are so many times when it is convenient to use this concept that most good teachers and books find themselves using it even when trying to avoid doing so. If the reader goes back and reviews the material presented so far in this book, he will find use of the word "set" in connection with geometry (sets of points), algebra (solution set), arithmetic (sets of numbers), logic (sets of statements), probability (sets of events), and other contexts. There has been no conscious effort to introduce the word; in fact, quite the contrary. Certainly it would have been possible to say everything that has been said without using that word, but it would not have been as easy.

With this much preamble regarding the usefulness of sets and caution against using them to obscure bad mathematics or bad teaching of mathematics, let us try to summarize some of the important concepts regarding sets. The reader will notice that many of these concepts were discussed earlier in order to talk about other things. Here we shall simply summarize and extend the discussion.

First, a set is simply a collection of objects. The reader might ask whether it is not necessary for the objects to have something in common. In the usual sense of having something in common it really is not, but on the other hand, if the objects are all members of the same set, they have one thing in common—being members of the same set. It is not necessary, however, for the objects to have something like color, size, location, etc., in common. For example, we can talk about the set that consists of George Washington, The Rock of Gibraltar, the planet Pluto, a particular cow named Bossie, and the small oak tree in one's back yard. These objects certainly do not seem to have anything in common other than membership in the same set, yet it is proper to refer to this set. It may not be useful to talk about such a set, but it is proper to do so. In beginning the study of sets, it is pedagogically desirable to consider useful sets rather than such useless ones as that described. One restriction which might be put on sets is that they be well-defined collections of objects. For example, it would not be correct to talk about the set of all beautiful women in the world unless we had a very specific definition of what is a beautiful woman. For some people, the set might consist of only one object, whereas for others it might consist of many millions of objects. Therefore, when using the word "set" in mathematics, we shall always try to define the set in such a way that there is no doubt as to what is and what is not a member of the set in question.

## Notation

As discussed earlier, there are several ways to name a set, among which are the following:

1. Listing the names of the elements between set brackets: $\{1, 3, 5, 7, 9\}$.

2. Using a variable and description of elements: $\{x | x$ is an odd natural number less than $10\}$.

3. Giving a partial list of the elements: $\{1, 3, \ldots, 9\}$.

In this case, the pattern should be reasonably clear to both writer and reader. If the set is finite, it is customary to write the name of the last element at the end, while the absence of the name of a last member is taken to indicate that the pattern goes on forever.

In general, we shall use capital letters, $A$, $B$, $C$, etc., to name sets. The symbol "$\in$" is used to indicate that something is an element of a particular set. Thus, in order to say that 8 is an element of the set $A$, we write "8 $\in$ $A$." There are two operations which are usually defined for sets. We shall define them and indicate a symbol which is sometimes used for each operation.

## $\cup$ Union

The union of two sets is the set of all elements which are in either of the sets. For example, if $A = \{a, b, c\}$ and $B = \{a, c, e\}$, then $A \cup B = \{a, b, c, e\}$. Notice that even though an element may be in both sets, it is counted only once.

## $\cap$ Intersection

The intersection of two sets is the set of all elements which are in both of the sets. From the previous example, $A \cap B = \{a, c\}$.

There are times when it is necessary to talk about a set that does not have any elements at all. For example, the set of unicorns has no members. It also happens that the set of apples on the author's desk has no members. Although the two descriptions sound quite different, there is only one set involved, since the elements of the first set are the same as the elements of the second. The set without any elements is called the *null set* or the *empty set* and is designated by the symbol $\emptyset$. There are also times at which it is convenient to talk about the set of all objects under consideration. This set is usually called the *universe*, or, when a variable is involved, the *replacement set* or domain of the variable. A unary operation which can be defined for sets is complementation. The complement of a set $S$ (with respect to the universe) is the set of all elements in the universe that are not in $S$. Thus, if the universe is the set of all integers, then the complement of the set of all even numbers is the set of all odd numbers. We shall use the symbol $\bar{S}$ to indicate the complement of $S$.

Set $A$ is said to be a subset of set $B$ (written $A \subseteq B$) if every element of $A$ is an element of $B$. Is every set a subset of itself? Since the word "subset" gives most people the impression that the subset should be smaller than the original set, the fact that a set is a subset of itself may seem surprising; however, this is the most convenient definition for the word "subset." If it is required that set $A$ not be the same as set $B$, but still be a subset of it, we call set $A$ a proper subset of set $B$ (written $A \subset B$).

If $A \subseteq B$ and $B \subseteq A$, can we say that everything that is an element of $A$ is an element of $B$ and everything that is an element of $B$ is an element of $A$? Would the two sets have to be the same set? One possible definition for equality among sets is the previous one. A different way of saying this is to require the two sets to contain precisely the same elements. Thus, $A = B$ if and only if $A$ and $B$ have exactly the same elements.

In discussing sets and operations on sets, a device known as a Venn diagram is often helpful.[7] In such a diagram, circles are drawn with the inside of the circles representing given sets. In Fig. 8.6, for example, the inside of the large circle represents the universe, the small circle (vertical hatching) represents the set $A$, and the horizontally hatched area represents the complement of $A$ with respect to the universe.

In Fig. 8.7, the two overlapping circles represent sets $A$ and $B$, the horizontally hatched area represents the union of the two sets and the area that has both vertical and horizontal shading is the intersection of the two sets. (The reader will no doubt notice that we are using the word circle here as an abbreviation for "the interior of the circle." We shall continue to use this abbreviation when no possible confusion could result.)

We can use Venn diagrams to find out more information about the operations on defined sets. For example, we may be interested in learning whether the operation of union is distributive over the operation of intersection. To do this we must find out if the statement

$$A \cup (B \cap C) = (A \cup B) \cap (A \cup C)$$

is true. In Figs. 8.8 and 8.9, three circles represent the three sets ($A$, $B$, and $C$). In general, we shall not draw the circle for the universe unless it is of importance in the discussion. In the Fig. 8.8, $B \cap C$ is shaded

---

[7] Named after the English logician John Venn, 1834–1923. Some people distinguish between Euler diagrams and Venn diagrams according to whether or not the universe is indicated, but we will not do so here.

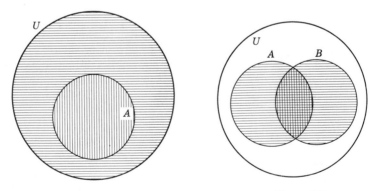

Figure 8.6          Figure 8.7

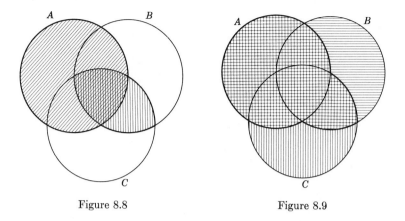

Figure 8.8                              Figure 8.9

with vertical lines and $A$ is shaded with diagonal lines. Thus, the union of $A$ and $B \cap C$ is represented by all the shaded area. In Fig. 8.9, $A \cup B$ is shaded with horizontal lines, whereas $A \cup C$ is shaded with vertical lines. Thus, the intersection of $A \cup B$ and $A \cup C$ is the area shaded with both vertical and horizontal lines. It should now be clear from the figures that $A \cup (B \cap C)$ and $(A \cup B) \cap (A \cup C)$ are in fact the same set. Other interesting facts about the operations on sets and the relations among sets can be discovered through similar methods.

## Exercises

1. Use Venn diagrams to show that intersection and union are commutative and associative.

2. Is intersection distributive over union? Use a Venn diagram to substantiate your answer.

3. Give a simpler name for each of the following sets:
(a) $P \cup \bar{P}$
(b) $P \cap \bar{P}$
(c) $\bar{\bar{P}}$ (that is, the complement of the complement of $P$)

4. What is the relationship between the statement "$P \subseteq Q$" and the statement "$\bar{Q} \subseteq \bar{P}$"? *Hint:* The statement "$P \subseteq Q$" can be indicated using a Venn diagram by drawing a circle for $P$ inside a circle for $Q$. In Fig. 8.10, the horizontally shaded area is the complement of $Q$. Is $\bar{Q}$ a subset of $\bar{P}$? Do the two statements seem to be equivalent?

5. Which pairs of the following statements are equivalent? Check all cases.
(a) $P \subseteq Q$
(b) $\bar{P} \cup Q = U$
(c) $P \cap \bar{Q} = \emptyset$

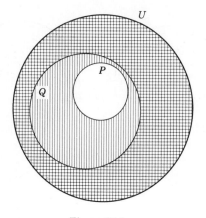

Figure 8.10

6. Pick out the pairs of equivalent sets from the following:

(a) $\overline{P \cup Q}$

(b) $\overline{P \cap Q}$

(c) $\bar{P} \cup \bar{Q}$

(d) $\bar{P} \cap \bar{Q}$

7. Look back at the valid statement formulas on p. 206 of this chapter and see if you can find any connection between the exercises you have just done and the formulas.

As the exercises show, there is a close connection between formal logic and elementary set theory. In fact, if the operations and relations are considered in a formal way, the two systems behave in much the same manner. To help clarify this statement, look at the following table.

| Sets | $P \cup Q$ | $P \cap Q$ | $\bar{P}$ | $P \subseteq Q$ | $P = Q$ | $\emptyset$ | $U$ |
|---|---|---|---|---|---|---|---|
| Logic | $P \vee Q$ | $P \,\&\, Q$ | $\sim P$ | $P \rightarrow Q$ | $P \leftrightarrow Q$ | $F$ | $T$ |

In explanation of the last two correspondences, a valid statement formula, which is always true, corresponds to a set which is the universe, whereas the negation of a valid statement formula (a statement formula that is always false) corresponds to the null set. Scanning the previous exercises with this in mind, we should find that the answers correspond closely to the valid statement formulas on p. 206.

A correspondence between two systems such as described is called an *isomorphism*. Essentially, we have an isomorphism between two systems if two people working corresponding problems in the systems must come up with corresponding answers (if they do the problems correctly). We shall talk about isomorphisms again in the next chapter, but it is worth noting here that one reason for studying a formal logic system and a system of sets is to see an example of an isomorphism that does not seem as artificial to the pupil as that between one set of numbers and another set of numbers that may seem identical to the first set. With a good group of high school pupils who have some extra time (in a mathematics club or a class), this might be a worthwhile project. Remember, however, that in set notation, "$\subseteq$" and "$=$" designate relations and cannot be thought of as operations (as was the case with "$\rightarrow$" and "$\leftrightarrow$" in formal logic).

## Relations and Functions

Although perhaps this topic could more appropriately be put off until a chapter on algebra, it seems to belong here because of its relationship to sets and also its connection with careful language.

One of the numerous changes in many of the newer textbooks is the definition of relation and function. Most people have some intuitive idea of what these two words mean before they encounter them in mathematics. Of course, the average nonmathematician may not distinguish the two concepts, but if he does give the matter serious consideration for a while, he will probably decide that when one thing is a function of another, it depends on the other in some sense. For example, wage raises in some industries are a function of the cost of living index. The person would also probably concede that if one thing is a function of another there is a relation between them, but he would probably want to add that a relation is a more general thing. In other words, there may be a relation between two things, and yet one may not be a function of the other. This is a rather vague description of the sort of intuitive ideas one may expect to find among junior high and high school pupils. These concepts can, and should, be developed more fully by considering various physical examples; relationships such as cousin, brother, father, child, etc., are often good examples, but there are many others, such as date to temperature, height to weight, etc. Among these relationships, some are different in the sense that whenever we know the first part of the relation, we can tell exactly what the second is. An example is the relationship denoted by "_____ has _____ as his (her) father." If we know how the first blank is to be filled, the name which should go in the second blank is determined. We call the general kind of relationship a *relation* in mathematics, whereas we call the kind of relation in which the first part determines the second a *function*.

Having developed our intuitive concepts of a relation and a function to this extent, we may wish to formalize these ideas so that we will be able to be absolutely sure whether we have a relation or function. For any given relation there will be pairs of objects which are in the relation to each other and other pairs which are not. Furthermore, the order in which the two objects are considered makes a difference. For example, in the relation "_____ is the father of _____," it is perfectly clear that if Joe is the father of Max, then Max cannot be the father of Joe (assuming the names apply to the same individuals in each case). Therefore, ordered pairs of objects are of some importance in relations and functions. Besides the ordered pairs of objects, there are the sets from which the objects come. For example, in the "_____ is the father of _____" relation, the first elements must be taken from the set of males who have had children, whereas the second set would naturally be the set of all people (or animals, if we wished to broaden our horizons). In general, we refer to the set of first elements as the *domain* of the relation or function, and the set of second elements as the *range* of the relation or function.

The way in which elements are paired with each other should also be considered. From all of this, some people would conclude that in order to have a relation, we must have a set of ordered pairs, a domain and range, and a method of pairing the elements of the range with those of the domain. However, closer consideration will indicate that we do not really need this much, for if we have all of the ordered pairs, the first members of the ordered pairs make up the domain, while the range is simply the set of all second members. Furthermore, if the ordered pairs are all available, the way in which elements are paired is determined. Of course, in the case of infinite sets, how members are being paired may not be obvious to an ordinary mortal. In this case, it will certainly be convenient to have some rule for pairing, even though in theory no such rule is needed if the ordered pairs are all available. Therefore, in a strict sense, it is possible to define a relation as a set of ordered pairs. Nothing more is really needed. On the other hand, this is a rather austere definition for youngsters, and if it is used, there ought to be a great deal of accompanying informal and intuitive discussion.

If the ordered-pair definition of a relation is accepted, the definition of a function is relatively simple. A function is a relation in which the first elements of no two ordered pairs are the same. Thus, the "_____ has _____ as a father" relation is a function because once we know that

Max has Joe as a father, we can be quite certain that we are not going to find out later that Max also has George as a father (again, assuming the names stand for the same individuals and our original information was accurate).

Before leaving this topic, let us consider two mathematical relations, one of which is a function and one of which is not a function. First, consider the relation $\{(x, y) \mid x^2 + y^2 = 1\}$. In general, we shall use parentheses around a pair to indicate that it is an ordered pair. Thus, this relation can be described in words as: the set of all ordered pairs, $(x, y)$, such that $x$ squared plus $y$ squared is one. When the relation is written in this manner, it is customary to indicate the universe from which the elements are taken, but we usually assume the universe is the set of real numbers when no other indication is supplied, as here. Figure 8.11 is a graph of the relation $\{(x, y) \mid x^2 + y^2 = 1\}$. Notice that given one value of $x$, say $\frac{1}{2}$, there are often two different corresponding values of $y(\sqrt{\frac{3}{4}}$ and $-\sqrt{\frac{3}{4}})$. Thus, this relation is not a function.

Now, consider the relation $\{(x, y) \mid y = 3x + 2\}$. In this case, if we graph the relation as in Fig. 8.12, we find that given any particular value of $x$, there is only one value for $y$. Another way to distinguish between a relation and a function is to consider all possible vertical lines. If any one of those lines crosses the graph in more than one point, the relation is not a function. But, if no vertical line crosses the graph in more than one point, the relation is a function. In this case, it is

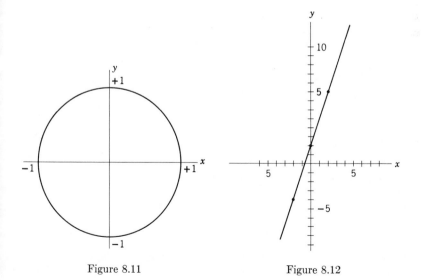

Figure 8.11                    Figure 8.12

clear that no vertical line will cross the graph in more than one point, whereas in the case of $\{(x, y)\,|\,x^2 + y^2 = 1\}$, many vertical lines would cross the graph in more than one point.

## Infinite Sets

A topic that never seems to lose its fascination is the subject of infinity. Undoubtedly, the mystical aspects of this topic account, in part, for that fascination, but the teacher can take advantage of that interest in teaching some good mathematics. The first time many pupils discuss infinity in a mathematics class is when some teacher, or other adult, tells them that any number divided by zero is infinity. Needless to say, a certain basic misconception may easily arise from such a statement. If, for example, 3 divided by 0 is infinity and 4 divided by zero is also infinity, then we have the equation $\frac{3}{0} = \frac{4}{0}$, and multiplying both sides of the equation by zero, we get $3 = 4$. Obviously, something must be wrong. The example shows why three divided by zero simply cannot be defined as a number. Some people will say that infinity is not a number, so that it is acceptable to define $\frac{3}{0}$ as infinity. If the definition of infinity is "something which can't be defined," it is possible that calling $\frac{3}{0}$ infinity can be justified. However, it seems far more reasonable simply to say that division by zero is undefined than to use words that are likely to have double meanings. As far as we are concerned, infinity has nothing to do with division by zero.

Later, when discussing limits, the symbol "$\infty$" is of some use in indicating that a variable takes on values that increase without bound. Thus, the statement, "$\lim_{x \to 0^+} \dfrac{1}{x} = \infty$" is simply interpreted "the limit of $1/x$ as $x$ approaches zero from above is infinity." In the interpretation "$x$ approaches zero from above" means that no matter how small a positive number one chooses, $x$ will get closer to zero than that number while remaining positive, and "the limit of $1/x$ is infinity" means that no matter how large a positive number one selects, $1/x$ will become greater than that number. This discussion may give some indication of the reason for the division by zero notion of infinity, but certainly does not justify it. Here the use of the word "infinity" is considerably closer to our intuitive idea than in the previous case.

A third use of the word "infinity" pertains to infinite sets. To many people, this use seems even closer to the intuitive notion than the one associated with limits.

Before considering infinite sets, let us view some basic ideas about counting. In kindergarten classes, it is common to ask pupils to draw pictures of their families. Even though a child is not yet able to count beyond two or three he is usually able to draw a picture of his family which is accurate in the sense that it has the right number of figures. He might draw a figure for his father (maybe with a pipe, but almost certainly larger than any other member of the family), his mother (long hair, skirt, and next largest), several older brothers and sisters (skirts distinguish the girls, and ordinarily size is in decreasing order of age), himself, and several younger brothers and sisters (with the youngest one or two perhaps lying down having their diapers changed). Having drawn a picture of his family, a child generally has no difficulty deciding whether his family is larger or smaller than that of the child sitting next to him—even though he is not able to count the number of members in either family. The process the child uses is what the mathematician calls a one-to-one correspondence. He simply draws a figure for each member of his family; thus for each one person there is exactly one figure which suggests the name "one-to-one." Then, in order to compare his family to that of the child next to him, he simply pairs off each member of his family with one member of the other child's family until he runs out of members of either family. If he runs out of members of both families at the same time, there is a one-to-one correspondence between the two sets, and the families are the same size. If he runs out of one before the other, the family with members left over is the larger of the two.

Although this does not seem to be a deep or difficult concept, the idea of a one-to-one correspondence is important in mathematics and has been used in impressive ways. One example is in the comparison of various infinite sets. In general, we say that two sets are the same size if we can find a one-to-one correspondence between them. With finite sets, if we try to set up a one-to-one correspondence between two sets and fail, one is larger than the other. As it turns out, this is not necessarily the case with infinite sets.

Let us compare two infinite sets to see if they are the same size. Let set $N$ be the set of all natural numbers ($\{1, 2, 3, \ldots\}$) and $E$ the set of all even natural numbers ($\{2, 4, 6, \ldots\}$). At first glance, it seems obvious that the set $N$ is larger than the set $E$. Actually, there is an obvious one-to-one correspondence that pairs a member of $N$ with each member of $E$ but leaves out half of the members of $N$, namely, 2 with 2, 4 with 4, 6 with 6, etc. However, according to our definition, the failure to find a one-to-one correspondence on the first try does not necessarily mean the sets are not the same size.

Let us now pair 2 from the set $E$ with 1 from the set $N$, 4 with 2, 6 with 3, and in general, the number $2n$ with the number $n$. Have we left out any member of the set $N$? Or of the set $E$? Notice that it is not possible to "go to the other end and look at all the members of $N$

which are left over." Since every even number is paired with a natural number, and every natural number is paired with an even number by this process, there is a one-to-one correspondence between the elements of sets $N$ and $E$. Therefore, we conclude that there are as many even natural numbers as there are natural numbers. This conclusion should not seem at all obvious to the intuition, even though it is based on simple intuitive ideas.

Similarly, it is possible to show that the set of all integers is the same size as the set of natural numbers. The reader may wish to try his hand at proving this fact.

Even more surprising is the finding that there are as many ordered pairs of natural numbers as there are natural numbers. This can be seen in the following way. Arrange the ordered pairs of natural numbers as in Table 8.5. If we say that there are $\aleph_0$[8] natural numbers, then there are clearly $\aleph_0$ ordered pairs of numbers in the first row, $\aleph_0$ in the second row, and, in fact, $\aleph_0$ in each row. If there are $\aleph_0$ rows, and $\aleph_0$ ordered pairs in each, there are apparently $\aleph_0 \times \aleph_0$ or $(\aleph_0)^2$ ordered pairs of natural numbers. This certainly seems to be a larger set than the set of natural numbers. Yet, there is a one-to-one correspondence between this set and the set of natural numbers. This correspondence can be set up as follows: pair 1 with $(1, 1)$, pair 2 with $(1, 2)$, pair 3 with $(2, 1)$, pair 4 with $(1, 3)$, pair 5 with $(2, 2)$. The reader should now try to guess the pattern and predict the next pairing. We shall continue to list a few more pairs before describing the method: 6 with $(3, 1)$, 7 with $(1, 4)$, 8 with $(2, 3)$, 9 with $(3, 2)$, 10 with $(4, 1)$, 11 with $(1, 5)$, 12 with $(2, 4)$, etc.

Pictorially, we are starting in the upper left hand corner and running diagonally down from right to left, counting off the ordered pairs as we go. Thus, on the first "diagonal" we get the ordered pair $(1, 1)$, on the second "diagonal," $(1, 2)$ and $(2, 1)$, etc. The reader should have no trouble seeing the pattern if he consults Table 8.5 as he tries

[8] "$\aleph$" is the first letter of the Hebrew alphabet, and "$\aleph_0$" is read "aleph nought" or "aleph subzero." The symbol was first used in this way by Georg Cantor, 1845–1918, the German mathematician who created the materials on which this discussion is based.

**Table 8.5**

$(1, 1), (1, 2), (1, 3), (1, 4), (1, 5), \cdots$
$(2, 1), (2, 2), (2, 3), (2, 4), (2, 5), \cdots$
$(3, 1), (3, 2), (3, 3), (3, 4), \cdots$
$(4, 1), (4, 2), \cdots$
$(5, 1), \cdots$
$\cdots$

to follow this discussion. Now, if we consider any particular ordered pair, it is clear that sooner or later some natural number will be paired with it. Therefore, there is a one-to-one correspondence between the sets.

Since there is a one-to-one correspondence between the set of all ordered pairs of natural numbers and the set of natural numbers, there are apparently as many ordered pairs of natural numbers as natural numbers. This fact can be used to show that the set of rational numbers is indeed the same size as the set of natural numbers.

From these facts, it would be easy to jump to the conclusion that all infinite sets are the same size. However, Cantor showed that this was not the case. Actually, he showed that there were an infinite number of sizes of infinite sets. Here we will be content with showing that there are more real numbers than rational numbers.

We shall begin by limiting attention to those real numbers between 0 and 1. If there are more real numbers between zero and one than there are natural numbers, there will surely be altogether more real numbers than there are natural numbers. Recall that in order to prove there are more real numbers than natural numbers, it is not enough to try to find a one-to-one correspondence, fail, and then conclude there is no such correspondence. We must prove, rather, that nobody, under any circumstances, could ever find a one-to-one correspondence between the set of real numbers and the set of natural numbers. To do this, we shall start by assuming that somebody has found such a correspondence, and show that he must have failed because he omitted some real numbers.

Say that somebody has set up a one-to-one correspondence between the real numbers (between zero and one) and the natural numbers. Assuming that such real numbers can be written as never-ending decimals (for example, .33333 . . . , .01001000100001000001 . . .), we can indicate any real number between 0 and 1 in this manner: $.a_1a_2a_3a_4a_5$ . . . , where "$a_1$" stands for a digit (0, 1, 2, . . . 9), "$a_2$" stands for a digit (maybe the same as $a_1$, maybe different), and so on. If somebody pairs the natural numbers with the real numbers between zero and one, his pairing could be represented as follows:

$$1 \text{ with } .a_1a_2a_3a_4a_5a_6a_7 \cdots$$
$$2 \text{ with } .b_1b_2b_3b_4b_5b_6b_7 \cdots$$
$$3 \text{ with } .c_1c_2c_3c_4c_5c_6c_7 \cdots$$
$$4 \text{ with } .d_1d_2d_3d_4d_5d_6d_7 \cdots$$
$$\cdots \cdots \cdots \cdots \cdots$$
$$n \text{ with } .q_1q_2q_3q_4q_5 \cdots q_nq_{n+1} \cdots$$
$$\cdots$$

The contention is that some real numbers must have been missed. To show this, all we need to do is construct one real number (between zero and one) which is not in the list. This may be accomplished in the following way: consider the digit $a_1$. It must be one of the digits from 0 to 9. Select any one of the other digits, and call it $\overline{a_1}$. Thus, if $a_1$ is 3, $\overline{a_1}$ can be 0, 1, 2, 4, 5, 6, 7, 8, or 9. Choose $\overline{b_2}$ in the same way (some digit other than $b_2$), and continue in a like manner with $\overline{c_3}$, $\overline{d_4}$, and so on, including $\overline{q_n}$, since $q_n$ is the $n$th digit in the numeral paired with $n$. The never-ending decimal formed by $.\overline{a_1}\,\overline{b_2}\,\overline{c_3}\,\overline{d_4}\,\cdots\,\overline{q_n}\,\cdots$ certainly stands for a real number between 0 and 1. Moreover, it is quite clear that this number is not mentioned in the list, since if it were paired with any natural number (say $n$) it would differ in at least one digit (the $n$th) from the number paired with $n$. As there were nine choices for each of the digits $\overline{a_1}$, $\overline{b_2}$, etc., we really have shown that there are $9 \times 9 \times 9 \times 9 \times \cdots = 9^{\aleph_0}$ real numbers between 0 and 1 which have been left out of the previous list.

The foregoing discussion shows some interesting aspects of mathematics which can be considered through the use of simple properties of sets. Although the process can be pursued in an ordinary high school classroom, there is no need to do so unless there is time and interest. However, like the isomorphism between formal logic and elementary set theory, this is good and interesting mathematics which is relatively new (Cantor did most of this work in the last quarter of the nineteenth century) and is not terribly hard to follow.

One further question may have occurred to the reader. At no point did we define an infinite set or a finite set. We assumed that the reader probably knew what we were talking about, and therefore we did not bother. Actually, had we tried to define an infinite set before undertaking the discussion, we would probably have had to use some obscure definition such as "a set in which there is no end to the elements." Although this might have been helpful to somebody who had never heard the word "infinite" before, it would not have been of any use to most readers of this book. On the other hand, we now have material which permits a precise definition of an infinite set. The reader undoubtedly noticed that for finite sets the idea of putting a set into one-to-one correspondence with a proper subset of itself would have seemed ridiculous; in fact, when we first did this with infinite sets, there may have been raised eyebrows. However, it quickly became clear that some sets could be put into one-to-one correspondence with proper subsets of themselves, and that these sets were invariably what we think of as infinite sets. As it turns out, the simplest definition of an infinite set is precisely this: An infinite set is a set that can be put into one-to-one correspondence with a proper subset of itself. A finite set can now be defined as a set that is not infinite. If the reader objects to this double negative sort of definition of finite set, he should try to come up with a better one which is not obscure.

## Summary

Careful language, correct logic, good arguments, and set language combined with some elementary set theory, are important in the mathematics of this century. All of these are also important in the teaching of elementary mathematics. However, no top-notch mathematician can get along only on formalism without a good intuitive understanding of the basic concepts underlying the formalism. In a similar way, no school pupil of mathematics can be expected to understand and appreciate good mathematics unless adequate informal background is laid for formally expressed thoughts. Therefore, although we must employ all of the aforementioned important aids in teaching a good mathematics course, it is more important for children to understand and appreciate the important underlying ideas involved in the mathematics, and have the feeling that it all makes sense—almost the feeling that "I could have created this if only I'd lived a few hundred years earlier" (highly unlikely in actual fact, but a good feeling for a pupil to have). Indeed, the teacher should never allow formalism to take the place of well-developed intuitive understandings.

## Teaching Hints

The material in this chapter is largely background material for the teacher, and should not be taught, as is, to junior or senior high school mathematics pupils. However, it is important that teachers be aware of the place of language, rigor, logic, and sets in mathematics and the teaching of mathematics. When these topics can be used to help children understand, they should be used. On the other hand, they should not be taught just for the sake of teaching something that seems to be modern or difficult.

Whenever a teacher is teaching, he should listen carefully to pupils questions (and answers) for any indications of confusion due to language—either language that is not careful enough or language that is too careful. Insofar as possible, he should try to use the same language the textbook uses, so as to avoid confusing the children by calling something a different name from the name the book uses.

In changing from one textbook series to another, one may find that the new book uses different terminology from that used by the old book. At first, this may seem to be a good reason for not changing series. However, as students progress in mathematics (and in life) they will have to get used to the fact that different people use different words to mean the same thing. Thus, if the terminology is not too drastically different, the change will be educational. Of course, the fact that the change has occurred should be discussed, and it might be interesting to carry on a discussion as to why one author thought a particular word was better than the other. For example, why do some people call the numbers 0, 1, 2, 3, . . . the natural numbers, whereas others omit 0 from the set of natural numbers? During such a discussion, the place of words in mathematics (and other communication) should be discussed. The fact that a word can be defined to mean precisely what its user wants it to mean is an important concept and one which many pupils (and many adults) are not aware of. Of course, the discussion would be incomplete if it were not pointed out that, by convention, we usually try to use words the same way everybody else does so as to avoid confusion.

As a general rule, rigor should be introduced only after pupils have seen a need for it. This means that when a topic is first introduced, the pupil's intuition should be relied on rather heavily. When difficulties arise, and the pupil realizes that these difficulties exist, that is the time for being more careful. For example, if the pupil is not worried about which of three points on a line lies between the other two (and he should not be—mathematicians were not worried about this for almost 2000 years), then it should not be brought up at the beginning of a geometry course. At a later time, it is probably desirable to go back and consider whether there may have been difficulties with the original system, and how these difficulties might be remedied. The important thing to remember is that there is usually a good reason for the introduction of more rigor or better axioms. Since the reasons do exist, it is desirable that the pupils understand the reasons before memorizing the axioms and rigorous proofs. In fact, if they really understand the reasons, the need for a good memory should be minimal.

One of the most important concepts in mathematics is that of a function. The ordered-pair definition of a function is correct and convenient to use; however, it has serious defects from a pedagogical point of view. The ordered-pair idea gives a static impression to the pupil, where a dynamic impression is far more appropriate. Even though it may not be as elegant, or as formally simple, a dynamic impression of a function will be far more appealing to children, and will put them in a much better position to use their knowledge about functions. One of the best intuitive definitions of a function (which is severely criticized by advocates of a great deal of rigor) is a machine, or "meat grinder," definition. Here, the function is thought of as a machine into which

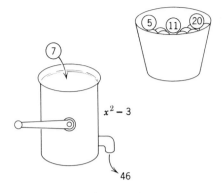

Figure 8.13

one drops a number or other object taken from a given domain (represented by the basket of numbers), turns the crank, and out comes a number. Then, the difference between a function and a relation is that when we drop a number into a function, we know what is going to come out, but when we drop a number into a relation, there are several different possibilities as to what might come out. Of course, a more formal definition of function also ought to be made available for the pupils, but this one will give them an intuitive feeling for what is happening.

The concept of limit is very important in higher mathematics, and is becoming more important in the mathematics that is useful to many different people. Surely this concept is important enough to begin studying, informally, at an early age. For example, determining the area of a circle, given the circumference (in terms of the radius), is an enjoyable and worthwhile exercise in the junior high school. Determining the limit of $(x^2 - 9)/(x - 3)$ as $x$ approaches 3 is something which junior high pupils can do quite well (by making successive approximations). If a good, firm, intuitive foundation is established in the early grades, the formal definition should come quite naturally and without great pain at a later time.

A discussion of infinity and infinite sets is fascinating to pupils of all ages. However, it does not really fit in to the main stream of the mathematics that students learn in school. With this in mind, the topic probably ought to be reserved for the mathematics club.

### Exercises

1. What, if anything, is wrong with each of the following statements?
(*a*) 3 plus 1 is 31.

(*b*) "5" plus "0" is 5.

(*c*) Half of *X* is *V*.

(*d*) Half of "*X*" is "*V*."

2. Discuss each of the following statements.

(*a*) Two negatives make a positive.

(*b*) In the equation $3x = 1.5 + 3$, cancel the 3's and you get $x = 1.5$.

(*c*) All students aren't smart.

3. Give two examples of functions and two examples of relations that are not functions from everyday life—neither the domain nor the range should be a set of numbers.

4. Using the following translations for *p*, *q*, and *r*, translate each of the following sentences into a statement formula.

> *p*:  modern mathematics is interesting
> *q*:  modern mathematics is difficult
> *r*:  modern mathematics is good

(*a*) Modern mathematics is interesting or difficult.

(*b*) Modern mathematics is either difficult or it is not difficult.

(*c*) If modern mathematics is good, then it is not interesting.

(*d*) If modern mathematics is difficult, then it is not interesting.

(*e*) To say that modern mathematics is interesting is equivalent to saying that it is good.

(*f*) Modern mathematics is interesting, good, and not difficult.

5. Show that there is a one-to-one correspondence between the set of natural numbers and the set of all integers.

6. Show that there is a one-to-one correspondence between the set of all integers and the set of integers divisible by 100.

7. Following the correspondence indicated on p. 222 between the set of natural numbers and the set of ordered pairs of natural numbers, what ordered pair corresponds to 13? to 16?

8. In the proof that there are more real than natural numbers, replace the set of reals by the set of rationals. Where does the proof break down?

9. Show that there are as many points on a line as on a line segment. (*Hint:* Figure 8.14 may be helpful.)

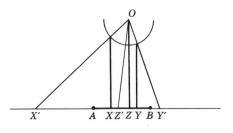

Figure 8.14

10. Show that there are as many points in a plane as there are in the interior of a square.

11. Show that there are as many ordered pairs of real numbers in which each number is between 0 and 1 as there are real numbers between 0 and 1. (*Hint:* Represent each real number as a never-ending decimal. Construct a single never-ending decimal from two such decimals and vice versa.)

12. Are there more complex numbers than real numbers?

## Questions for Further Thought and Study

1. Study *"Gödel's Proof"* by Nagel and Newman and *"The Mathematician"* by John von Neumann. Discuss the place of rigor in mathematics and mathematics education in light of these essays. What standards of rigor should be followed by mathematicians? What standards of rigor should be required of school children?

2. Construct a formula (not just a procedure) which defines a one-to-one correspondence between the natural numbers and the set of all ordered pairs of natural numbers.

## REFERENCES

Exner, Robert M., and Myron F. Rosskopf. *Logic in Elementary Mathematics*, McGraw-Hill, New York, 1959. An introduction to the important ideas of logic for secondary school teachers of mathematics. Correct, but relatively easy to read.

Kemeny, John G., J. Laurie Snell, and Gerald L. Thompson. *Introduction to Finite Mathematics*, Prentice-Hall, Englewood Cliffs, N.J., 1957. Designed for college freshmen who may not be continuing in mathematics or the physical sciences, this book is a unique contribution to mathematical education since it considers applications to the biological and social sciences. Either this or the later book, *Finite Mathematical Structures*, should be studied by secondary school mathematics teachers. Chapters 1, 2, and 3 pertain to logic and sets.

McShane, E. J. "Operating with Sets," *Insights into Modern Mathematics*, NCTM, Washington, D.C., 1957, pp. 36–64. A good elementary introduction to sets and some of the uses of sets in mathematics. Includes operations, induction, functions and relations, correspondences, and infinite sets.

Newman, James R. (ed.). *The World of Mathematics*, 4 vols., Simon and Schuster, New York, 1956. This collection of essays and excerpts from the works of the great mathematicians and others who had some interest in mathematics should be in the library of every mathematics teacher. The magnitude of the survey is impressive, the selection is excellent, and the commentaries (by Newman) are superb. Everybody, from the most sophisticated of mathematicians to the least sophisticated junior high school pupil, should be able to find something of interest to him in the collection. Part 10 has to do with infinity and Parts 11 through 19 pertain more or less to logic and mathematical thought. Included are *Goedel's Proof*, by Nagel and Newman, *How to Solve It*, by Polya, *The Mathematician*, by von Neumann, and *Can a Machine Think?* by Turing, as well as many other articles of a similar nature.

Wilder, Raymond L. *Introduction to the Foundations of Mathematics*, 2nd ed., John Wiley and Sons, New York, 1965. An excellent, relatively easy to read introduction to origin and nature of fundamental concepts of modern mathematics. Shows how formalism grew out of intuitive concepts and why the formalism was necessary. Although this is not precisely recreational reading, it can be read and appreciated with a minimum of formal training.

# EXPANDING THE NUMBER
# SYSTEM

From the time a child is born until rather late in his formal mathematical education his number system is expanding and his understanding of it is (or should be) improving. At first, the number system is expanded by the haphazard annexing of new numbers. The numbers $\frac{1}{2}$, $\frac{1}{4}$, $\frac{3}{4}$ may easily be annexed to his system before the number $1000$, simply because he may have use for them first.

During the early stages of life, the child is not concerned with such things as whether the sum will be a number in his system if he adds a couple of numbers, and other such formalities. He is simply interested in whether he has the necessary numbers to carry on the activities in which he wants to participate. In general, insofar as he thinks about these things at all, the young child seems to assume that when he needs new numbers, they will be there waiting for him, in much the same way as he assumed that when he needs food, love, or some other necessity of life, it will be waiting for him.

In traditional mathematics programs, it was not until the introduction of negative numbers in the ninth grade that pupils first grew suspicious of the source of these new numbers. Undoubtedly, this suspicion stemmed partially from the general rebellion against adult authority which commonly occurs sometime between the ages of twelve and

231

fifteen. Part of the difficulty also came from the children's increased intellectual awareness of what was happening when new numbers were annexed to the system, not the least of these happenings being the increased work which would be available with the new numbers.

Whatever the reasons for the children's interest in the source of these new numbers, the introduction of signed numbers in the junior high school (they are presently being introduced in all three grades—7, 8, and 9—of the junior high, as well as earlier in some programs) offers an excellent opportunity to discuss the annexation of new numbers, the reasons for annexing them, the rules that ought to be followed, and the advantages which will accrue when the number system has been expanded.

Essentially two different procedures are now in common use for expanding the number system. Neither of these is incorrect; each can be justified mathematically, but one involves elegant, formal, mathematics, whereas the other is more pedestrian and probably more appropriate for young pupils. We shall consider the more pedestrian approach first and will then return to the other one in a later section.

### Annexing New Numbers

What is the root of the equation $x + 1 = 0$?

Readers are probably answering in unison, "negative one!" with perhaps a few "minus one's" thrown in for good measure. But is $-1$ really the root of this equation, or is this an equation which happens not to have a root? If the question is being asked of a pupil who has never before heard of negative numbers, as far as he is concerned, the equation does not have a root. Furthermore, if the question had been asked of a good sixteenth century mathematician, he would very likely have agreed with the pupil: the equation does not have a root.

The important question is not "what is the root of this equation?" but does this equation have a root in the number system which we are using? If the answer is "no," and there is good reason to want the equation to have a root, is it desirable to expand the number system so that the equation will have a root in the expanded system? Is such a procedure fair? We have rules which we are supposed to be following, and now it looks as though we were about to change those rules because it is convenient to do so. An important point to be made is that one of the major functions of a mathematician is to invent new "games" or new rules for old "games," but to devise them in such a way that they will be significant, and have some bearing on the physical world or at least on some other mathematics which in turn may be related to something related to the real world. The mathematician is not necessarily trying to be useful, but to be significant, which in the long run amounts to almost the same thing. Therefore, if we can create a new system that has all of the advantages of the old system, plus some other good features, we should certainly feel free to do so. By doing so, we will be acting, to some extent, like mathematicians.

But what are the important features of the old number system? Well brought up children who have been exposed to a "modern" mathematics program will believe that the commutative, associative, and distributive laws are of great importance. If the children are not quite so well brought up, they will still agree that the laws are true (with the possible exception of the distributive law, and they can rather easily be convinced of that) but they may not know their names. Of course, the names are not important, but on the other hand, if we are going to talk about these properties, it may be handy to have some names. Hence let us agree to call these properties the usual names. Another property which will be important is closure. What this says is that when we add two numbers in our system, we would always like to get a unique number in the system. We would also like a corresponding property for multiplication.

## Integers

Now we are ready to begin the important work. We would like the equation $x + 1 = 0$ to have a solution in our new system. We know that it does not have a solution in the old system because when we add two numbers together in that system we always get a number that is at least as great as either addend. Let us therefore create a new number and call it "$\bar{1}$," which we shall designate "negative one" for the time being. All we know about this new number is that $\bar{1} + 1 = 0$ and that the basic properties of mathematics are supposed to work in the new system.

What is $\bar{1} + \bar{1}$? We know that $\bar{1} + 1 = 0$, and therefore that $(\bar{1} + 1) + (\bar{1} + 1) = 0 + 0 = 0$. By reusing the associative and commutative laws for addition several times, we can rewrite this $(\bar{1} + \bar{1}) + (1 + 1) = 0$, or $(\bar{1} + \bar{1}) + 2 = 0$. Apparently, $\bar{1} + \bar{1}$ is the number which we can add to 2 in order to get zero. If a teacher asks the children what they think this number should be called and the symbol to be used for it, he will certainly get the answers "negative 2," and "$\bar{2}$." Likewise, the children can convince themselves that for any number in the old system, there should be a new number in the new system such that the sum of the two numbers is zero. Furthermore, both the symbol and the name for each of these new numbers should seem quite reasonable to the pupils.

Now we have a great many new numbers. How can we work with them? We know that the new numbers, which we shall call negative numbers, behave in much the same way as the old ones when two of them are added. From previous discussion we have seen that if $3 + 4 = 7$, then $\bar{3} + \bar{4} = \bar{7}$, and so on. What happens if we add a negative number to one of the old numbers which we shall call positive?

$$\bar{5} + 8 = ?$$

Let the pupils try to play with this for a while. They may guess several different answers, but the teacher should insist that they try to convince the other pupils that they are right. The teacher should not accept the correct answer just because it happens to be correct. If none of them is able to come up with a convincing argument, the teacher might suggest that they break the number 8 into two parts which would be more convenient. They will almost certainly hit on the following procedure:

$$\bar{5} + 8 = \bar{5} + (5 + 3) = (\bar{5} + 5) + 3 = 0 + 3 = 3.$$

In a similar way, they should quickly arrive at the following argument to show that $\bar{8} + 5 = \bar{3}$:

$$\bar{8} + 5 = (\bar{3} + \bar{5}) + 5 = \bar{3} + (\bar{5} + 5) = \bar{3} + 0 = \bar{3}.$$

Having seen this much, the pupils are now ready to do a number of exercises in adding numbers in the new system. At first glance, the adding process may seem a little cumbersome, but if the reader compares it with the procedure he uses in adding two numbers of opposite sign he will see a close connection. Subtracting the number with smaller absolute value has the effect of "breaking up" the one with larger absolute value. Of course, if the pupils find short cuts, there is little reason to stop them from using these as long as they understand the basic procedure and can relate the short cut to that understanding. But we should not try to force the short cut on the pupils before they understand the procedure; otherwise they will memorize the short cut and forget the understanding.

There are several ways to handle subtraction. One of these is to define subtraction as adding the additive inverse of the subtrahend. This procedure is both efficient and correct, but the pupils will feel that a teacher is trying to put something over on them, and that this has no obvious connection with what they consider subtraction. It is probably best to go back to the student's own idea of subtraction and try to build from that.

For example, what does a pupil mean when he says $8 - 3 = ?$ Is he looking for the number that can be added to 3 in order to produce the total of 8? If so, what we really want is a number, $x$, such that $3 + x = 8$. Let us try the same thing with the problem $8 - \bar{3}$. Apparently, what we want is a number, $x$, such that $\bar{3} + x = 8$. We know that we must add 3 to $\bar{3}$ in order to get 0, and that we must add 8 to 0 in order to get 8. Therefore, we must add $3 + 8$ in order to get from $\bar{3}$ to 8. Other problems of this sort can be similarly solved by the pupils using their understanding of subtraction from the old number system. Most likely, the pupils will figure out some short cut involving changing the sign and adding, and, of course, this fits right into the procedure used. To explain this specific case more fully we know that we must add the additive inverse of $\bar{3}$ to get to 0, and then 8 to get to 8. Thus what we have really done is to add the additive inverse of the subtrahend to the minuend. This same procedure and same explanation will suffice no matter what sort of numbers (positive, negative, large or small absolute value) we start with.

Before leaving addition and subtraction, it is worth mentioning that in developing the negative numbers, the teacher should use a large number of physical examples for motivation. Among these will be several which will suggest the number line. Furthermore, the number line will undoubtedly have been used quite often, and therefore, the pupils will be familiar with it. Certainly, it would be wise to use this in helping the pupils to add and subtract more efficiently and with greater meaning. Subtraction, especially, is made easier by reference to the number line. However, if we are really trying to introduce pupils to a process of building a system according to orderly rules, it is not fair to have them justify their procedures from physical examples. It is convenient and reassuring to go to physical models only to see that we have not strayed afar in our considerations. On occasion, we go to these models for clues to what might be an appropriate procedure to try. If some pupils are actually learning to manipulate the new numbers through physical examples this is not necessarily bad, but the brighter pupils should also begin at this time to get a feeling for creating and expanding mathematical systems.

Having learned to add and subtract the new numbers, we might now try to see if we can multiply in the new system. Let us try $7 \times \bar{5}$. Some pupils might suggest adding $\bar{5}$ to itself, doing this over, and continuing till we have used $\bar{5}$ as an addend seven times. This will give the correct answer and the pupils should be complimented, but one can point out that this procedure resulted in difficulty when considered as a method of multiplying fractions: adding $\frac{3}{4}$ to itself $\frac{5}{7}$ times did not make much sense; the problem is even worse with irrational numbers. Therefore, let us see if we can use our basic properties to decide what the product of 7 and $\bar{5}$ ought to be. We know that $5 + \bar{5} = 0$, and that the distributive law ought to work in the new system. We further know that the product of zero and any number is zero. Can we think of an interesting way to use all of this information? With this much of a hint, several pupils will probably suggest that 7 ought to be multiplied by $(5 + \bar{5})$ yielding $7 \times (5 + \bar{5}) = 7 \times 0 = 0$. Then, using the distributive law, $(7 \times 5) + (7 \times \bar{5}) = 0$, or $35 + (7 \times \bar{5}) = 0$. But we know that $\overline{35}$ is the number that can be added to 35 in order to get zero, so $7 \times \bar{5}$ must be $\overline{35}$.

A similar procedure will work for the product of any positive number multiplied by a negative number. The commutative law for multiplication will take care of the situation in which a negative number is to be multiplied by a positive number, and a variation of the preceding discussion will show that the product of two negative numbers must be positive: for $\bar{7} \times \bar{5}$, $0 = \bar{7} \times (5 + \bar{5}) = \overline{35} + (\bar{7} \times \bar{5})$, and therefore, $\bar{7} \times \bar{5}$ must be the number that can be added to $\overline{35}$ to get 0, or it must be 35.

The process of division is probably handled best by using multiplicative inverses (after rational numbers have been considered) simply because this procedure is so like multiplication and has been thought so by children for a long time. Dividing by 3 and multiplying by $\frac{1}{3}$ will seem to be essentially the same thing to most junior high school pupils.

Several comments should be made about the foregoing procedure. First, the procedure has much to recommend it in the sense that it gives the pupils a feeling for the sort of thing a mathematician might do. Second, a large number of physical examples will help the children to understand the operations involved and the connection between mathematical considerations and physical models. It is fine to get ideas from the physical models, but if we want to satisfy certain mathematical rules, we must consider these apart from the physical situation. Other than the number line, physical models which may prove helpful include elevators with the ground-floor numbered zero and several floors below ground level, various machines which run forward and backward, such as cars, motor boats, etc., moving pictures running forward or backward, bank accounts in the black or red, and a thermometer. As an example of a physical model for the product of two negative numbers, suppose a man lost 20¢ per hand in 5 hands in a poker game, he would have "gained" $5 \times \overline{20}$ or $\overline{100}$ cents after the five games. Now suppose that we have been taking moving pictures of his losing the money and proceed to run these backwards, thus running through five games backward, or $\bar{5}$ games. After the $\bar{5}$ games in which he lost 20¢ per game ($\overline{20}$ cents) he will be better off by 100 cents. Thus, $\overline{5} \times \overline{20}$ apparently ought to equal 100.

A third comment to be made is that we have gone over this work rapidly and skipped many important details. For example, we assumed that we started with the numbers 0, 1, 2, 3, . . . , or the natural numbers, with 0 annexed. This is reasonable in terms of what the pupils know at this time, but may seem a little awkward. Some authors refer to the natural numbers as the set {0, 1, 2, 3, . . .} rather than leave 0 out, because of this set's usefulness. There is no obvious logical or historical reason for preferring one set over the other; there are times when either is convenient, and therefore, it is helpful to have a name for each set. Those who call {0, 1, 2, 3, . . .} the set of natural numbers usually call {1, 2, 3, . . .} the set of counting numbers; while those who call {1, 2, 3, . . .} the set of natural numbers often call {0, 1, 2, 3, . . .} the set of cardinal numbers.

A fourth comment concerns the symbol "$\overline{8}$" and others like it. The objection to starting off by writing negative eight "$-8$" is that the pupils will almost certainly think of the minus sign as indicating subtraction. However, it is desirable that they distinguish between the subtraction operation and part of a new numeral. Otherwise, considerable confusion may result when it appears that several operations are being carried on simultaneously with only one pair of numbers ($-4 - 7$, for example). For the same reason, it is preferable to use the word "negative" when talking about the new numbers and the word "minus" when talking about subtraction. If the new number system is developed as it was above, it might seem desirable to have some term for the old numbers other than "old numbers." We call the numbers 1, 2, 3, . . . positive, with zero being neither a positive nor a negative number. We call the whole set {. . . , $-2, -1, 0, 1, 2, 3, . . .$} the set of integers. Of course, we shall begin writing negative eight "$-8$" reasonably soon, simply because that is the standard way of doing it, and we shall use parentheses around numerals if any possible confusion could result. It is probably desirable to continue to refer to negative numbers as "negative numbers" rather than as "minus numbers" throughout the ninth grade.

Fifth, the fact that the sum of two numbers was zero was important. Indeed, $-7$ (or $\overline{7}$) was *defined* to be the number that could be added to 7 in order to get a sum of zero. If the commutative law holds, then 7 and $-7$ have the interesting relationship to each other that either can be added to the other to attain a sum of zero. Such numbers are of some importance in mathematics, and we refer to them as additive inverses of each other. Thus, the additive inverse of 7 is $-7$ and the additive inverse of $-7$ is 7. On occasion, we shall wish to designate the additive inverse of a number that is represented by a variable, for example, the additive inverse of $x$; it seems natural to call the additive inverse of $x$, "$-x$" but it should also be made clear to the pupils that $-x$ is not necessarily a negative number. For example, if $x$ is the number $-7$, then the number that can be added to it to give 0 is 7; thus the additive inverse of $-7$ is 7, or $-(-7) = 7$. This is not a case of "two negatives making a positive," but the result of the definition of additive inverse and $-7$. The rule about "two negatives . . . " can confuse pupils when applied in the wrong place (adding two negative numbers, for example). Thus, we have three uses for the minus sign: one to designate the operation of subtraction, one to serve as part of numerals for negative numbers, and one to signify the additive inverse of a number. The last one can probably be saved until the pupils are familiar with the first two.

Finally, it is important to notice that what we have been doing has been to create a new system which would probably have the properties we wanted it to have, namely, closure; commutative, associative, and distributive properties; and including 0 and 1 with the usual properties for these. If we wished to prove that the system did have the properties desired, we would have to give precise definitions for the operations of addition and multiplication of the new numbers, as well as the definitions for the new numbers themselves, and then set out to prove that the new system really possessed those properties. From the way in which it is constructed, pupils will probably believe that the system has these properties, but it may be worth pointing out that using some of the properties to make the definitions does not necessarily indicate that the definitions will satisfy all of the properties. On the other hand, with an average or even an above average group of ninth graders, it is probably not worthwhile trying to prove that all of the desired properties are really satisfied—the procedure would be quite tedious and of relatively little value.

The rational numbers present a different sort of problem from the integers. Pupils carry on operations with positive rationals beginning in elementary school and have some idea of how to add $\frac{3}{4}$ and $\frac{5}{7}$, or so we assume. The corresponding operations with positive and negative rational numbers will be so similar that they do not present a great challenge. Therefore, it might be interesting to get the pupils to develop a reasonably formal definition of equality, addition, and multiplication for rational numbers and then prove that the system has the desired properties.

If this procedure were followed, the teacher might start by asking what the relationship is between $\frac{2}{3}$ and $\frac{4}{6}$. The children would decide that the two are equal to each other. The same is true of $\frac{7}{8}$ and $\frac{14}{16}$. In the case of $\frac{12}{28}$ and $\frac{15}{35}$ they might decide the two were equal if they reduced each one to lowest terms and got the same result. The teacher might then see if the children could develop a more formal definition of equality for rational numbers. Noting they said that $\frac{2}{3} = \frac{4}{6}$, he might ask what is the product of 2 and 6? Of 3 and 4? Do the children notice anything interesting? Noting further that they said $\frac{7}{8} = \frac{14}{16}$, what is the product of 8 and 14? Is 7 $\times$ 16 also 112? The teacher next might try this with $\frac{12}{28}$ and $\frac{15}{35}$. In general, does it seem that $a/b = c/d$ if and only if $ad = bc$? Here we adopted the convention of omitting the "$\times$" sign between variables. This is a significant abbreviation when first used, and should be discussed thoroughly and implemented by considerable practice. After this definition of equality has been made to seem reasonable for positive rational numbers, it would be assumed for all rational numbers, and some practice should be provided.

The teacher should then ask the class how to add $\frac{3}{7}$ and $\frac{5}{8}$. Is the common denominator 7 $\times$ 8? Does the numerator of the first fraction become 3 $\times$ 8 (or 24)? Is the numerator of the second fraction 5 $\times$ 7 (or 35)? If so, could the answer be represented as follows: $\dfrac{(3 \times 8) + (5 \times 7)}{7 \times 8}$? Can the same thing be done with $a/b + c/d$? Is the common denominator $bd$? Is the numerator of the first fraction $ad$? Is $bc$ the numerator of the second fraction? If so, can this sum be represented as follows: $(ad + bc)/bd$? Let us agree to use this as the definition of addition for rational numbers.

Eliciting a definition for multiplication of rational numbers is relatively simple, and we have the following three definitions:

DEFINITION 1.   $a/b = c/d$ if and only if $ad = bc$.
DEFINITION 2.   $a/b + c/d = (ad + bc)/bd$.
DEFINITION 3.   $(a/b)(c/d) = ac/bd$.

Still missing is a definition of rational numbers themselves. In general, pupils will find it natural to think of rational numbers in connection with division. From a mathematical point of view, they will get into no trouble doing so. From the pure mathematics standpoint, it may seem a coincidence that the arithmetic of rational numbers and the arithmetic of quotients happen to be the same,[1] but from a practical

---

[1] Some authors of elementary textbooks would use this argument to maintain that the quotient approach ought not to be used, leaving the ordered-pair approach as the way to introduce rational numbers. This approach will be discussed later.

standpoint, there is great doubt that the arithmetic of rational numbers would have been of much interest had it not happened to be essentially identical to the arithmetic of quotients. Therefore, it seems perfectly reasonable to define a rational number as the quotient of two integers.

One problem remains. As we saw earlier, division by zero is essentially not definable. If we define $\frac{3}{0}$ to be some number, $n$, then we know that $3 = n \cdot 0$. But it can be proved that the product of zero and any other number ($n$) is zero, and therefore, $3 = 0$. As this cannot be, $\frac{3}{0}$ is not defined. For similar reasons, $a/0$ is not defined when $a$ is any number other than 0. In the case of $\frac{0}{0}$, the conflict does not occur. If we let $\frac{0}{0}$ equal 1, $0 = 0 \cdot 1$ which is true. But it would be just as good to define $\frac{0}{0}$ to be 2 (since $0 = 0 \cdot 2$), or $\pi$, or any other number. Hence, $\frac{0}{0}$ is also not usually defined. Therefore, we shall define a rational number as the quotient of two integers, with the divisor not equal to zero.

DEFNITION 4.    A rational number is the quotient of two integers $(a/b)$ with $b \neq 0$.

Logically speaking, it is clear that the fourth definition should have come before the other three, but in a teaching situation, it might be easier to be vague about what a rational number is until after some of the earlier discussion has occurred. Now, let us see if using the definitions and our knowledge of integers we can actually prove that the system of rational numbers has the desired properties.

Addition is commutative: that is, for any rational number $a/b$ and $c/d$,

$$\frac{a}{b} + \frac{d}{c} = \frac{c}{d} + \frac{a}{b}$$

By definition, $a/b + c/d = (ad + bc)/bd$, and $c/d + a/b = (cb + da)/db$. Therefore, we must show that $(ad + bc)/bd = (cb + da)/db$. Before doing this, let us comment briefly on the operations of addition and multiplication, and the relation of equality. In the foregoing definitions, addition for rational numbers is in terms of addition and multiplication for integers; multiplication for rational numbers is defined in terms of multiplication for integers; and even equality for rational numbers is defined in terms of multiplication and equality for integers. We are assuming, in this discussion, that we know all about the operations and relations for integers and that we are simply trying to find out things about the operations and relations for rational numbers. Therefore, it is not circular reasoning to use the commutative law of addition for *integers* to prove the commutative law of addition for *rational numbers*. It is important for children to realize this, otherwise they will have badly confused notions of what constitutes a proof. It may be helpful to use different symbols for the operations in different systems at the beginning of the study; for example, $\oplus$ could signify addition of rationals.

With that much warning, let us continue. $ad + bc = bc + ad$ by the commutative law of addition for integers, $bc + ad = cb + da$ by the commutative law of multiplication for integers, and $bd = db$ by the commutative law of multiplication for integers. Therefore, $(ad + bc)/bd = (cb + da)/db$, which was to be proved, and addition is commutative for rational numbers.

Using the preceding definition, the reader may be interested to show in a similar manner that addition of rational numbers is associative and multiplication is commutative and associative. We shall only demonstrate here that multiplication is distributive over addition. To show this, we must prove that for any three rational numbers, $a/b$, $c/d$, and $e/f$, $(a/b)(c/d + e/f) = (a/b)(c/d) + (a/b)(e/f)$. Using the definitions for addition and multiplication on the left side and the same definitions in opposite order on the right side, we get:

$$\frac{a}{b} \frac{cf + de}{df} \stackrel{?}{=} \frac{ac}{bd} + \frac{ae}{bf}$$

or

$$\frac{acf + ade}{bdf} \stackrel{?}{=} \frac{acbf + bdae}{bdbf}$$

This will be a true equality on the condition that

$$(acf + ade)(bdbf) = (bdf)(acbf + bdae)$$

Through employment of the distributive law and the commutative and associative laws of multiplication for integers, the left and right members each become $ab^2cdf^2 + ab^2d^2ef$. Therefore the two rational numbers are equal, and multiplication is distributive over addition for rational numbers.

One fact that may have bothered the reader throughout the preceding discussion is not imposing a restriction that the denominators not equal zero. Actually, this is not generally necessary if we are given rational numbers to begin with, since our knowledge that they are rational tells us that the denominator cannot be zero. On the other hand, there is no harm in reminding the pupils of this fact at regular intervals, even if it is not mathematically necessary to mention it. Along these lines is the question of whether some of the rational numbers that were considered in the various proofs were necessarily rational—that is, could their denominators have been zero? Since addition and multiplication are closed for rational numbers, all additions and multiplications in such a proof must have resulted in rational numbers. We will leave it to the reader to prove that addition and multiplication are, indeed, closed under the operations of addition and multiplication for rational numbers. In order to do this, we must show (for addition) that if $a$, $b$, $c$, and $d$ are integers with $b \neq 0$ and $d \neq 0$, then $ad + bc$ is an integer and $bd$ is an integer not equal to zero. We may use the closure rules for integers and also the fact that if the product of two integers is zero then one of the integers is zero.

### Real Numbers

The real numbers cause great difficulties. From a practical point of view, there is no need for them. It would be perfectly possible for industries to continue functioning, armed forces to wage war, governments to calculate the national debt, and physicists to carry out all pertinent or interesting measurements without irrational numbers. For any practical use, a rational number will always do. In estimating the quotient of the circumference of a circle divided by the diameter, 3.14 will do for most purposes ($3\frac{1}{7}$ is a little better) and 3.14159 for almost all.

However, there are many theoretical problems, often closely associated with practical problems, which occur without the real numbers. From the mathematician's standpoint, these problems can be summed up by saying that not every set of rational numbers which has an upper bound has a least upper bound in the set of rational numbers. From the high school pupil's standpoint this statement might seem obscure, and when he found out what a least upper bound was he might easily react "so what?"

The difficulties that will have the most meaning to a high school

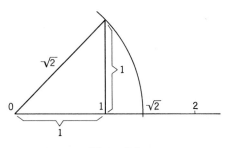

Figure 9.1

pupil are the same ones that disturbed the Pythagoreans about 500 B.C. Consider, for example, an isosceles right triangle with legs one unit long (Fig. 9.1). By the Pythagorean theorem, the hypotenuse has length $\sqrt{2}$. Now, if there is a number for every point on the line (which seems reasonable in theory if we are to measure lengths correctly), there must be a number for $\sqrt{2}$. But it can be proven that there is no such number among the rational numbers, and therefore there must be other numbers which are not rationals. As it turns out, if there are points on the line only where there are rational numbers, there will be more holes in the line than points. This is a rather surprising fact, to say the least,[2] especially in light of the fact that between any two rational numbers there is always another one; this can be shown by taking the arithmetic mean of the two. Therefore, there are an infinite number of rational numbers between any two.

There are several proofs that the square root of two is irrational. Most of these are variations on Euclid's well-known proof which, in essence, goes like this: Assume that $\sqrt{2}$ is a rational number and therefore can be represented as the quotient of two integers, $a/b$; and assume that $a/b$ has been reduced to lowest terms (so $a$ and $b$ have no factors in common).

Then, $a^2 = 2b^2$. But, if $a^2$ is even, then $a$ is even (most high school pupils will accept this, but see lemma following for proof). Since $a$ is even, let $a = 2c$ where $c$ is an integer. Then, $a^2 = (2c)^2 = 4c^2$. But, since $a^2 = 2b^2$, by substitution, $4c^2 = 2b^2$, and $2c^2 = b^2$. Now, $2c^2$ is clearly an even integer, and therefore, $b^2$ is even. But, if $b^2$ is even, then $b$ is even and $a$ and $b$ have a factor (2) in common. Thus, it is impossible to express $\sqrt{2}$ as the quotient of two integers reduced to lowest terms.

A step in the foregoing proof which may need a little more work is the statement that if $a^2$ is even then $a$ is even. This can be proved in the following way: Assume that $a$ is not even. Then, since $a$ is an integer, it must be odd. Let $a = 2n + 1$ where $n$ is an integer. Then $a^2 = (2n + 1)^2 = 4n^2 + 4n + 1 = 2(2n^2 + 2n) + 1$. By closure for addition and multiplication of integers, $2n^2 + 2n$ is an integer and therefore $2(2n^2 + 2n) + 1$ is an odd number. Thus, the statement that $a$ is not even implies $a^2$ is not even. By our knowledge of the contrapositive, we can conclude that $a^2$ is even implies $a$ is even.

[2] This follows from the fact, proved in the previous chapter, that there are more real numbers than rational numbers, from which it can be shown that there must be more irrational numbers than rational numbers. It happens that there are more transcendental numbers (numbers which are not roots of any algebraic equation, $a_0 x^n + a_1 x^{n-1} + \cdots + a_n = 0$, where $n$ is a positive integer and the coefficients are any integers) than algebraic numbers; there are only $\aleph_0$ algebraic numbers.

Ordinarily, this would be proved as a lemma[3] prior to the main theorem, but since that step is fairly obvious, perhaps children should not be burdened with this detail until they have a good understanding of the principal theorem.

For those who are interested in methods of proof, we point out that the proof that the square root of two is irrational is an honest-to-goodness indirect proof, since we start with the negation of the theorem and show that it leads to a contradiction ($a$ and $b$ have no factors in common, but $a$ and $b$ are both divisible by 2); whereas the proof of the lemma is a proof by contrapositive in which the negation of the conclusion implies the negation of the hypothesis. Many persons would tend to call both of these indirect proofs, though they are essentially different. For teachers, this point is worth noting since the lemma is sometimes proved before the theorem to help the pupils understand indirect proofs. Yet this hardly seems appropriate since that proof does not happen to be an indirect proof. In fact, it is not surprising that some pupils are badly confused by this course of events.

The proof that the square root of two is irrational is likely to be well above the heads of many of the pupils in an algebra class. Therefore, a simpler approach might be more appropriate. This approach had the advantage that it provides for a relatively simple "construction" of the real numbers. Essentially, this approach is based on the assumption that every number (real number, of course) can be written as a never-ending decimal, and that every never-ending decimal is the name for some number. It can be shown, rather easily, that every rational number is represented by a repeating decimal. Therefore, if we can give an example of a nonrepeating decimal, we will have shown that there are numbers which are not rational. Hence we will simply assume that the set of all distinct never-ending decimals corresponds to the set of all real numbers. This seems to be the simplest way to get at the real numbers and still not leave the pupils with any misconceptions.

First, let us show that any rational number can be represented as a repeating decimal. By "repeating decimal" we mean that as we read the decimal from left to right, beyond some decimal place the same pattern repeats itself in a given number of places. For example, ".234638121212121212121212 . . ." is a repeating decimal if the "12" continues to repeat in the same way. However, the earlier repetition of the "3" is not important in determining rationality.

Consider the rational number $\frac{1}{7}$. In order to get a decimal repre-

---

[3] A lemma is a sort of helping theorem—usually proved to make the main proof of a theorem seem less complicated. Ordinarily, a lemma is used only to prove the theorem that follows it.

sentation of this number, using long division, we divide in the following way:

```
       .142857
  7)1.0000000000000
     7
     ─────
     ③0
     2 8
     ─────
      ②0
      1 4
      ─────
       ⑥0
       5 6
       ─────
        ④0
        3 5
        ─────
         ⑤0
```

Before continuing with the division, let us stop to see what we have done so far. Each remainder in this long division has been circled. Is any remainder greater than 7? Could any remainder be greater than or equal to 7 if 7 is the divisor? Then, what are the possible remainders? If the remainder is ever zero (after the decimal point has been passed so that the digit "brought down" is always a zero), does that mean that the quotient will thereafter contain nothing but zeros? We will call a decimal with nothing but zeros after a certain place a repeating decimal, though some people would call it a terminating decimal. Then, if none of the remainders happens to be zero, are the only possible remainders 1, 2, 3, 4, 5, 6? After all of these remainders have been used up, must one of them recur as the next remainder? When that happens, the process of division will look exactly the same as at some time previously, and therefore the process will begin to repeat itself, thus leading to a repeating decimal for the quotient. In a similar way, it can be seen that for any positive integral divisor and dividend, a repeating decimal would have to result from the process of long division. Therefore any rational number can be represented as a repeating (or terminating[4]) decimal.

We now present two examples of nonrepeating decimals.

First: .10100100010000100000100000010000000100000001 . . .
Second: .1234567891011121314151617181920212223242 5 . . .

─────
[4] It is easy to show that so-called terminating decimals are equal to true repeating decimals with "9" as the repeating part. For example, .50000 · · · = .49999 · · · · . This will be left as an exercise, but the method of proof will become obvious from the discussion very shortly.

Clearly the first decimal is not repeating since if it were it would have to repeat in some number, $n$, places. But suppose it repeats in $n$ places; if we go far enough to the right, we will get to a place where there are $n$ 0's together. But if there are $n$ 0's in a row and the decimal is repeating in $n$ places, all the digits after that point must be 0's. But it is clear from the method of construction that there will always be 1's in the decimal after any particular place. Therefore, the decimal cannot be a repeater. The argument for the second decimal is similar.

To leave the subject of rational numbers and repeating decimals without discussing the fact that every repeating decimal is the representation for some rational number would be unfortunate. Thus, let us show how to convert a repeating decimal into the quotient of two integers.

Consider the repeating decimal $37.284392392392392392392 \ldots$. The repeating portion repeats in three places. Let us multiply this number (which we will call $p$) by $10^3$ or 1000. Thus,

$$10^3p = 37284.39239239239239239239 \ldots$$

and
$$p = 37.28439239239239239239 \ldots$$

Subtracting, we get
$$1000p - p = 37247.108$$

or
$$999p = 37247.108$$

or
$$999000p = 37247108$$

and
$$p = \frac{37247108}{999000}$$

which is the quotient of two integers, or a rational number. Of course, this can be reduced, but the point is that the procedure can be used for any repeating decimal. If the decimal repeats in $n$ places, multiply by $10^n$, subtract, multiply both sides of the equation by whatever is necessary to eliminate decimal fractions, and divide.

Real numbers, then, should probably be introduced into high school mathematics as those numbers represented by infinite (repeating or nonrepeating) decimals. There are other methods of introducing real numbers which are mathematically superior, but the subtleties involved are such that these would not be appropriate for high school children. The best known of such introductions are due to Cantor and Dedekind (a contemporary of Cantor). Dedekind's method is remarkably similar to that used by Eudoxus more than 2000 years earlier. Of course, Eudoxus' work was geometric in nature, whereas Dedekind's was algebraic. For a further discussion of this, see Chapter 14.

### Complex Numbers

One motivation for each new system of numbers was an unsolved equation. For the integers (from the natural numbers) $x + 1 = 0$

was a motivating problem. For the rationals (from the integers) $2x = 1$ could be used as a motivating problem. For the reals (from the rationals) $x^2 = 2$ was used as motivation. Let us consider the equation $x^2 + 1 = 0$. It has many things in common with the previous equations, and certainly does not *look* much more difficult, but it cannot be solved in the system of real numbers. We know that the square of any nonzero real number is positive, therefore, $x^2 + 1$ cannot be zero if $x$ is a real number. Thus, the root of the equation $x^2 + 1 = 0$ must be a new kind of number. Actually, there should be two roots to this equation, but let us concentrate on only one of them for the time being. It would be natural to call this root $\sqrt{-1}$, but it is usually called "$i$." Therefore, by definition, $i^2 = -1$.

Following an analogous procedure to that used for integers, we try to maintain as many of the properties of the old system as possible. Thus, by closure for multiplication, $i^3$ must be an element of the system, and it is natural to say that $i^3 = i^2 \cdot i = (-1)i = -i$. Similarly, it is clear that $i^4$ should be equal to $(i^2)^2 = (-1)^2 = 1$. Also, $i^5 = i^4 \cdot i = 1 \cdot i = i$; $i^6 = i^4 \cdot i^2 = -1$, etc. From this, it is clear that the other root of $x^2 + 1 = 0$ is $-i$.

Continuing to assume closure, we can easily see that all numbers that can be expressed in the form $a + bi$, where $a$ and $b$ are real numbers, are in the system. Then, treating these in much the same way as we treat binomials, we can deduce the rest of the properties of the complex number system. One problem that must be solved first, however, is the matter of what else the system contains. Since it is closed under multiplication, $(a + bi)(c + di)$ should also be in the system. This can be rewritten as $ac + adi + bci + bdi^2$; but $i^2 = -1$, and therefore, $(a + bi)(c + di) = ac - bd + (ad + bc)i$, which is in the form $A + Bi$. Therefore, we can continue to multiply numbers such as $a + bi$ by each other without creating numbers which cannot be represented in that form. Similarly, if addition is defined as follows: $(a + bi) + (c + di) = (a + c) + (b + d)i$, addition can be seen to be closed for complex numbers. Equality for complex numbers is quite simple: $a + bi = c + di$ if and only if $a = c$ and $b = d$. Using these definitions, we can show that the system of complex numbers is a field. That is, the operations of addition and multiplication are commutative and associative with multiplication being distributive over addition; there are identity elements (0 and 1) for addition and multiplication, and there are inverses with respect to both addition and multiplication, except, of course, that 0 does not have a multiplicative inverse.

Most of the properties of a field will be left for the reader to discover, but the question of multiplicative inverses is interesting enough to be considered here. How does one ordinarily write the multiplicative inverse of $a + bi$? Is $1/(a + bi)$ a complex number? The symbol certainly does not look right. Let us multiply numerator and denominator by $a - bi$. The number $a - bi$ is known as the conjugate of $a + bi$. With a reasonable amount of time, the right hints, and some experimentation, high school pupils can figure out for themselves that this is the proper step:

$$\frac{1}{a + bi} \cdot \frac{a - bi}{a - bi} = \frac{a - bi}{a^2 + b^2} = \frac{a}{a^2 + b^2} - \frac{bi}{a^2 + b^2}$$

Now, from our knowledge of real numbers we know that if $a^2 + b^2$ is not zero, $a/(a^2 + b^2) + [(-b)/(a^2 + b^2)]i$ must be a complex number. But, the only way that $a^2 + b^2$ could be zero (with $a$ and $b$ real numbers) is for both $a$ and $b$ to be zero, but that would mean that $a + bi = 0$. Since we only want to be able to find multiplicative inverses for nonzero numbers, we have shown that all complex numbers except zero have multiplicative inverses. Thus, the complex number system is a field and contains the square root of $-1$. In fact, $n$ $n$th roots of every complex number (to be shown in a later chapter) are contained in the system. Even stronger is the fact that every algebraic equation has a root in the system of complex numbers.

Several interesting things about the complex number system should be called to the attention of any person who is teaching this material. In particular, not everything which is true of the real number system is true of the complex number system. One example of this is the statement: for all $a$ and $b$, $\sqrt{ab} = \sqrt{a}\sqrt{b}$. This happens to be true for real numbers, but not for complex numbers. Some years ago, *Scientific American* presented a paradox based on this fact which was the bane to the existence of many mathematics teachers until they figured out the difficulty. To show that this property does not hold for complex numbers, consider the quantity $\sqrt{(-4)(-9)}$ which is equal to $\sqrt{36} = 6.$[5] On the other hand, $\sqrt{-4}\sqrt{-9} = (2i)(3i) = 6i^2 = (6)(-1) = -6$. Apparent paradoxes are easy to construct using the assumption that $\sqrt{ab} = \sqrt{a}\sqrt{b}$ when $a$ and $b$ are negative numbers, but the moral of this for pupils, and teachers, is that if complex numbers are converted to the $a + bi$ form rather than being left in radical form, such difficulties cannot occur.

Another fact of interest about complex numbers is that they are not ordered. This might seem apparent from the fact that order

[5] The radical symbol always signifies the positive square root if one exists and is *not* to be thought of as containing a built in "plus or minus sign." If it were this ambiguous, mathematical work with radicals would be chaotic.

appears to have something to do with position on a line, and that real numbers have taken up all the space. Actually, it is possible to string the complex numbers out along a line in *an* order;[6] the difficulty lies in that any ordering of the complex numbers cannot have the usual relationship to the operations of addition and multiplication. In particular, an ordered field has a subset of elements, $S_p$ (the positive elements), which is closed under addition and multiplication such that each element, $x$, of the field satisfies exactly one of the following: $x = 0$, $x \in S_p$, $-x \in S_p$, where $-x$ designates the additive inverse of $x$. It can also be shown that for any field $(-x)^2 = x^2$. Since either $x \in S_p$ or $-x \in S_p$, and $S_p$ is closed under multiplication, either $x^2 \in S_p$ or $(-x)^2 \in S_p$, But since $x^2 = (-x)^2$, both must be elements of $S_p$, and therefore the square of any nonzero element of an ordered field must be an element of $S_p$. If the complex number system is an ordered field, $1^2 \in S_p$, but since $1^2 = 1$, $1 \in S_p$; from the trichotomy, therefore, $-1 \notin S_p$. But $i^2 \in S_p$, and therefore, since $i^2 = -1$, $-1 \in S_p$. This is a contradiction. Hence, the assumption that the complex number system is an ordered field must be false.

The procedures used to annex new numbers to an old system, thus creating a new system, are somewhat haphazard and quite informal.

[6] It is possible to create a one-to-one correspondence between the complex numbers and the real numbers and then replace each real number by the corresponding complex number. A one-to-one correspondence can be created between the reals, $r$, from 0 to 1 and the ordered pairs $(a, b)$ in which $a$ and $b$ are between 0 and 1 by using the decimal representations: $a = .a_1a_2a_3 \ldots$, $b = .b_1b_2b_3 \ldots$, $r = .r_1r_2r_3r_4r_5 \ldots$; then, $r$ is paired with $(a,b)$ if $a_1 = r_1$, $a_2 = r_3$, $a_3 = r_5$, etc., and $b_1 = r_2$, $b_2 = r_4$, $b_3 = r_6$, etc. Since complex numbers can be thought of as ordered pairs of reals, this produces a one-to-one correspondence between the reals from 0 to 1 and the complex numbers in which each component is between 0 and 1. There are simple geometric proofs for the fact that there is a one-to-one correspondence between the points on a line segment and the points on an entire line (see Fig. 9.2), and for the fact that there is a one-to-one correspondence between the points inside a square and the points in an entire plane (analogous to the first proof). Thus, there is a one-to-one correspondence between the reals and the complex numbers.

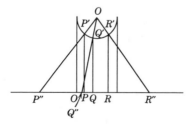

Figure 9.2

In each case, we have, in effect, used the procedure that was most convenient and which would also teach the pupils something about the way in which men create number systems and deduce facts from formal assumptions. This procedure is not elegant from the mathematical point of view but seems to be appropriate pedagogically.

## Constructing New Numbers from Old Numbers

Another procedure, which is more elegant mathematically, is actually to create a new number system from the old one and then show that a subsystem of the new system is isomorphic to the old system. This procedure involves equivalence classes, some subtleties involving names and objects, and a necessity of proving that isomorphisms exist between certain systems. It is probably not the best way to develop number systems for young children, though it has some appealing features. We shall discuss this procedure rather briefly as it applies to the construction of several new systems. The principal reason for using this procedure is to be able to produce consistency proofs for the new system assuming the old system to be consistent. Since this activity does not seem appropriate for school pupils, the entire procedure is probably not appropriate for them.

## Equivalence Relations and Sets

We have already indicated that a relation can be thought of as a set of ordered pairs, but ordinarily, there is some sentence associated with the relation which tells us that a first member of an ordered pair has the given relation to the second. If, for example, "$\sim$" were the name of a relation, we would write "$a \sim b$" to indicate that $(a, b) \in \sim$, or the ordered pair $(a, b)$ was an element of the relation $\sim$. "$a \sim b$" is read "$a$ has the relation $\sim$ to $b$." "$a \not\sim b$" will mean that $(a, b)$ is not an element of $\sim$, or that $a$ does not have the relation $\sim$ to $b$. In general, $a$ and $b$ will be taken from a specified universe.

An equivalence relation is a special kind of relation which is of considerable importance in mathematics. A relation, "$\sim$," is an equivalence relation (for the set $S$) if it has the following three properties for all elements, $a$, $b$, and $c$, of the universe ($S$).

1. $a \sim a$                                 ($\sim$ is reflexive)
2. If $a \sim b$, then $b \sim a$        ($\sim$ is symmetric)
3. If $a \sim b$, and $b \sim c$, then $a \sim c$   ($\sim$ is transitive)

When $\sim$ is an equivalence relation, we often read "$a \sim b$" as "$a$ is equivalent to $b$."

There are many examples of equivalence relations. The relation of equality happens to be one, but others include examples such as similarity among geometric figures: _____ has the same parents as _____; congruence among geometric figures: _____ lives on the same block as _____, and so on. Equality, as it is used in elementary mathematics, is a much stronger relationship, in that $a = b$ is interpreted to mean that "$a$" and "$b$" are names for the same object.

If an equivalence relation ($\sim$) is defined for a set ($A$), then the subset of $A$ which consists of all elements of $A$ that are equivalent to an element $a$ of $A$ is called an equivalence set (or sometimes an equivalence class) of $A$. Such an equivalence class will be denoted $[a]$.

This definition can be written:

$$[a] = \{x \mid x \in A \text{ and } x \sim a\}$$

From the definition of equivalence set (and equivalence relation) many facts can be proved about equivalence sets. For example

$$[a] = [b] \text{ if and only if } b \in [a]$$

Since this is an "if and only if" statement, it can be proved as two conditionals. First, the "if" part: $b \in [a]$ implies $[a] = [b]$.

*Proof.* If $b \in [a]$ then, by definition of an equivalence set, $b \sim a$. Now, suppose that $x \in [b]$, then $x \sim b$ (definition of equivalence set) and by the transitive property, $x \sim a$. But, if $x \sim a$, then, $x \in [a]$ (definition of equivalence set), and therefore, any element of $[b]$ is an element of $[a]$. On the other hand, if $y \in [a]$, then $y \sim a$. $a \sim b$ (by the symmetry property), and therefore, $y \sim b$ (transitivity) and $y \in [b]$ by definition of equivalence sets. Therefore, any element of $[a]$ is an element of $[b]$. We have now shown that $[a] \subseteq [b]$ and $[b] \subseteq [a]$, and therefore, $[a] = [b]$.

The "only if" part of the theorem says: $[a] = [b]$ implies $b \in [a]$.

*Proof.*    If $[a] = [b]$, then every element of each set is an element of the other, so $b \in [a]$ because it is an element of $[b]$ ($b \in [b]$ by the reflexive property and the definition of equivalence sets). Therefore, we have proved both parts of the theorem.

## Construction of the Integers

Using equivalence sets, we can construct the system of integers from the system of natural numbers and then show that the latter is isomorphic to a subsystem of the integers. Notice that this procedure is essentially different from that used previously. With this procedure, a natural number will not actually *be* an integer, it will only be like an integer—so similar, in fact, that for all practical purposes, it will not make any difference if we do not distinguish between positive integers and natural numbers.

In this discussion, $a$, $b$, $c$, etc., are to be thought of as natural numbers, and we shall assume the properties of the natural number systems.

Let $H$ be the set of all ordered pairs, $(a, b)$, of natural numbers. Two such ordered pairs, $(a, b)$, and $(c, d)$, will be equivalent, that is $(a, b) \sim (c, d)$, if and only if $a + d = b + c$. If the reader wishes to think of an ordered pair $(a, b)$ as $a - b$, he will find that nothing said in the future contradicts that thought. Of course, someone who knows nothing about negative numbers would say that $b$ must be less than (or equal to) $a$ in that case, but if the reader insists on thinking of $(a, b)$ as $a - b$, then he must give up this limitation on $b$. Officially, we shall think of $(a, b)$ simply as an ordered pair of natural numbers.

The imaginative reader should now be able to figure out an appropriate definition of addition and multiplication for these ordered pairs, and would probably find the exercise worthwhile. Meanwhile, we shall prove that $\sim$ really is an equivalence relation. In order to do this, we must prove that it is reflexive, symmetric, and transitive.

*Reflexivity:* $(a, b) \sim (a, b)$ if $a + b = b + a$, which is true by the commutative law of addition for natural numbers.

*Symmetry:* If $(a, b) \sim (c, d)$, then $a + d = b + c$, and since equality is symmetric (for natural numbers), $b + c = a + d$. By the commutative law of addition for natural numbers, $c + b = d + a$, and therefore, $(c, d) \sim (a, b)$.

*Transitivity:* If $(a, b) \sim (c, d)$, and $(c, d) \sim (e, f)$, then $a + d = b + c$, and $c + f = d + e$. Adding corresponding members, we obtain $(a + d) + (c + f) = (b + c) + (d + e)$, and by several uses of the associative and commutative laws of addition for natural numbers, we can obtain $(a + f) + (c + d) = (b + e) + (c + d)$. A cancellation law for addition, which is true of natural numbers, can now be applied, or $(c + d)$ can be subtracted from each member, with the restriction that the remainder must still be a natural number. In either case, the result is: $a + f = b + e$, which implies $(a, b) \sim (e, f)$.

Therefore, since it is reflexive, symmetric, and transitive, $\sim$ is an equivalence relation. Let $I$ be the set of all equivalence classes on $H$ with respect to $\sim$, and denote the equivalence class which contains $(a, b)$ in the usual fashion: $[(a, b)]$.

If we look again at what is happening from an informal point of view, we would think of the ordered pair $(7, 3)$ as standing for the integer 4 $(7 - 3 = 4)$; and the ordered pair $(9, 5)$ would also stand for 4, and so on. However, all such pairs are equivalent under our definition, and therefore, the equivalence class $[(7, 3)]$ is the same as the equivalence class $[(9, 5)]$, or $[(7, 3)] = [(9, 5)]$. In other words, $[(7, 3)]$, $[(9, 5)]$, and so on, are just different names for the integer 4. In a similar way, $[(2, 8)]$, $[(1, 7)]$, and so on, are names for the integer we think of as $-6$.

If the reader has been thinking about the definitions of addition and multiplication, he can check his definitions with the following; if he has not, he should. In any case, the definitions for addition and multiplication for the equivalence sets are:

$$[(a, b)] + [(c, d)] = [(a + c, b + d)]$$

and

$$[(a, b)] \cdot [(c, d)] = [(ac + bd, ad + bc)]$$

Intuitively, the reader should find these definitions appealing if he has been thinking of the ordered pair $(a, b)$ as the binomial $a - b$. However, we must still show formally that we have defined an operation with each of the preceding definitions. Thus, we must show that the results of applying one of the operations is indeed a unique element of our set.

For addition, it is clear that $a + c$ and $b + d$ are natural numbers since addition of natural numbers is closed; the remaining question is whether we could get two different answers by adding the same two equivalence classes. To check this, assume $(a, b) \sim (x, y)$, and $(c, d) \sim (z, w)$. Then, we must show that

$$[(a, b)] + [(c, d)] = [(x, y)] + [(z, w)]$$

From our hypothesis, we know that $a + y = b + x$, and that $c + w = d + z$. Adding corresponding sides, we have:

$$(a + y) + (c + w) = (b + x) + (d + z)$$

The conclusion will be true if and only if

$$[(a + c, b + d)] = [(x + z, y + w)]$$

which is true if and only if $(a + c, b + d) \sim (x + z, y + w)$, and this, in turn, is true if and only if $(a + c) + (y + w) = (b + d) + (x + z)$. By several uses of the associative and commutative laws of addition for natural numbers, the last statement can be seen to be the same as the statement derived from the hypothesis. Therefore, the two equivalence sets are the same, and addition is a properly defined operation (both closed and unique). A similar argument can be used to show that multiplication, as defined, is an operation.

It is easy to show that the commutative and associative laws hold for both addition and multiplication, and an abbreviated proof of the fact that multiplication is distributive over addition follows:

We must show that

$$[(a, b)] \cdot ([(c, d)] + [(e, f)])$$

equals

$$[(a, b)] \cdot [(c, d)] + [(a, b)] \cdot [(e, f)]$$

Working on each side separately, we have

$$[(a, b)] \cdot [(c + e, d + f)] \stackrel{?}{=} [(ac + bd, ad + bc)] + [(ae + bf, af + be)]$$
$$[(a(c + e) + b(d + f), a(d + f) + b(c + e))] \stackrel{?}{=}$$
$$[(ac + bd + ae + bf, ad + bc + af + be)]$$
$$[(ac + ae + bd + bf, ad + af + bc + be)] \stackrel{?}{=}$$
$$[(ac + ae + bd + bf, ad + af + bc + be)]$$

Because of the reflexive property of equivalence relations, it is clear that the two equivalence sets are equal, and therefore, multiplication is distributive over addition.

This system has a multiplicative identity element as does the system of natural numbers. An interested reader should be able to guess at least one name for that element.[7] In order to show that $(2, 1)$ is a multiplicative identity element, we must show that $[(2, 1)] \cdot [(a, b)] = [(a, b)]$ for all $a$, $b$. By definition of multiplication, the left-hand member is $[(2a + b, 2b + a)]$; and this is equal to $[(a, b)]$ because $2a + b + b = 2b + a + a$.

The natural number system was missing an additive identity element and additive inverses. We shall now show that the new system has both. First, a name for the additive identity is $[(1, 1)]$. To show that $[(1, 1)]$ is an additive identity element, we must show that $[(1, 1)] + [(a, b)] = [(a, b)]$. Since this is fairly easy and quite similar to the last proof, we leave it for the reader.

For any equivalence set, $[(a, b)]$, the additive inverse is $[(b, a)]$. In order to prove this, we must show that for all $a$, $b$, $[(a, b)] + [(b, a)] = [(1, 1)]$. This can be shown as follows: $[(a, b)] + [(b, a)] = [(a + b, b + a)]$, which is equal to $[(1, 1)]$ because $a + b + 1 = b + a + 1$.

We have shown that the new system has all of the important properties of the natural numbers plus the added properties of having an additive identity element and additive inverses. It is still desirable to show that a subsystem of the new system is isomorphic to the system of natural numbers. In particular, if the natural number $n$ is paired with the equivalence class $[(n + 1, 1)]$, then operations carried out in

---

[7] Notice that $(1, 0)$ will not suffice since 0 is not a natural number. An alternate construction using 0 might be simpler for this reason.

one system will give results which correspond to the results of corresponding operations in the other system. It is worth noting that the indicated pairing (or mapping) is a one-to-one correspondence since $[(n + 1, 1)] = [(m + 1, 1)]$ if and only if $n + 1 + 1 = 1 + m + 1$, or $n = m$.

To show that corresponding operations give corresponding results, consider first addition.

$$[(a + 1, 1)] + [(b + 1, 1)] = [(a + 1 + b + 1, 1 + 1)]$$
$$= [(a + b + 2, 2)]$$

this is equal to $[(a + b + 1, 1)]$, since $a + b + 2 + 1 = 2 + a + b + 1$. The corresponding operation in the natural number system, of course, gives $a + b$ as the sum of $a$ and $b$. But our correspondence pairs the natural number $a + b$ with the equivalence set $[(a + b + 1, 1)]$, and therefore, the two systems are equivalent under addition. For multiplication,

$$[(a + 1, 1)] \cdot [(b + 1, 1)] = [(ab + a + b + 1 + 1, a + 1 + b + 1)]$$

which can be shown to equal $[(ab + 1, 1)]$. Therefore, the isomorphism between the system of natural numbers and this subsystem of the new system is shown to be complete. Because of this, it is common to call the elements of the subsystem of the new system by the names of the corresponding natural numbers. In particular, $[(1 + 1, 1)]$ is called 1, $[(2 + 1, 1)]$ is called 2, $[(3 + 1, 1)]$ is called 3, and so on. The equivalence set $[(1, 1)]$ will be called 0, and the additive inverse $[(1, a + 1)]$ of $[(a + 1, 1)]$ will be called $-a$. Now, we have the system of integers, as we usually think of it with all of the usual properties.

Several comments should be made about the foregoing procedure. First of all, it is not necessary to make it as austere as it appears here. If we use a number line for the natural numbers, the ordered pairs can be thought of as trips along the line. For example, a trip from the point corresponding to 3 to the point corresponding to 7 would be represented by the ordered pair (7, 3), and it is clearly the same size trip as the trip indicated by the ordered pair (8, 4). These trips are trips of the same size, but in the opposite direction from the trips corresponding to (3, 7) and (4, 8) which makes the additive inverse property seem reasonable, and so on.

Although the ordered-pair approach can be made relatively palatable, it has no particular advantage over the other method of introducing new numbers except for making it possible to carry out proofs that belong in an advanced course in foundations of mathematics. This would be sufficient reason if pupils fully appreciated the subtleties surrounding the use of equivalence classes and proofs (including the final isomorphism proof), but there is good reason to believe that twelve- and thirteen-year-old pupils require a great deal of time and effort to appreciate these things, and that the time and effort could better be spent doing something else. At a later time, in college, perhaps, it would be possible for those who were really interested in such things to come back to the topic of introducing new numbers and do it with considerable mathematical elegance.

If the procedure is used to introduce integers, it would also be used to introduce rational numbers. It makes more sense with rational numbers, since the ordered pair $(a, b)$ will turn out to correspond to the number we all think of as $a/b$. This causes some difficulty, however, since the names we finally hit upon for rational numbers are the ordered pairs with which we started. Thus, we start by saying $(2, 3) \sim (4, 6) \sim (6, 9)$, etc. Then, we define equivalence classes so that $[(2, 3)] = [(4, 6)] = [(6, 9)]$, etc. and change the name of this equivalence class to $\frac{2}{3}$, with $\frac{4}{6}$, $\frac{6}{9}$, etc., being other names for it. The question may arise, since $\frac{2}{3}$ seems to be only another way to write the ordered pair $(2, 3)$, should we say $\frac{2}{3} = \frac{4}{6}$ or $\frac{2}{3} \sim \frac{4}{6}$? The answer depends on whether we are talking about the ordered pairs or the equivalence classes of ordered pairs. This problem can be avoided if care is taken, but often it is not. Furthermore, unless the pupil has sufficient maturity to avoid the problem himself, there is some question whether he will understand the development well enough to make it worth the effort.

The interested reader should have no great difficulty in constructing the rational number system from the integers using ordered pairs, but he should be careful to remember that the second member of an ordered pair ought not to be zero. We shall leave the development of the rational number system from the system of integers and the development of the complex number system from the real number system to the exercises.

An ordered-pair construction does not, in any way, help in the construction of the real number system unless, perhaps, it makes the pupils age faster, thus making them more mature. Therefore, we shall not discuss the real number system further at this time.

The introduction of number systems is important, because of the mathematics that can be learned as systems are created and also because the number systems are useful in and of themselves. The teacher should not forget that although the underlying structure is of great importance, the ability to use the number system is also highly valuable. Thus, it is not sufficient to say that in the future we will all be able to use computers and hence, not need to add, subtract, multiply, and divide. Any reasonably educated person *ought to* be able to carry on simple computations—not necessarily long, difficult computations, or with great rapidity—but he should be able to add up a column of figures, keep a checkbook balanced, and do the arithmetic involved in making out an income tax blank. Therefore, besides learning about the structure of number systems, pupils should be exposed to sufficient practice in operating with numbers.

### Teaching Hints

It is important for the teacher to remember that there are both physical and logical reasons for expanding our number system. The introduction of negative numbers, for example, as well as the introduction of rational numbers, has important physical applications. In light of this fact, and the fact that many pupils find it easier to understand physical models than the formal logic, both physical examples and logic should be used to motivate the introduction of, and computation with, new numbers.

In the case of the integers, there are many obvious applications. For example, the thermometer; this is not only a good motivation for the numbers themselves, but also helps with simple calculations. It has the added virtue of being quite similar to the number line. For simple additions it is natural to give a temperature and then add an increase or decrease to this. (As in the case of clock arithmetic, there is a question whether the elements are the same sorts of things, but this usually does not bother children; if it does, it can be handled in the same way as the clock arithmetic problem was handled, considering motions from zero.) Subtractions can be thought of as "undoing" a recent change. For example, if the weatherman says that an hour ago the temperature was $-5°$, and it has gone down $7°$ in the hour, then we add $-5$ and $-7$, getting $-12$. Now if we have the result, $-12$, and the weatherman announces that he made a mistake, the temperature did not really fall $7°$, but stayed constant, what is the true temperature? It must be $-12 - (-7)$. But we also know that it must be the same as it was an hour ago. Therefore, $-12 - (-7) = -5$. This, and many similar examples will help the pupils to understand the physical basis for computations with signed numbers.

It is worth noting that pupils find it easier to associate multiplication (and division) with whole numbers than with the real (or rational) numbers. With this fact in mind, it is better to take examples that seem to involve counting rather than examples that involve real measurements. In particular, an example involving nondiscrete motion (such as a car or boat moving forward or backward, but not a whole number of units) will be less appealing than an elevator that stops only at a floor, or a thermometer that is assumed to be at a particular whole degree measure (the closest one), or a bank account that has a certain number of dollars (positive or negative) in it at a time. Some of these examples involve nonintegral numbers, but the pupils do not notice that, and therefore follow the discussion more easily.

Other physical models can be constructed indefinitely, if the teacher will simply give his imagination free rein. One example which tends to be very real to children in our grade-conscious society is the following: suppose a teacher gives between 0 and 5 points for each of twenty tests. If a pupil gets 3 out of 5 points on each of the twenty tests, what is his total score? Suppose the teacher lost the grades for five tests; now what is the pupil's score? (Negative times positive.) Now, suppose the teacher starts each child with 100 points and *subtracts* between 0 and 5 points for each test, etc.

One important point to remember when trying to justify the four fundamental operations is that the rules for multiplication and division happen to be simple. With this in mind, it is more important to justify addition, and particularly subtraction, than the other two operations. Even with a program based largely upon memory, children seldom forget how to multiply and divide signed numbers. Of course, it is still desirable to justify these operations, but one of the major reasons for careful justification is to help the children remember in the future. If they will remember anyway, that reason is not so important.

The material in this chapter will be introduced over a long period of time in the education of a pupil. It is therefore desirable that the various teachers involved find out how the others are handling the topic—not that they must do it the same way, but so they will at least be aware of things the pupils have been exposed to. For example, there is a strong tendency to use the number line in the elementary school. If the whole numbers and many of the fractions have been located on the number line, it will seem natural to locate any additional positive rationals there, and the discussion about "holes in the number line" which usually accompanies the introduction of real numbers will seem appropriate. Further, it will not be surprising to find that some of the elementary school teachers have extended the number line in the negative direction. This comes naturally out of a discussion of temperature, at least in the colder climates. Probably the operations involving these numbers will not have been considered in any serious sense, but it should not be unusual to find that the numbers have been considered.

The close connection between geometry and numbers is important both from the mathematical and pedagogical points of view. Many children find it easier to "think from a picture" than just to use symbols. With that in mind, the early introduction of the number line is highly desirable, and early introduction of geometric representations of complex numbers (see Chapter 12), when that number system is under consideration, is equally desirable. In fact, the history of mathematics shows that few mathematicians took complex numbers at all seriously until they had seen their geometric representation.

In the logical justification and development of new number systems, the distributive law plays an important role. One of the reasons the distributive law seems so important is that it is the only one of the five basic laws (two commutative laws, and two associative laws, and the distributive law) that does not seem to be obviously true to pupils. In light of this, it is worth trying by physical example to convince pupils that the distributive law is true. This probably ought to be done early in the elementary school, but if it has not been done, or if the pupils have forgotten, it can be done in the junior or senior high school. The essentials of the procedure are as follows.

To show that $3(5 + 7) = 3(5) + 3(7)$, consider a pile of five objects, and a pile of seven objects; now, consider two more pairs of piles with the same numbers.

||||| ||||||| ||||| ||||||| ||||| |||||||

If we combine the piles in pairs, the result corresponds to $(5 + 7) + (5 + 7) + (5 + 7)$, or $3(5 + 7)$. On the other hand, if all the piles of five are combined first, and then the piles of seven, the result corresponds to $(5 + 5 + 5) + (7 + 7 + 7)$, or $3(5) + 3(7)$. Almost all children will believe that the number of objects has not been changed by the procedure, and that $3(5 + 7) = 3(5) + 3(7)$. Since the argument does not depend in any essential way on the numbers involved, this should be a convincing demonstration that the distributive law holds for all numbers, or at least, all whole numbers. Again, most pupils will assume that it is true of all numbers. This sort of assumption ought not to be discouraged below the college level, even though it does not necessarily follow logically. An interesting fact for teachers of young pupils is that at an early age, not many pupils believe that the number of objects in a pile remains unchanged when objects are rearranged. Thus, demonstrations of the sort described here may not be very effective for four-, five-, and six-year-old pupils.

## Exercises

1. Give two physical models (not found in the text) to illustrate the fact that:
(a) the product of two positive numbers is positive.

(b) the product of a positive and a negative number is negative.

(c) the product of a negative and a positive number is negative. (*Note:* In physical examples, b and c will seem quite different from each other.)

(d) the product of two negative numbers is positive.

2. Show that using Definitions 1, 2, 3, and 4:

(a) addition is closed and unique for rationals.

(b) multiplication is closed and unique for rationals.

(c) addition of rationals is associative.

(d) multiplication of rationals is commutative.

(e) multiplication of rationals is associative.

3. Prove that $\sqrt{3}$ is irrational.

4. Try to adapt the proof that $\sqrt{2}$ is irrational to $\sqrt{4}$. Where does the proof fail?

5. Represent each of the following as a repeating decimal:

(a) $\frac{2}{7}$, (b) $\frac{1}{13}$, (c) $\frac{2}{13}$.

6. Are any of the remainders for 5b the same as a remainder for 5c? If a remainder in the division for 5b were the same as a remainder for 5c, would the repeating portions of the two decimals have to be the same thereafter? Try to produce a proof that the decimal corresponding to $\frac{1}{13}$ must repeat with a period of one of the following: 12, 6, 3, 2, or 1. Use a similar argument to show that the decimal corresponding to $\frac{1}{19}$ must have a period of 18, 9, 6, 3, 2, or 1.

7. Write the first 50 digits of five irrational numbers that are not equal to those indicated in the text.

8. Write each of the following as the quotient of two integers.

(a) .272727272727 . . .

(b) .0236236236236236236 . . .

(c) 8.2314141414141414 . . .

(d) 73.29764764764764764764 . . .

(e) .49999999999 . . .

9. Using the definitions of addition, multiplication, and equality for complex numbers (p. 247), show that:

(a) addition of complex numbers is commutative and associative.

(b) multiplication of complex numbers is commutative and associative.

(c) there is an additive identity element and a multiplicative identity element.

(d) each complex number has an additive inverse.

10. What is wrong with the following argument?

(a) $-1/1 = 1/-1$

(b) $\sqrt{-1/1} = \sqrt{1/-1}$

(c) $\sqrt{-1}/\sqrt{1} = \sqrt{1}/\sqrt{-1}$

(d) $\sqrt{-1/1} = 1/\sqrt{-1}$

(e) $\sqrt{-1} = 1/\sqrt{-1}$

(f) $\sqrt{-1}\,\sqrt{-1} = 1$

(g) $-1 = 1$

11. What is wrong with the following proof that if a relation ($\sim$) is symmetric and transitive, then it is reflexive?

(a) $a \sim b$ implies that $b \sim a$.   (symmetry)

(b) $a \sim b$ and $b \sim a$ implies $a \sim a$.   (transitivity)

(c) Therefore, $a \sim a$.

(*Hint:* "$p$ implies $q$" is true whenever $p$ is false.)

12. Describe a relation (with its universe) that is symmetric and transitive but not reflexive.

13. What is a relation that is both reflexive and symmetric but not transitive?

14. What is a relation that is reflexive and transitive but not symmetric?

15. Show that if equivalence classes $[a]$ and $[b]$ have at least one element in common, then $[a] = [b]$.

16. If $a \in S$ and $\sim$ is an equivalence relation on $S$, of how many equivalence classes (of $S$ with respect to $\sim$) is $a$ an element? Prove it.

17. Show that according to the definitions of addition and multiplication of ordered pairs of natural numbers (p. 253) both operations are commutative and associative.

18. Show that $[(1, 1)]$ is the additive identity element for the system considered on pp. 252–256. (*Note:* This requires showing that $[(1, 1)]$ is an additive identity element and that if $[(e, f)]$ is an additive identity element, then $[(e, f)] = [(1, 1)]$.)

19. Construct the rational numbers as a set of equivalence classes of ordered pairs of integers.

20. Construct the complex numbers as a set of equivalence classes of ordered pairs of real numbers.

## REFERENCES

Courant, Richard, and Herbert Robbins. *What Is Mathematics?* Oxford University Press, New York, 1941. A classic which should be in the library of every mathematics teacher. Chapters I and II pertain to numbers and number systems.

Levi, Howard. *Elements of Algebra*. Chelsea Publishing Co., New York, 1953. A short, austere, axiomatic development of the real number system and its subsystems.

Niven, Ivan. *Numbers: Rational and Irrational*, School Mathematics Study Group: New Mathematical Library 1, Random House, New York, 1961. Development of our number systems at a level which is appropriate for high school teachers.

Smith, David Eugene, *A Source Book in Mathematics*, 2 vols., Dover Publications, New York, 1959. See references 5 in Chapters 4 and 5. See also references for Chapter 10.

# ALGEBRA

Many pupils distinguish mathematics from word problems and contend they can handle the former if spared the latter. This distinction is wholly artificial. If we were to describe the mathematician's work, we would say it is more similar to solving word problems than to manipulating symbols. Nevertheless, the manipulation of algebraic symbols in accordance with certain rules is essential to anyone who intends to go on in mathematics or the physical sciences.

Equipping youngsters with technical facility in equations and the other elements of algebra is certainly a worthwhile enterprise. However, these techniques can either be learned with understanding or simply by rote as a set of unrelated, clever tricks which neither the teacher nor the pupil comprehends. If they are learned with understanding, they are likely to be remembered longer, to be more useful in courses both in and out of mathematics, and generally, to encourage a better grasp of mathematics. Every mechanical manipulation in algebra has a reason; keeping this in mind will enhance an individual's teaching and give his pupils a better feeling for mathematics. Sometimes it may not be appropriate to discuss the reasons in detail, but if a teacher can present algebra whenever possible in terms of reasons and understanding, his pupils will doubtless learn more readily, retain ability longer, and make better use of mathematics.

There are innumerable examples of rules which are stated, memorized, and used in countless exercises by pupils. Most traditional textbooks are full of such things. For example, in discussing signed numbers, a typical textbook, after considering a number line and the idea of oppositeness, might offer the following definition of absolute value:

The *absolute value* of a number is its arithmetic value without regard to the sign. Or, even worse, the *absolute value* of a number is the number with the sign dropped.[1]

Besides some of the technical difficulties involving the proper use and definition of words, these definitions are confusing to a pupil. True, they get the pupil over the immediate problem of operations with signed numbers rather quickly and informatively, but they leave him floundering in the more complicated procedures. What, for example, is the absolute value of $-x$? Most pupils would not hesitate to say that it was $x$ (even if they had reason to believe that $x$ was a negative number) on the basis of the foregoing definition.

Having presented a definition for absolute value, the traditional book might then produce several rules for the addition and subtraction of numbers, such as the following:

To add two numbers with the same sign, find the sum of their absolute values and prefix to this their common sign.

To add two numbers having unlike signs, find the difference between their absolute values and prefix to this the sign of the number which has the greater absolute value.

There might or might not be any discussion about the source of these rules, but in any case, most pupils end with the feeling that there is something mystical to the way in which these rules appear. But the pupils do not have much time to ponder the matter before they are compelled to employ the rules on 100 or more exercises which are meant to help them remember the rules. Of course, the authors are careful not to include any exercises that do not happen to fit these rules ($-3 + 3$, or $0 + (-2)$, for example), and nobody cares whether the pupils think there is any reason for any of these manipulations. The pupils are supposed to accept these procedures because they have been told to do so by someone who has more experience than they. Of course, the pupils who are likely to become mathematicians, tend to ask "why?" Even when discouraged from asking aloud, they continue

---

[1] The usual definition of absolute value is: $|x| = x$ when $x \geq 0$ and $|x| = -x$ when $x \angle 0$. With a few examples (which he would use with pupils) the reader can see that the absolute value of a number is always nonnegative.

to ask themselves this question, and therefore, do not seem to be seriously hurt by the procedures. However, many pupils who might gain more facility in mathematics—perhaps even some who might become good mathematicians—decide that it would be easier to memorize a foreign language than to memorize mathematics, and leave the study of mathematics as quickly as possible.

This set of rules and exercises is not an isolated example. Almost every page of many traditional textbooks consists of a rule (perhaps with some attempt at explanation), one or two worked out examples, and as many exercises as would fit conveniently onto the page. Such rules might include: The product of two binomials of the form $(ax + b)$ is the product of the first two terms plus the sum of the cross products (these are *not* angry products, as the reader is undoubtedly aware) plus the product of the second terms. The examples worked out just below the statement of the rule would presumably clarify what the author was talking about.

What is wrong with the previous procedures? Several basic difficulties are involved. First of all, the sort of thing that we are teaching pupils to do through such techniques can be done more efficiently by a machine; and if that is all the child is learning to do, we would be better advised to spend our time constructing a machine which would carry on these activities. It would be cheaper to create and maintain the machine. On the other hand, if the pupil is understanding the procedures and even figuring them out for himself, he will be able to do things no machine has yet been able to do. He will be able to associate real physical problems with his mathematics; he will be able to figure out new concepts which he has not been taught;[2] and he will be able to explain what he is doing, and why, to other people.

A second difficulty with the traditional procedure is that human memory is somewhat faulty. If a person has to rely entirely on memory to recall a particular fact, he is likely to forget it or get it confused. But if he can rely partially on memory, and then figure out, at least in part, whether his memory serves him well or whether he has confused some basic notions, he is more likely to get the concept correct.

A more modern approach to the rules of operation for integers was presented in Chapter 9, and the discussion about multiplying binomials can be handled with relative ease if we agree that the distributive law and other basic laws apply to polynomials. In this case, $(ax + b)(cx + d) = (ax + b)cx + (ax + b)d$ by use of the distribu-

---

[2] It is true that some machines can do this sort of thing on an elementary level, but they do not seriously compare with the human mind in this respect—not yet, anyway.

tive law, and this, in turn, is equal to $(axcx + bcx) + (axd + bd)$ by use of the left-hand distributive law which can be easily proved using the other laws. This is equal to $acx^2 + (bcx + adx) + bd$, by use of the associative laws and the commutative law of multiplication, which equals $acx^2 + (bc + ad)x + bd$ by the distributive law. Admittedly, this takes more time to develop than just *telling* the pupils, but this procedure should require less time for them to learn and understand. They will use essentially the same procedures to solve similar problems, rather than having to memorize a new trick for each new one. Of course, children will have to have a fair amount of practice in order to make the newly learned concept a part of themselves, but practice with understanding will be far more profitable in the long run then practice without it.

## Equations and Word Problems

Many teachers of mathematics have said that the most difficult thing about teaching algebra is the word problems, and many of their pupils have agreed with them. Some teachers have avoided this difficulty simply by skipping the word problems or de-emphasizing them on the basis that "they really aren't mathematics anyway." Interestingly enough, the techniques that these teachers then proceed to teach are precisely those that are often done by machine in our society, whereas those that are skipped (the translation of a real life problem into mathematical symbolism) are the ones that require human intelligence.

There is no simple, all inclusive, method of teaching pupils how to solve problems. However, many suggestions can be made about what to do and what not to do to make algebra more comprehensible to the children.

Two places to look for trouble in solving word problems is in the reading and understanding of the problem and in the understanding of the mathematics. In effect, what we have just said could be paraphrased: if we wish to translate from one language to another, it is desirable to know and understand both languages. But it is not enough to know only the vocabulary of the two languages; we must have a feeling for both of them. Similarly, in translating a problem from English into mathematics, the pupil must first understand clearly what information is available and what is being asked for. To teach him that "is greater than" is always going to mean either $>$ or $+$ will obviously get him into trouble when the other interpretation should be used. For example, "$x$ is greater than 5," is translated $x > 5$, and "$x$ is greater than 5 by exactly 7" is translated "$x = 5 + 7$." It seems essential that pupils know the English language well and understand their mathematics if they are to become adept at translating word problems into mathematical symbolism.

If the pupil is lacking competence in English, he may spend his time more profitably in a remedial reading class than in the mathematics classroom. In our society a person can survive with almost no formal knowledge of mathematics, but it is almost impossible for him to exist without being able to speak, read, and write his mother tongue. Thus, the most important single thing the schools can do for pupils is to teach them to read, write, and speak so that they can communicate effectively with their fellow man. If the schools have not accomplished this before the pupil reaches junior high school, it is time for a really concentrated effort on the problem. To have the child go through the motions of attending other classes in which reading is a prerequisite (or ought to be) is farcical. Although undoubtedly we can teach some mathematics to an illiterate, it probably is not worth the effort.

If the pupil can read English with a reasonable amount of understanding and still seems to be having difficulty with word problems in the mathematics class, there are some things the teacher can do to help him. Part of this involves asking appropriate questions. For example, what are we trying to find? What information is available? Have we used all of the available information? Is all this information really necessary? Is the problem similar to any other we have solved? What would be a reasonable answer to the problem? If we try that answer, what happens? How can we go about getting a better one?

After the pupil has solved the problem, there are additional questions which will help him to become a better problem solver. For example, is there some other way to solve the problem? Is there some way to generalize the solution? Is there some principle which may be pertinent for future problems? And so on.

One technique suggested by two of the questions in the paragraph preceding the previous one is the process of guessing a reasonable answer and testing it for correctness. The process has two obvious advantages. First, it makes the pupil think about what type of answer will be right. Second, testing for correctness will often suggest an equation which might be solved to determine the right answer.

For example, consider the following typical "I'm thinking of a number" problem: I'm thinking of a number. Two more than three times the number is 19. What is the number?

Suppose the pupil guesses that the answer is about 5, which is really quite reasonable. How does he check to see if he is right? Presumably he multiplies 5 by 3, getting 15, and then adds 2, getting 17. He notes that this is not correct, but he also notices the procedure he used. Suppose, instead of starting with 5 as a guess, he starts with $x$; he would multiply $x$ by 3, getting $3x$, and add 2. Thus, $3x + 2$ should be 19 if $x$ is the correct answer. Now all that is necessary is that the pupil solve the equation $3x + 2 = 19$.

Sometimes the problem occurs because the pupil does not really understand the algebra. He may have learned to solve equations in a mechanical way, but he has no real idea of what he has done once he has solved the equation. Thus, we start children out in algebra by giving them easy problems (such as $5x + 2 = 22$) to solve, and when they say, "I know, the answer is 4," we ask them how they got it. If they do not get it by the method of our preference, we treat them like criminals. Obviously, any reasonably bright thirteen-year-old will have no difficulty solving the equation $5x + 2 = 22$ without algebraic manipulations, if he understands the problem. If he does not understand the problem, why would he be interested in solving it anyway, except to pass the course?

Rather than discourage the process of guessing, we really should encourage it, but at the same time encourage other methods of solving the same equation. If the pupil understands both the guessing and manipulatory techniques (substract 2 from each member and then divide each member by 5) he will certainly find cases where he prefers to use the latter technique, unless he is extremely clever or the teacher is poor at making up or finding good problems. Furthermore, if the pupil really understands both techniques, he will have a much better appreciation of what an equation is and its relation to a word problem.

At least one good teacher, who was teaching a unit on linear equations, ran into one boy who was quite successful with a method of guessing which was not at all clear to the teacher. The teacher had given the boy a problem such as $3x + 2 = 19$, figuring that the non-integral answer would keep him from guessing the right answer. The boy came up with the answer almost instantly, and the teacher asked him to explain how he got it. The boy said "I guessed." Suspecting something deeper than a random guess, the teacher pressed the point further, asking whether that was the boy's first guess? "Well, no," the boy replied, "my first guess was 5, but that came out wrong by 2, and since I multiplied the 5 by 3, I decided the answer was $5\frac{2}{3}$." The teacher, assuring the boy that he had just been lucky and that it would not happen again, went on with the class while the boy kept right on "guessing" and getting the answer before anyone else in the class.

The interesting thing about the boy's procedure, is that it is perfectly general and will work with any linear equation ($ax + b = c$), and with variations can be made to work with a large number of other equations. It is essentially the method of false position which was used by the ancient Egyptians to solve precisely this type of problem. Expressed algebraically, the boy was solving the equation $ax + b = c$, by replacing the $x$ by some number, $q$, getting $aq + b$ equal to some number $c'$. He then decided that $x$ must be equal to $q + (c - c')/a$. The reader can check to see that the procedure actually does work by replacing $x$ by the quantity $q + (c - c')/a$ in the equation $ax + b = c$, and then replacing $c'$ by $aq + b$. The pupil in question later majored in mathematics in one of our leading universities, and has since learned how to solve equations in the usual way; in fact, there is some reason to believe that he already knew how to do them properly, but was just trying to be difficult, or interesting. The point is that if we teach with understanding and try to encourage the children to understand and question, we achieve better results in the long run.

Procedures used with problems involving systems of equations are similar to that used with problems that require only one equation. However, one warning ought to be made. Often we teach children to solve problems by using only one equation when solutions could also be found by using two equations.

For example, the larger of two numbers is twice the smaller. The sum of the two is 21. What are the numbers?

> *Solution:*   Smaller number: $x$
> Larger number: $2x$
> Therefore, $x + 2x = 21$, $3x = 21$, and $x = 7$, $2x = 14$.

Later, we try to force the children to solve the exact same type of problem using two equations in two unknowns and cannot understand why they object:

> Smaller number: $x$
> Larger number: $y$
> Therefore, $y = 2x$
> $$x + y = 21$$

By substitution, (or subtraction): $3x = 21$, and $x = 7$; therefore, $y = 2(7) = 14$.

A quick glance at the length of the two methods should tell anybody why the pupils prefer the former to the latter. Even if the former were not taught first, pupils might very easily prefer it. Of course, there are many problems which are much more complicated and for which any normal person will have to use more than one equation, but we do not usually begin with those.

What should we do in a case like this? There are several answers. First, if we have made it a habit to encourage the pupils to try to solve each problem in several ways, rather than solving several problems in one way, they will not find it unusual or unreasonable to be asked to solve this type of problem in more than one way. Second, to show them the advantage of the new method of solving problems (using several equations in several unknowns) the teacher should try to present complicated problems rather quickly and encourage the class to use both methods in solving them. This must not be offered as a challenge indicating an attempt to ruffle those who refuse to accept the teacher's assertion that this is a better way to work the problem. Such a tactic is demoralizing. If the pupils can do the problems their way, they will maintain that their procedure is easier, simply to counter the teacher's opinion. The best approach is to give them the problem and let them solve it by as many means as they can before deciding without pressure from the teacher which is the preferable method.

Once the pupils are able to set up an equation, or a system of equations, there will be several ways in which they can go about solving them. Perhaps the procedure that involves most understanding and yet is mechanical enough so that the majority of pupils can become quite proficient at it is the method of *equivalent equations* (or equivalent inequalities). Equivalent equations are equations having identical solution sets. It can be shown that certain operations performed on both members of an equation produce an equivalent equation; then, the procedure of producing a simple equivalent equation is similar (hopefully with more understanding) to older methods of solving equations.

For systems of equations, two basic principles are used. First, if any equation of a system is replaced by an equivalent equation, then the new system is equivalent to the old system. This fact seems clear from the definitions of equivalent equations and equivalent systems. Second, if an equation of a system is replaced by its sum with another equation of the system, then the new system is equivalent to the old one. This is not quite so obvious as the first principle. It can be demonstrated in the following way.

Suppose $(x_1, y_1, z_1, \ldots w_1)$ is a member of the solution set of the system:

$$1. \quad ax + by + cz + \cdots + ew + g = 0$$
$$2. \quad hx + jy + kz + \cdots + mw + n = 0$$
$$\cdots\cdots\cdots\cdots\cdots\cdots\cdots\cdots\cdots\cdots\cdots$$
$$px + qy + rz + \cdots + sw + t = 0$$

Now, suppose that equations 1 and 2 are added together; by this we mean that the left members are added and the right members are added to give the left and right members of a new equation. If $(x_1, y_1, z_1, \ldots w_1)$ makes both equations true statements, which would have to be the case if it is a member of the solution set of the system, then by the rules for real numbers it would also have to make the sum a true statement. Therefore, if Equation 1 is replaced by the new equation, the new system will have $(x_1, y_1, z_1, \ldots w_1)$ as a root and also any other roots from the old system. Thus, anything that was a root of the old system will also be a root of the new. By a similar argument (multiplying each member of equation 2 by $-1$ and adding to the new equation) it can be shown that anything that is a root of the new system is a root of the old, too.

Using the principles for equivalent systems, we would show that the following systems are equivalent:

$$\text{I} \begin{cases} 2x + 3y - 7 = 0 \\ 5x + 6y + 2 = 0 \end{cases} \qquad \text{II} \begin{cases} -4x - 6y + 14 = 0 \\ 5x + 6y + 2 = 0 \end{cases}$$

$$\text{III} \begin{cases} x + 16 = 0 \\ 5x + 6y + 2 = 0 \end{cases} \qquad \text{IV} \begin{cases} -5x - 80 = 0 \\ 5x + 6y + 2 = 0 \end{cases}$$

$$\text{V} \begin{cases} -5x - 80 = 0 \\ 6y - 78 = 0 \end{cases} \qquad \text{VI} \begin{cases} x = -16 \\ y = 13 \end{cases}$$

The principle of replacing an equation by an equivalent equation shows that I is equivalent to II, III is equivalent to IV, and V is equivalent to VI; and the principle of replacing an equation by its sum with another equation in the system shows that II is equivalent to III and IV is equivalent to V. From a purist point of view, we have accomplished nothing so far. From a practical point of view, the root of the system $(-16, 13)$ is more obvious from VI than from I.

Conceivably the reader can develop a more efficient method of finding the root of the previous system, but this method has the advantage of being quite general, easily justified, and easy to understand, and sufficiently similar to procedures with matrices (or determinants) to be used in justifying more advanced mathematical procedures at a later time.

## Inequalities

In many of the newer mathematics textbooks, equations and inequalities are treated together or in close proximity to one another. This is desirable, since much modern usuage of equations is in association with inequalities. Working with inequalities has generally become very important, not only in higher mathematics courses, but also in practical problems of industry, physical sciences, social sciences, and almost everywhere that mathematics is used.

Simple inequalities with one variable are now introduced rather commonly in the junior high school mathematics classes. Certainly, every child entering the ninth grade should have seen, and be familiar with, the symbols ">", "<", "$\geq$", and "$\leq$." Furthermore, he should have had enough experience graphing inequalities on a number line so that he could graph the solution set of $x < 5$ and perhaps even determine that the graph of the inequality is the same as the graph of $2x < 10$. Formal manipulations with such inequalities then become reasonably easy to justify. The most difficult of these is the one concerning multiplication of both members of an inequality by a negative number. This says that if $a > b$, and $c < 0$, then $bc > ac$. In general, pupils will believe that if $a > b$, then $ac > bc$ for all values of $c$ until they see an example to the contrary. Probably the best way to convince them that their conception is false is to give them several specific examples. First, they might be given $5 > 3$, and told to multiply by 7, getting $35 > 21$. This is fine. Next, $5 > 3$, multiply by zero, getting $0 > 0$. Since zero is different from other numbers in a lot of ways; they may believe it is the only exception. Now, try $5 > 3$, multiply by $-1$, and $-5 > -3$, or multiply by $-7$, and $-35 > -21$. Something must be wrong.

Let us take a look at the number line. Suppose, in Fig. 10.1, that $b > a$ and both $a$ and $b$ are positive:

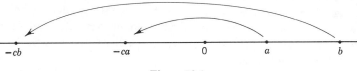

Figure 10.1

Notice that in multiplying by a negative number the products are relatively the same distance from zero as the multiplicands but on the opposite side of the origin; therefore if $b > a$, and $-c < 0$, then $-ca > -cb$. In a similar way, if one number is positive and the other negative, both will change sides and therefore their order. If both are negative, the situation is similar to that pictured in Fig. 10.1.

If a fairly formal definition of order has been used, it is possible to prove the foregoing result rigorously. The reader will recall our saying that order, in the usual sense, has a close connection with the operations of addition and multiplication. In particular, a field such as the rational or real number system is said to be ordered if it has a subset $P$ (the positive numbers) such that $P$ is closed under addition and multiplication, and every element, $n$, of the field satisfies precisely one of the following: (1) $n \in P$, (2) $n = 0$, (3) $-n \in P$. Now, we say that $p > q$ if and only if $(p - q) \in P$.

To prove that if $a > b$ and $c > 0$, then $ac > bc$, we proceed as follows.

$(a - b) \in P$, and $(c - 0) = c \in P$ by the definition of $>$.
$c(a - b) \in P$ because $P$ is closed under multiplication.
$(ca - cb) \in P$ by the distributive law (and substitution).
$ca > cb$ by the definition of $>$.

The proof for the other case is similar:

THEOREM.    If $a > b$ and $c < 0$, then $bc > ac$. By definition,

$$c < 0 \text{ means } 0 > c$$

*Proof.*    $(a - b) \in P$ and $(0 - c) = -c \in P$ (definition)
Therefore            $(-c)(a - b) \in P$    (closure for $P$)
and                        $(-ca + cb) \in P$
So                          $(bc - ac) \in P$

and by the definition of $>$, $bc > ac$.

This definition of order is somewhat austere for ninth graders since it does not seem to have much to do with their experience. However, it would seem reasonable to use it with eleventh graders, after they have had some experience with formal definitions. The definition is convenient to use in proofs involving inequalities and makes the concept of order quite specific.

Solving inequalities that involve more than one variable is interesting, useful, and at times, a little tricky. It is surprising how often good teachers with excellent backgrounds in mathematics are led into an attempt to solve a system of linear inequalities in two unknowns by purely algebraic means.

For example, to solve the system of inequalities,

$$\begin{cases} x + 2y > 7 \\ x - 2y > 5 \end{cases}$$

such an individual would add the inequalities to get $2x > 12$, or $x > 6$; and subtract the inequalities to get $4y > 2$ or $y > \frac{1}{2}$. Thus, the simple pair of inequalities

$$\begin{cases} x > 6 \\ y > \tfrac{1}{2} \end{cases}$$

replaces the more complicated system

$$\begin{cases} x + 2y > 7 \\ x - 2y > 5 \end{cases}$$

Of course, this procedure is entirely incorrect, and the teacher should be careful to avoid it. He should also know the reason it does not work in case some pupil suggests it. It is true that if $a > b$ and $c > d$, then $a + c > b + d$; therefore, it is true that anything that satisfies the first pair of inequalities must also satisfy the inequality $x > 6$. However, it is not true that if $a + c > b + d$, then $a > b$, and $c > d$. For example, $6 + 6 > 7 + 3$, but it is not true that $6 > 7$ and $6 > 3$. Thus, it would be quite surprising if the new system of equations turned out to be equivalent to the old. The second operation (subtraction) performed on the two inequalities is wrong in both ways: it is not true that if $a > b$ and $c > d$, then $a - c > b - d$, nor that if $a - c > b - d$, then $a > b$ and $c > d$. The reader can find counterexamples for both propositions without much difficulty.

Generally, the procedure used to solve a pair of linear inequalities (or any system of inequalities containing more than one variable) is to graph the solution sets of the inequalities, and the intersection of the solution sets will be the solution set of the system. Usually, there is no simple algebraic way to write down such an answer, but the graphic solution will make it relatively easy to decide whether a particular ordered pair is in the solution set.

To use the graphic approach to the foregoing problem, we would start by graphing the two equations $x + 2y = 7$ and $x - 2y = 5$ (Fig. 10.2). The resulting lines each divide the plane into two parts. It is possible to convince children that one of those parts must be the graph of the solution set of $x + 2y > 7$. This can be done as follows: Suppose an ordered pair, $(x, y)$ satisfied the equation $x + 2y = 7$; what would we know about the graph of the pair $(x, y)$? The pair is a point on the line with equation $x + 2y = 7$. Suppose the pair $(x, y)$ did not satisfy the equation $x + 2y = 7$; what about the point and the line then? The point would not be on the line. Suppose the ordered pair $(x, y)$ *almost* satisfied the equation—that is, $x + 2y$ turned out to be 7.001—where would the point be? It would be very close to the line. If the children have trouble on this one, several examples may be used. Now what will happen to the point if the value of $x$ increases so that the value of $x + 2y$ increases? It will move farther away from the line. But what if the value of $x$ decreases until the sum is 7 again, and then continues to decrease until the value of $x + 2y$ becomes less than 7? The point gets closer to the line, then is on the line, and eventually crosses over to the other side.

Continued pursuit of this line of questioning with both $x$ and $y$ changing in various ways will leave the pupils convinced of the appropriate result.

The only remaining question is, which side of the line corresponds to the solution set of $x + 2y > 7$? Many pupils will respond that it must be the side above the line, since the $>$ symbol was used. Even though the answer happens to be correct in this case, the reason is not correct; by that reasoning, the solution set of $7 < x + 2y$ would be below the line, which contradicts the previous answer. This procedure would also not work for the second half of this problem. Rather, we choose one point, not on the line, replace the variables in the inequality with its coordinates, and see whether it is in the solution set. If it is, the point is on the correct side. If it is not, the point is on the wrong side. We might try the point (4, 2). Since (4) + 2(2) = 8 which is greater than 7, the point with coordinates (4, 2) must be on the correct side of the line, and the graph of the solution set for $x + 2y > 7$ is the half-plane above the line. Notice that the arithmetic involved in using such numbers as 4 and 2 might get a little complicated with more complex inequalities, and, more important, it is not always clear which side of the line such a point is on, without careful plotting.

One point has simple coordinates, and is already plotted on the graph. Usually, it is not necessary to call this to the attention of pupils; some of them will find out for themselves rather quickly that the origin is convenient to use for this purpose. Had we tried the coordinates of the origin in the inequality $x + 2y > 7$, we would have found that for this pair the inequality says that $0 > 7$ which is false, and therefore, the origin is not a point on the graph of the solution set. In a similar way, the graph of $x - 2y > 5$ can be plotted, and the intersection of the solution sets is shown in Fig. 10.2 by the cross-hatching.

From the graph in Fig. 10.2 it should be clear that no simple pair of inequalities such as $\begin{cases} x > 6 \\ y > \frac{1}{2} \end{cases}$ could possibly have the same solution set, since the lines corresponding to $x = 6$ and $y = \frac{1}{2}$ are parallel to the axes. Therefore, the solution set of this new pair of inequalities must be the interior of a right angle that has sides parallel to the axes—clearly not the desired solution set.

Once pupils have learned to solve simple systems of linear inequali-

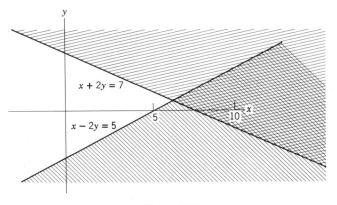

Figure 10.2

ties, there is no reason why they cannot solve problems in linear programming. To be sure, the problems will have to be kept simple, but the relevant principles they contain can be brought out, and the problems made realistic enough to give the pupils a feeling for the usefulness of such procedures. Consider the following example, for instance.

A farmer has 200 acres to plant and 300 hours of labor with which to do the work. He wishes to plant two crops, one of which (crop $B$) takes one hour per acre to plant and the other of which (crop $A$) takes two hours per acre to plant. If the profit per acre on crop $B$ is $5, and the profit per acre on crop $A$ is $8, how much of the acreage should be planted with crop $A$ and how much with crop $B$? What will the farmer's profit be?

*Solution.*    Let $x$ be the number of acres planted with crop $A$ and $y$ the number of acres planted with crop $B$.

What is the least number $x$ can be? What is the least $y$ can be? Then, must the following inequalities be satisfied by the solution: $x \geq 0$, and $y \geq 0$? If there are only 200 acres to be planted, what can we say about the sum of $x$ and $y$? If it takes two hours per acre to plant crop $A$ and $x$ acres are planted, how many hours are required to plant crop $A$? How many hours are required to plant crop $B$? Then, how many hours are required to plant both crops? Must this number be less than or equal to 300? Then, the following four inequalities must be satisfied.

$$x \geq 0$$
$$y \geq 0$$
$$x + y \leq 200$$
$$2x + y \leq 300$$

The graph of the solution set of these four inequalities appears in Fig. 10.3.

To avoid unnecessary confusion, inequalities such as $x \geq 0$ and $y \geq 0$ are not usually plotted, and we simply limit consideration to the first quadrant if these inequalities are to hold. However, we still do not know what is the best answer for the farmer, we simply know the possible answers. From the graph, it is clear that he could plant all 200 acres in crop $B$ but would then not use up all of his hours of labor; or he could plant 150 acres in crop $A$; or could plant 50 acres of each (in which case he would not use up either his labor or his land); etc. But which of the possible cases will result in the most profit?

Let us suppose that the farmer decides he wants to make a profit of \$1000. Can he do it, and if so, how? We know that he makes a profit of \$8 per acre on crop $A$ and \$5 per acre on crop $B$, so his total profit $(P)$ must be $P = 8x + 5y$ dollars. If $P$ is supposed to be 1000, we can plot the graph of $1000 = 8x + 5y$ to see whether it intersects our solution set (Fig. 10.4). The graph of $1000 = 8x + 5y$ does intersect the solution set in many points. If the farmer wanted to make a profit of \$1000, he could do it by planting all 200 acres in crop $B$; he could do it by planting 125 acres in crop $A$; he could do it by planting 100 acres in crop $A$ and 40 acres in crop $B$, and so on. However, there is doubt that \$1000 is the greatest profit the farmer can make.

Suppose he wanted to make a profit of \$1500, how would he check to see if he could do that? Presumably, he would graph the line corresponding to $8x + 5y = 1500$. What relation would this line have to

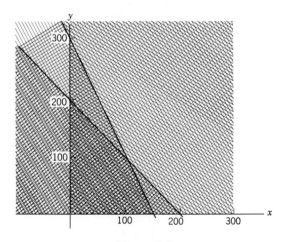

Figure 10.3

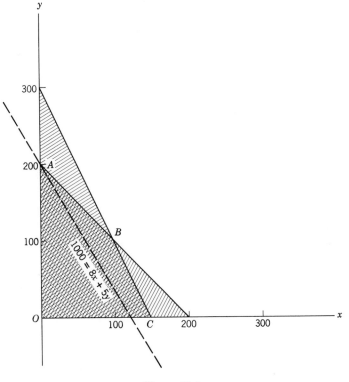

Figure 10.4

the one already graphed? Would the two be parallel? In fact, would all of the profit lines be parallel to each other? Then, would the profit line that is farthest to the right and up but still passing through a point of the solution set be the one representing the greatest profit the farmer could make? Through what point would such a line pass? From the graph, it looks as though it would be either point $B$ or point $C$—probably point $B$. Let us check. At point $C$, with coordinates (150, 0), the profit would be $8(150) + 5(0) = 1200$. At point $B$, with coordinates (100, 100), the profit would be $8(100) + 5(100) = 1300$. The greatest profit can be made by planting 100 acres of each crop, and the profit is $1,300.

Let us reconsider the procedure. We noticed that all of the profit lines are parallel to each other. Since the solution set of the system of inequalities is a convex polygon and its interior, it seems clear that the profit line representing the greatest profit will either go through one vertex of the polygon or along one side of the polygon. If it goes along one side of the polygon, it must go through two vertices. In any case, it seems that we can find the greatest profit simply by checking all of the vertices (without constructing profit lines). In this case, the vertices have coordinates (0, 0), (0, 200), (100, 100), and (150, 0). The corresponding profits are 0, 1000, 1300, and 1200. Therefore, the best answer is (100, 100) with a profit of $1300.

If the market changed so that the profit for crop $A$ was $10 per acre, what would the best solution be? Suppose the market changed again so that the profit per acre on crop $A$ was $12.50 per acre, what is the best solution and what is the profit? The reader can figure out the answers to these questions quite easily, but he should notice that in some cases there will be more than one possible solution, and the mathematics does not tell us which one to use. In other cases, it may seem that we are wasting either land or labor, since we do not use all that is available; however, if the desire is to create the largest profit, it may just happen that we will run out of time or land before the other is exhausted.

The procedure used here is not difficult, and has been taught with considerable success to ninth-grade pupils. It certainly gives them a feeling for one good practical use of inequalities.

### Systems and Proofs

Up until the beginning of the nineteenth century, algebra consisted largely of a set of rules and tricks for manipulating symbols in order to solve various problems. Mathematicians had learned to solve quadratic, cubic, and fourth-degree equations by use of radicals. However, they were not able to take the next step and solve the general fifth-degree equation. The world of algebra was waiting for a mathematician to come along who was clever enough, or lucky enough, to figure out how to solve the fifth-degree equation. Mathematicians had learned to get approximate roots for such equations using graphic methods, but there seemed to be no solution which used radicals. Then, in 1824, the young Norwegian mathematician, Neils Henrik Abel, proved that it was not possible to solve the general fifth-degree equation using a finite number of algebraic operations (including radicals). Abel died five years later (at the age of twenty-six) before seeing the more general work of the even younger French mathematician, Evariste Galois. Galois provided necessary and sufficient conditions for the solution by algebraic means of any polynomial equation. Tragically, Galois died in a duel at the age of twenty (in 1832), terminating another great mathematical career. Before their untimely deaths, these two young men had set the stage for the appearance of modern algebra.

In order to produce their remarkable results, the two mathematicians looked for properties of the equations they were considering without limiting their view to the specific numerical coefficients. Thus, they began to look at the basic properties of the system from which their elements were taken. Galois created a theory of groups noting that it was not the individual elements of the group which provided important properties, but rather the relations among elements of the group (a group is a set of elements with one operation defined which satisfies certain basic properties; groups will be discussed more fully in the next several pages).

Thus, a little over 100 years ago, mathematicians realized that they could learn more about algebra by studying the basic underlying structure of mathematical systems than by trying to discover new tricks to solve specific problems. This emphasis on structure is now finding its way into the elementary algebra of the high school where it is being used to unify the topic of algebra and make it more meaningful to pupils.

In Chapter 9, we considered various number systems, and their underlying structures were summarized in a set of axioms or principles. Three of the number systems considered were fields (the rational number system, the real number system, and the complex number system), whereas the other two (the natural number system and the system of integers) had some of the properties of a field, but not all. Such development of number systems with great reliance on the underlying structure is typical of modern algebra. In the school mathematics course, reliance on structure provides pupils with a few general reasons rather than hundreds of tricks and puts the emphasis on thinking and proving rather than remembering and manipulating. Of course, it is still necessary to develop the ability to manipulate, but it is done with understanding.

In this section, we shall consider another structure which is closely related to a field, and give examples of different systems from elementary mathematics which have this structure.

A *group* is a set of elements having one binary operation defined. Each group is closed, associative, has an identity element, and has inverses (with respect to the operation). Thus, one example of a group is the set of integers with the operation of addition. Another example of a group is the set of nonzero rational numbers under the operation of multiplication. Notice that this system is closed under multiplication since the product of two numbers cannot be zero unless one of them is zero (and multiplication was closed for the rational numbers before we removed zero). There are many other systems with which the reader is familiar that are also groups—it may be of interest for him to find some of these on his own, and show that they really are groups.

If the reader had never heard of a group before, he would probably be surprised at the omission of an important property from the list of properties of a group. Is not a group commutative? All of the groups considered above are commutative. However, there are many groups which are of interest that do not happen to have the property of commutativity. Therefore, when a group has this property, we give it a special name—we call it a commutative group, or an abelian group (after Abel).

Now, let us consider a group in which the elements and operation are reasonably familiar to the high school algebra student, but that is not abelian (or commutative). Consider the set of all linear functions (in which the second element of an ordered pair is determined from the first by using an expression of the form $ax + b$ where $a$ and $b$ are real numbers and $a \neq 0$). As our operation, let us use composition of functions. By composition we mean that if the function $f$ is determined by $ax + b$ and the function $g$ is determined by $rx + s$, then the composition, $f$ of $g$ (also written $f(g(x))$) is determined by $a(rx + s) + b$.

First let us show that our system is closed under the operation of composition. $a(rx + s) + b = arx + as + b = (ar)x + (as + b)$. If $a$, $b$, $r$, and $s$ are real numbers ($a, r \neq 0$), then so are $ar(\neq 0)$ and $as + b$, and the system is closed.

Before tackling the associative law, some notation will help. When we wish to indicate the composition of two functions, $f$ and $g$, we will sometimes write "$f°g$" to indicate the function $f(g(x))$; this will reduce the need for some parentheses, as well as making the operation of composition look more like the usual operations with which we are familiar. To show that composition is associative, we must show that $f°(g°h) = (f°g)°h$ for any linear functions. Let $f$ be determined by $ax + b$, $g$ by $cy + d$, and $h$ by $rz + s$.
Then,

$$g°h = c(rz + s) + d = crz + cs + d$$

and

$$f°(g°h) = a(crz + cs + d) + b = acrz + acs + ad + b$$

On the other hand,

$$f°g = a(cy + d) + b = acy + ad + b$$

and therefore,

$$(f°g)°h = ac(rz + s) + ad + b = acrz + acs + ad + b$$

Therefore, composition of linear functions is associative.

The identity element for composition of linear functions is obviously the function determined by $x$ (or $1x + 0$). In order to show that there are inverses for the operation of composition, let us find the inverse of a function determined by the expression $ax + b$. If $cx + d$ is to be the inverse of $ax + b$, $a(cx + d) + b$ must equal $x$, and $c(ax + b) + d$ must also equal $x$. Considering the first condition, we find that $acx + ad + b = x$, and therefore, since two linear functions are equal only if the coefficients of corresponding terms of the defining expressions are equal, $ac = 1$, and $ad + b = 0$. From this we find that $c = 1/a$ and $d = -b/a$. Therefore, the inverse of the function defined by $as + b$ is apparently the function defined by $(1/a)x - b/a$. In order to check this, we must consider two cases:

1. $a(1/a\ x - b/a) + b = x - b + b = x$.
2. $(1/a)(ax + b) - b/a = x + b/a - b/a = x$.

Since both cases are satisfied, and both $1/a$ and $-b/a$ are real numbers ($a \neq 0$ from the definition of a linear function), every linear function has an inverse.

It is worth noticing that both cases had to be considered since we had not considered commutativity yet. Actually, it can be proved that in a group (commutative or not) if case 1 holds, then case 2 must hold, but that proof is somewhat advanced for high school pupils.

Is this group commutative? If it is, $a(cx + d) + b = c(ax + b) + d$ for all real numbers $a$, $b$, $c$, and $d$ ($a, c \neq 0$). But this means that $acx + ad + b = cax + cb + d$, which requires that $ad + b = cb + d$ for all real numbers $a$, $b$, $c$, and $d$ ($a, c \neq 0$). It is easy to find a counterexample for this last statement: choose $b = 0$ and $a$ equal to any number but 1, for example. Thus, the group is not commutative.

There are other noncommutative groups which can be constructed from the materials of high school mathematics. One of these is the group of distance-preserving geometric transformations. It can be shown that all such transformations can be written as a composition of rotations (rotating the plane about a point), translations (moving the plane in one direction), and reflections (pairing each point of a plane with its mirror image in a line of the plane, or rotating the plane in three dimensions 180° around the line or axis of symmetry). The system of such transformations under the operation of composition is a group, but is again a noncommutative group.

This last group and the group of linear functions are closely associated, since the group of linear functions is, essentially, a group of transformations on a line (thought of as a number line, in this case). If $a = 1$, the transformations are translations; if $a = -1$ and $b = 0$, the transformation is a reflection; and if $a = -1$ with $b \neq 0$, the transformation can be thought of as a reflection followed by a translation. Of course, there are no rotations (unless a reflection is to be thought of as a rotation of 180° in the second dimension) on a line. The linear transformations include expansions and contractions when $a$ is not 1 or $-1$.

Many other systems can be thought of as groups, including such things as furniture moving and positions of a triangle (under rotations and reflections). Having studied a basic algebraic structure, we can find many examples of that structure throughout mathematics and the real world. If we have proved some theorems about the structure from several basic principles, we will know that those theorems are true about any other system that satisfies the same general principles. This not only is a saving in time and energy, but it can also lead us to discover facts which we would never have suspected if we had not looked at a situation from the abstract point of view.

Mathematical structure will continue to play an increasingly important role in modern mathematics and in the teaching of contemporary high school mathematics courses. The teacher will do well to study mathematical systems as systems, to understand the role of structure in modern mathematics, and to communicate this understanding to his pupils.

### Exponential and Logarithmic Functions

One of the topics of algebra which has changed most in the past several years is the topic of logarithms. One hundred years ago, the principal reason for teaching logarithms was to enable students to carry out long computations quickly and easily. At present, most such computations are not done with logarithms. They may be done with slide rules when a small degree of accuracy is needed, otherwise they may be carried out with high speed computers. This does not mean that the study of logarithms is no longer desirable, but that acquiring a great deal of proficiency in computing with logarithms is no longer important enough to spend long hours learning laborious calculations. High school pupils can spend their time and energy learning more important things.

There are important facts to be learned about logarithms. In general, the logarithmic function should be studied as a function, and its relation to the exponential function should be considered in some detail—with a careful study of each in its own right. In studying the exponential function in high school, it is necessary to be a little vague about the question of real number exponents, since a thorough development of this topic is well beyond the scope of a normal high school mathematics curriculum. Once this obstacle has been passed, and the pupils have agreed that real number exponents ought to follow the same rules as rational number exponents, it is possible to pursue a reasonably extensive study of exponential functions. If the formula $y = b^x$ determines the function, various values of $b$ can be considered to show that if $b > 1$, the function is always increasing (monotonically increasing) whereas if $1 > b > 0$, the function is decreasing (the graph "falls" as we move from left to right). If $b = 1$, the function is a constant, and is not really of much interest except as the limiting case as $b$ approaches 1. For $b < 0$, the exponential function is not defined in elementary mathematics, since there would be some question, for example, as to whether $-2\pi$ is a positive or negative number.

Having considered the exponential function, the pupils are now ready to tackle the inverse of the exponential function. Notice that one advantage of the ordered pair approach to functions is that it is so easy to define the inverse of a function: we simply interchange the members of each ordered pair. From this definition, there is no guarantee that the inverse of a function is necessarily a function, but since the interesting cases of the exponential function are either monotonically increasing or monotonically decreasing for a given value of $b$, there is exactly one value of $b^x$ for every value of $x$, and for every value $b^x$ which is defined ($b^x > 0$), there will be exactly one value of $x$. The inverse of an exponential function is therefore a function. For a particular value of $b$, say 2, we can graph the exponential function and its inverse to see the relationship between the two (Fig. 10.5).

From Fig. 10.5, the relationship between a function and its inverse becomes apparent. The graphs are symmetric in the line $x = y$, which is what one would expect since the $x$ and $y$ values have been interchanged. Using the information acquired about the exponential function, we can find out many things about the new logarithmic function. In general, if the pupil will keep the definition of the logarithmic function firmly in mind, he should have little trouble determining all of the salient facts about logarithms. That is, if the pupils will remember that (for $b > 0$, and $b \neq 1$) $x = \log_b y$, if and only if $y = b^x$, he can derive most of the other important facts about logarithms from his knowledge of exponents.

We shall not take the time to consider all the facts about logarithms

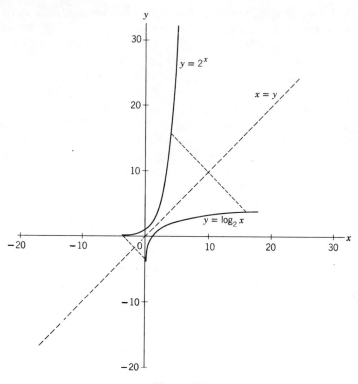

Figure 10.5

here, but the pupil should have some practice carrying on simple operations with logarithms to a base other than 10 (2, for example) to get a feeling for the topic before he goes into the base-10 logarithms. Then some discussion of which base would be most convenient might easily follow, with the fact that if, for example, logarithm (base 10) of 1.732 were known, then the logarithm of 17.32 would be greater by one, the logarithm of 1732 would be three greater than the logarithm of 1.732, and so on. Thus, a relatively compact table could be used to find the logarithms to the base 10 of many numbers in a rather simple way. On the other hand, if two is used as the base, and the logarithm of 1.732 is known, the logarithm of $2 \times 1.732$ is one more than that, and the logarithm of $8 \times 1.732$ is three more than the known logarithm. None of these are convenient facts to know.

Once the pupils have decided that logarithms to the base 10 are convenient, they should undertake some practice using them in simple exercises such as multiplying two numbers, dividing one number by another, multiplying several numbers together, and carrying on other operations. However, the huge numbers of practice exercises which were once insisted upon are no longer appropriate. Rather, the pupils should spend some time finding roots and large powers of numbers, since logarithms are particularly well suited for this sort of thing, and exponential equations could easily be studied in some detail because of the applicability of logarithms to this topic. Furthermore, some applied problems (compound interest, a few triangle solutions, etc.) could also be included with some benefit.

## Induction and the Binomial Theorem

The word "induction" means many different things. When associated with proofs, it is most commonly thought of as the procedure by which we jump to a conclusion about a whole population after having observed only a part of it. For example, after having seen 100 dogs and noticing that they all weigh more than ten pounds, we might conclude that all dogs weighed more than ten pounds. Or, having noticed that the sun rises every morning (though sometimes behind clouds) we might reach the conclusion that the sun will always rise in the morning. This procedure is often called scientific induction or even logical induction. It is not the same thing as mathematical induction which we shall discuss in this section. A proof by mathematical induction is a real proof (a *deductive proof*, in fact), and it is not possible by continuing to observe more cases to find an exception to a rule that has been proved by mathematical induction.

In mathematical induction, we know that a certain statement (or theorem) is true for the number 1 and we also know that whenever the statement is true of a number ($n$) it must be true of the next number ($n + 1$). Thus, since we know that the statement is true of 1, it must be true of the number after 1, or 2; now, since we know it is true of 2, it must be true of the number after 2, or 3; but, if it is true of 3, then it must be true of 4; and if it is true of 4 it must be true of 5; and so on. From this, we conclude that the statement is true for all natural numbers.

Before actually using the induction principle to prove a theorem, let us first show that it must be true. In order to do this, we assume that every nonempty subset of the positive integers has a least element. This assumption is usually acceptable to high school pupils; in fact, if it is not mentioned explicitly, they will not even notice its use in the following proof.

Given: The theorem $T$ is true of the number 1; we write this fact:

$T(1)$. If $T$ is true of $n$, then it is true of $n + 1$, written: $T(n)$ implies $T(n + 1)$.

To prove: $T$ is true of all positive integers.

*Proof.*    Suppose $T$ is not true of all positive integers. Then there must be a least positive integer, call it $q$, for which $T$ is not true. $q$ cannot be 1, since we know that $T(1)$. Therefore, $q - 1$ must be a positive integer for which $T$ is true (since $q - 1$ is less than $q$ and $q$ is the least integer for which $T$ is not true). But, by hypothesis, if $T(q - 1)$ is true, then $T(q)$ is true in contradiction to the assumption that $T(q)$ is not true. Therefore, $T$ must be true of all the positive integers.

It may take some doing to convince all pupils, no matter how bright they are, that a proof by induction really works. Examples such as standing up a set of dominoes so that if one is knocked down the next one will be knocked down and then asking what will happen if the first one is knocked down may be of some help. Of course, it is not really necessary to set the dominoes up—describing the experiment should be sufficient.

Once most of the pupils have accepted the principle, it can be used to prove some simple theorems. For example, what is the sum of the first $n$ odd integers?

$$1 = 1$$
$$1 + 3 = 4$$
$$1 + 3 + 5 = 9$$
$$1 + 3 + 5 + 7 = 16$$
$$1 + 3 + 5 + 7 + 9 = 25$$
$$1 + 3 + 5 + 7 + 9 + 11 = 36$$
$$1 + 3 + 5 + 7 + 9 + 11 + 13 = 49$$

Is there a pattern? What is it? Is the sum of the first four positive integers equal to $4^2$ or 16? Would the sum of the first eight positive integers be $8^2$ or 64? Does it seem reasonable to suppose that the sum of the first $n$ integers is probably $n^2$? So far, we have proved nothing. In fact, what we have done is to use scientific induction to reach a conclusion. There is nothing wrong with this procedure—mathematicians use it all the time—but it is not a mathematical proof. We have only conjectured so far. Probably the reason mathematical induction is given that name is because scientific induction so often plays an important role in determining what we ought to try to prove by mathematical induction.

Our theorem says that the sum of the first $n$ odd numbers is $n^2$. We know that this is true (trivially) for the integer 1. Let us see if we can prove that when it is true for some integer $q$ it is true for $q + 1$.

Assume

$$1 + 3 + 5 + 7 + 9 + 11 + \cdots + (2q - 3) + (2q - 1) = q^2$$

(Notice that $2q - 1$ is the $q$th positive integer, and $2q + 1$ is the $(q + 1)$th integer.) If the theorem is to be true for $q + 1$, $1 + 3 + 5 + \cdots + (2q - 3) + (2q - 1) + (2q + 1)$ must equal $(q + 1)^2$. Add $(2q + 1)$ to both members of the equation in our assumption, then:

$$1 + 3 + 5 + \cdots + (2q - 3) + (2q - 1) + (2q + 1)$$
$$= q^2 + 2q + 1 = (q + 1)^2$$

which was to be proved. We have shown that the sum of the first odd integer is $1^2$, and that if the sum of the first $q$ integers is $q^2$ then the sum of the first $(q + 1)$ odd integers is $(q + 1)^2$. Therefore, we can conclude, from the principle of induction, that the sum of the first $n$ odd positive integers is $n^2$.

The reader should keep in mind several facts about this discussion. First, the discovery of what theorem to prove is an important part of the procedure; in fact, in many respects, it is the most important part of the procedure. No matter how good we are at proving things, if we do not know what to prove, there is not much to accomplish. Second, the question of notation is important. It would have been correct to use the variable $n$ where we have used $q$ but it would have been confusing. One thing that annoys pupils most about mathematical induction is that in the second part, we seem to assume what we are trying to prove. That is, we want to prove that the theorem is true for all positive integers, $n$, and assume that it is true for $n$. This difficulty can be partially overcome by the careful choice of variables, but if it persists, we must have a discussion of inductive proof and implication. In the second part of the induction proof, what we are proving is that *if* the theorem is true for some number *then* it is true for the next one. We make no claim that it *is* true for any number at this time, nor do we *assume* that it is true for any number. As discussed in Chapter 8, there is no need for $p$ to be true in the statement "$p$ implies $q$," yet if $p$ happens to be true, $q$ must also be true. Having proved the theorem (or subtheorem) that if our statement is true about $n$ then it is also true of $n + 1$, and the theorem that our statement is true about 1, we can conclude (by mathematical induction) that our statement is true of all positive integers.

Induction is usually thought to be a difficult topic to teach or learn and, in fact, is not easy to learn. On the other hand, it is important enough in mathematical proofs and is used commonly enough in elementary college courses so that any high school pupil who has majored in mathematics should have met the principle of mathematical induction before he graduates.

Once the principle of mathematical induction is known, it seems a shame not to use it to prove the binomial theorem, even though there are other, simpler ways of persuading pupils that the binomial theorem is true. Again, let us start by trying to find a pattern.

$$(a + b)^1 = a + b$$
$$(a + b)^2 = a^2 + 2ab + b^2$$
$$(a + b)^3 = a^3 + 3a^2b + 3ab^2 + b^3$$
$$(a + b)^4 = a^4 + 4a^3b + 6a^2b^2 + 4ab^3 + b^4$$

and so on.

Undoubtedly, pupils seeing this for the first time will need a considerably greater number of examples, but these will be enough for our purposes here. Let us begin by deciding what sort of information we need in order to be able to expand any binomial. In looking at the pattern, it seems reasonable to suppose that if the binomial $(a + b)$ is being raised to the $n$th degree, the first term will be $a^n$, if the terms are arranged in the same order as they are here. Then, there will be various terms arranged in descending order of the exponent of $a$, and it seems that the exponent of the factor $b$ will be increasing as we read from left to right. Finally, the last term will apparently be $b^n$. The coefficients, meanwhile, seem to get larger for a while and then get smaller. These observations are informal and disorganized—about the way pupils might notice them in a classroom situation, if somebody were asking appropriate questions.

The important thing is that the pupils notice the order of the terms and the fact that we would like to know something about exponents and about coefficients. The order is obvious, and most pupils will quickly notice that the sum of the exponents in any one term is always $n$ and be able to explain why. The major remaining problem is the coefficients. However, it is not desirable to pass over these first two items too quickly in order to get to the coefficients, because if these items are not understood, the rest of the formula will not serve much purpose.

After several more examples [probably up to $(a + b)^9$ or so] and being asked the right questions, pupils will begin to recognize how to get from the coefficient of one term to the coefficient of the next, and finally, after more discussion, may come up with the following formula, or one like it. In this formula, we label the first term as term number 0, the next as term number 1, and so on. The reason for this is that the formula is easier to figure out that way; then if anyone wants to convert to the usual way of counting, he should have no great difficulty.

| Term number: | 0 | 1 | 2 | 3 |
|---|---|---|---|---|

$$(a + b)^n = a^n + na^{n-1}b + \frac{n(n-1)}{2!} a^{n-2}b^2 + \frac{n(n-1)(n-2)}{3!} a^{n-3}b^3 + \cdots +$$

$$\underset{i}{\underline{\frac{n(n-1)(n-2) \cdots (n-i+1)}{i!}}} a^{n-i}b^i + \cdots + \underset{n-1}{na b^{n-1}} + \underset{n}{b^n}$$

Notice that the $i$th term is easy to figure out by looking for a pattern in the early terms. In each of the early terms, the exponent of the $b$ is the same as the number of the term, and the denominator of the coefficient is also the same (remember that $0! = 1$). Since the sum of the exponents is $n$, the exponent of $a$ can be determined easily once that of $b$ is known. The numerator of the coefficient (except in the zeroth term) begins with a factor of $n$ and continues with 1 subtracted from each factor until the last factor has a number one less than the exponent of $b$ subtracted from $n$. The explanation is more complicated than the formula, but some such discussion may help some pupils to see the pattern. Through knowledge of permutations and combinations (perhaps with probability), the coefficient of the $i$th term as numbered here would simply be written $\binom{n}{i} = \frac{n!}{(n-i)!i!}$, which is correct even for the zeroth term.

If the binomial theorem is to be proved using induction, it is desirable to get the preliminary work out of the way before beginning the proof itself, and then introduce the proof at the beginning of a period. The pupils should use the theorem a few times on exercises so that they are familiar with it, and do some simpler proofs using induction. This way they may finish the proof and discussion in a single period. The proof is shown as follows: $(a + b)^1 = a + b$. Therefore, the theorem is true for $n = 1$. Assume

$$(a + b)^n = a^n + na^{n-1}b + \frac{n(n-1)}{2!} a^{n-2}b^2 + \cdots + nab^{n-1} + b^n$$

and multiply both members by $a + b$, getting $(a + b)^{n+1}$ on the left, and the following sum on the right:

$$a^{n+1} + na^n b + \frac{n(n-1)}{2!} a^{n-1}b^2 + \cdots + na^2 b^{n-1} + ab^n$$

$$+ a^n b + na^{n-1}b^2 + \frac{n(n-1)}{2!} a^{n-2}b^3 + \cdots + nab^n + b^{n+1}$$

Collecting terms, we have

$$a^{n+1} + (n + 1)a^n b + \left(\frac{n(n - 1)}{2!} + \frac{2n}{2!}\right) a^{n-1}b^2 + \cdots$$

$$+ (n + 1)ab^n + b^{n+1}$$

The coefficient $[n(n - 1)]/2! + 2n/2!$ can be rewritten

$$\frac{n(n - 1 + 2)}{2!} = \frac{(n + 1)n}{2!}$$

In order to make the coefficients and exponents look more like the proper formula for the expansion of $(a + b)^{n+1}$, we could replace occurrences of $n$ by $(n + 1) - 1$ but it should be clear even without this that the numbers are right as far as they go. We still have the general term to worry about—and that, needless to say, is the most important one. In fact, if that comes out right, the rest must come out right.

Consider the $(i + 1)$th term of the expansion of $(a + b)^n$. It is

$$\frac{n(n - 1)(n - 2) \cdots (n - i + 1)(n - i)}{(i + 1)!} a^{n-i-1}b^{i+1}$$

When multiplied by $a$, it becomes

$$\frac{n(n - 1)(n - 2) \cdots (n - i + 1)(n - i)}{(i + 1)!} a^{n-i}b^{i+1}$$

When multiplied by $b$, the $i$th term becomes

$$\frac{n(n - 1)(n - 2)(n - 3) \cdots (n - i + 1)}{i!} a^{n-i}b^{i+1}$$

Multiplying numerator and denominator of the second of these terms by $(i + 1)$, adding the two terms, and using the distributive law, we have

$$\frac{(i + 1 + n - i)n(n - 1)(n - 2)(n - 3) \cdots (n - i + 1)}{(i + 1)!} a^{n-i}b^{i+1}$$

$$= \frac{(n + 1)(n)(n - 1) \cdots (n + 1 - i)}{(i + 1)!} a^{n-i}b^{i+1}$$

From the way in which it was constructed, this should be the $(i + 1)$th term. Let us see if it is correct for the $(i + 1)$th term of the expansion of $(a + b)^{n+1}$. The exponent of $b$ should be $i + 1$, and it is; and the exponent of $a$ should be $(n + 1) - (i + 1)$, which it is. The denominator of the coefficient should be $(i + 1)!$, which it is; and the numerator of the coefficient should contain factors from $(n + 1)$ down to $[(n + 1) - (i + 1) + 1]$ or $[(n + 1) - i]$, which it does. Therefore, we have shown that if the binomial theorem works for $n$, then it works for $n + 1$. We have also shown that it is true for 1, and therefore, by induction, is true for all positive integers. The theorem is also true for other numbers, but probably should neither be proven nor used in the high school for exponents other than positive integers.

The binomial theorem is not particularly modern or is this treatment of it outstandingly novel. However, the theorem is important; the method of mathematical induction is an important method of proof; a mathematics teacher should be familiar with both; and a good mathematics student should be exposed to both during his high school education.

Often, the topic of sequences and series is included with induction and the binomial theorem. This is entirely appropriate, but we have decided to put it off until a later section on limits, since the topic is also closely related to limits. (See Chapter 14.)

As we have seen in this chapter, the mathematician's view of algebra has changed greatly in the past 140 years, and this change is beginning to affect the high school algebra courses. Although we should not neglect the development of facility with algebraic techniques, we should develop that facility as an adjunct to the study of structure of systems, rather than as an end in itself to be acquired through rote.

## Teaching Hints

Algebra and arithmetic are intimately associated. In fact, there are times when it is hard to decide whether a problem is an algebraic or an arithmetical problem. Rather than being a disadvantage, this fact can be used to help the pupils acquire a better understanding of both topics. For example, the multiplication of two binomials is quite similar to the multiplication of two two-digit numbers. To multiply $2x + 3$ by $7x + 4$, we could proceed as on the left in the following, whereas a similar problem with integers is done on the right.

$$
\begin{array}{r}
2x + 3 \\
7x + 4 \\
\hline
12 \\
8x \\
21x \\
14x^2 \phantom{000000} \\
\hline
14x^2 + 29x + 12
\end{array}
\qquad
\begin{array}{r}
23 \\
74 \\
\hline
12 \\
80 \\
210 \\
1400 \\
\hline
1702
\end{array}
$$

In each case, the algorithm has been performed in a long way, without any of the usual shortcuts, thus making the similarity more apparent. Once pupils have seen the similarity, they should find it easier to understand both procedures and easier to see the importance of the number ten in our numeration system. Of course, shortcuts would be introduced (preferably by the pupils) very shortly.

The problem of producing word problems which are interesting and meaningful to the pupils, and also within the scope of their ability to solve, is both important and difficult. The teacher may find that it is worthwhile to check local businesses and industries to see if somebody there can describe the sorts of problems involving elementary algebra which must be solved in that particular enterprise. It is surprising how many problems in business can be solved using elementary algebra. It may also be interesting for the pupils to make up their own word problems (with or without solutions). Some of the things the pupils will learn from such procedures include the meaning of words in problems, the necessity for being careful when stating problems, and an understanding of the fact that the really significant step is to get from the physical problem to the mathematical symbolization. Thus, the rote memorization of gimmicks for translating certain words into certain mathematical symbols is useless. If the child really understands the physical situation and the mathematics, it is entirely possible that he can take this important step without ever verbalizing the problem—or, at least, without stating it with great precision. Even if the problem is beyond the child's present ability to solve, the process of thinking about it, and describing what sort of mathematical problem must be solved in order to solve the physical problem will be of great value to him. It may also help to motivate later sections in the algebra course.

In discussing systems of equations, an enlightening procedure is to start with a pair of equations, say

$$\begin{cases} x + 2y = 6 \\ 4x - 3y = 2 \end{cases}$$

and have the pupils graph both. Then, form a new equation by adding those two (getting $5x - y = 8$). Now they should graph this new equation. Ask the children if they notice anything at all surprising. Then have them multiply both members of the top equation by 2. What does the graph of $2x + 4y = 12$ look like? Now, form the sum again ($6x + y = 14$). Have them graph it. Do they notice anything unusual? Do they believe that the graph of the sum of two equations will always go through the point of intersection of the graphs of the original equations? Try additional examples to see if the pupils become more convinced that this will always happen. Ask if anybody thinks he can produce a convincing argument that this must always happen. (The argument involves considering a pair of numbers which satisfies both equations. If it makes both of them true, must it make their sum true? Etc.) Now, consider what sort of equation would be easy to solve (for example, something like $x = 2$), and the pupils can work out the whole procedure themselves. This method is particularly appropriate because the pupils first find out about an important principle, and then discover a way to use it. Often, if they first discover how to use a principle to get the answer, they are less interested in why the procedure works and therefore fail to learn. With less understanding, they use it less effectively, and forget it more readily.

In the linear programming section, many pupils will contend that they can guess the answer without actually trying all cases. With students like this, we can usually show them that guessing will not always work by making the slope of the profit line either equal to, or almost equal to, the slope of the graph of one of the conditions. If this does not work, make up a problem in which there are many conditions so that a polygon of many sides results. This can be done by first drawing the polygon, and then making a condition for each desired inequality.

Although there is a great deal of work on structure in the newer mathematics courses, this does not require teachers to teach pupils all of the properties of a field (or a ring, etc.) in the seventh grade. Rather, it is more desirable that the pupils begin to become familiar with the important principles of their number system as a structure and then, if they continue in mathematics, come back to the topic in a more formal manner at a later time. Thus, the formal study of groups, rings, and fields ought not to be undertaken until a great deal of informal work with structures (number systems, etc.) has been done. With the present curricula, this formal study probably ought to be put off until about the twelfth grade.

One of the practical results of studying logarithms ought to be a familiarity with the workings of a slide rule. A good way to introduce the slide rule is to start with a slide rule for addition. This simply involves two rulers fastened together in an appropriate fashion—or, if negative numbers are to be included, special rulers will be needed; these are easily constructed. This slide rule may be of considerable help in discussing the addition and subtraction of signed numbers, as well as the introduction of multiplicative slide rules. Once addition on the slide rule is understood, and the basic principles of logarithms have been studied, it should take a relatively small flight of imagination for pupils to see how these principles can be combined to produce a standard slide rule. Then, of course, some practice is desirable, and a discussion of the other scales will be helpful.

The topic of mathematical induction is one of the most difficult in elementary mathematics to teach. Some of the brightest pupils always seem to have serious reservations about the procedure. This may have something to do with the idea of proving something about an infinite set, but usually seems to be less basic than this. The proof that appears in the book can be modified so as to be appropriate for high school pupils, and will convince some, but there will still remain a few who are not convinced. Actually bringing a set of dominoes to class and trying the obvious experiment, discussing each part of induction in the process, will be helpful to some; showing how the experiment might fail is an important part of this. Actually using the induction theorem to prove things that the pupils suspect are true may be helpful to some. No matter how hard we try, some good pupils may never be convinced that the induction principle really makes sense, though the teacher may be able to get them all to say they believe it.

**Exercises**

1. Show that the method of false position described on pp. 267–268 is a correct one for solving a linear equation.

2. Solve the following systems of equations using equivalent systems and explain why each system in your work is equivalent to the previous system.

(a) $\begin{cases} 3x + 2y = 7 \\ 7x - y = 11 \end{cases}$    (b) $\begin{cases} x + y + z = 5 \\ 2x - 3y - z = 8 \\ 3x + y - 3z = 0 \end{cases}$

3. In the linear program problem on p. 275, if crop $A$ produces a profit of \$10 per acre, and crop $B$ produces a profit of \$8 per acre, what is the most profitable number of acres to plant in each crop?

4. If the market changes so that the profit on crop $A$ is \$12.50 per acre, what is the most profitable distribution of crops?

5. Consider some set of elements (other than numbers) and a binary operation (for example, the set of statements with some logical operation) and decide whether the set and operation constitute a group. If the answer is yes, is the system a commutative group?

6. Use a logarithm table to solve the following for $x$.

(a) $(1.2)^{23} = x$    (b) $7^x = 5$    (c) $\sqrt[5]{18} = x$    (d) $\log_2 10 = x$
(e) $\log_2 1.5 = x$    (f) $\log_2 .75 = x$    (g) $\log_2 3 = x$    (h) $\log_2 5 = x$

7. What is the sum of the first $n$ even positive integers? Prove that your answer is correct using mathematical induction.

8. What is the sum of the first $n$ positive integers? Prove it.

## Questions for Further Thought and Study

1. Study the work of Hamilton (with quaternions) and Cayley. What is a number system? Must it be a field? What place did these two men have in the formalization of algebra?

2. Formulate a method for solving problems and then choose several particular problems and show how your method applies to those problems. You may find the *Twenty-First Yearbook of the National Council of Teachers of Mathematics* and some of Polya's work helpful.

## REFERENCES

Bechenbach, Edwin, and Richard Bellman. *An Introduction to Inequalities*, School Mathematics Study Group: New Mathematics Library 3, Random House, New York, 1961. Inequalities approached from a rigorous point of view and then used in important problems of analysis and geometry.

Birkhoff, Garret, and Saunders MacLane. *A Survey of Modern Algebra*, rev. ed., Macmillan Co., New York, 1953. The granddaddy of the college modern algebra textbooks, but not necessarily recommended for bedtime reading.

Kemeny, John G., Hazelton Mirkil, J. Laurie Snell, and Gerald L. Thompson. *Finite Mathematical Structures*, Prentice-Hall, Englewood Cliffs, N.J., 1959. Similar to *Finite Mathematics* (see references for Chapter 8) but more advanced with considerable work on linear algebra and a chapter on continuous probability theory. Chapters 4 and 5 would be appropriate for somebody who wishes to learn more about algebra—especially linear algebra and linear programming.

Kelley, J. L. *Introduction to Modern Algebra*, Van Nostrand Co., Princeton, 1960. Used as the textbook for the algebra course on Continental Classroom. Well written introduction to modern algebra with emphasis on linear algebra. Does not require a strong background.

MacLane, Saunders. "Algebra," *Insights into Modern Mathematics*, Twenty-third Yearbook of the National Council of Teachers of Mathematics, NCTM, Washington, D.C., 1957, pp. 100–145. A brief but informative article on modern mathematics including groups, rings, fields, some work with number theory, and a consideration of systems involving geometric transformations.

McCoy, Neal H. *Introduction to Modern Algebra*, Allan and Bacon, Boston, 1960. An elementary introduction to modern algebra and linear algebra. The teacher who has not had much exposure to modern mathematics at the college level would find this relatively easy to study.

Polya, G. *How to Solve It*. Princeton University Press, Princeton, 1945. Probably the best book ever written on the topic of problem solving. This book should be read by every teacher of mathematics.

Sawyer, W. W. *A Concrete Approach to Abstract Algebra*, W. H. Freeman and Co., San Francisco, 1959. Well written axiomatic development of modern algebra for the secondary school teacher. Considerable work with vectors and vector spaces.

Smith, David Eugene. *A Source Book in Mathematics*, 2 vols., Dover Publications, New York, 1959. See references 5 in Chapters 4 and 5. The algebra section (pp. 201–306) includes work with cubic and biquadratic equations, the work of Abel and Galois, Fermat's last theorem, and the Fundamental Theorem of Algebra. As mentioned earlier, Quaternions are considered in the last section (Calculus, Functions, and Quaternions).

# GEOMETRY

"Euclid alone has looked on Beauty bare."

These words of Edna St. Vincent Millay, perhaps more than any others, typify the place geometry has held in the minds of educated men for over 2,000 years. Yet, Euclid has been attacked sharply and not only by advocates of modern mathematics. In 1869, J. J. Sylvester, one of England's great mathematicians, said "I shall rejoice to see . . . Euclid honourably shelved or buried 'deeper than e'er plummet sounded' out of the schoolboy's reach."

Why the difference of opinion? Why do some people feel that the only real mathematics course in the secondary school curriculum is geometry, while others feel that most of the geometry taught in high school "has just as much relevance to what mathematicians (pure and applied) are doing today as magic squares or chess problems!"[1]?

Interestingly enough, the reason seems to lie as much with the teaching of other mathematics courses as with the teaching of geometry. Most adults who love and understand mathematics caught their first

[1] Jean Dieudonné, in *New Thinking in School Mathematics*, Organization for European Economic Cooperation, Office for Scientific and Technical Personnel, Paris, 1961, p. 36.

glimpse of "real mathematics" in a course in plane geometry. In arithmetic, they were asked to memorize rules and compute quickly and accurately; in algebra, there were more rules, more tricks, and more computations. Not until geometry were there reasons. Never was there a discussion of "why"; there were only a great number of statements and examples as to "how." Then geometry came on the scene with its axioms (however incomplete), its proofs (however imperfect) of theorems (however useless), and its original exercises which allowed the pupil to try his own hand at creating proofs. Here was an opportunity for the pupil who wanted to think. Here was an opportunity to see the beauty of mathematics. Here, in short, was the pupil's first opportunity to do some mathematics which he could do better than a machine. Is it any wonder that many of us have found a place in our hearts for our tenth-grade geometry course?

On the other hand, those who go on to more formal mathematical education find few places where their study of Euclidean plane geometry is of help, and they usually knew the few facts that are helpful prior to beginning the geometry course. Furthermore, the study of proof and structure is being taken over by algebra courses in which the proofs and the structure are much simpler, and more easily understood. Actually, if the geometry of Euclid is made rigorous according to modern day standards, it becomes so difficult as to be far beyond the capacity of even the brightest schoolboy to learn in a one-year course; and if it is not correct, can we justify studying it as a model of mathematical and logical thinking?

## What's Wrong with Euclid

Euclid's *Elements* was the first attempt to incorporate all of the important mathematics of the time into a single work, arranged systematically with assumptions explicitly stated, definitions, and proofs of theorems. It is also the last time a person is likely to accomplish this feat,[2] since the body of mathematical knowledge is expanding so rapidly that no one individual can even hope to understand it all, much less write about it. Without question, the contributions of Euclid are magnificent. His work has served as a model for mathematicians and nonmathematicians to follow in presenting ideas logically. According to the standards of his time, his work was rigorous and complete. Yet, according to the standards of the twentieth century, there are many flaws in the *Elements*, and even more flaws in the versions written for high school pupils. Let us consider some of the mistakes of Euclid.

---

[2] Although the Bourbaki group has made valient efforts along this line during this century.

One of Euclid's errors was that he apparently tried to define everything. For example, he defined a line as "length without breadth." How, then, would we define "length" and "breadth?" Are the words "length" and "breadth" to be taken as undefined, basic words? If so, why are they not used thereafter in the development? Apparently, what Euclid was doing was to give intuitive descriptions of the undefined objects in his system. If this is, in fact, the case, it would have been better to separate the intuitive descriptions from the formal definitions. This is really a minor point, but it is certainly desirable for a person studying geometry as an example of a mathematical system to be aware that it is *not* possible to define everything. Authors and teachers should keep this in mind when planning a geometry course.

A second error of Euclid was that some of his axioms were not stated precisely. For example, "It is possible to produce (extend) a finite straight line continuously in a straight line." Suppose the line segment is extended $\frac{1}{2}$ its length, and then $\frac{1}{4}$ of the original length, and then $\frac{1}{8}$ of the original length, and so on. Does this constitute extending it continuously? Since Zeno had preceded him, it is surprising that Euclid was not precise enough about his postulate to avoid this sort of interpretation. Clearly, from later usage, the interpretation given here would not suffice. More important, though less obvious, is whether it would be possible for the line to "come back on itself," like a great circle on a sphere, if it were extended far enough. There is nothing in Euclid's geometry which prevents this possibility.[3] Again, this can be corrected rather easily, but it is well to remember that such lapses should be corrected. In mathematics, we should say what we mean.

Undoubtedly, the most important flaw in Euclid is the fact that his set of assumptions is incomplete. It is not possible to prove the theorems of Euclid's *Elements* from his axioms, although it is possible to prove things which ought not to be true by the methods he used.

The first proposition in the elements is to construct an equilateral triangle given one of the sides $(\overline{AB})$. The construction is simple (Fig. 11.1)—a circle is drawn with each endpoint as center and $AB$ as the radius. If $C$ is a point of intersection of the two circles, then $ABC$ is an equilateral triangle. But what guarantee is there that the two circles actually intersect? There is nothing in any of Euclid's axioms which requires them to intersect. Suggesting that it is obvious from the drawing is not fair, since a figure is not to be used as part of a proof— only the assumptions and logic are. Whether the circles intersect is

---

[3] A spherical geometry is prevented by the assumption that two points determine precisely one straight line (also more loosely stated than desirable in Euclid), but a line "coming back on itself" is not prevented by any of the assumptions.

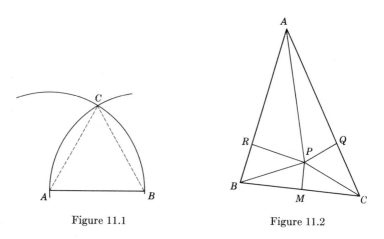

Figure 11.1                    Figure 11.2

partially a question of continuity, but also of whether one circle could be entirely on one side (inside or outside) of the other. Unfortunately, Euclid makes no assumption about this question.

Another example of incompleteness in Euclid's axioms concerns the process known as "superposition." This procedure (essentially picking up a triangle and placing it on top of another triangle) is used for the first couple of congruency theorems and then dropped "like a hot potato." In fact, many pupils try to prove later theorems by this method and are told not to, because "we don't use that method except for the first two theorems." Why not? Essentially, because there is nothing in any of Euclid's axioms that allows us to do it, (not with angles, anyway). Why did Euclid do it? He had to; there was no other way to prove the congruent triangle theorems from his assumptions. It is possible to correct this difficulty either by assuming two of the congruent triangle theorems (or slightly weaker postulates which are quite similar), or by making a series of assumptions which allow motion (or something equivalent) of geometric figures.

Probably the most important omission from Euclid's axiom system is the omission of any assumption about "betweenness." This omission allows such peculiarities as the following proof using Fig. 11.2 that all triangles are isosceles.

Given: $\triangle ABC$
To prove: $AB = AC$

1. Construct the perpendicular bisector ($\overleftrightarrow{MP}$) of $\overline{BC}$.
2. Construct the bisector ($\overrightarrow{AP}$) of $\angle BAC$.

3. $\overset{\leftrightarrow}{AP}$ and $\overset{\leftrightarrow}{MP}$ meet in a point, $P$ (if they were parallel we could easily prove that $\triangle ABC$ is isosceles and the lines coincide).

4. Drop perpendiculars from $P$ to $\overset{\leftrightarrow}{AB}$ and $\overset{\leftrightarrow}{AC}$ ($\overset{\leftrightarrow}{PR}$ and $\overset{\leftrightarrow}{PQ}$, respectively).

5. Draw lines $\overset{\leftrightarrow}{PB}$ and $\overset{\leftrightarrow}{PC}$.

6. $BP = CP$ (Since $P$ is on the perpendicular bisector of $\overline{BC}$, it is equidistant from the endpoints.

7. $PR = PQ$ ($P$ is on the angle bisector of $\angle BAC$)

8. $\angle PRB$ and $\angle PQC$ are right angles (construction)

9. $\triangle PRB \cong \triangle PQC$ (right $\triangle$ with two pairs of corresponding sides congruent)

10. $BR = CQ$ (corresponding parts of congruent triangles)

11. $PA = PA$

12. $\angle s\ ARP$ and $AQP$ are right angles (construction)

13. $\triangle PRA \cong \triangle PQA$ (same as 9)

14. $RA = QA$ (same as 10)

15. $BR + RA = BA$, and $CQ + QA = CA$ (the whole equals the sum of its parts)

16. $BR + RA = CQ + QA$ (equals added to equals are equal)

17. $BA = CA$ (substitution)

18. Triangle $ABC$ is isosceles (definition)

What, if anything, is wrong with this proof? First it is clear that if every triangle is isosceles, the resulting geometry is going to be most peculiar. Furthermore, it is not at all hard to work from this conclusion to a contradiction. Certainly, something has to be wrong with the proof. The question is what? Is there any step that was taken at any time which is not justified by Euclid's axioms? This depends partially on what we mean by "justified." Certainly every step taken here is as justified by Euclidean axioms as are the steps taken in most proofs in high school text books, and they are also as justified as many of the steps taken in proofs appearing in the *Elements*.

The explanation which many people like to give for this paradox is that the figure is drawn incorrectly. But the figure is not supposed to have anything to do with the proof—a proof is to be independent of the figure. One of the first things students learn in a plane geometry course is that their eyes may play tricks on them, so they are not to rely on the figure. Are we going to change this rule now, just because an incorrect figure got us into trouble? Incidentally, what is the matter with the figure anyway? Suppose $P$ falls outside the triangle. Then, as in Fig. 11.3 we would see that the proof is exactly the same as before, except that $RA - RB = AB$, and $QA - QC = AC$, in step 15; thus step 16 is changed to read: $RA - RB = QA - QC$ (equals subtracted from equals are equal). But the rest of the proof remains the same, and the theorem is still true. Apparently there was nothing wrong with Fig. 11.2.

Of course, if the reader has drawn a careful figure with a triangle that is not close to being isosceles, he will find that neither Fig. 11.2 nor Fig. 11.3 is correct. But there is nothing in Euclidean geometry that tells us that we must draw our figures carefully, nor is there anything in Euclid's assumptions that tells us that there is anything wrong with either of these figures. We need more axioms.

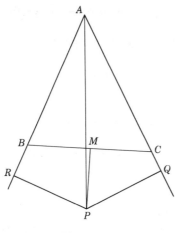

Figure 11.3

If the reader has not yet discovered the difficulty, he will find that if he constructs a carefully drawn figure, point $P$ will always be outside of the triangle (assuming the triangle is not isosceles— if it is, $\overleftrightarrow{AP}$ and $\overleftrightarrow{PM}$ will coincide) and precisely one of the points $R$ and $Q$ will be between the endpoints of a side of the triangle. That is, if $R$ is between $A$ and $B$, then $Q$ will not be between $A$ and $C$; and, if $R$ is not between $A$ and $B$, then $Q$ is between $A$ and $C$. Missing from the *Elements* is a concept of "betweenness." More than any other omission this is a serious blow to geometry as it has been studied for two thousand years. There are many proofs in the *Elements* which depend on "betweenness"; these are apparently carried out with the assumption that a well-drawn figure will take the place of an axiom. It is particularly surprising that Euclid could have made an error of this sort when we consider that Eudoxes had preceded him, and Eudoxes' handling of the incommensurable case (which Euclid used) was based essentially on the concept of "betweenness."

There are several different ways to correct the mistakes of Euclid. One of the best known was produced by David Hilbert,[4] an outstanding mathematician of the late nineteenth and early twentieth centuries.

[4] David Hilbert, *Grundlagen der Geometric*, Seventh Edition, Teubner, 1930. Translated into English by E. J. Townsend (*Foundations of Geometry*).

Hilbert patched up Euclid by supplying the axioms that Euclid left out. However, Hilbert's goal was to leave Euclid alone as much as possible, only to patch it up where it was necessary. If one starts with Hilbert's version of Euclid, and then waters it down considerably by either assuming a great deal more than is necessary or making mistakes, or both, one can finish a year of geometry. But why should we bother to correct Euclid, and then make the result incorrect again? If we are going to teach an incorrect geometry, Euclid's is probably as good as anybody's and a good deal better than most.

A second major contribution to the correction of Euclid's errors was made by George David Birkhoff (a renowned mathematician in his own right and father to another) in 1932.[5] Birkhoff's point of view was that since the Greeks did not have and use numbers as we know them today, and since many of the properties which are difficult to develop properly in geometry are essentially similar to the properties of the real numbers, we should use the real number system in developing geometry. He proposed axioms of linear measure (ruler) and of angle measure (protractor) which do not require a great deal more understanding than how to use a ruler and protractor. Of course, tenth-grade students do not usually understand fully the implications of the real number system, but they have (or can be taught) a good enough intuitive understanding of this system to proceed with a correct geometry. Birkhoff and Beatley included considerable discussion of logic and three-dimensional geometry, and handled congruence as a special case of similarity (factor of proportionality is 1). The number of theorems was cut drastically, and many of these were supposed to be assumed the first time through and proved at a later time, when the pupils had acquired a better idea of proof and mathematical structure. All in all, the Birkhoff-Beatley text was a most remarkable achievement. It is a sad commentary on the state of mathematical education that it took twenty years before large numbers of schools began to accept books using that approach.

There have been other attempts to write geometry textbooks which were both rigorous and at a proper level for high school pupils. In

---

[5] G. D. Birkhoff, "A Set of Postulates for Plane Geometry, Based on Scale and Protractor," *Annals of Mathematics*, vol. XXXIII, April 1932, pp. 329–345. In 1933, Birkhoff collaborated with Ralph Beatley, also a professor at Harvard, to write a geometry based on these postulates; this was planographed by Spaulding-Moss Co., Boston. Later, in 1940, a revision was published under the title *Basic Geometry* by Scott Foresman Company. The book was out of print almost immediately—unfortunately, it was 20 years ahead of its time. More recently, several commercial texts and at least one noncommercial text have used the same approach with a great deal of success.

1958, Howard Levi wrote a geometry that incorporated all of the important facts of elementary geometry, trigonometry, and analytic geometry into one course. This material has been taught to several tenth-grade classes with considerable success, one difficulty being that teachers tend to have some trouble with it because it is so novel. Levi starts with the real numbers and states several of his basic assumptions in terms of the real number system. This is certainly the most algebraic of the three geometries mentioned here, and is, in many respects, the most efficient and straightforward.

## Must Euclid Go?

Euclid's *Elements* are incorrect by modern standards. The *Elements* are ponderous by any standards at least for young children, for whom they were not originally written. There is little of a factual nature in geometry which pupils do not already know when entering the tenth grade from a good mathematics program, and what is left can easily be learned in a few hours. Geometry as taught in the high schools is not in the mainstream of present-day mathematics.

The arguments for Dieudonne's point of view ("Euclid must go!"[6]) seem overwhelming. What is there to say in defense of Euclid? *"We liked it when we went to school"* is not sufficient. First of all, there are many people who *didn't* like it; and second, the changes that are occurring in the curriculum at other levels have as a primary purpose to put into algebra, and even seventh- and eighth-grade mathematics, the very things we say were so appealing about Euclid's geometry. What, then, is left for Euclid?

Two basic arguments favor Euclid. The first is historical. For 2,000 years, educated men everywhere read and studied geometry as written by Euclid. Although it is possible to read the great literature of the past 2,000 years without a knowledge of Euclid, such a knowledge certainly makes much of that literature more comprehensible and worthwhile. Thus, from the point of view of a general education, geometry holds a unique place among the mathematics courses offered in the high school. Although algebra and arithmetic fit more readily into the mainstream of present-day mathematics, they do not have as great a significance in the cultural history of our civilization. Undoubtedly, the cultural aspects of geometry can be comprehended in less than a year, but to try to compress this part of geometry into a few hours or weeks of study would surely miss the mark—for it is the flavor of geometry, not the facts alone, which have seemed significant to the great minds of history.

[6] *New Thinking in School Mathematics*, O.E.E.C., Paris, 1961, p. 35.

The second, and overriding, argument in favor of keeping geometry in the curriculum relates to the sort of objects studied in geometry. In arithmetic and algebra, we study numbers, symbols for numbers, combinations of symbols, axioms about symbols (and the rather obscure things for which the symbols stand), and systems involving symbols. Do we really have any feeling for the fact that $5 + 7 = 12$? That is, suppose that there were five people at a party and seven more came. Would we notice the difference if there were not twelve people at the party a moment later? Not unless we counted, or had them all sit down at a table where there were twelve place settings. In other words, we would not be likely to be upset by failure of the people at the party to obey the fundamental rules of arithmetic unless we had studied those laws carefully and then taken the trouble to apply them to the situation—and it *would* be troublesome to apply them.

On the other hand, when a child first begins to crawl, he knows what the shortest distance between two points is; in fact, he knew before this time, he just did not have the physical facility to demonstrate his knowledge. When children see railroad tracks going off into the distance, they really know, though it may not *look* that way, that the two tracks will never meet unless one or both of them bend in toward the other. In general, the basic assumptions and many of the theorems of geometry are about familiar objects, and the facts involved in them seem to be obviously true, for the most part. Therefore, the study of geometry has much of its basis in what might be thought of as obvious facts about physical objects which are familiar to all of us. Rather than deterring the study of geometry, knowing many of the facts of geometry actually aids it. The idea that we can prove statements that do not seem at all apparent (the Pythagorean Theorem, or some of the theorems about circles, for example) from obvious statements is exciting to children and many adults. Is it really possible to get excited about the fact that the sum of two even numbers is even? Is it not a fact that the theorem is at least as obvious as the axioms?

Geometry, then, offers an opportunity to study proof and mathematical structure in a setting which is familiar to the pupil. It offers the chance to prove nonobvious facts from obvious ones. That the mathematician does not really insist on the axioms' being more obvious than the theorems is not important; the child insists on this if he is to be impressed with the structure we are building. Then, once he appreciates the concepts of proof and mathematical structure, he will have time enough to go back and reduce the number of postulates to a minimum.

Geometry still has a place in the mathematics curriculum of the high school. It is a place which cannot be taken by the abstract study of algebra and arithmetic, a place it will not satisfactorily fill if it becomes so abstract and so preoccupied with considerations of a trivial nature that it is no longer concerned with the mathematics of the space surrounding the pupil.

If we are going to defend the teaching of geometry on the grounds stated here, there is a serious question whether it is necessary or desirable to correct all the mathematical errors of Euclid. Certainly, it is necessary to correct some of the pedagogical errors—for example, proving theorems in the early part of the course which are more obvious to the pupil than the methods used to prove them. But there seems to be no excuse for considering whether a point is between two other points when it is obvious from the drawing that it is. Surely, no ordinary fifteen-year-old will be worried about such a question as whether the angle bisector of one angle of a triangle intersects the opposite side of the triangle. Obviously it does. Later, after the main body of geometry has been discovered and proved, the pupil can come back to see how it is really possible to make the study rigorous. But it would be tedious and unprofitable for him actually to go through the entire course and make every proof rigorous. It is hard to imagine a high school sophomore, just beginning the study of geometry, who is excited about the proof of the fact that if three points are on the same straight line, one of them is in the middle.

### A Course in Geometry

A high school course in geometry should emphasize mathematical creativity and insight on the part of the pupil rather than formalism and form of proofs. It should give the pupil a feeling for deductive reasoning without so much rigor that *rigor mortis* sets in. It should consider geometry of three dimensions as well as geometry of one and two dimensions, since we live in a three-dimensional world. Having achieved these goals, the course should probably include some consideration of algebraic or analytic geometry, since this is the sort of geometry that is most commonly used in mathematics today. Certainly, there should be no attempt to compartmentalize the subjects of algebra and geometry. On the other hand, if we turn to a completely algebraic geometry, we shall probably lose a great deal of the intuitive spontaneity that comes in a traditional geometry course. The following brief outline and discussion concerns the sort of course in geometry that might be appropriate for the tenth grade.

First, a brief review of the facts of geometry which pupils have learned in their previous courses might be appropriate, especially if the teacher is not sure how much the pupils know. If he asks the right questions, the teacher may be amazed at what he learns. The teacher should also consult with junior high school teachers to find out what *they* think the pupils should know. Included in this review would certainly be such topics as measuring angles and lines, and the congruence theorems for triangles; these were probably discovered by cutting out triangles or performing simple constructions in junior high. It would probably be best to convince the pupils of the truth of these statements through use of constructions. Give them some parts of a triangle and let them go to work. In some cases they will find they have too much information, whereas in others, they will find that they do not have enough. The pupils should be able to come up with the usual congruency theorems with proper help from a good teacher.

Some simple proofs should come next. Such theorems as supplements of equal angles are equal, vertical angles are equal, etc., might be included here. Although the theorem being proved may be immediately obvious to the pupils, the reason is that they "see" the proof themselves. The "proofs" that would be included here would be simple situations in which the teacher would first ask whether the children thought something was always true or not, and when they said that it was true, the teacher would ask "why?" The answer a pupil would give would presumably be a proof, in the sense that we refer to proof here. If some other pupil were not convinced by the proof, the proving pupil would have to furnish something better, if he could.

At about this time, the pupils would have a large number of facts at their disposal, and the teacher would encourage them to produce a list of assumptions they would like to make in order to proceed with the rest of the course. It is essential that the teacher have a pretty good idea of what sort of assumptions are needed at this point, and he would do well to use the axioms out of any regular plane geometry book for this purpose. Undoubtedly, assumptions about betweenness would *not* be included. If some pupil suggests such assumptions, the teacher might reasonably suspect him of having an older sibling who had studied such things or a father who is a professor of mathematics. If this is not the case, he should probably be sent on to college—he is wasting his time in high school.

## A Sequence of Theorems

Next, we would develop a reasonably formal geometry in which several basic theorems would be proved and studied rather thoroughly in class, and many more would be derived and proved by the pupils.

As good a sequence as any for the basic theorems was produced by the Commission on Mathematics of the College Entrance Examination Board, and we shall quote it here for the convenience of the reader.

THEOREM 1.    The base angles of a triangle are equal if and only if the triangle is isosceles.

THEOREM 2.    An exterior angle of a triangle is greater than either remote interior angle.

THEOREM 3.    Two lines are parallel if and only if a transversal makes a pair of alternate interior angles equal.

THEOREM 4.    The sum of the interior angles of a triangle equals two right angles.

Relations among lines and planes in two and three dimensions: intersection, perpendicularity, parallelism; methods of representation (drawing); intuitive discussion largely, using classroom model to develop space perception; a few simple three-dimensional proofs.

ASSUMPTION.    A line is parallel to the base of a triangle if and only if it divides the other two sides into proportional segments.

THEOREM 5.    Two triangles are similar if two angles of one are respectively equal to two angles of the other.

THEOREM 6.    An altitude drawn to the hypotenuse of a right triangle forms two triangles, each similar to the original.

THEOREM 7.    A triangle is a right triangle if and only if the square on the largest side is equal to the sum of the squares on the other two sides.[7]

It is clear that many logical ideas would be needed in order to go through this program, and these would be discussed at the appropriate time. For example, the ideas of converse, and if and only if, would have to be discussed in connection with the first theorem, and would be used for several others. Surely the idea of "if _____ then _____" reasoning would arise in this discussion, as would various other questions of proof. Hopefully, the proofs would be about as rigorous, but probably not any more rigorous, than proofs used to be in traditional plane geometry courses. The big differences would be in the number of proofs the pupils had done for them; the way in which the theorems were acquired (stating and proving one theorem that is not in the book should be worth at least two that are); the number of assumptions made (there are many more in this procedure because we quite frankly assume some things which are hard to prove); and the number of

[7] *Report of the Commission of Mathematics: Program for College Preparatory Mathematics,* College Entrance Examination Board, New York, 1959, p. 38. For a further discussion of this sequence, see pp. 114 and 115 of the *Appendices* to the report.

theorems the pupil is expected to remember (this number has been cut to a bare minimum).

Now is the time to consider what has been done. Show the pupils that from a small number of assumptions, we have proved many theorems. Trace some of the reasons back to the original axioms, and show that each one ultimately depends on one of the assumptions made at the beginning of the course. Then discuss the concept of proof again, and begin to consider some of the omissions of the first time through—such as questions of betweenness. For example, the proof that all triangles are isosceles might be presented and discussed. Then, some of the basic theorems might be discussed in terms of any concepts of betweenness which were assumed in their proofs. Perhaps a discussion of how various people have corrected these problems, including a list of Hilbert's axioms or Birkhoff's might be considered. There should be no attempt to correct all of the proofs; perhaps one or two could be handled correctly, but there would be no point to going through the entire program again.

## Incidence Geometry

With this new emphasis on rigor, a miniature mathematical system might be considered. Probably the easiest and most worthwhile system would be a geometry of incidence. Almost everything that could possibly be called a geometry satisfies the following *incidence* postulates (so-called because they consider questions of points, lines, and planes falling upon one another).

1. A line is a set of points containing at least two points.
2. Two distinct points lie in one and only one line.
3. A plane contains at least three distinct noncollinear points.
4. Three distinct, noncollinear points lie in one and only one plane.
5. If a plane contains two distinct points of a line, it contains the line.
6. If two planes contain a point in common, they have another point in common.

From these postulates of incidence it is possible to prove several theorems. For example, two lines intersect at most in one point; two distinct planes are either parallel or have a line in common (with parallel defined as having no point in common); if a line intersects a plane not containing it, the intersection is a single point; etc. These theorems can be proved with great rigor and with no reference to drawings. In fact, once the proofs have been carried out, it might be interesting for the pupils to try to find different physical models for the undefined objects, point, line, and plane. It might be possible, for example, to set up a committee structure within a school which would have the required properties. The universe would be the school, the planes would be classes, the lines would be committees, and the points would be the children. Or a more geometrical interpretation might consist of only three points, as in Fig. 11.4. The points are $A$, $B$, and $C$; the lines are $\{A, B\}$, $\{A, C\}$, and $\{B, C\}$; and the only plane is $\{A, B, C\}$. The lines which have been drawn, of course, are meant to suggest appropriate sets of points and have no further meaning. There are not supposed to be points between $A$ and $B$, for example. Clearly, this is the smallest geometry satisfying the six postulates which contains at least one of each kind of the undefined objects (points, lines, and planes).

If the pupils want more than one of each kind of undefined object, they should be able to construct a geometry such as that indicated by Fig. 11.5. There are four points, six lines, and four planes. One theorem which the pupils might be interested in proving, for example, is that if there is more than one plane in such a system then there must be at least four planes.

In order to expand the geometry to one in which the parallel postulate (through a point not on a line there is one and only one line parallel to the given line) is true, at least four points (in one plane) are needed. Figure 11.6 indicates such a geometry. Notice that line $AC$ is parallel to line $BD$, even though they do not "go in the same direction." The only question is whether the lines have a point (of our universe) in common.

Having considered the methods of proof and the completeness of the postulates, we can now consider what might happen if some of the postulates were not true. The first candidate, which will come to the mind of the reader, for a postulate to be thrown out is the parallel postulate. There has been so much written on non-Euclidean geome-

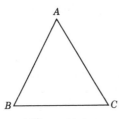

Figure 11.4

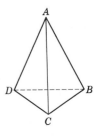

Figure 11.5

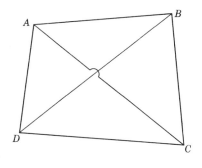

Figure 11.6

tries lately that it is hardly appropriate for us to go into the topic here.[8] In a classroom, we should try to get the children to develop their own model for a non-Euclidean geometry. Since this would almost certainly be spherical geometry, it would be necessary to remove at least one more axiom from the system in use, namely, the second incidence postulate (two distinct points lie in one and only one line). If betweenness postulates are included in the system, there will be need to revise these also, since each of three points on a great circle (line) would appear to be between the other two. However, the important idea to get across is that there are perfectly good physical models of geometries which do not satisfy our postulates.

At this point, most of the major objectives in teaching a course in plane (and solid) synthetic geometry have been achieved. Some time will probably remain in the year, and in that time, there are many interesting things to do. In general terms, the important things which might be considered at this time are more facts of plane and solid geometry, and an introduction to coordinate geometry. The relationship between synthetic and analytic geometry could easily be brought out during this further development by first developing coordinate geometry (the Pythagorean Theorem is crucial in any such development; this is the reason for ending the earlier section with that theorem) and then allowing the pupils to use either synthetic or analytic proofs for the remaining theorems. In fact, it would be good to encourage both types of proofs for as many theorems as possible. The facts of solid geometry would be brought out along with those from

[8] For a particularly good discussion of this topic, see Gould, S. H., "Origins and Development of Concepts of Geometry," in *Insights Into Modern Mathematics*, Twenty-Third Yearbook of the National Council of Teachers of Mathematics, NCTM, Washington, D.C., 1957. Pages 286–298 are on the topic of non-Euclidean geometry.

plane geometry, but not necessarily with formal proofs. Ordinarily, the proofs in synthetic plane geometry would involve about the same amount of rigor as was used to develop the seven basic theorems. Teachers and pupils would have agreed that it is possible to do such proofs rigorously, that somebody else has probably done them that way, and that both teacher and pupil should be satisfied with that arrangement.

### Coordinate Geometry

By the time they reach the tenth grade, pupils will have done a good deal of graphing and will be familiar with the basic assumption involved in making a graph, namely, that there is a one-to-one correspondence between the points of a plane and the set of all ordered pairs of real numbers. Ordinarily the children will have used rectangular coordinates and will often have used the same scale on each axis, though in some cases they will have found it more convenient to use different scales. For simple graphic work, there is no need to have the scales the same, but we are accustomed to rectangular coordinate systems even in graphing. When we use coordinate systems in coordinate geometry, it is generally desirable to use rectangular coordinate systems in which the scale is the same on each of the axes. Technically this is not necessary, but if the figures are going to look like the figures we expect, it is imperative. The graph of $x^2 + y^2 = 1$ will look like a circle if the same scale is used on both axes and will look like an ellipse if different scales are used. If we use the same scale on both axes and look at the figure from an angle instead of from directly above, it will look like an ellipse rather than a circle anyway. And if we use different scales and look at the figure from the appropriate angle, it is possible to make it look like a circle. In theory, therefore, there is no need to use the same scale on both axes.

It is not necessary to point this out to the pupils, unless one enjoys such discussions. Rather, it is a good idea to agree at the beginning of a unit in coordinate geometry that rectangular coordinates with the same unit on each axis will be used. Actually, many of the incidence properties can be more easily proved using nonrectangular coordinates with a convenient scale on each axis. If this is considered at all, it probably ought to be saved until after some of the other work with coordinates has been completed.

Before beginning the geometric proofs using coordinate systems, it is desirable to develop some preliminary material. Included in this would be the definition of the slope of a line (with respect to a particular coordinate system); parallel and perpendicular lines (equal slopes and slopes that are negative reciprocals); midpoints; the equation of a straight line from various bits of information (two points, one point and slope, intercepts); the distance formula (between two points); and the derivation of the equation of a circle. This should be enough preliminary work to prove most of the theorems to be considered. If more such material is needed later, it can be developed by methods similar to those used to develop the foregoing. Except for definitions, the pupils should be able to figure out most of the concepts if they are asked a few questions, and even the definitions should seem natural to them.

Probably the hardest of the facts for the pupils to discover for themselves would be the relation between the slopes of perpendicular lines. We might start by drawing several pairs of perpendicular lines on the board as in Fig. 11.7 and have the pupils estimate the slope of each line in each pair. Fairly quickly, it should become obvious to the pupils that if one slope is positive, the other is negative, and if the absolute value of one is greater than 1, the absolute value of the other is less than 1. During this discussion, it should also be brought out that if the slope of one of the lines is zero, the slope of the other line is not defined; and if the slope of one is not defined, then the slope of the other will be zero. (This is not to be interpreted as meaning that

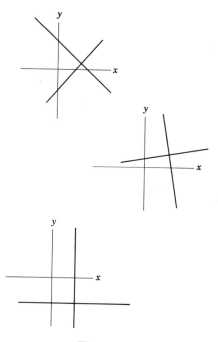

Figure 11.7

the negative reciprocal of "undefined" is zero, though the converse is, in a sense, true.) Very likely, the pupils will actually be able to guess the correct relationship. If they cannot, then the teacher can set out to derive it after building the proper foundation, even if the pupils do not know precisely what the formula is going to be.

Start by drawing a pair of perpendicular lines which intersect the $x$-axis of a pair of coordinate axes. As in Fig. 11.8, take the intersection of one line with the $x$-axis as having coordinates $(a, 0)$ and the intersection of the other line with the $x$-axis as have coordinates $(b, 0)$. Then, draw perpendiculars to the $x$-axis from the points $(a + 1, 0)$ and $(b + 1, 0)$. Are triangles $ADC$ and $FBE$ similar? Then, $CD/AC = BE/EF$. If the slope of $AD$ is $m$, what are the coordinates of $D$? What are the coordinates of $F$ if the slope of $BF$ is $m'$? Then, $CD = m$, $AC = 1, BE = 1,$ and $EF = -m'$ (assuming we are thinking of directed line segments which is necessary when considering slopes; this would have been discussed earlier when the topic of slopes was first brought up). By substitution, $m/1 = 1/-m'$ or $m$ and $m'$ are negative reciprocals. Note that this proof will not work if one of the lines is parallel to the $x$-axis. Very likely, several bright pupils will be able to provide a derivation for this formula with only the figure, or one like it, to guide them. There are, of course, many different derivations for this formula, and it might be interesting for the pupils to try to find others. Also, the converse of this theorem (if the slopes are negative reciprocals, then the lines are perpendicular) should be proved, preferably by the pupils.

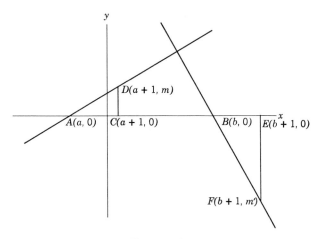

Figure 11.8

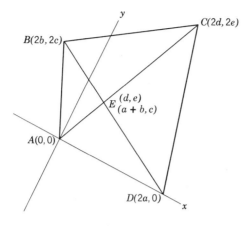

Figure 11.9

After these preliminaries, the pupils are ready to begin the proofs of geometric theorems. Several facts should be kept in mind when constructing a proof involving the use of coordinates. First, the coordinate system is, in general, something the individual pupil brings to the problem. He may choose his own coordinate system in which ever way he wants, as long as doing so does not alter the problem. Thus, if it is convenient to choose a particular point as the origin, choose that point. If it is convenient to take a particular ray (which has the proper end-point) as the positive $x$-axis, such a choice is entirely legitimate. Even the unit can be chosen by the pupil working the problem, but usually that is not done because it does not really help much in most cases; however, if it would help, it would be perfectly proper. It is also fair for the pupil working the problem to choose the direction in which the positive $y$-axis is to go, thus assuring himself that certain coordinates will be positive. Again, this is often no help, but it is legitimate.

With all this freedom, it would seem as though we could do almost anything with the coordinate axes, and this is true as long as we do not put any special restrictions on the original figure. However, the pupil must be careful not to assume more than is given. Let us take a particular example and show the kind of manipulating of coordinates which is legitimate and describe some other activities which would not be proper.

In order to prove that if the diagonals of a quadrilateral bisect each other the quadrilateral is a parallelogram, we start with the quadrilateral $ABCD$ (Fig. 11.9), with the midpoints of $AC$ and $BD$ coinciding (point $E$). We select point $A$ as the origin and ray $\overrightarrow{AD}$ as the $x$-axis.

In all probability, every reader will tilt either his head or the book slightly (whichever is more convenient) when he looks at Fig. 11.9 with the axes "at an angle." This is because of the rigid notion we all have that the $x$-axis is always horizontal and the $y$-axis vertical. However, if we are bringing the axes to the quadrilateral, we have to accept the quadrilateral as it is. Therefore, to emphasize that the axes are placed there for the convenience of the problem solver after the figure is determined, the teacher should arrange the figure so that the axes on occasion will be "tilted."

For a quadrilateral, it is possible to choose the positive $y$-axis so that the $y$-coordinates of $B$ and $C$ will be positive, but we can make no restriction on the $x$-coordinates of those points. Actually, there is no particular advantage to such a restriction in this case. Since the unit has not yet been chosen for the coordinate system, it is possible to decide that the $x$-coordinate of $D$ will be 1, or 2, or $\pi$, or whatever number we chose to make it. Again, no great simplification results from such a decision. We only remark that it would be possible, and perfectly correct to do this.

Now, we must assign arbitrary numbers to the remaining coordinates. That is, the $x$-coordinate of $D$, and both coordinates of $B$ and $C$ must be assigned a variable which could be replaced by any real number. It would be natural to let the variable $x$, for instance, stand for the $x$-coordinate of $D$, but since $x$ would be a real number, $x/2$ would also be a real number, and we could write the coordinates of $D$ as $(2 \cdot x/2, 0)$, if we so desired. Instead, let $a$ be half the $x$-coordinate of $D$ so that $2a$ becomes the $x$-coordinate. Again, nothing in this procedure restricts the generality of the original quadrilateral.

But why bother? We looked ahead and saw that we were going to have to find the coordinates of a midpoint, and therefore would have to divide by 2; and what is easier to divide by 2 than $2a$? For the same reason, we choose the coordinates of $B$ to be $(2b, 2c)$ and the coordinates of $C$ to be $(2d, 2e)$. If a child does not see the point of such shortcuts, or does not plan ahead well enough to be so shrewd (or lazy) as to take advantage of them, the teacher must not force the issue. He should permit the pupil to work with the messy fractions, after calling his attention to the other possibility. The practice in working with rational expressions will be good for him, and when he sees how easily others do the problem, it may encourage him to plan more carefully henceforth.

Working the problem is easy once the preliminaries have been handled. The midpoint of $\overline{AC}$ has coordinates $(d, e)$ and the midpoint of $\overline{BD}$ has coordinates $(a + b, c)$. Since these two midpoints coincide,

$d = a + b$, and $e = c$. The slope of $\overset{\leftrightarrow}{AD}$ is 0, and the slope of $\overset{\leftrightarrow}{BC}$ is $(2e - 2c)/(2d - 2b) = (e - c)/(d - b)$. Since $e = c$ and $d \neq b$ (if $d = b$, points $B$ and $C$ would coincide and there would be no quadrilateral), the slope of $\overset{\leftrightarrow}{BC}$ is 0. In a similar way, it can be shown that the slopes of the other two sides of the quadrilateral are both $c/b$ and the quadrilateral is a parallelogram.

In working this problem, the pupil would not go through all of the explanation. He would simply draw the figure and write out the calcuations of the previous paragraph. If using the figure is supposed to be taboo, he might indicate in the proof the points that were to have what coordinates, but this seems unnecessarily formal.

There are many other theorems which happen to be rather easy to prove analytically, but which are quite difficult to prove synthetically. The Commission of the CEEB listed many such theorems (pp. 133–135 of the Appendices), but it would really be more interesting to let the pupils decide for themselves which method they each would prefer for each theorem. If we follow this procedure, we will probably get advocates of each method in a class, and the resulting discussions will be of much more interest and value to the pupils than having somebody tell them which method is supposed to be the easier for a particular theorem. Remember, we are trying to develop individual initiative and inventiveness in this course.

The remaining facts generally brought out in a plane geometry course would be discussed during the rest of the year, with the children having access to either a synthetic or analytic type proof for any problem or theorem. As various topics are considered, analogues in three dimensions would be considered too. For example, when circles are studied, spheres, cylinders, and cones might be considered. The pupils would have enough background and ingenuity to figure out the formulas for the areas and volumes for the cylinder, and the area for the cone (with a slight hint, perhaps).

In discussing three-dimensional geometry, it is desirable for the pupils to learn to draw figures of three-dimensional objects in two dimensions, and to visualize these objects and their relationships to one another.

If tenth-grade pupils can successfully complete the course in geometry outlined here and really understand the basic underlying concepts being developed, they will have indeed increased their understanding of mathematics and their appreciation of the subject. If there is still time left before the course ends, which seems unlikely, it could be spent reviewing concepts of proof, investigating other non-Euclidean geometries, studying geometric transformations (translations, rotations, and reflections) and the system formed by considering composite transformations, or developing some simple concepts of trigonometry from a geometric point of view.

There have been many attacks on geometry as a full-year course in the high school, and there will undoubtedly be more. Considering the way in which it is taught (memorizing theorems, proofs, and other "important concepts"), in many instances there would seem to be good justification for such attacks. However, if the teacher will remember what he is trying to accomplish with this course and will teach it in a way that encourages imagination and understanding rather than imitation and memorization, there are many who believe that geometry can be a very worthwhile venture in the education of any person.

### Teaching Hints

One of the advantages that geometry has over other topics studied in mathematics is its immediate appeal to the learner's knowledge of the real world. With this in mind, it seems a shame not to use the real world to help the pupils understand the mathematics. In geometry, more than any other topic, the use of physical models is appropriate and useful. There are many two- and three-dimensional models which can be purchased through commercial companies (NDEA funds will help in the purchase of these—check with the principal), and the pupils can be given extra credit or otherwise encouraged to make their own, probably a more educational method of getting the models (NDEA funds are also available for buying materials for this).

There are many models available with no more effort than looking for them, as well as the obvious models, such as those suggested. For example, the room in which one teaches has models of parallel and perpendicular planes; parallel, perpendicular, and skew lines; lines perpendicular to a plane; all the planes containing a given line (rotate a door on its hinges); etc. Some rooms may have unique features which can be used to help develop certain concepts. For example, if the floor or ceiling is tiled, that fact can be useful in the study of area and in the development of a coordinate system. If the tiles (as is often the case) have a design in which all the diagonals have been drawn, the special case of the Pythagorean Theorem in which the triangle is a right isosceles triangle can be seen easily.

There are many aids such as films and film strips that are available to help in the teaching of geometry, and there is certainly a place for good films in this field—for example, in the teaching of loci and the applications of geometry. However, one of the most useful visual aids we can use is an overhead projector. By cutting a circle out of a piece of cardboard, we can project a light beam which approximates a cone, and then intercept the beam with a screen at different angles, thus showing the various conic sections. In coordinate geometry, we can draw a figure, project it onto the screen, and *then* bring the coordinate system (on a prepared overlay) to the figure, thus impressing upon the pupils that the coordinate system is brought to the figure, not vice versa. We can consider some of the nonmetric properties of figures by projecting them onto a screen, and then changing the angle of the screen in order to see how the figure changes. Figures can be prepared in advance, using several different colors to help explain a proof or some other concept. The overhead projector has other advantages, such as allowing the teacher to face his class at almost all times, but these advantages are true for any subject. The one big disadvantage of an overhead projector is that it is not possible to leave a long proof within view of the pupils. However, this problem can be solved by using both the blackboard and the overhead projector.

When using the blackboard in geometry, it is wise to have several different colors of chalk available, since many figures are easier to understand if different parts of a figure can be distinguished in some relatively permanent fashion. For the same reason, it is desirable that the pupils have pencils of several different colors available. There are retracting automatic pencils which have four colors of lead in the same pencil, and if the pupils can be prevailed upon to buy these, they will be a big help to them.

Many other techniques will be picked up for making the teaching of geometry more effective by a teacher who is interested. One such technique which is helpful when corresponding parts of congruent triangles are going to be considered is to write the letters for the vertices of the triangles in the same order. Thus, $\triangle ABC \cong \triangle DEF$ means $AB = DE$, $BC = EF$, and $AC = DF$, as well as $\angle A \cong \angle D$, $\angle B \cong \angle E$, and $\angle C \cong \angle F$. Replacing $A$ by $B$ and $B$ by $A$ in the original statement would result in a substantially different statement and, in general, it would be false that $\triangle ABC \cong \triangle BAC$. This procedure has substantial advantages in terms of communication, and is a help to the individual working with congruent triangles, making it unnecessary to have to go back to the proof to check to see which side is congruent to which. There is also one very attractive proof that the base angles of an isosceles triangle are congruent which is based upon the notation described here. Given that $AB = AC$, the proof consists of showing that $\triangle ABC \cong \triangle ACB$ (sas), and thus, $\angle B \cong \angle C$.

In teaching geometry, as in teaching any subject, it is good to keep the goals in mind. In geometry, most teachers say that they are teaching pupils a concept of proof and also to think logically. If this is so, the pupils ought to have an opportunity to construct many original proofs, and to see proofs others have constructed. One of the most useful theorems for this purpose is the Pythagorean Theorem. Pupils should be encouraged to construct their own proofs of this important theorem, and see how many different ones can be produced in one class. Then, they can set out to find other proofs which have been produced by other people. They will discover that this particular theorem has many many proofs, including one by a President of the United States, a blind girl, and many other interesting people. Seeing the large number of different proofs, all valid, should help to convince pupils that there is no one right way of doing a proof, and that imagination and ingenuity play a more important part in mathematics than memory does.

It is also desirable to teach the students to "think logically" outside, as well as inside, a mathematics class. For example, they might each be asked to bring in an example of an argument (or several arguments) that they have heard put forth on the radio, television, or in the newspaper. There are many sources of such arguments—advertisers, politicians, editorial writers, lawyers, etc. Presumably some of the arguments will seem logical, and some will seem less so. Some will be based on assumptions that seem reasonable; some will be based on assumptions that seem highly dubious. This sort of discussion should not be all destructive; the reward should be at least as great for finding a valid argument as for finding an invalid one. However, it should help the pupils to evaluate other people's arguments about nonmathematical topics, and it should help them to construct their own arguments in a more logical manner. The information now available on transfer of training indicates that without this sort of application, the teaching of geometry is not likely to have a substantial effect on the thinking of pupils outside the geometry class.

### Exercises

1. Prove Theorems 1 to 7 (p. 308). You may wish to refer to the *Appendices of the Commission Report*, pp. 114–115.

2. State and prove at least five theorems based on the incidence axioms 1 to 6 (p. 309).

3. Choose at least three theorems from plane geometry and prove each by synthetic means and also by analytic means.

## Questions for Further Thought and Study

1. Compare commercial geometry textbooks based on Euclid's work, Hilbert's variations on Euclid and Birkhoff's axioms. Which, if any, seems most appropriate for high school pupils?

2. What do you think is the place of geometry in the secondary school mathematics curriculum? What are the purposes of a course in geometry and how could these purposes best be achieved?

## REFERENCES

Birkhoff, G. D. "A Set of Postulates for Plane Geometry Based on Scale and Protractor," *Annals of Mathematics*, **XXXIII** (April 1932), 329–345. See comments in text.

Birkhoff, G. D., and Ralph Bentley. *Basic Geometry*, Scott, Foresman Co., 1940. See comments in text.

Blumenthal, L. M. *A Modern View of Geometry*, W. H. Freeman and Co., San Francisco, 1961. Modern postulational geometry of the plane including the coordinatization of affine and projective planes.

Curtis, Charles W, Paul A. Daus, and Robert J. Walker. *Studies in Mathematics*, Volume II—*Euclidean Geometry Based on Ruler and Protractor Axioms*, School Mathematics Study Group under a grant for the National Science Foundation, New Haven. A sound mathematical discussion, for high school teachers, of the Birkhoff geometry as adapted by the SMSG high school textbooks.

Glicksman, Abraham M. *Vectors in Three-Dimensional Geometry*, NCTM, Washington, D.C., 1961. Vectors are used to develop important ideas of three-dimensional geometry. In light of recent recommendations in Europe and this country, this approach to geometry and the vector algebra which is also developed are of particular interest.

Gould, S. H. "Origins and Development of Concepts of Geometry," *Insights into Modern Mathematics*, Twenty-third Yearbook of NCTM, Washington, D.C., 1957, pp. 273–305. A review of geometry from Pythagoras to the present with a discussion of incommensurables and Eudoxus, geometric algebra, the place of axiomatics in geometry, the attempts to prove the parallel postulate and non-Euclidean geometries and projective geometry.

Heath, Sir Thomas L. *Euclid's Elements of Geometry*, 3 vols., Dover Publications, New York, 1956. Translation of the *Elements* and subsequent mathematical development.

Hilbert, David. *The Foundations of Geometry* (translated by E. J. Townsend), Open Courts Publishing Co., La Salle, Illinois, 1947. This is Hilbert's successful attempt to "patch up" Euclid. Although it later turned out that the axioms are not independent, the work is mathematically correct and very impressive. Not the easiest reading available.

Kazarinoff, Nicholas D. *Geometric Inequalities*, School Mathematics Study Group: New Mathematics Library 4, Random House, New York, 1961. This book is an outgrowth of a seminar for high school pupils held in Ann Arbor by the author in 1958. Although the basic ideas presented are not difficult, the problems (some still unsolved) require a creative imagination and a good mind.

Prenowitz, Walter. "Geometric Vector Analysis and the Concept of Vector Space," *Insights into Modern Mathematics*, Twenty-third Yearbook of the National Council of Teachers of Mathematics, NCTM, Washington, D.C., 1957, pp. 145–199. From a physical and geometric concept of vector, Prenowitz moves smoothly into the algebra of geometric vectors and then into a more abstract study of vector algebra and vector spaces.

Reid, Constance, *A Long Way from Euclid*, Thomas Y. Crowell Co., New York, 1963. Written for a reader with only a knowledge of Euclidean geometry, the book delves into many historically interesting geometric developments and uses geometry to consider other important mathematical concepts.

Smith, David Eugene. *A Source Book in Mathematics*, 2 vols., Dover Publications, New York, 1959. See reference 5 in Chapter 4. Section III (pp. 307–545) is on geometry and includes the beginnings of projective geometry, non-Euclidean geometry, analytic geometry, topology, as well as some work with trigonometry and the number $\pi$.

Organization for European Economic Cooperation, *New Thinking in School Mathematics*, Office for Scientific and Teaching Personnel, Paris, 1961. Euclidean geometry is generally degraded, though not condemned by all members, to the extent that Dieudonne condemns it.

CHAPTER

12

# CIRCULAR FUNCTIONS
# AND TRIGONOMETRY

For approximately 2000 years trigonometry was used almost entirely as an accessory to astronomy and as a device for making measurements. Probably the first study of trigonometric functions as functions stems from the work of sixteenth-century mathematicians who created tables which allowed them to find the product of two numbers by adding two other numbers. This work was the precursor of present-day logarithms.

Although trigonometry is still used for mensurational purposes and for astronomy and navigation, it is studied principally as a set of functions having interesting and important properties. The sine curve is used commonly to describe various wave motions such as alternating electric current, sound waves, or other vibrations. Most mathematical descriptions of recurring events involve some form of trigonometric function. Therefore, the emphasis in the study of trigonometry in the high school is changing from the study of measurement to the study of functions. Furthermore, since the study of algebra tends to concentrate more heavily on the functional approach, the combining of the two topics is quite natural. Thus, recommendations of various study groups point toward an integrated course in algebra and trigonometry for the eleventh grade with more emphasis on trigonometric functions as functions than before the second half of the twentieth century.

Chapters are still found near the end of eighth- or ninth-grade text-books on mensurational trigonometry. This is as it should be, since many pupils who do not continue on to further study of mathematics may find some future use for the mensurational aspects of trigonometry. Furthermore, since these aspects of trigonometry have historical precedence, there is some reason to believe that they ought to come first in the education of young minds. However, by the time pupils have progressed through a good mathematics program to the eleventh grade, they are ready for a solid mathematical approach to trigonometric (or circular) functions.

### The Wrapping Function

As we may recall, a function can be defined as a set of ordered pairs in which no first member appears more than once. A unit in trigonometry might start with the creation of a certain function which is often called the wrapping function. This function is defined as a set of ordered pairs in which the first member is a number and the second member is itself an ordered pair (namely, the coordinates of a point).

Consider the unit circle (a circle with radius of one unit, and center at the origin of a two-dimensional coordinate system) and a one-dimensional coordinate system on a line which is tangent to the circle at the point with coordinates $(1, 0)$ as in Fig. 12.1. Assume that the one-dimensional coordinate system has the same basic unit as the two-dimensional coordinate system. Imagine the one-dimensional co-ordinate system to be on a string of infinite length and the circle to be a wheel around which the string can be wrapped. The string can be wrapped around the wheel in a counterclockwise direction. Since we start with the 0 of the string at the point $(1, 0)$ of the circle or wheel, what point of the string will fall on the point $(1, 0)$ the next time around? We know the radius of the circle is one unit, and that the circumference of the circle is given by the formula $C = 2\pi r$. Most pupils will have no difficulty discovering that the point of the string with coordinate $2\pi$ will also fall on the point of the circle with co-ordinates $(1, 0)$ as will points with coordinates $4\pi$, $6\pi$, $8\pi$, etc. Once they have discovered this fact, they will have little difficulty observing that the number $\pi$ will fall on the point of the circle with coordinates $(-1, 0)$ which is halfway around the circle from the point at which the wrapping process started. Other numbers that will fall on the point $(-1, 0)$ are $3\pi$, $5\pi$, etc.

The next step is for the pupils to try to find some other member of the function. So far, they know that any number of the form $2n\pi$, where $n$ is a positive integer or zero will fall on the point with coordinate

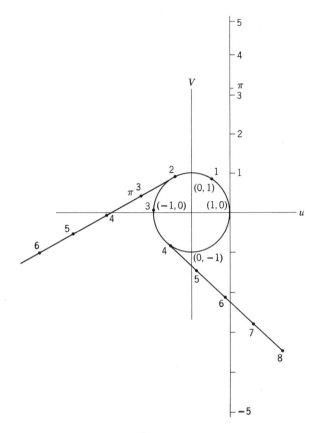

Figure 12.1

(1, 0) and that numbers of the form $\pi + 2n\pi$ will fall on the point with coordinates $(-1, 0)$. It will be easy for them to find out that numbers of the form $\pi/2 + 2n\pi$ will fall on the point with coordinates $(0, 1)$ and that numbers of the form $3\pi/2 + 2n\pi$ will fall on the point $(0, 1)$.

Consider the number $\pi/4$. Where will it fall? Will it fall on the point of the circle which is midway around the circle between the points $(1, 0)$ and $(0, 1)$? Suppose that point is called point $P$. What is the measure of angle $POR$ in degrees (Fig. 12.2)? Now drop a perpendicular from $P$ to the $x$-axis; in right triangle $OPQ$, what is the measure of angle $OPQ$? Since two angles of the triangle have the same measure (namely 45°), the legs of the right triangle are congruent, or if $(u, v)$ are the coordinates of $P$, $u = v$. From the Pythagorean Theorem and the knowledge that the radius of the circle is one, we can derive the

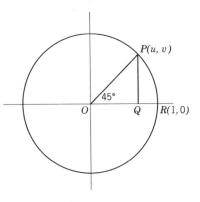

Figure 12.2

fact that $u = 1/\sqrt{2}$ or $\sqrt{2}/2$. Therefore, the coordinates of $P$ are $(\sqrt{2}/2, \sqrt{2}/2)$.

Several points in the preceding paragraph are of interest to the teacher. First, the pupils should have enough knowledge of geometry to tell immediately that if the length of $\overline{OP}$ is one unit, the lengths of the legs are equal to $\sqrt{2}/2$ units. Had they faced this problem in geometry they would have had no trouble solving it; however, experience shows that a large portion of the class will be lost if we make this assumption in the eleventh grade. Apparently there are two reasons for this loss of memory. When children have not used certain knowledge for several months, they often tend to forget it; further, they tend to think of geometry as one subject, algebra as an entirely different one, and trigonometry as still a third. The result is that pupils often object if a problem in one subject has a solution that comes from the other. One of our major goals in teaching a "modern mathematics program" is to show that there are no walls between these various subjects. In any case, the teacher will probably find it expedient to discuss carefully the reason why the coordinates of point $P$ are $(\sqrt{2}/2, \sqrt{2}/2)$.

Usually there will be one or more pupils in the class who will be able to go through the proof to the satisfaction of the other pupils. When this happens, such a procedure is desirable. If there are no pupils in the class who can do this by themselves, the teacher can often draw the proof out of the pupils simply by asking the right questions along the way. (For example, what is the measure of angle $POQ$? Then, what is the measure of angle $OPQ$? What do we know about the sides opposite two congruent angles of a triangle? Then, if $u$ stands for the length of $\overline{OQ}$, what is the length of $\overline{PQ}$? What is the length of $\overline{OP}$? From the

Pythagorean Theorem, what is the relationship of these three lengths to each other? Solve for $u$.)

If a pupil solves the equation $u^2 + u^2 = 1$ and decides that the roots are $1/\sqrt{2}$ and $-1/\sqrt{2}$, he is right, but he will almost certainly find a good deal of opposition in the class. There will be two objections: first, from the problem it is known that $u$ is a positive number; and second, he did not rationalize his answer. The first objection is indeed correct, but a teacher may be able to encourage a lively discussion about other points around the circle from a consideration of the negative values for $u$. The second objection is interesting mostly because if the teacher asks why the number must be rationalized, the answer is almost certain to be something like "because that's the way you're supposed to do it." Needless to say, this answer does not represent the type of thinking we wish to encourage in mathematics. Usually there is a reason for doing things the way they are done in mathematics; and if the pupils are encouraged to look for those reasons, they will find mathematics a much more interesting subject as well as an easier one to learn.

In this case, the teacher might ask the pupils to find a decimal approximation of $1/\sqrt{2}$ to three places. He would encourage them first to divide 1 by 1.414 and then let them divide 1.414 by 2, after having rationalized. After this, they will see a justification for rationalizing. However, this does not mean that they should always rationalize every fraction they see. The major reason for rationalizing a fraction is to find a decimal approximation for it. If they are not planning to find such an approximation, there is no particular reason, in general, for rationalizing. Indeed, there are times when it is convenient to "unrationalize" a fraction. That is, we might start with a fraction in which there is a radical in the numerator and multiply by something so as to make a radical appear in the denominator instead. This procedure is often used in determining a limit when the limit of both the numerator and denominator of the original fraction is zero.

Coming back to the wrapping function, pupils should now be able to determine the coordinates of points on which such numbers as $\pi/4$, $3\pi/4$, $5\pi/4$, etc. will fall. There is one other important class of numbers which ought to be considered before going on with the study of circular functions. Consider the number $\pi/6$. Where will it fall on the unit circle? Since it is one-third of the way between 0 and $\pi/2$, the number $\pi/6$ should be one-third of the way along the arc from the point $(1, 0)$ to the point $(0, 1)$. In that case, pupils will readily agree that angle $POQ$ in Fig. 12.3 has a measure of $30°$, and therefore, angle $OPQ$ has a measure of $60°$. If they recall certain facts about a "30-60-90" triangle, they will be able to determine the coordinates of point $P$.

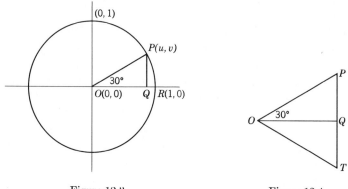

Figure 12.3                    Figure 12.4

On the other hand, the teacher will probably find it necessary to go through a brief derivation of the necessary information for some of the pupils. In Fig. 12.4 consider point $T$ such that $Q$ is the midpoint of $\overline{PT}$. Then $\triangle POT$ is equilateral, $PQ$ is one-half of $PT$, and therefore, $PQ = PO/2$. Or in Fig. 12.3, if $PO = 1$ and $v$ is the ordinate of $P$, $v = \frac{1}{2}$ and $u$ (the abscissa of $P$) satisfies the condition that $1^2 = (\frac{1}{2})^2 + u^2$. Thus, the coordinates of $P$ are $(\sqrt{\frac{3}{2}}, \frac{1}{2})$.

Having been led this far, the pupils should be able to find coordinates of points corresponding to such numbers as $\pi/3$, $2\pi/3$, $5\pi/6$, $7\pi/6$, etc.

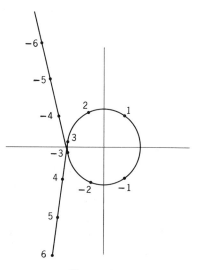

Figure 12.5

### Table 12.1

| $x$ | $0$ | $\frac{\pi}{6}$ | $\frac{\pi}{4}$ | $\frac{\pi}{3}$ | $\frac{\pi}{2}$ | $\frac{2\pi}{3}$ | $\frac{3\pi}{4}$ | $\frac{5\pi}{6}$ | $\pi$ | $\frac{7\pi}{6}$ | $\frac{5\pi}{4}$ | $\frac{4\pi}{3}$ | $\frac{3\pi}{2}$ | $\frac{5\pi}{3}$ | $\frac{7\pi}{4}$ | $\frac{11\pi}{6}$ |
|---|---|---|---|---|---|---|---|---|---|---|---|---|---|---|---|---|
| $W(x)$ | $(1, 0)$ | $(\sqrt{\frac{3}{2}}, \frac{1}{2})$ | | | | | | | | | | | | | | |

| $x$ | $2\pi$ | $\frac{13\pi}{6}$ | $\frac{9\pi}{4}$ | $\frac{7\pi}{3}$ | $\frac{5\pi}{2}$ | $\frac{8\pi}{3}$ | $\frac{11\pi}{4}$ | $\frac{17\pi}{6}$ | $3\pi$ | $-\frac{\pi}{6}$ | $-\frac{\pi}{4}$ | $-\frac{\pi}{3}$ | $-\frac{\pi}{2}$ | $-\frac{2\pi}{3}$ | $-\frac{3\pi}{4}$ |
|---|---|---|---|---|---|---|---|---|---|---|---|---|---|---|---|
| $W(x)$ | | | | | | | | | | | | | | | |

Before making a table of the known values for the wrapping function, let us return briefly to the wrapping process itself. We will recall that the positive half of the string was being wrapped in a counterclockwise direction around the unit circle. At the same time, imagine that the negative half is being wrapped around the unit circle in a clockwise direction (Fig. 12.5). Then, the number $-2\pi$ will fall on the point $(1, 0)$, the number $-\pi$ will fall on the point $(-1, 0)$, the number $-\pi/2$ will fall on the point $(0, -1)$, $-3\pi/2$ will fall on the point $(0, 1)$, $-\pi/6$ will fall on the point $(\sqrt{\frac{3}{2}}, -\frac{1}{2})$, etc. Thus, the pupils are now able to fill out a table such as Table 12.1.

In the wrapping function, the first member of each ordered pair is a number, but the second member is itself an ordered pair of numbers, namely, the coordinates of a certain point on the unit circle. Another way of arriving at the same function is to imagine a point moving in a counterclockwise direction around the circle starting at the point with coordinates $(1, 0)$; then the first member of an ordered pair is the distance the point has traveled and the second member is the coordinates of the point after it has traveled the given distance.

### Sine and Cosine Functions

Once the wrapping function is understood, creating the sine and cosine functions is quite simple. The cosine function is the set of ordered pairs in which the first member is a real number and the second member is the abscissa of the point corresponding to that real number under the wrapping function. Thus, Table 12.2 is a partial list of the cosine

### Table 12.2

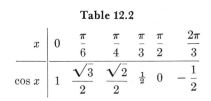

| $x$ | $0$ | $\frac{\pi}{6}$ | $\frac{\pi}{4}$ | $\frac{\pi}{3}$ | $\frac{\pi}{2}$ | $\frac{2\pi}{3}$ |
|---|---|---|---|---|---|---|
| $\cos x$ | $1$ | $\frac{\sqrt{3}}{2}$ | $\frac{\sqrt{2}}{2}$ | $\frac{1}{2}$ | $0$ | $-\frac{1}{2}$ |

function. Similarly, the sine function can be defined as the set of ordered pairs in which the first member is a real number and the second member is the ordinate of the corresponding point. Thus, given a number $x$, sin $x$ can be evaluated by considering the point which is $x$ units in a counterclockwise direction from the point $(1, 0)$ on the unit circle. The ordinate of that point is sin $x$. The abscissa of that point is cos $x$. (In this book, we will follow the usual convention of abbreviating sine $x$ and cosine $x$ as sin $x$ and cos $x$.)

Historically, the sine and cosine functions were defined for angles of right triangles, then for angles larger than 90°, and still later for angles larger than 180°. However, for pupils who are studying the properties of the functions, rather than trying to solve mensurational problems, the definitions given here are more appropriate. Notice that only the one definition of the sine function is needed; after that sin $x$ can be determined for numbers greater than $\pi$ as easily as for numbers between 0 and $\pi/2$. Also, when these functions are considered in mensurational problems involving angles, radian measure seems much more natural to the pupils than it did when the trigonometric functions were approached only in terms of angles (measured in degrees).

The periodicity of the trigonometric functions is seen quite easily from our definitions. For example, if we start with a point $a$ units from $(1, 0)$ on the unit circle and go $2\pi$ units farther, we get back to the point at which we started. Thus, sin $(a + 2\pi)$ and sin $a$ must be the same number, or sin $(a + 2\pi) = $ sin $a$. Similarly, cos $(a + 2\pi) = $ cos $a$.

From simple considerations of geometry, such formulas as sin $(x + \pi) = -$ sin $x$, sin $-x = -$ sin $x$, etc., follow easily. Since the cosine and sine functions are such good examples of even and odd functions, this is probably as good a place as any to digress slightly and discuss them. We could start by considering the function defined by $f(x) = x^2$. From a few numerical examples, the pupils will quickly realize that $f(-x) = f(x)$. Furthermore, for any function defined by $f(x) = x^{2n}$, where $n$ is an integer, $f(-x) = f(x)$. Thus, it seems natural to call any function $g$, an even function if $g(-x) = g(x)$. In a similar way, pupils can be shown that it is natural to call any function $h$ for which $h(-x) = -h(x)$ an odd function. From these definitions and our knowledge that cos $-x = $ cos $x$, we see that cosine is an even function. What kind of function is sine? Is $|x|$ an even or an odd function? There are, of course, many functions which are neither even nor odd; for example, the function defined by $y = x^2 + x$ is neither even nor odd.

Having seen that cosine is an even function and sine an odd function, and that both are periodic, we can, with the help of the values already determined for these functions and our intuitive notion that functions defined in this way must be continuous, graph both the sine and the cosine functions. If any pupils have ever seen an oscilloscope in action, the graphs should look familiar to them. Even if they have not, the graphs will look like a good representation of wave motion, or the path of an earth satellite plotted on a flat map, or various other familiar phenomena.

## Other Circular Functions

The other four trigonometric functions can be defined in terms of the two now known. Thus, $\tan x = \sin x/\cos x$; $\cot x = \cos x/\sin x$; $\sec x = 1/\cos x$; and $\csc x = 1/\sin x$. From these definitions, many of the values of these four functions can be derived and their graphs drawn. Furthermore, many of the properties of these four functions can be determined. For example, since sine and cosine are both periodic (with period $2\pi$), the other four functions must also be periodic. This can be seen easily in the case of tangent: $\tan (x + 2\pi) = \sin (x + 2\pi)/\cos (x + 2\pi) = \sin x/\cos x = \tan x$. However, many pupils will tend to jump to the conclusion that the period of the tangent function is exactly $2\pi$. This, of course, is not the case since the smallest number $p$, such that $f(x + p) = f(x)$ for all $x$, is said to be the period of $f$. What is the period of tangent? Try to prove that $\tan (x + \pi) = \tan x$.

## Simple Identities

Since pupils will know the distance formula, they should have no trouble applying it to the distance from the origin to a point on the unit circle having coordinates $(\cos x, \sin x)$, thus arriving at the formula: $(\sin x)^2 + (\cos x)^2 = 1$. The difference between $\sin x^2$ and $(\sin x)^2$ can and probably should be discussed through numerical examples. Then the convention of writing $(\sin x)^2$ as $\sin^2 x$ in order to avoid putting in the parentheses can be introduced.

From the basic formula $\sin^2 x + \cos^2 x = 1$, we can derive various interesting facts. First, the pupils' knowledge of real numbers and squares of real numbers should tell them that $-1 \leq \sin x \leq 1$ (which they probably saw intuitively from the definition of $\sin x$) as well as the corresponding fact concerning $\cos x$. Second, some simple algebra, combined with the definitions of other functions, will enable the pupils to derive such formulas as $\tan^2 x + 1 = \sec^2 x$. With this much information, many simple identities can be proved by the pupils. However, there is an important point to be remembered when we begin to consider identities. Not all equations which are normally thought to be identities are true for all values of the variable. For example, the "identity" $\tan^2 x + 1 = \sec^2 x$ is true only when $\tan x$ and $\sec x$ are defined. Since $\tan x = \sin x/\cos x$, and $\cos \pi/2 = 0$, $\tan \pi/2$ is not defined. Therefore, the statement $\tan^2 \pi/2 + 1 = \sec^2 \pi/2$ is meaningless. In such instances, we should be careful to mention the values of $x$ for which the statement is true (or more simply, indicate the values of $x$ for which the statement is not true). Thus, we would say $\tan^2 x + 1 = \sec^2 x$ for all $x$ except $x = \pi/2 + n\pi$ where $n$ is any integer (positive, negative, or zero). Notice that in this case, $\sec x$ is undefined in precisely the places $\tan x$ is undefined, and, of course, 1 is always defined. Therefore, the restriction we have indicated is sufficient.

In the past, some people made the error of defining $\frac{1}{0}$ as a number written "$\infty$." They also defined $\frac{2}{0}$ as the same number. This leads to the fascinating result that $\frac{1}{0} = \frac{2}{0}$, and multiplying each side of the equation by 0 we arrive at nonsense. The symbol "$\infty$" has a perfectly good meaning in calculus; $\lim_{x \to \infty} f(x)$ signifies the limit as $x$ gets large without bound of $f(x)$. In talking about limits, it is appropriate to say that the limit as $x$ approaches 0 from the positive side of $1/x$ is $\infty$, or that $1/x$ gets large without bound as $x$ approaches 0 from the positive side. However, it is misleading to give pupils the impression that $\infty$ is the resulting number when we divide some number by 0. It is correct to say that we do not get any number when we divide by 0, or more simply, that division by 0 is not defined. See Chapter 8 for further discussion of infinity and infinite sets.

### Sum and Difference Formulas

We have yet to mention angles in connection with the circular functions and can continue to study these functions without recourse to angles. However, from a pedagogical point of view, the relation between these functions and angles probably ought to be introduced before much more work is done. Although these functions are important as functions from the real numbers to the real numbers, they are also useful in connection with angles. Hence we do not want to go to the opposite extreme from what formerly was done, and completely ignore the relation between circular functions and angles. Yet, the sum and difference formulas can be easily derived without reference to angles, as we shall see. In Fig. 12.6, assume $A$ is $x$ units in a counterclockwise direction from $R$ along the unit circle, and $B$ is $y$ units from $R$ (if $x$ or $y$ is a negative number, the following argument will still hold; however, pupils may find it difficult at first to see that going negative three units in a counterclockwise direction is the same as going three units in a clockwise direction). Pick point $C$ so that it is $x - y$ units from $R$.

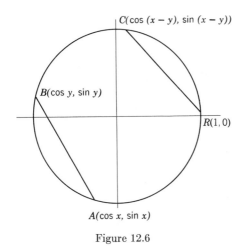

Figure 12.6

Then, the coordinates of $A$, $B$, and $C$ respectively are: $(\cos x, \sin x)$, $(\cos y, \sin y)$, and $[\cos (x - y), \sin (x - y)]$. Since arcs $AB$ and $RC$ have the same measure and are therefore congruent, segment $\overline{AB}$ is congruent to segment $\overline{CR}$. Therefore, by the distance formula,

$$(\cos y - \cos x)^2 + (\sin y - \sin x)^2 = [\cos (x - y) - 1]^2 + \sin^2 (x - y)$$

Simplifying this formula through algebra and the fundamental pythagorean identity $(\sin^2 x + \cos^2 x = 1)$, we get

$$\cos (x - y) = \cos x \cos y + \sin x \sin y$$

By substituting $-y$ for $y$ in the foregoing formula, we can find the formula for $\cos (x + y)$. Further, by replacing either $x$ or $y$ by $\pi/2$ in each of these formulas we can derive interesting relations between the sin and cos functions. An observant pupil may have noticed these relations when he was graphing the two functions.

In order to find the formula for $\sin (x + y)$, we note that $\sin (x + y) = \cos [\pi/2 - (x + y)] = \cos [(\pi/2 - x) - y] = \cos (\pi/2 - x) \cos y + \sin (\pi/2 - x) \sin y = \sin x \cos y + \cos x \sin y$. The formula for $\sin (x - y)$ follows easily.

From these formulas, the formulas for the other four functions of sums and differences follow with the aid of the definitions, as do the "double angle" formulas from the sum formulas.

## Exercises

1. Copy and complete Table 12.2.

2. Using the same values of $x$ as in Exercise 1, make a table of values for $\cos x$; $\sin x$.

3. Rewrite the tables in Exercise 2 using decimal approximations (the nearest hundredth will be sufficient) and then graph the sine and cosine functions. (One needs only as much of a table as is necessary, considering periodicity and one's knowledge of even and odd functions, for this problem.)

4. Create a table for each of the other four circular functions similar to those in Exercise 2.

5. Follow the procedure of Exercise 3 to graph the tangent, cotangent, secant, and cosecant functions.

6. Using a traditional trigonometry book, turn to the section on identities and determine what restrictions must be made on the variable(s) in order for each identity to be true for all real numbers. In each case, would it be sufficient to say that the identity is true whenever all functions are defined?

7. Fill in the missing steps in the derivation of the formula for $\cos (x - y)$.

8. Using the formula for $\cos (x - y)$, derive the formulas for $\cos (x + y)$, $\sin (x - y)$, $\sin (x + y)$, $\cos (\pi/2 + x)$, $\cos (\pi/2 - x)$, $\sin (\pi/2 + x)$, $\sin (\pi/2 - x)$. Derive these in whatever order is convenient, but do not use a formula which is not yet derived.

9. Given these approximate values: $\sin .3 = .30$, $\cos .3 = .96$, $\sin .5 = .48$, $\cos .5 = .88$, find approximations for the following:

(a) $\sin .6$   (b) $\cos .6$   (c) $\tan .3$   (d) $\cos .2$
(e) $\cot .5$   (f) $\csc .2$   (g) $\sin (.3 + \pi/2)$   (h) $\sec (\pi/2 - .8)$

10. Derive the formulas for $\sin 2x$ and $\cos 2x$; from the latter and the formula $\sin^2 x + \cos^2 x = 1$, derive the formulas for $\sin x/2$, $\cos x/2$ and $\tan x/2$.

## Circular Functions and Angles

Even if pupils have never studied any trigonometry before (which is unlikely for good pupils in the eleventh grade), they will certainly notice a connection between how we find the value of $\cos \pi/2$ or $\sin \pi/2$ and a 90° angle. Similarly, they will notice a connection between $\pi/4$ and a 45° angle, $\pi/3$ and a 60° angle, etc. (Fig. 12.7). Therefore, making this connection should not be a particularly difficult task. From the theorem in plane geometry which says that central angles with equal measure intercept arcs with equal measure (on a circle), we can see that there is a simple proportion relating angle measure to the measure of the intercepted arc on the unit circle. Since we know that an angle of 180° intercepts an arc on the unit circle with a measure of $\pi$, the desired proportion must be: $180/\pi = \theta/x$, where $x$ is the measure of the intercepted arc and $\theta$ is the measure of the central

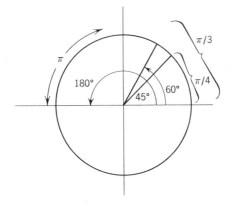

Figure 12.7

angle in degrees. Recalling that in geometry we occasionally measured arcs in degrees, the pupils will probably not be too surprised to find that we sometimes find it convenient to measure angles in units derived from the way in which we have been measuring arcs on the unit circle. Specifically, a central angle that intersects an arc of length one on a unit circle is said to have a measure of one radian. Or more generally, since we can always take the unit to be the length of the radius for any given circle, a central angle has a measure of one radian if it intersects an arc that has a length equal to the radius of the circle. Clearly, the formula established for converting arc length to degree measure of a central angle of the unit circle will also work for converting radian measure of an angle to degree measure of an angle.

If we use radian measure for our angles, the circular functions can now be thought of as functions of angles rather than of lengths of arcs. However, if we measure angles in degrees, we have a different set of functions. For example, the sine function as defined earlier has such members as $(\pi/2, 1)$, $(\pi/3, \sqrt{3}/2)$, $(\pi/4, \sqrt{2}/2)$, etc.; if we think of the first number as the measure of an angle in radians, the same ordered pairs are members of our function. However, if we wish to carry on the measuring procedure for angles in degrees, we must make some changes in the first members of the function in order to have a corresponding situation. Thus, the corresponding members of the new sine function would be: $(90°, 1)$, $(60°, \sqrt{3}/2)$, $(45°, \sqrt{2}/2)$, etc.

From the direct relationship between the measure of an angle in degrees and in radians, we can see that all the statements made about circular functions would also be true of these new functions which have as their domain the set of angle measures in degrees. Consequently, we use the same name to apply to each function—that is, we will say sin $45° = \sqrt{2}/2$ just as we say $\sin \pi/4 = \sqrt{2}/2$. No difficulties should arise because of this double use of the term "sin" or of the other words used to designate the circular functions. It is also possible to handle this situation more formally by considering the function $R$, which converts degree measure to radian measure and then thinking of sin 45° as a composite function $(\sin [R(45°)])$.

### Solving Triangles

The procedure for finding the sine of an angle whose measure in degrees is $\theta$ involves creating a set of axes with origin at the vertex of the angle, and $x$-axis along one side of the angle. Then, we must construct a unit circle and determine the ordinate of the point at which the terminal side of the angle intersects the unit circle. Since angles are measured in a counterclockwise direction, it is necessary to be sure that the *first* side $(\overrightarrow{OR'})$ of the angle is the one on the positive $x$-axis. This procedure may not always be convenient. Let us simplify it. In Fig. 12.8, if the smaller circle is a unit circle and the other one has a radius of length $b$ (which could be either greater than or less than 1), we see that triangle $OPQ$ is similar to triangle $OP'Q'$ and therefore, if $a$ is the ordinate of $P'$, $1/b = (\sin \theta)/a$ or $\sin \theta = a/b$. Thus, if an angle $(R'OP')$ is in standard position (vertex at origin and first side along positive $x$-axis), we can determine its sine by dividing the ordinate of any point on its terminal side by the distance of that point from the origin.

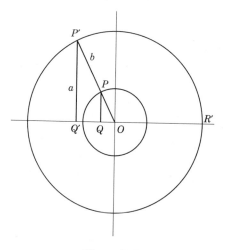

Figure 12.8

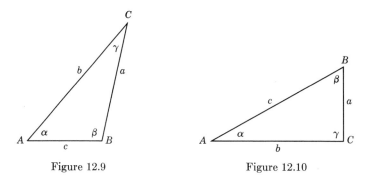

Figure 12.9                    Figure 12.10

Using the information of the previous paragraph, we can derive the law of sines. In Fig. 12.9, the angles and sides of triangle $ABC$ have the following measures: $A:\alpha$, $B:\beta$, $C:\gamma$, $AB = c$, $BC = a$, and $CA = b$. If we imagine a set of coordinate axes with origin at $A$ and $x$-axis along the ray $\overrightarrow{AB}$, the altitude of triangle $ABC$ drawn from $C$ to the extension of $\overleftrightarrow{AB}$ is the ordinate of point $C$. Therefore, $\sin \alpha$ = altitude (to $\overleftrightarrow{AB}$) $\div$ $b$, or the altitude equals $b \sin \alpha$. Similarly, if we imagine a set of coordinate axes with origin at $B$ and $x$-axis along ray $\overrightarrow{BC}$, the altitude from $A$ to $\overleftrightarrow{BC}$ can be shown to be $c \sin \beta$. Finally, the altitude from $B$ to $\overleftrightarrow{AC}$ can be shown in a similar way to equal $a \sin \lambda$. Since there are three bases and three altitudes of the triangle, there are three ways of finding its area, namely, $\frac{1}{2}cb \sin \alpha$, $\frac{1}{2}ac \sin \beta$, and $\frac{1}{2}ba \sin \lambda$. Since the area of the triangle does not change when we use different methods of computing it, we can set the first two areas equal to each other and by a proper division get $(\sin \alpha)/a = (\sin \beta)/b$. Setting the second and third equal to each other, we get $(\sin \beta)/b = (\sin \gamma)/c$. We can combine these two to get $(\sin \alpha)/a = (\sin \beta)/b = (\sin \gamma)/c$, or the law of sines.

In a right triangle, with $\gamma = 90°$, $\sin \gamma = 1$; hence $(\sin \alpha)/a = 1/c$, and $\sin \alpha = a/c$; or, the sine of an acute angle of a right triangle is equal to the length of the side opposite the angle divided by the length of the hypotenuse. This is the traditional definition of the sine of an angle. The other traditional definitions follow readily. For example, $\cos \alpha = \sin (90° - \alpha) = \sin \beta = b/c$, and the cosine of an acute angle of a right triangle is equal to the length of the adjacent side divided by the length of the hypotenuse. In this derivation, we must remember that $90°$ corresponds to $\pi/2$, and therefore, the statement that $\cos \alpha = \sin (90° - \alpha)$ follows from a previous theorem. Having come this far, we can easily find the values of the other functions in terms of the sides of a right triangle (Fig. 12.10). For instance,

$$\tan \alpha = \frac{\sin \alpha}{\cos \alpha} = \frac{a/c}{b/c} = \frac{a}{b}$$

With these formulas, and a table of values for the trigonometric (or circular) functions, pupils should be able to "solve right triangles." That is, given that one angle of a triangle is a right angle, the length of any of the three sides, and the measure of any of the other parts, a pupil can find the measure of each of the remaining parts. Probably, this is the best place for pupils to start becoming familiar with the standard trigonometry tables for angles between 0° and 90°.

Somewhere in the study of trigonometric functions, the pupils should become familiar with the standard inverse functions. Perhaps the best time to do so is immediately after graphing the circular functions. On the other hand, the pupils will be likely to use the inverses of trigonometric functions more commonly (at first, anyway) with angles, and therefore they should certainly discuss the inverse functions after beginning to use standard trigonometry tables. If they keep in mind that the inverse of a function can be acquired simply by reversing the members of each ordered pair, they should have no trouble with this concept. Thus, if one member of the tangent function is approximately (30°, .577) then the corresponding member of the inverse of this function is (.577, 30°). They will, however, need ample practice with interpolation, especially with the inverses of decreasing functions such as the cotangent.

There are two common ways of naming the inverse of each trigonometric function, for tangent, they are "arctan" and "tan⁻¹." Since both are commonly used, pupils should be exposed to both, but probably the term "arctan" is less likely to cause confusion since "$-1$" of "tan⁻¹" is indistinguishable from an exponent. Clearly, if we use the term "$\tan^{-1} x$" to signify the angle whose tangent is $x$, we must abandon that symbol as another way to write $1/\tan x$.

The fact that the inverse of a function is not necessarily a function is worth repeating. In fact, no periodic function has an inverse which is a function; therefore, none of the trigonometric functions has an inverse which is a function.

Before turning to solutions of oblique triangles, we shall consider the law of cosines. In the classroom, there would probably be some advantage in first using the law of sines to solve several triangles so as to show both the general procedure involved and the need for another tool to solve some triangles. Given any triangle, we can consider a coordinate system with its origin at one vertex and its $x$-axis along one side of the

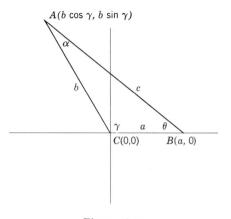

Figure 12.11

triangle. In Fig. 12.11, the coordinates of $C$ are $(0, 0)$, the coordinates of $B$ are $(a, 0)$ because the length of $CB$ is $a$, and since the measure of angle $ACB$ is $\gamma$ and the length of $AC$ is $b$, the coordinates of $A$ are $(b \cos \gamma, b \sin \gamma)$. From the distance formula we know that

$$c^2 = (b \cos \gamma - a)^2 + (b \sin \gamma)^2 = b^2 \cos^2 \gamma - 2ab \cos \gamma + a^2$$
$$+ b^2 \sin^2 \gamma = a^2 + b^2(\sin^2 \gamma + \cos^2 \gamma) - 2ab \cos \gamma$$

or

$$c^2 = a^2 + b^2 - 2ab \cos \gamma$$

Now, we have the necessary tools to solve all the triangles soluble by means of trigonometry. However, there are several comments which we should keep in mind as we teach this part of trigonometry. First, we have been discussing two different kinds of angles. In geometry, angle $ABC$ and angle $CBA$ are congruent, and the idea of a "sensed" angle does not occur at least not in most ordinary geometries now taught in the schools. In trigonometry, the sense of the angle is quite important; thus, an angle of $70°$ is an entirely different angle from one of $-70°$. Nevertheless, when we apply trigonometry to the solution of triangles, we think of all of the angles as not being sensed (nonsensed angles, as some irreverent pupils have been known to put it). Therefore, we assume that all the angles with which we deal in this study have a measure between $0°$ and $180°$, thus making the trigonometric study of triangles conform to that of plane geometry.

Since all of the angles we are considering have measures between $0°$ and $180°$, we can determine the angle uniquely if we are given the cosine of an angle; however, if we are given the sine of an angle, there are, in general, two angles that may have that sine. For example, if we know that $\sin \theta = \frac{1}{2}$, $\theta$ could be either 30° or 150°. Thus, if triangle $ABC$ has the measures $\alpha = 30°$, $c = 8$, $a = 6$ (Fig. 12.12), we have the interesting possibility that the person who is solving the triangle is thinking of a different triangle from the one which the questioner has in mind. Thus, we have the so-called ambiguous case. Notice that with the same numbers except with $a = 4$, we do have a unique right triangle with the appropriate properties. Also, if we are given the same measures with $a$ changed to 2, there is no triangle at all.

The ambiguous case is interesting for several reasons. First, the close connection between solving triangles and the congruency theorems (or postulates, as the case may be) from plane geometry is nowhere seen more clearly than in the connection between the ambiguous case in trigonometry and the SSA nontheorem (two triangles are congruent if two sides and a nonincluded angle of one are respectively congruent with two sides and a nonincluded angle of the other) from plane geometry. In trigonometry, whenever we are given three independent parts (that is, anything but three angles) of a triangle, we can find the others except in the ambiguous case; in geometry, two triangles are congruent when three independent parts of one are congruent to the corresponding parts of the other except in the SSA nontheorem. Thus, the two situations are entirely analogous, as, indeed, we have every right to expect. This connection should be brought to the attention of the pupils and probably discussed at some length.

One question that may arise from the preceding discussion is, if we are given three parts, how do we know whether there is a triangle containing these parts? Looking at Fig. 12.12, we see that if we are given $\alpha$, $c$ and $a$, then in order to have precisely one triangle, $a$ must equal $c \sin \alpha$ or be greater than $c$. If $c > a > c \sin \alpha$, there will be two triangles, and if $a < c \sin \alpha$, there will be no triangle. If two sides and an included angle are given (or two angles and an included side), it is clear that precisely one triangle will have the required properties; if

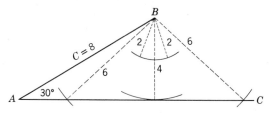

Figure 12.12

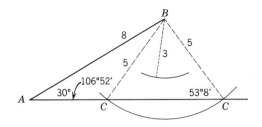

Figure 12.13

the lengths of the three sides are given, in order to have a triangle, the sum of the lengths of any two must be greater than the length of the third. Does this mean that before proceeding to solve a triangle we should first check the conditions to see that we do have a triangle? In the long run, we would probably waste more time checking then if we did not. There is no danger in simply proceeding, since whenever there is no triangle, this fact will always appear in the subsequent algebra. For example, if $\alpha = 30°$, $c = 8$ and $a = 3$, as in Fig. 12.13, we try to solve the triangle through the law of sines, getting: $(\sin 30°)/3 = (\sin \gamma)/8$ or $\sin \gamma = (8 \cdot \frac{1}{2})/3 = \frac{4}{3}$. Since we know that there is no angle with a sine equal to $\frac{4}{3}$, we conclude that no triangle has the given properties. If the value of $a$ had been 5, we would have found that $\sin \gamma = \frac{4}{5} = .8$. Reference to a table tells us that one angle that has a sine of about .8 is an angle of 53° 8′. However, we know that if the measure of an angle lies between 0° and 180°, its supplement will have the same sine as it does. Thus, an angle of 106° 52′ will have a sine of about .8, and, as we can see from Fig. 12.13, there are two triangles satisfying the given conditions.

In the case of two angles and an included side, the measure of the third angle can be found easily, assuming the sum of the first two is less than 180°. Finding the other two sides requires the use of the law of sines. If we are given $\beta$, $\gamma$, and $a$, and have found $\alpha$ then from the law of sines, $b = (a \sin \beta)/\sin \alpha$. Assuming that $\alpha$ is neither 0° nor 180°, $\sin \alpha$ is not zero, and the formula for $b$ will produce a real number in all cases, we find no possible difficulty in this case, as predicted.

In the case of two sides and the included angle, showing that we always have a unique triangle is somewhat more difficult. Assume we are given the values of $\alpha$, $b$ and $c$. Then, by the law of cosines, $a^2 = b^2 + c^2 - 2bc \cos \alpha$. In order for $a$ to be a real number, $a^2$ must be greater than or equal to zero, or $b^2 + c^2 - 2bc \cos \alpha \geq 0$. Assuming $b$ and $c$ are positive numbers, this is obvious when $\cos \alpha \leq 0$. When

$0 < \cos \alpha \leq 1$, we have

$$b^2 + c^2 - 2bc \cos \alpha \geq b^2 + c^2 - 2bc = (b + c)^2 > 0$$

Therefore, $a$ is a positive number when $b$ and $c$ are positive numbers and we can always find a positive real value for $a$.

This does not finish the potential difficulties, however. We must still find the measure of the other two angles. From a theorem in plane geometry, we know that the largest angle will lie opposite the largest side; therefore, we can determine which angle has the greatest measure. If angle $A$ has the greatest measure, then we can be sure that both of the other angles are acute; finding them using the law of sines leads to no ambiguity. If angle $A$ does not have the greatest measure, but angle $B$ does, then we know that angle $C$ is acute and can find it using the law of sines with no ambiguity. The measure of angle $B$ can be found from our knowledge of the sum of the measures of the angles of a triangle.

Finally, if we are given the measures of the three sides of a triangle, we will use the law of cosines to determine the measure of an angle. Solving $a^2 = b^2 + c^2 - 2bc \cos \alpha$ for $\cos \alpha$, we have: $\cos \alpha = (b^2 + c^2 - a^2)/2bc$. Since we know that $\cos \alpha$ must be a number between 1 and $-1$, the triangle will exist when

$$-1 < \frac{b^2 + c^2 - a^2}{2bc} < 1 \quad \text{or} \quad -2bc < b^2 + c^2 - a^2 < 2bc$$

thus, $a$, $b$, and $c$ must satisfy both of the following conditions (and their equivalent conditions) at the same time.

(1)
$$-2bc < b^2 + c^2 - a^2$$
$$0 < b^2 + 2bc + c^2 - a^2$$
$$0 < (b + c)^2 - a^2$$
$$0 < (b + c - a)(b + c + a)$$

since $b + c + a$ is positive, the above restriction requires that $b + c - a$ be positive or: $b + c > a$

(2)
$$b^2 + c^2 - a^2 < 2bc$$
$$b^2 - 2bc + c^2 - a^2 < 0$$
$$(b - c - a)(b - c + a) < 0$$

since $a > 0$, it is impossible that

$$b - c - a > 0 \quad \text{and} \quad b - c + a < 0$$

at the same time. Therefore,

$$b - c - a < 0 \quad \text{and} \quad b - c + a > 0$$

or

$$b < c + a \quad \text{and} \quad b + a > c$$

These three conditions taken together are equivalent to saying that the sum of the lengths of any two sides of the triangle must be greater than the length of the third side, as we had expected.

Algebra tells us that we can solve triangles in those cases where it is obvious from geometric considerations that we can solve them. In general, therefore, we do not have to decide in advance whether a triangle with the given conditions exists; if instead we carry out the algebra and do not run into an equation which has no solution in the desired universe, we can rest assured that a triangle does exist. Similarly, if we find that in order to solve the triangle, we must solve an equation which has no solution in our universe, we know that there is no triangle satisfying the given conditions.

One last comment on solving triangles. The reader has seen that we have in the law of sines and the law of cosines (and in our knowledge about the sum of the angles of a triangle) enough equipment to solve any soluble triangle; and yet, he undoubtedly recalls that there is another well-known law which is sometimes used in solving triangles, the law of tangents. The law of tangents says:

$$\frac{a - b}{a + b} = \frac{\tan \frac{1}{2}(\alpha - \beta)}{\tan \frac{1}{2}(\alpha + \beta)}$$

It has been used in solving triangles where two sides and an included angle were given, and the numbers were complicated enough so as to make the use of logarithms desirable. For example, suppose we are given $a$, $b$, and $\gamma$, we can find $\frac{1}{2}(\alpha + \beta)$ by subtracting $\gamma/2$ from $90°$. Then $\tan \frac{1}{2}(\alpha - \beta) = \tan \frac{1}{2}(\alpha + \beta) \times (a - b)/(a + b)$, and we can find a value for $\frac{1}{2}(\alpha - \beta)$. Since we have a value for both $(\alpha - \beta)$ and $(\alpha + \beta)$, we can solve for $\alpha$ and $\beta$ and use the law of sines to find the value of $c$. Although, from a theoretical point of view, this procedure is obviously more complicated than using the law of cosines, squaring the numbers $a$ and $b$, adding them and so on, as required by the law of cosines, is likely to require messy calculations, and because of the additions and subtractions involved, the law of cosines does not lend itself readily to the use of logarithms.

On the other hand, if we use the law of tangents, only multiplications and divisions are required, except for simple additions and subtractions at the beginning. We can find the logarithms of the given data at the beginning of the problem, carry on our calculations, and then reconvert at the end. Before the advent of desk calculators, this procedure saved considerable time when the numbers given were cumbersome. However, in the present age, any person who is asked to solve any large number of triangles will certainly avail himself of the services of a calculator. Therefore, as mentioned in the discussion of logarithms, there seems to be no particular point in spending large amounts of time studying methods of simplifying difficult computations by hand when almost certainly none of the pupils will ever be faced with such computations, anyway. Although the law of tangents was very helpful at one time, and is still of interest historically and in some problems in physics, we should spend little time on it in a course in high school trigonometry.

### Exercises

1. Copy Fig. 12.8, and put in the three sets of coordinate axes mentioned in the text. Determine the length of each altitude of the triangle, and find the area in the three ways suggested. Set these equal to each other in pairs and derive the law of sines.

2. Given triangle $ABC$, consider a set of coordinate axes with origin at $A$ and positive $x$-axis along the ray $\overrightarrow{AB}$. Using a procedure similar to that of the text, derive the law of cosines (using the angle with measure $\alpha$, of course).

3. List all possible sets of three parts of a triangle (that is, two angles and included side, two angles and nonincluded side, three angles, etc.), in each case stating whether or not there is a theorem in plane geometry pertaining to the congruency of triangles with these parts congruent. State whether or not we can be sure at least one triangle exists when these three parts are given. If not, what conditions are necessary to solve the given triangle if it can be solved? Describe the procedure used. If the solution is not unique, indicate how many noncongruent triangles might satisfy the given conditions.

### Vectors

Long used in the physical sciences, vectors have recently won some popularity in the teaching of certain topics of high school mathematics. Various suggestions have been made as to when and how vectors should be studied and used, but we shall limit ourselves to discussing some of their properties and the relation of their study to some of the other mathematics taught in the secondary schools of this country.

A vector is often thought of as a distance and a direction, or as a line segment with an arrow at one end which points in a particular direction

(Fig. 12.14). In order to avoid confusion later, let us make clear what we have in mind when we say vector $\overrightarrow{AB}$ (we shall use the half-arrow for vectors to distinguish it from the whole arrow which designates a ray). If we mean the specific segment $\overline{AB}$ with the direction from $A$ to

B, the vector $\overrightarrow{AB}$ and the vector $\overrightarrow{CD}$ in Fig. 12.14 are not the same and are therefore not equal. However, these two vectors do have many of the same properties. Actually, they have all the same properties which are of importance in the study of vectors. Therefore, we say that a vector is a direction and a distance, and a specific segment with an arrow to indicate direction is only its representation. We could get the same effect by use of equivalence classes with the segment-direction approach, but we would simply add to our difficulties by doing so. Hence, we shall think of vectors as directions and distances.

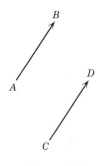

Figure 12.14

The negative of a vector is often thought of as the vector acquired by putting the arrow on the other end. Intuitively, this is correct, but in careful development, there would be some doubt that the sum of a vector and its negative were necessarily zero without some accurate definitions of addition, zero, and "putting the arrow on the other end." To approach vectors on a reasonably sound pedagogical basis, we should probably start with the intuitive notion of arrows having fixed direction and length, then "define" addition as the placing of the tail of one arrow at the head of another, and consider the sum to be the vector from the tail of the first to the head of the second. Pupils will then obtain an idea of what these terms mean. For purposes of rigor, we should define a vector as an ordered pair (distance, direction) and actually specify and derive the operations and properties desired. If teachers plan to use vectors in the study of geometry and to help introduce trigonometry, as suggested in the *Report of the Commission on Mathematics* of the College Entrance Examination Board (1959), they are largely restricted to the intuitive approach. On the other hand, if vectors are not studied until after trigonometry, a more rigorous approach is available.

From an intuitive idea of addition of vectors emerges the basis for a precise definition of addition. In Fig. 12.15, the vectors $(r, \theta)$ and $(s, \phi)$ are broken into their components: $r \cos \theta$ and $r \sin \theta$ for the first and $s \cos \phi$ and $s \sin \phi$ for the second. A representation of $(s, \phi)$ appears in the appropriate spot for addition and the resultant vector

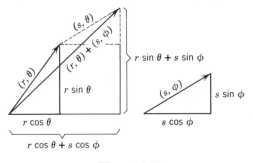

Figure 12.15

is marked $(r, \theta) + (s, \phi)$. Notice that the sum of the horizontal components of the original vectors is the horizontal component of the sum, and similarly, the vertical component of the sum equals the sum of the vertical components. Therefore, the length of the new vector is

$[(r \cos \theta + s \cos \phi)^2 + (r \sin \theta + s \sin \phi)^2]^{\frac{1}{2}}$
$= [r^2 \cos^2 \theta + 2rs \cos \theta \cos \phi + s^2 \cos^2 \phi + r^2 \sin^2 \theta$
$\qquad\qquad\qquad\qquad + 2rs \sin \theta \sin \phi + s^2 \sin^2 \phi]^{\frac{1}{2}}$
$= [r^2 + s^2 + 2rs(\cos \theta \cos \phi + \sin \theta \sin \phi)]^{\frac{1}{2}}$
$= [r^2 + s^2 + 2rs \cos (\theta - \phi)]^{\frac{1}{2}}$

Looking back at Fig. 12.15, we see that the angle of the new vector has a tangent equal to $(r \sin \theta + s \sin \phi)/(r \cos \theta + s \cos \phi)$. From these considerations, the following definition seems reasonable:

$(r, \theta) + (s, \phi) = (\sqrt{r^2 + s^2 + 2rs \cos (\theta - \phi)},$
$$\arctan \frac{(r \sin \theta + s \sin \phi)}{(r \cos \theta + s \cos \phi)} \Big)$$

This definition is certainly not a simple one and is not worth memorizing, but it gives a clear, concise statement of what is meant by addition of vectors.

Let us see if this operation has the properties associated with an operation called addition. First, is the operation closed? There are two ways in which the definition might lead to lack of closure: the first is that the distance may turn out to be a nonreal number (the radicand might be negative); the second possibility is that the number $r \cos \theta + s \cos \phi$ might be zero, in which case we would have to find the arctangent of a nonnumber.

We know $\cos (\theta - \phi)$ lies between $-1$ and $+1$, or $\cos (\theta - \phi) \geq$

$-1$, and $r^2 + s^2 + 2rs \cos (\theta - \phi) \geq r^2 + s^2 - 2rs = (r - s)^2 \geq 0$. Therefore, the distance will always be a real number, and the first difficulty is removed.

The second problem is more complicated. Actually it is possible for $r \cos \theta + s \cos \phi$ to be zero. Several possibilities occur. First, if the numerator of the fraction $(r \sin \theta + s \sin \phi)/(r \cos \theta + s \cos \phi)$ is zero at the same time as the denominator is zero, we can prove that the distance will also be zero. We shall say that the sum is the zero vector which we shall simply write "0" with no direction indicated. Since we define this as a vector, we have no trouble with closure when both numerator and denominator of the fraction are zero. If the numerator of the fraction is a positive number and the denominator is zero, we shall say that the angle of the sum is 90°, and when the numerator is negative with a zero denominator, we shall say the angle is 270°. Thus, by the simple expedient of definition, we assure closure. Notice, that these definitions correspond with intuition, and therefore, we shall probably preserve the other properties desired.

Having discussed closure, we next turn to uniqueness. Certainly, when adding two vectors, we expect to get only one result. Probably the first step in this direction is to eliminate extra names for a single vector. Thus, (2, 10°) and (2, 370°) would not both be used since they stand for the same vector. Let us agree to use only angles with non-negative measure less than 360°; that is, the second member, $\theta$, of an ordered pair is such that $0° \leq \theta < 360°$. From our knowledge of the real number system we know that all of the operations to determine the distance are unique (including finding $\cos (\theta - \phi)$, since cos is a function). Therefore, the result will always be a unique, nonnegative real number. However, given any number, we can find two angles that have that number for a tangent and are in our universe. How shall we decide between them? From geometric considerations, it is clear that whenever the numerator of the fraction $(r \sin \theta + s \sin \phi)/$ $(r \cos \theta + s \cos \phi)$ is positive, the angle will lie between 0° and 180° and when negative, the angle will lie between 180° and 360°. Furthermore, when the numerator is zero, the angle will be 0° if the denominator is positive, and 180° if the denominator is negative. We have now imposed enough conditions on the definition of addition to assure both closure and uniqueness.

The procedure used to assure closure and uniqueness may seem untidy, yet it is instructive, both to a bright high school pupil and to the college student who has never seen any reason for fussing over closure and uniqueness when defining a new operation. We would like addition of vectors to be closed and unique; otherwise, calculations will lead to utter confusion, even if the student is capable of performing all of the mechanical tasks. Therefore, when the definition left us without either closure or uniqueness, we had to improve on it while still leaving it essentially the same. Furthermore, the improvements all fit our intuitive ideas reasonably well.

Let us try an example to see how we would use the definition in a specific case. Suppose we wished to add (3, 30°) and (4, 80°).

$$(3, 30°) + (4, 80°) = \left[ \sqrt{9 + 16 + 24 \cos 50°}, \arctan \left( \frac{1.50 + 3.94}{2.60 + .69} \right) \right]$$

$$= (\sqrt{40.36}, \arctan 1.66) = (6.35, 59°)$$

Figure 12.16 shows that the answer found is close to the one we would expect. There are several places in the calculations which called for decision. First, why did we choose cos 50° and not cos −50°? Does it make any difference? Second, there are two angles with tan of 1.66—what are they? How did we decide which to use? Finally, throughout the calculations we used tables in the appropriate spots. Our answer is only an approximation, and we could find a more accurate approximation by using more precise tables.

If we let $r = 0$ in the definition of addition, we get

$$(0, θ) + (s, φ) = \left( \sqrt{0 + s^2 + 0}, \arctan \frac{\sin φ}{\cos φ} \right) = (s, φ)$$

Thus, as we had assumed when defining the zero element, the angle of the zero element makes no difference, and any vector $(0, θ)$ is an identity element for addition. As we said before, we will say there is only one such element and designate it 0. To be entirely correct, we should also show that $(r, θ) + (0, φ) = (r, θ)$, since we have not yet shown that addition is commutative. The reader may provide this proof for himself if he wishes.

To show that addition of vectors is commutative, we simply use the fact that addition of real numbers is commutative and also notice that $\cos (θ − φ) = \cos (φ − θ)$ because the cosine is an even function.

The proof that addition of vectors is associative is considerably more

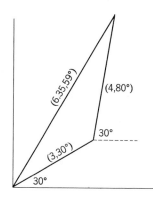

Figure 12.16

complicated. However, if we refer to the original "derivation" of the definition of addition, and use the equivalent forms for the length and angle of the sum which first appeared in those "derivations," the proof is fairly straightforward.

Finally, to show that every vector has an additive inverse, we simply display the inverse. We contend that $(r, \theta + 180°)$ is the additive inverse of $(r, \theta)$. To prove this we note that

$$(r, \theta) + (r, \theta + 180) = (\sqrt{r^2 + r^2 + 2rr \cos (180°)},$$

$$\arctan \left[ \frac{r \sin \theta + r \sin (\theta + 180°)}{r \cos \theta + r \cos (\theta + 180°)} \right]) = \left( \sqrt{2r^2 - 2r^2}, \arctan \frac{0}{0} \right) = 0$$

(If $\theta > 180°$, then $(\theta + 180°)$ should be interpreted as $\theta - 180°$.)

Thus, the set of vectors is a commutative (or abelian) group with respect to addition.

Having established the group properties for addition of vectors, we move on to multiplication of vectors. Unfortunately, there is no immediately obvious way to define multiplication among vectors. One type of multiplication involving vectors which is well known is called scaler multiplication. This is a procedure of successive additions of a vector to itself. Thus, $3 \times (r, \theta) = (3r, \theta)$, or a vector three times as long as the vector $(r, \theta)$ but in the same direction as $(r, \theta)$. Of course, when we multiply by irrational real numbers such as $\sqrt{2}$, we can no longer say we have added the vector to itself $\sqrt{2}$ times, but intuitively the idea is much the same. When we multiply a set of vectors by a real number, the vectors end up looking much like the originals except for a change in size; their directions are still the same. Thus, multiplying by a real number has the effect of changing the scale. Therefore we call the real number a scaler, and as mentioned previously, this type of multiplication is called scaler multiplication. The properties of this type of multiplication are immediately obvious from our knowledge of real numbers. A set of vectors with addition as previously defined and multiplication by real numbers is called a vector space.

Another way of representing a vector $(r, \theta)$ is by an ordered pair in which both members are real numbers. Considered with respect to a set of coordinate axes, these numbers could be thought of as the $x$ and $y$ components of the vector. Thus, $(r, \theta)$ would be represented as $(r \cos \theta, r \sin \theta)$. Or, if we are given the representation $(a, b)$ in the new system (Fig. 12.17), the representation in the old system would be $(\sqrt{a^2 + b^2}, \arctan b/a)$. In this new system, there is another type of multiplication in which the result is called the inner product or the dot product. Given two vectors $(a, b)$ and $(c, d)$, the inner product is

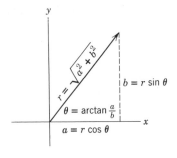

Figure 12.17

defined as $(a, b) \cdot (c, d) = ac + bd$. Notice that the dot product of two vectors is *not* a vector, but rather a real number.

The set of vectors is a subset of the set of objects known as matrices. Within this larger set there is still another operation known as multiplication. However, we shall not discuss that topic here. There has been some suggestion that for bright high school pupils, a course in matrix algebra is appropriate; see, for example, the School Mathematics Study Group booklet, *Mathematics for High School, Introduction to Matrix Algebra*.

### Exercises

1. Define addition of vectors algebraically in such a way that the set of vectors is a commutative group with respect to addition. (Hint: Combine the various restrictions scattered in this section.) Show that your results do define a commutative group.

2. Using the definition in Exercise 1, add the following:

(a) $(\sqrt{2}, 45°) + (2, 240°)$
(b) $(5, 150°) + (2\sqrt{2}, 135°)$
(c) $(8, 140°) + (10, 320°)$
(d) $(5, 75°) + (8, 15°)$

3. Show that if $r \sin \theta + s \sin \phi$ and $r \cos \theta + s \cos \phi$ are both zero, so is $\sqrt{r^2 + s^2 + 2rs \cos (\theta - \phi)}$

### Complex Numbers

The study of complex numbers relates several apparently divergent topics including the study of number systems, circular functions, and exponents. Recall that complex numbers can be represented either in the usual form of $a + bi$, where $a$ and $b$ are real numbers or as the ordered pair of real numbers $(a, b)$. If we decide to try to plot the complex number $(a, b)$ on a pair of coordinate axes, we can think of the vertical axis as the pure imaginary axis and the horizontal axis as the real one. Then the complex number $(a, b)$ or $a + bi$ is represented as in Fig. 12.18. The similarity between vectors and complex numbers is immediately obvious. From this graphic representation, another way of writing complex numbers is suggested. An ordered pair

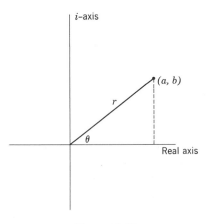

Figure 12.18

that gives us the same information as the pair $(a, b)$ is the pair $(r, \theta)$, where $r = \sqrt{a^2 + b^2}$ and $\theta = \arctan a/b$. Thus, we have another ordered pair representation of a complex number. Notice that if we are given the complex number $(r, \theta)$ and wish to convert it to standard form, we simply note that $a = r \cos \theta$ and $b = r \sin \theta$; therefore, the complex number can be written $r \cos \theta + ri \sin \theta$ or $r(\cos \theta + i \sin \theta)$. This is sometimes referred to as the polar form of a complex number since graphing it on polar coordinates is particularly easy in this form.

Adding complex numbers in polar form is not easy, however. It is essentially the same process as used for adding vectors. Indeed, we can always reconvert to the standard (or rectangular form) to add complex numbers in the usual way. However, multiplying complex numbers in polar form is surprisingly easy, and the procedure leads to some interesting results involving powers and roots of complex numbers.

Consider the two complex numbers $r(\cos \theta + i \sin \theta)$ and $s(\cos \phi + i \sin \phi)$. The product of these numbers is

$$r(\cos \theta + i \sin \theta) \cdot s(\cos \phi + i \sin \phi)$$
$$= rs[\cos \theta \cos \phi - \sin \theta \sin \phi + i(\cos \theta \sin \phi + \cos \phi \sin \theta)]$$

From our knowledge of the formulas for the sine and cosine of the sum of two angles, we can simplify this to $rs[\cos (\theta + \phi) + i \sin (\theta + \phi)]$. Thus, we see that the product of the two complex numbers represented by $(r, \theta)$ and $(s, \phi)$ is $(rs, \theta + \phi)$. Because of the common occurrence of "$\cos \theta + i \sin \theta$" in the study of complex numbers, we abbreviate this: "cis $\theta$" when it is convenient to do so. Thus, the result can be written: $r$ cis $\theta \cdot s$ cis $\phi = rs$ cis $(\theta + \phi)$.

The number $r$ is often called the modulus of the complex number $r$ cis $\theta$ and $\theta$ is called its amplitude.[1] The number $r$ is also defined to be the absolute value of $r$ cis $\theta$. Since we know that $r = \sqrt{a^2 + b^2}$, we can show that this definition of the absolute value of a complex number does not contradict the definition for real numbers. If $|a + bi| = \sqrt{a^2 + b^2}$, then when $b = 0$, $|a| = |a + 0i| = \sqrt{a^2} = |a|$.

Having established a formula for multiplying two complex numbers, we turn next to finding powers of complex numbers. Suppose we wished to find the eighth power of $2 + 2i$. We could multiply $(2 + 2i) \times (2 + 2i)$, getting $4 - 4 + 8i = 8i$; then multiply $8i \times 8i$ getting $-64$, and finally multiply $-64 \times -64$ getting 4096 as the answer. Another way of attacking the problem is to convert $2 + 2i$ to polar form: $2\sqrt{2}$ cis $45°$. Then,

$$(2\sqrt{2} \text{ cis } 45°)^8 = (2\sqrt{2})^8 \cdot \text{cis } (8 \times 45°) = 2^{12} \text{ cis } 360° = 4096$$

We have not actually proved that we can use this procedure for raising to a power, but in light of our work with products, it should seem reasonable.

The theorem we used to find the eighth power of $2 + 2i$ is known as De Moivre's Theorem which says:

The $n$th power of a complex number $(r$ cis $\theta)$ is a complex number with the $n$th power of the given modulus as its modulus and $n$ times the given amplitude as its amplitude, or, $(r$ cis $\theta)^n = r^n$ cis $n\theta$

In order to prove De Moivre's Theorem for all natural numbers $n$, we use induction.

Clearly the statement is true for $n = 1$, since

$$(r \text{ cis } \theta)^1 = r \text{ cis } \theta = r^1 \text{ cis } 1 \times \theta$$

Next, suppose that it is true that $(r$ cis $\theta)^k = r^k$ cis $k\theta$. What is $(r$ cis $\theta)^{k+1}$?

$$(r \text{ cis } \theta)^{k+1} = (r \text{ cis } \theta)^k \cdot r \text{ cis } \theta = (r^k \text{ cis } k\theta) \cdot r \text{ cis } \theta$$
$$= r^k \cdot r \text{ cis } (k\theta + \theta) = r^{k+1} \text{ cis } (k + 1)\theta$$

Therefore, since the theorem is true for $n = 1$ and for $n = k + 1$, whenever it is true for $n = k$, the theorem is true for all natural numbers $n$ by the induction theorem.

Suppose we wished to find an $n$th root of the number $s$ cis $\phi$. This

---

[1] The modulus is also commonly called the absolute value, whereas the amplitude is sometimes called either the argument or the angle of the complex number.

would mean that we wished to find some number $r$ cis $\theta$ such that $(r \text{ cis } \theta)^n = s \text{ cis } \phi$. From De Moivre's theorem, we know that $s = r^n$ and $\phi = n\theta$. Therefore, we should be able to find an $n$th root of $s$ cis $\phi$ by taking the $n$th root of the real number $s$ as our modulus and dividing $\theta$ by $n$ in order to find the amplitude. For example, suppose we wished to find a cube root of $i$. We know $i$ could be written in the form 1 cis 90°. Therefore, a cube root of $i$ can be found by taking the cube root of 1 (which is 1) for a modulus and one-third of 90° (or 30°) for an amplitude. Thus, the number 1 cis 30° ought to be a cube root of $i$. If we convert this number to standard form, we have $\sqrt{3}/2 + i/2$ or $(\sqrt{3} + i)/2$. Let us check to see that this really is a cube root of $i$.

$$\left(\frac{\sqrt{3} + i}{2}\right)^2 = \frac{2 + 2\sqrt{3}i}{4} = \frac{1 + \sqrt{3}i}{2}$$

Multiplying this product by $(\sqrt{3} + i)/2$, we get

$$\frac{\sqrt{3} - \sqrt{3} + i + 3i}{4} = \frac{4i}{4} = i$$

Are there any other cube roots of $i$? We know that, in general, we expect three roots to a cubic equation. Therefore, we might expect to find two more cube roots of $i$. However, the procedure just used seems to yield only one root. If we recall that when we started talking about vectors we made the assumption that we ought to use only non-negative angles less than 360°, we notice that precisely the same convention is needed for polar representations of complex numbers. In fact, we have been tacitly assuming this convention throughout our discussion of complex numbers. Yet, another way to represent the complex number $i$ is as the ordered pair (1, 450°) or 1 cis 450°. Now, the cube root of $i$ turns out to be 1 cis ($\frac{1}{3} \cdot 450°$) or 1 cis 150°. If we convert this number to standard form, we have $-\sqrt{3} + i/2$. The reader can easily convince himself, by multiplication, that this number is, in fact, a cube root of $i$.

A third cube root of $i$ can be found by representing the complex number $i$ by 1 cis 810°, in which case the cube root is 1 cis 270° which can be converted to $-i$. Again, a simple multiplication will prove to the reader's satisfaction that $-i$ is really a cube root of $i$.

The reaction of a high school pupil to the preceding argument is likely to be "if all we have to do is add another 360° to the amplitude of the last representation of a complex number in order to get a new representation which will give rise to a different root, why can't we go on finding new roots indefinitely?" The answer is to let the pupil try.

He will quickly find that upon applying this procedure to 1 cis 1170°
he gets an answer of 1 cis 390°, which is another representation of the
first root found, or $(\sqrt{3} + i)/2$. Continued use of this procedure will
simply repeat the other roots already found.

If we try to generalize the foregoing procedure, we notice that in
order to find the $n$th roots of a complex number in polar form, $r$ cis $\theta$,
we take the $n$th root of the real number $r$ as our modulus and use $\theta/n$,
$\theta/n + 360°/n$, $\theta/n + 2 \cdot 360°/n$, etc., as our amplitudes. Since $n$ is
assumed to be a natural number, sooner or later one of the ampli-
tudes is certain to be $\theta/n + n \cdot 360°/n$ or $\theta/n + 360°$. Since we have
agreed to use only amplitudes that are less than 360°, and $\theta$ itself was
originally assumed to be a nonnegative angle less than 360°, we can
rewrite this last amplitude as $\theta/n$ and recognize it as a repeat of our
first amplitude. This procedure can be depended on to give us exactly
$n$ $n$th roots of any complex number.

An interesting but rather unexpected dividend comes from the formula for finding the $n$th power of a complex number. If we apply
De Moivre's Theorem to $(1 \text{ cis } \theta)^3$, we find the result is 1 cis $3\theta$. However, we can also multiply $(\cos \theta + i \sin \theta)^3$ the long way getting
$\cos^3 \theta - 3i \cos^2 \theta \sin \theta - 3 \cos \theta \sin^2 \theta - i \sin^3 \theta$. We know that these
two results must be equal and further, that two complex numbers are
equal if and only if their real parts are equal *and* their pure imaginary
parts are equal. Therefore, we can conclude that $\cos 3\theta = \cos^3 \theta -
3 \cos \theta \sin^2 \theta$ and $\sin 3\theta = 3 \cos^2 \theta \sin \theta - \sin^3 \theta$. Thus, we have de-
rived the standard formulas for the sine and cosine of three times an
angle. The same procedure can be used for any multiple of an angle.
Sometimes these formulas are simplified by recalling that $\sin^2 \theta +
\cos^2 \theta = 1$, and the first formula becomes $\cos 3\theta = 4 \cos^3 \theta - 3 \cos \theta$,
whereas the second formula becomes $\sin 3\theta = 3 \sin \theta - 4 \sin^3 \theta$.

With extensive use of the various theorems on limits or a great
reliance on the faith of one's audience, a teacher can derive the series
expansion for sin $x$ and cos $x$ by using De Moivre's Theorem on cis $n\theta$
and letting $n\theta = x$ (a constant) while $n$ gets very large. Although both
the procedure and results are interesting, there is some doubt that
this sort of study is the best use of a high school pupil's time, especially
if no thorough discussion of limits accompanies the study. Similarly,
a discussion of complex exponents, although interesting, is undoubtedly
beyond the scope of a normal high school program.

### Teaching Hints

An effective model of the wrapping function can be made by taking
a bicycle wheel of radius 12 inches (if the radius is slightly less, it can

be built up using cloth and black electrical tape) and a long tape measure, preferably calibrated in hundredths of a foot. The wheel should be fastened firmly so it does not spin and the tape can be wrapped around it in the appropriate direction. Using either a coordinate system, if one is available, or just a yard stick and some care, the pupils can find close approximations for such numbers as sin 1, cos 2, sin −7, etc. This will impress upon them the fact that we are not limited to rational multiples of $\pi$ for numbers in the domain.

When the pupils are trying to evaluate values of the wrapping function (and later, sine and cosine), the use of angle measures in degrees must not be discouraged. It is natural and desirable for them to see the connection between the real numbers they are using and degree measure of an angle. This will make the connection between radian measure and degree measure seem natural when it is brought up.

Although the law of tangents is not of very much practical use in the solving of triangles now, it does have some important applications in physics, notably in optics. Perhaps it would be appropriate to develop a unit in conjunction with the physics teacher which involves the law of tangents and other theorems which he would like to have discussed in the mathematics class—or perhaps the unit should be taught in the physics class.

A unit on complex numbers and trigonometry, such as that described, is one of the most cohesive in elementary mathematics. It brings together such important strands of mathematics as geometry, functions, algebra, extension of the number system, and exponents. This is an ideal opportunity to discuss the unity of mathematics, and to review important concepts. Notice, however, that it is not necessary to spread the trigonometry evenly through an algebra book in order to integrate the two. In fact, it is preferable to start the trigonometry only after sufficient background in algebra has been acquired.

## Exercises

1. Compute each of the following using De Moivre's Theorem and a table where necessary:

(a) $(-3 + 3i)^5$

(b) $(\sqrt{3} - i)^7$

(c) $(3 + 3\sqrt{3}\,i)^8$

(d) $(-5 + 5i)^4$

(e) $(3 - 2i)^{11}$

(f) $(3 + 2i)^{11}$

2. Find all of the indicated roots (convert answer to standard form):

(a) The three cube roots of 1

(b) The six-sixth roots of 1

(c) The twelve-twelfth roots of 1

(d) The six-sixth roots of 64

(e) The three cube roots of $-8i$

(f) The two square roots of $-36i$

(g) The five-fifth roots of $i$

(h) The seven-seventh roots of $2 + 5i$

3. Using De Moivre's Theorem derive the formulas for the following:

(a) $\sin 2\theta$        (b) $\cos 2\theta$        (c) $\sin 4\theta$        (d) $\cos 4\theta$
(e) $\sin 5\theta$        (f) $\cos 5\theta$

## Questions for Further Thought and Study:

1. Discuss the various objects called angles in high school mathematics. Give a definition of each and describe their relation to one another. Also, discuss the measurement of the angles.

2. In this chapter, symbols such as "$\theta$" were used. Did these symbols stand for real numbers, for real numbers with some sort of unit attached, or for something else? Would you have used the symbols to stand for the same thing as here, or would you prefer to use them differently? Justify your answer in either case, and if you would use them differently, mention the changes which would have to be made in how they were used.

3. In light of the recommendations regarding vectors made by various groups, when do you think is the most appropriate time to introduce vectors into the mathematics curriculum of the high school? How would you introduce vectors (what would be your definitions, rules for operations, etc.)? Would you use vectors in studying other topics; if so, what topics and how would you use vectors? If not, why would you introduce vectors at all? If you decide you would prefer not to introduce vectors into the school mathematics curriculum, explain why the various groups that have recommended them are in error.

4. Pick some scientific journal (or book) and scan about one year's set of issues for uses of trigonometry (until you have found at least ten such occurrences). Discuss the uses to which trigonometry is put and tabulate the number of times trigonometry is used principally as a mensurational aid as opposed to an aid in studying functions. Could any of the problems occurring in this journal be adapted for use in a high school trigonometry course? If so, list them.

5. Draw a picture for the proof of the formula for $\cos(x - y)$ for each of the following pairs of values for $x$ and $y$:

| $x$ | $\dfrac{3\pi}{2}$ | $-\dfrac{\pi}{2}$ | $-\dfrac{\pi}{2}$ | $\dfrac{3\pi}{2}$ | $\dfrac{3\pi}{2}$ | $-\dfrac{3\pi}{2}$ |
|---|---|---|---|---|---|---|
| $y$ | $\dfrac{5\pi}{6}$ | $\dfrac{5\pi}{6}$ | $-\dfrac{7\pi}{6}$ | $-\dfrac{7\pi}{6}$ | $-\dfrac{5\pi}{6}$ | $\dfrac{5\pi}{6}$ |

Discuss the changes that must be made in the proof for each of these cases.

## REFERENCES

Commission on Mathematics of the College Entrance Examination Board. *Program for College Preparatory Mathematics*, College Entrance Examination Board, 1959, pp. 28–29, 37, 41–43. Suggests a study of numerical trigonometry in the junior high school or early in the eleventh grade followed by a more formal study of trigonometry in the eleventh and twelfth grades. Recommends a change of emphasis from triangle solving and identities to vectors and functional properties.

————. *Appendices*, College Entrance Examination Board, 1959, pp. 175–233. Presents material on various topics which may be of help to a teacher trying to teach a "modern" course in trigonometry. Topics included are an introduction to vectors, coordinate trigonometry, complex numbers, some simple applications of vectors, derivation of trigonometric formulas, the circular function approach, and a discussion of the relations between circular functions, exponential functions, and infinite series ending with the formula $e^{2\pi i} - 1 = 0$.

Organization for European Economic Cooperation, *Synopses for Modern Secondary School Mathematics*, Office for Scientific and Technical Personnel, Paris, 1961. Pp. 89, 132 ff.: Use of vectors in geometry and study of vectors with respect to group properties. Pp. 172–186: Proposed program of vector and linear algebra for late senior high age group. Pp. 201–219: An axiomatic description of affine spaces in which, starting with the notion of an abstract vector space, Dr. Artin derives properties of a general affine geometry. This is very difficult material even for bright high school seniors.

Courant, Richard, and Herbert Robbins. *What is Mathematics?* Oxford University Press, New York, 1941, pp. 88–103. Study of complex numbers ending with fundamental theorem of algebra.

Fehr, Howard F. *Secondary Mathematics, A Functional Approach for Teachers.* D. C. Heath and Co., New York, 1951, pp. 254–296. Relates the complex number system to trigonometry, including De Moivre's theorem, series expansions of sine and cosine, Euler's formula, complex exponents and logarithms, and closure of the complex number system.

Levi, Howard. *Foundations of Geometry and Trigonometry*, Prentice-Hall, Englewood Cliffs, N.J., 1960; see particularly pp. 100 ff., 137–152, 202–266. A unique and careful approach to trigonometry from a geometric point of view with geometry, in turn, approached from an algebraic point of view. Makes a careful distinction between angles and sensed angles.

# PROBABILITY AND
# STATISTICAL INFERENCE

Our world is full of numbers. Unfortunately, most people are afraid of numbers and are equally afraid of anybody who seems to know what he is doing with them. Thus, many people will accept any "fact" if it is supported by "statistics." Advertisers, newspapers, large corporations and labor unions, business groups find it easier to persuade others with statistics. Sometimes these statistics are easy to interpret, even for the uninformed "man in the street"; sometimes even the expert is hardpressed to interpret them correctly.

One purpose of a high school course in probability and statistics is to help the consumer of statistical reports to interpret them intelligently. For this reason, a course in probability and statistics is likely to be more appropriate for "remedial" or slow pupils than a course in elementary algebra. Even for the college-bound pupil who is not going to major in mathematics or one of the closely allied physical sciences, such a course will be of considerable value if it is taught with understanding. For the pupil who is planning on continuing his mathematics education in college for several years, a course in probability might be of more value if it were to come after a course in calculus. However, even for this individual, a preview would likely provide a good intuitive foundation for later studies. But if only the arithmetical calculations are considered, with no understanding of how they can be used to interpret (or misinterpret) data, the pupils will be little better off than with a course in formal algebra.

## Organizing and Reporting Data

There are many ways to report a set of data to someone else. Interestingly enough, one name, "average," is used to designate several different numbers which often describe a set of data. For example, suppose a small factory employs ten people. A labor union announces that the average worker gets a salary of only $3000 per year, while the company says that the average wage is $7300 per year. Which one is lying? Actually neither. The "average" used by the labor union is the *mode*, while the "average" used by the company is the *mean*. A third measure, the *median*, is also called an average, and is usually more appropriate in cases of this sort.

Let us suppose that the figures giving rise to the above facts were the following: $3000, $3000, $3000, $3500, $4000, $4500, $6000, $6000, $15,000, and $25,000. The mode is found by looking through the figures to see which one appears most often. It is clear that $3000 is the most common wage in the factory, and is therefore the mode of the wages. To find the mean, we add up all of the salaries and divide by 10 getting $7300. To determine the median, we arrange the salaries in order and count off half of them. Half of these figures are greater than $4250 and half are less than that; therefore, $4250 is said to be the median. If there were a salary exactly in the middle, we would use that as the median, but in a case of this kind, it is common to take the mean of the two middle figures.

Which of these three statistics seems fairest? Certainly, the $3000 figure does not seem fair, since every worker in the plant earns at least that much, and most of them earn more. On the other hand, $7300 does not seem much fairer, since only two of the employees make more than $7300, and those two are almost certainly managers (probably the owner and his son). Yet, in a sense, the $7300 figure gives considerable information; in conjunction with the knowledge that there are ten employees, it tells us that the company spends $73,000 per year on salaries. This figure does not, however, indicate much about the economic condition of the employees. Probably, the fairest figure which does give some general information about the economic condition of the employees is the median. This figure tells us for sure that half of the employees earn more than $4250 a year, and half earn less.

In teaching a course in statistics, it is common to mention the three kinds of averages, but it is not common to discuss how these averages can be used to tell entirely different stories. For the pupil, it is as important to have the latter information as it is to know how to compute the averages.

## Variability and Reliability

If the mean of a set of data is accompanied by some measure of the dispersion or variability of the data, the mean becomes a more significant figure. For example, if the mean of the salaries in a plant is $7300, and the range of salaries is $600, then the reader can be fairly certain that most of the employees have a salary somewhere between $7000 and $7600. It is possible that there would be one person who had a salary of $7800 and five with salaries of $7200, but we would still agree that the $7300 figure was a reasonable indication of the kind of salary paid to the employees of the firm. On the other hand, if the range is $22,000 and the mean is $7300, the mean does not really seem to be so good an indicator of the financial condition of the employees, but the two pieces of information together give the reader some idea as to the kind of a distribution that must have produced them. We can assume that no employee gets less than $0, and in this day and age it would be unlikely that any would be drawing less than $2000 per year. In that case, if the range is $22,000, the top salary must be approximately $24,000, or more. If we know that there are only ten employees in the firm, and the top salary is at least $24,000 with an average of $7300, it is clear that the total payroll is $73,000 (10 × 7300) and about one-third of it is going to one employee. That means that the mean of the salaries other than the $24,000 is roughly $5500. Thus, the information about the mean and range gives a much more accurate picture than the mean alone.

There are other, more sophisticated, measures of variability. For example, the mean absolute deviation is a good indicator. To find the mean absolute deviation, we find the positive difference between the mean and each of the measures, then add them all, and divide by the number of measurements. For example, in our illustration, the absolute differences are 4300, 4300, 4300, 3800, 3300, 2800, 1300, 1300, 7700, and 17,700. The sum of these is 50,800, so the mean absolute deviation is $5080—or "on the average," the salaries differ from the mean by about $5000. This is a rather substantial deviation considering the size of the mean. On the other hand, if there had been five salaries of $7000 and five of $7600, the mean absolute deviation would be $300, indicating a much smaller dispersion.

The measure of dispersion in common use is the standard deviation rather than the mean absolute deviation. The principal reason for this is that the standard deviation is much more convenient from the point of view of advanced computations. Moreover, it has various interesting properties which the other measures do not have. The standard deviation is calculated by finding each difference as before, squaring it, adding the squared deviations, dividing the sum by the number of cases, and taking the square root. It sounds much more complicated, and is for elementary problems attacked with elementary methods, but it remains in common usage because of its convenience. For simple problems, it will give about the same kind of information as the mean absolute deviation.

Once the various measures of dispersion have been mentioned, it is important that pupils keep in mind what these mean. There are formulas for use in simplifying the calculation of the standard deviation; in fact, when using a desk calculator and the proper formula, the standard deviation is relatively simple to calculate. However, it is not our major aim (or should not be) to teach the children to calculate quickly. It is more important that they know what the end result means. In the standard deviation, the derivation of simpler formulas is interesting and shows the pupils how some knowledge of algebra can simplify their work considerably, but it is also important that they be reminded, every now and then, what the standard deviation tells them. For this purpose, Chebyshev's Theorem (there are various spellings of this name; translations from the Russian do not all agree) is of considerable interest. This theorem tells us that no more than $1/n^2$ of the measurements can lie more than $n$ standard deviations from the mean of the measurements. Thus, if we know that the mean of 100 measurements is 5000 and the standard deviation is 400, then we know that no more than $\frac{1}{9}$ of the measurements are outside the range 3800 to 6200. That is, at least 89 of the measurements must be within the range. The number of standard deviations used here is 3; $3^2 = 9$, and therefore, no more than $\frac{1}{9}$ of the measurements can be more than three standard deviations (or $3 \times 400$) from the mean (5000).

Chebyshev's Theorem is easy to prove and quite significant, especially when the nature of the underlying distribution is not known. Actually, if the distribution is known, or assumed, to be a so-called "normal distribution" then Chebyshev's Theorem is not particularly informative. But many of the distributions one encounters in everyday life are *not* normal. A normal distribution has a "bell-shaped graph" similar to the one reproduced in Fig. 13.1. In such a distribution, most of the measurements cluster around the mean, about which the graph

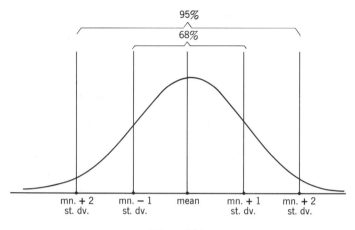

Figure 13.1

is symmetric. For such a distribution, the mean, median, and mode are the same number (or if the distribution is "almost normal," these averages are about the same). Thus, for a great deal of statistical work, any one of the averages is as good as the others, and the one usually used is the mean because of its mathematical simplicity. However, statisticians and laymen should not habitually think of these averages as being the same.

Ordinarily, such distributions as height, weight, and intelligence are assumed to be normal for a particular population. Actually, even these measures may show nonnormal tendencies for one reason or another. For example, if the population contains both men and women, or everybody, irrespective of age, is used to determine the statistics, the distribution may be distinctly not normal. But, if all male Americans who are twenty years old are taken as the population, it is likely that the distribution of their heights and weights would be close to being normal.

If a distribution is normal, or almost normal, approximately 68% of the measurements will be within one standard deviation of the mean and 95% of the measurements will be within two standard deviations of the mean. Essentially all (99.7%) of the cases will be within three standard deviations of the mean.

If more people knew more about distributions and deviations from the "average," there would be considerably more intelligent actions taken by society in light of statistical information. For example, the parent who finds out that his child's I.Q. is 95 is horrified by the fact that the child is below average, whereas the same parent may be delighted to find out that another child has an I.Q. of 102. Even assuming that these scores are correct (a topic which will be discussed shortly) and that they mean something significant about the child's intelligence (whatever that is), is there any reason to suppose that one child is a great deal brighter than the other, or that either is abnormal? The answer to both questions is "no." Actually, the first child would probably be brighter than about 40% of the population, whereas the second is brighter than about 54% of the population, assuming a standard deviation of about 20 on the I.Q. scores. These deviations vary from test to test, but this is not an unreasonable estimate for our purposes. Clearly, both children could be accurately described as being "average."

A more substantial difficulty with the assumption that the two children are drastically different in intelligence concerns the reliability of the figures. How certain can we be that the measurement given is the true measure (for the time being, we shall not discuss what the true measure is)? We know there is some error in any measurement. If we measure a football field, there is bound to be some variation in the measurements taken by different individuals, or by the same individual at different times. One measure might come out 100 yards and 5 inches, another might be 99 yards and 33 inches, and so on. The odds against the football field's actually being 100 yards are astronomical, but if it were, the odds against anyone's measuring it and getting a result, say, to the nearest $\frac{1}{8}$ of an inch, of 100 yards are also high. The fact is, that no matter how refined our measuring instruments, there is always some error in every measure. In industry and the physical sciences, it is important to know how large the error is likely to be. In the social sciences this is equally important. Unfortunately, the probable error is often not provided. With I.Q. scores, for example, the best of the I.Q. tests has a probable error of about 3%. This means that about 50% of the time the true score and the test score will be within 3% of each other and about 50% of the time they will not. Thus, it would be reasonable to say (with 50% certainty) that the first child has a score between 92 and 98, while the second child's true I.Q. is probably between 99 and 108. Remember, there is only a 50% chance that these statements are correct!

Actually, rather than the probable error, statisticians usually use the standard error (essentially the standard deviation of the errors) so that 68% of the cases will generally fall within one of these units of the true score. Thus, if the standard error on a test is 5, one can be

364 PROBABILITY AND STATISTICAL INFERENCE

reasonably confident (68% sure) that if a child scores 110 on the test his true score is somewhere between 105 and 115.

Perhaps a few definitions of terms would be appropriate. Probably the best definition of "intelligence" yet proposed by psychologists is "that which is measured by an intelligence test." Of course the maker of the intelligence test had something else in mind; he hoped to be able to predict how individuals would do certain tasks, such as going to school, working at certain jobs, etc., but definitions involving these concepts become difficult to check. Assuming the above definition is accepted, the true intelligence of an individual can be thought of as the average of the scores he would make in taking the test over and over indefinitely, without any recall of the previous test and therefore, no effects (good or bad) from having taken it previously. The limit of this average as the number of scores increases without bound is defined to be the true score. From this definition and various mathematical techniques, it is possible to determine the standard error and the likelihood that a particular score will be accurate to a certain degree. However, the calculations in this procedure are of less importance to the majority of citizens than the existence of such a procedure and a figure which can be given to the interested reader telling him how likely it is that a certain score is really within a particular distance of the true score.

If it were common knowledge that such techniques were possible, it would not be so common to hear a television commercial asserting "83% of the doctors responding to our questionnaire prescribe *Tantalizers* for their patients." If the public demanded information as to the certainty of the "independent laboratory" conducting the study that its information would be repeated in another poll of doctors in which *all* of them responded, the commercials would not bother with statements like this. In fact, no such statements would be made, since the reliability of the figures would probably be so low as to be preposterous.

All the topics discussed so far adapt themselves to a great deal of numerical calculation. However, if the teacher gets carried away with the calculations and forgets to emphasize the underlying theory of the topics, a course in statistics will deteriorate into a course in simple arithmetic; and if the pupils have not learned arithmetic by the time they reach high school, it seems unlikely that they will learn it then. Therefore, we have emphasized ideas rather than techniques throughout this discussion. The reader can find the techniques discussed at great length in many elementary probability and statistics books. This same emphasis on ideas will continue throughout the chapter.

## Pictorial Presentations

Because of the general mathematical and statistical illiteracy of the population, it has become customary to present much statistical data to the public in pictorial form. Almost everyone knows how to read a bar graph or a simple line graph, and variations on these usually are designed to make it easier to understand them while adding "eye appeal."

In school, we usually teach pupils to make bar graphs and line graphs, and teach them to make such graphs honestly. Having learned to make such graphs honestly, the child (and later the adult) assumes that everyone else will do likewise. Unfortunately, this does not follow. Let us consider a few ways in which it is possible to make a graph seem to say something entirely different from what it is saying—not with the idea of making dishonest graph makers out of people, but with the idea of helping them to recognize such graphs when they see them.

Figure 13.2 graphs the number of divorces granted in the United States during the years from 1954 to 1959.

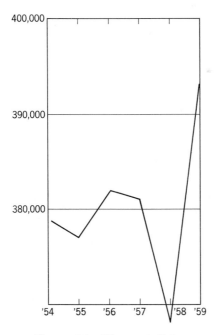

Figure 13.2    Divorce statistics

As we look at this graph, do we have the feeling that the number of divorces is on the increase? Is it our impression that the institution of marriage in the United States is in serious trouble and that something ought to be done—*quickly?* It certainly does seem that the number of divorces is skyrocketing. Now, let us look at a different graph. In Fig. 13.3, we find precisely the same information with the entire scale (from 0 to 400,000) included. This may still be a little disturbing, but presumably we do not get the same feeling of immediacy we obtained from the graph in Fig. 13.2. In fact, it looks as though the number of divorces has remained relatively stable over the five-year period.

But this is not the whole picture. Suppose, instead of limiting ourselves to those five years, we include a few years on either side of the time in question. Now, does it seem as though the number of divorces is on the increase or the decrease? Actually, Fig. 13.4 is as dishonest as Fig. 13.2, but notice that the reader gets an entirely different picture from a different source.

Finally, since we know that the population of the United States is increasing, let us consider the rate of divorce per 1000 population (Fig. 13.5). The reader will note that although there was a substantial upswing in number of divorces (on every graph) from 1958 to 1959, it is barely reflected in the rate. How could that be?

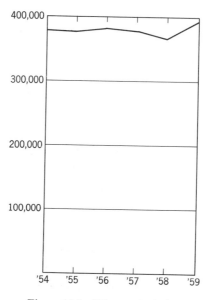

Figure 13.3   Divorce statistics

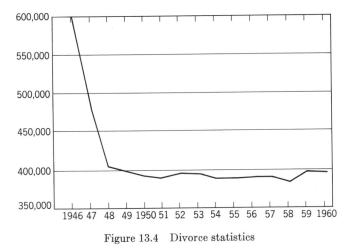

Figure 13.4    Divorce statistics

Could the number of babies born in 1959 have been so great as to have almost offset a rise of some 27,000 divorces? Would the babies be likely to be getting divorces? Then, is the graph in Fig. 13.5 a fair one? Probably not, but it may give the reader an idea as to the cause of some of the increase in number of divorces from 1958 to 1959. The numbers, in each case, referred to the total population of the United States, and in 1958 there were 48 states in the Union. The following year Alaska joined the Union (population about 226,000), and the year after, Hawaii (population about 633,000) joined.

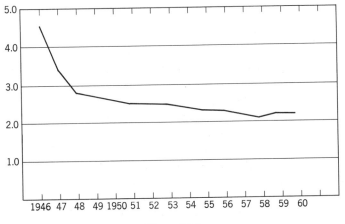

Figure 13.5

Many other things should probably be taken into consideration before jumping to a conclusion about the divorce rate in this country, but the important point is that one graph, though correct in every detail, can be very misleading.

Now, suppose we were trying to win support for a greater number of marriage counselors. Suppose also that we happened to believe that the ends justified the means. Which of the graphs would we be likely to use?

A better and more honest graph would produce the rate of divorces over a much longer period of time—starting, say, in 1890 with a rate of 0.5; 1900, 0.7; 1910, 0.9; 1920, 1.6; 1930, 1.6; 1940, 2.0; 1950, 2.6; 1960, 2.2. These figures on any kind of a graph would give a general feeling of the trend in divorces. The fact that the marriage rate has remained relatively constant (9.0 in 1890, to 12.0 and 12.1 in 1920 and 1940, and back down to 8.5 in 1960) makes these figures even more meaningful.

This discussion is not intended to make any judgments about the relative merits of divorces, marriage counselors, or even marriage. It is simply designed to show that the reporting of statistics can be misleading, and that we should look for potentially misleading forms of reporting, especially when the reporter has a bias of some sort to disseminate.

As well as the reporting of the statistics in the previous example, there are other possible sources of misconception. Are we interested in the total number of divorces, or are we really more interested in number of divorces as it relates to the number of people who might be getting a divorce? For example, in a society in which there was no marriage, there would presumably be no divorce—would this be our ideal? There was a substantial rise in the number of both divorces and marriages in 1959 and again in 1960. Is the rise in the number of divorces a cause of the rise in the number of marriages, or is the rise in the number of marriages a cause of the rise in the number of divorces? Probably neither. They are undoubtedly both results of the increase in the number of people of marriagable (and divorcable) age. Thus, we should always be careful about ascribing a cause- and effect-relationship to two events that happen to occur together. They may both be results of an entirely different cause. For example, several recent studies have shown that cigarette smokers have certain undesirable traits. One of these traits is nervousness. Is this an effect of smoking? Or is it a cause? Or, could it be that the large number of government reports about the bad effects of smoking have made cigarette smokers

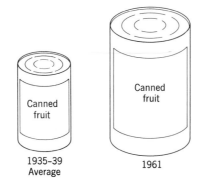

Canned
fruit

Canned
fruit

1935-39
Average

1961

Figure 13.6

nervous? The simple facts do not tell us whether there is any cause-and-effect relationship involved.

One commonly used, but sometimes misleading, form of graph is the graph that uses pictures to represent numbers. Picture graphs are not necessarily misleading, but when a two- or three-dimensional picture is used to represent a one-dimensional statistic, the results can be most remarkable. For example, suppose we wished to depict the fact that the number of pounds of canned fruit consumed in the United States increased from 15 pounds per person in 1935 to 1939 to 23.5 pounds per person in 1961. A simple bar graph could be used for this purpose, but a picture is more appealing. So we draw a can 1.5 centimeters tall and another 2.35 centimeters tall as in Fig. 13.6, to indicate the canned fruit consumption for the two periods. What is wrong with this? If we read only the words, it may seem that nothing is wrong. However, if we look at Fig. 13.6, we should have a vague feeling of uneasiness. It *looks* as though the increase has been considerably greater than it actually was. The reason for this can be found in a geometry course. If the ratio of lengths in two similar figures is 2 to 3, what is the ratio of areas? What is the ratio of volumes? In Fig. 13.6, the eye sees two areas which are in a ratio of 4 to 9, and the mind imagines two volumes in a ratio of 8 to 27. Thus, instead of a simple increase of a little more than 50%, the viewer imagines an increase of about 250%.

The presentation of statistics can be misleading in many other ways. For an excellent and entertaining review of many of these, the interested reader should consult *How to Lie with Statistics* by Darrell Huff.[1]

[1] Darrell Huff, *How to Lie with Statistics*, W. W. Norton & Company, New York, 1954.

## Probability

After acquiring a reasonable amount of familiarity with the collection, summarization, and presentation of data, the pupil should learn something about probability before continuing with his study of statistics. Some of the ideas presented in Chapter 7 (Probability for Junior High) may be of some help, but a more formal treatment is possible and desirable in the high school. Chapters 4 and 5 of *Introductory Probability and Statistical Inference for Secondary Schools*[2] present this sort of material well, as do several commercial textbooks. We shall not go into detail on these matters, but shall simply mention some of them and discuss one or two difficulties which might occur.

At the foundations of probability is the very definition of probability. This is a difficult concept to define with much rigor; however, the following definition will satisfy high school pupils and it is not incorrect. If there are $n$ equally likely possible outcomes to an event, such as flipping a coin, and $f$ of those are favorable (the result of "heads" for example), the probability of the favorable result is $f/n$. The most obvious difficulty with this explanation of probability is the question of "equally likely" events. How does one determine equally likely events? In physical situations, we often can attempt it. For example, in the case of flipping a coin, we ordinarily assume that the coin will come up heads half the time and tails the other half. Of course, this is not true for most coins and most people tossing them. In general, physical objects do not behave in precisely the way we expect because they are not made perfectly. Also, we have neglected the possibility that the coin will come out neither heads nor tails. The coin might land on its edge (not as unlikely as it may seem if the surface of the floor or table on which the experiment is being performed is not smooth) or be lost— it could roll down a hot air duct, be stolen by a dishonest observer, caught in midair by a large bird that happens to be passing by, or melted by the blast of an atomic bomb that happens to be going off in the neighborhood. Ordinarily, such possibilities are ignored in determining probabilities and are also ignored (or assumed not to count) in actual practice.

In order to determine whether a coin is "honest" (that is, has the same probability of coming up heads as tails) we would probably be inclined to try a large number of experiments.   If we flipped a coin one million times and came up with precisely 500,000 heads and 500,000

[2] Published in a preliminary edition and a revised preliminary edition by the Commission on Mathematics of the College Entrance Examination Board, New York. The first edition was published in 1957.

tails (a most unlikely occurrence, even if the coin is honest) we would probably assume that the coin was honest. On the other hand, if we flipped the coin one million times and got 800,000 heads and only 200,000 tails, we would very likely assume that there was something "dishonest" about the coin or the way in which it was flipped. This gives another possible definition of probability: namely, try the experiment a large number of times and the limit of the number $f/n$ (where $f$ is the number of favorable occurrences and $n$ is the total number of trials) as $n$ gets large without bound is the probability of the event. For many purposes, this is a better definition than the "equally likely events" definition.

In the end, we must have some undefined terms, and "probability" is perhaps as good an undefined word as any. Once the word "probability" has been discussed and accepted, and we have agreed that a probability will always be a number between 0 and 1 inclusive, the class is ready to begin further discussion.

Topics included in such a discussion would be the following.

*Complementary events.* If $A$ is an event, not $A$ or the complement of $A$ is the event that does not occur. Therefore, if $p(A)$ is the probability that $A$ occurs, then $p$ (not $A$) $= 1 - p(A)$.

*Independent events.* Intuitively, if events are independent, they have no effect on each other. Using the "equally likely events" idea of probability, we can show that if two events are independent, then the product of their probabilities is the probability of their conjunction. That is, $A$ and $B$ are independent if and only if $p(A) \cdot p(B) = p(A \& B)$. This is sometimes taken as the definition of independent events in probability.

*Conditional events.* What is the probability that event $A$ happens if $B$ has happened? This is usually written: "$p(A|B)$" and read "the probability of $A$ given $B$." By thinking carefully about the meaning of a conditional probability, it seems reasonable that the probability of $A$ given $B$ must be equal to the probability that both $A$ and $B$ will occur divided by the probability that $B$ occurs, or $p(A|B) = [p(A \& B)]/p(B)$. The intuitive reason for this is that given that $B$ occurs, $B$ becomes the universe, and if we know that $B$ occurs and we are interested in the cases where $A$ occurs, clearly both $A$ and $B$ occur. For the probabilities, each of the denominators would have an $n$ (the total number of trials) which would be divided (or canceled) out. Using conditional probability and the belief that $A$ and $B$ are independent if and only if $p(A|B) = p(A)$, we can make the definition of independent events shown previously seem reasonable; in fact, this is undoubtedly the preferable way of approaching the topic of independent events.

To repeat the illustration used in Chapter 7, suppose a certain high school's basketball team has a .2 probability of winning the conference championship and its baseball team a .3 probability of winning the conference championship. What is the probability that one or the other of its two teams will win the championship?

While the reader is considering that question, let us ask another. Suppose school $A$ has .2 probability of winning the basketball championship and school $B$ has a .3 probability of winning the same championship. What is the probability that either team $A$ or team $B$ will win the championship?

Do the two questions have the same answer or are they essentially different from each other? Let us consider another question. Suppose the basketball team of a certain school has a .7 probability of winning the conference championship and the baseball team of that school has .6 probability of winning the conference championship. What is the probability that either of the two teams will win a conference championship? Can it be greater than 1?

From these questions, a group of high school pupils can figure out an acceptable formula for the probability of the disjunction of two events. The pupil's first reaction (probably the same as many readers who did not give serious consideration to that first question) is simply to add the two probabilities. In fact, this is precisely what they have been doing right along. For example, the probability of getting a "3" with a single (6-sided) die is $\frac{1}{6}$. The probability of getting a "5" with the die is also $\frac{1}{6}$, and the probability of getting a "1" is also $\frac{1}{6}$. How do we find the probability of getting an odd number when a single die is thrown? Simply by adding $\frac{1}{6} + \frac{1}{6} + \frac{1}{6}$ and getting $\frac{1}{2}$. There is nothing incorrect about this, but the problem, like the problem of two teams in the same league, is quite different from the problem under discussion.

In order to see what is wrong, let us consider a problem involving dice again. The reason for using such an example is that it is often easier to see what is going on if the set of all possible outcomes and assigned probabilities can be written out in front of the class. Now the difficulty in the foregoing exercises (the ones involving the basketball team and the baseball team from the same school) seems to have arisen because the events were not mutually exclusive; it was possible for both events to occur at the same time and this, in turn, seemed to make it possible for the sum of the two probabilities to be greater than 1. Consider a similar situation with dice. What is the probability that if two dice are thrown one or the other will land with a 2 face-up? We know the probability of getting a 2 on the first die is $\frac{1}{6}$, and that the probability of getting a 2 on the second die is also $\frac{1}{6}$. We suspect that the probability that at least one die comes up "2" is not $\frac{1}{6} + \frac{1}{6} = \frac{1}{3}$. Consider Table 13.1. If the dice are honest and independent, it seems

**Table 13.1**

| | | | | | |
|---|---|---|---|---|---|
| (1, 1) | (1, 2) | (1, 3) | (1, 4) | (1, 5) | (1, 6) |
| (2, 1) | (2, 2) | (2, 3) | (2, 4) | (2, 5) | (2, 6) |
| (3, 1) | (3, 2) | (3, 3) | (3, 4) | (3, 5) | (3, 6) |
| (4, 1) | (4, 2) | (4, 3) | (4, 4) | (4, 5) | (4, 6) |
| (5, 1) | (5, 2) | (5, 3) | (5, 4) | (5, 5) | (5, 6) |
| (6, 1) | (6, 2) | (6, 3) | (6, 4) | (6, 5) | (6, 6) |

reasonable to say that each of the 36 pairs indicated in the table has an equally likely chance of occurring. From the way in which the table was set up, if we roll the two dice and are told that the result would be indicated in the first row, we know that the first die has a "1" up. The probability of this event is $\frac{1}{6}$—or from Table 13.1 it is $\frac{6}{36}$, since there are 36 equally likely events of which 6 happen to be favorable (that is, the first die has a "1" up). Similarly, the probability of being in the second row is also $\frac{1}{6}$. What is the probability of being in the second column? The table seems to indicate that the probability of getting a "2" with the first die is $\frac{1}{6}$ and also that the probability of getting a "2" with the second die is $\frac{1}{6}$, precisely as expected.

Now, from Table 13.1, what is the probability of getting a "2" with at least one die? The way to find out is simply to count, making sure not to include any case more than once. The reader can determine easily that the number of pairs in which at least one element is a "2" is 11. Since there are 36 possible cases, the probability of getting a 2 on one die or the other is $\frac{11}{36}$.

Why is the probability not $\frac{1}{3}$ (or $\frac{12}{36}$)? We would have arrived at the answer $\frac{1}{3}$ by adding $\frac{1}{6}$ to $\frac{1}{6}$. In other words, we would have added the number of cases in the second row to those in the second column, getting 12, and then dividing by 36. But if we did this, we would have counted the ordered pair (2, 2) twice, but it is only one possible outcome and therefore, we should count it only once. Thus, the probability of either of these two events occurring is the sum of their probabilities minus the probability that they occur together, or $(\frac{1}{6} + \frac{1}{6}) - \frac{1}{36} = \frac{11}{36}$.

This same reasoning should apply to any pair of events. If the events are mutually exclusive (for example, getting a "2" or a "3" on the same die), we simply add their probabilities, since the probability of their happening together is 0. On the other hand, if the events are not

mutually exclusive, we must find the probability that the two events occur together and subtract that probability from the sum of the two probabilities.
Thus,

$$p(A \text{ or } B) = p(A) + p(B) - p(A \text{ \& } B)$$

Applying this formula to the basketball and baseball team problem, we have

$p(\text{winning one or the other}) = p(\text{winning basketball})$
$+ p(\text{winning baseball}) - p(\text{winning both})$
$= .2 + .3 - p(\text{winning both})$

How do we determine the probability of winning both champion⁻ ships? If we could assume the two events are independent, this proba⁻ bility would be the product of .2 and .3. However, there is good reason to suppose that the two events are not independent. Very likely some of the same players are on both teams; certainly some of the cheering sections would be the same and their opponents would also be from the same schools. However, it is not clear what influence all these consider⁻ ations and others will have, and therefore, we will assume, rightly or wrongly, that the events are independent. Then, $p$ (winning one or the other) $= .2 + .3 - .06 = .44$.

For the second example, since the events are mutually exclusive (Team $A$ or Team $B$ might win the championship—but it is impossible for both to win it, excluding ties, of course), the probability is $.2 + .3 - 0 = .5$.

For the third example, $p$ (winning one or the other) $= .7 + .6 - .42 = .88$, assuming the events are independent.

There are many other things which a teacher will wish to cover in his discussion of probability. One is the binomial theorem, and binomial distributions and their relation to a normal curve. We have already considered the binomial theorem from an algebraic point of view, in⁻ cluding a proof by induction. In the development of permutations and combinations, the number $n!/[m!(n - m)!]$ turns out to be the number of combinations of $n$ things taken $m$ at a time (or the number of subsets with $m$ elements of a set with $n$ elements). The procedures for establish⁻ ing this fact are the same as those used in permutation problems in Chapter 7.

Consider the problem of expanding $(a + b)^n$. This can be rewritten

$$\overbrace{(a + b)(a + b)(a + b) \cdots (a + b)(a + b)}^{n \text{ factors}}$$

In carrying out this multiplication, we add together all possible products in which one factor comes from each of the binomial factors. Thus, one term is simply the product of all of the first terms, or $a^n$. Another term would be $a^{n-1}b$, where the $n - 1$ factors of $a$ were taken from the first $n - 1$ binomial factors, and the $b$ was taken from the $n$th binomial factor; another term would be $a^{n-1}b$, where the $b$ was taken from the second to the last binomial factor, and the $n - 1$ factors of $a$ were taken from the other binomial factors; etc. Some of these terms will be the same. Our problem is to find out how many terms of $a^{n-1}b$ there are, how many terms of $a^{n-2}b^2$, etc. But in order to find out the number of terms there are of $a^{n-1}b$, all we need to know is how many ways there are of choosing $n - 1$ things from $n$ possibilities, since the number of $a$'s to choose from is $n$, and we want only $n - 1$ of them. Each binomial factor from which no $a$ is chosen will contribute a $b$ to the product. In a similar manner, there are $n!/[m!(n - m)!]$ ways of obtaining a term with $m$ factors of $a$. Therefore, the binomial theorem can be written

$$(a + b)^n = \frac{n!}{n!(n - n)!}\, a^n + \frac{n!}{(n - 1)!(1)!}\, a^{n-1}b + \frac{n!}{(n - 2)!(2)!}\, a^{n-2}b^2$$
$$+ \cdots + \frac{n!}{(n - m)!m!} a^{n-m}b^m + \cdots + b^n$$

In order to use this formula, it must be remembered that $0! = 1$. This fact can be made to seem reasonable to children by noting that in general, $(n - 1)! = n!/n$; hence $0!$ should be $1!/1$ or $1/1$ or $1$. Also, the fact that this interpretation of $0!$ works so well in the binomial theorem ought to be convincing. Of course, we have not really proved that $0! = 1$; we have only shown that it is a reasonable and convenient way to define it. Therefore, mathematicians define it this way.

Several other comments should be made about probability before leaving the topic. First, "the law of probability" is one of the most often quoted or misquoted laws of mathematics. Generally, people tend to use it in the following way:

"We have had 17 children and all 17 have been boys; therefore, by the law of probability, the next one *has* to be a girl."

There is no law that says anything of the sort in probability theory. If the assumption is made that boys and girls are equally likely (not quite true) and that the sex of the various offspring of a couple are determined by independent events (definitely not true), then the probability of getting 18 boys in a row is $1/262{,}144$. But on these assumptions, if the first 17 were boys, there would still be precisely a $\frac{1}{2}$ probability that the next one would be a boy. Actually, if we flipped a coin 17 times and got 17 heads in a row, we would suspect that there was something slightly odd about the coin (though it may happen, on occasion, even with an honest coin) and that there was a rather high probability of getting heads on any one toss. By similar reasoning, if the first 17 children are boys, it would seem to be quite probable that the next one would be a boy, too. This fact has been borne out with somewhat smaller numbers by actual experience.

The law that people think of when they quote "the law of probability" is that $f/n$ tends to approximate the probability of event $A$ if $f$ is the number of favorable cases, $n$ is the number of trials, and $n$ gets large without bound. Thus, if one tosses an honest penny ten times, it may come up heads five times, or seven times, or any number of times between 0 and 10. But if we toss a penny one million times, the odds are extremely high (about 300 to 1) that the number of heads will be between 498,500 and 501,500, and thus to the nearest hundredth, $f/n$ is .50. All of this assumes that the penny really does have a $\frac{1}{2}$ probability of landing heads.

Another fact a teacher should remember when teaching a course in probability is that the topic presents many tricky problems. Over the years some of the best mathematicians have made mistakes in figuring out probability problems. With this in mind, the teacher is likely to make some mistakes if he does not insist on sticking close to a book or to types of problems which have been worked out in advance. This is not to suggest that the teacher should use only cut-and-dried problems, but that he should bring a certain sense of humility to the teaching of this topic. If he does not and still does a creditable job of teaching, he will almost certainly develop this quality quickly. We must not insist we have the right answer and refuse to consider someone else's, even if we *know* we are right. In probability, there is always a probability greater than zero of having made a mistake.

### Applications

Once the proper foundation has been laid, there are many applications of statistics and probability which can be explored. Such areas as sampling, testing hypotheses, confidence limits, significance tests, randomness, analysis of variance and covariance, and coefficients for regression lines can be investigated. Many of these require more background than indicated here, and most of them should not be seriously studied in the high school, but the pupils should begin to get an inkling of when statistics are appropriate in industry, science, politics, etc.

However, before the pupils become too absorbed in the mathematics involved in such discussions, they must be constantly reminded that a certain amount of common sense must go into all experiments in which statistical methods are going to be applied.   If the experimenter does not use good judgment, he will acquire incorrect information.   No matter how much statistical analysis he does on his data, he is not going to make them more useful; he will only make it easier to communicate his false information to others.

For example, if we want to find out what people say they do or think, we ask them. But if we want to find out what people *really* do or think, we will probably have to figure out some other way of acquiring the information. A telling example of this sort of thing occurred in a house-to-house survey in which the respondents were asked to tell which magazines were read in the household. It turned out that *Harper's* was read by a great many more people than *True Story*. However, publisher's sales figures showed that the contrary situation was true. If the publishers had relied on the data from the survey, they would have increased the production of *Harper's* and decreased that of *True Story*. Instead, they assumed the obvious: people had simply not told the truth. They wanted to impress the interviewer.[3] A similar incident occurred in a graduate education class at a large eastern university. A professor of psychology was talking to the class and impressing it with statistics. In order to show how significant his statistics were, he would first ask the class what they thought people believed and then would *tell* them what people really believed. One question was, "What percentage of people do you think believe that teachers should participate in politics?" Most of the answers from the class were below 25%. One student who had tired of the game said, "If you mean 'What percent *say* they believe that teachers should participate in politics?' I would say it must be at least 90%, but if you mean, 'What per cent actually *do* believe this; I'd guess it's closer to 20%." The professor looked a little sheepish, admitted that the only way he knew to determine what people believed was to ask them, and then came up with the figure 93% in answer to his question. Clearly, from the actions and reactions of people to teachers who run for public office or get deeply involved in political campaigns, it is not true that 93% of the people in this country believe that teachers should participate in politics, except, of course, to vote on election day.

Probability and statistics are topics of great importance in the world today. The interpretation and comprehension of statistical information are becoming an important part of our society. It is clear that a well-

[3] This example and many others like it are mentioned in Huff, *How to Lie with Statistics* (see p. 16).

educated citizen must know something about statistics. The sort of things he ought to know have been indicated in this chapter. For non-mathematically inclined individuals who have had only a smattering of algebra in previous courses, this course would be limited primarily to basic understandings and interpretations, with few proofs and relatively little complicated calculations. For more advanced mathematics pupils, more reliance would be placed on algebra, careful derivations, and proofs, but the important emphasis would still be on understanding the underlying principles and interpreting other people's data.

### Teaching Hints

In beginning a unit on statistics, it would be desirable for the pupils to collect statistics from various sources (newspapers, radio, television, encyclopedias, etc.) and analyze them. Questions such as what is meant by "average income," "average height," and "mean temperature" can be discussed and will give the pupils an insight into much of what goes on around them every day.

Another project which may be of value to the class at a later time would be to collect raw data (for example, heights of class members, grades in English of class members, sex of class members, etc.), assign appropriate numbers when these are not already implicit in the data, and calculate the mean and standard deviation of the data. Then, compare the results with the expected results for a normal distribution, and the predicted results from Chebyshev's Theorem. This should give the pupils some feeling for the types of populations that are likely to be approximately normal and also indicate those not likely to be normally distributed.

Many physical objects can be used to demonstrate principles in probability. In fact, one science book club recently gave away a free probability kit with every new subscription. Kits of this sort are available commercially and are both interesting and valuable; but, as with most such aids, it is also possible to make your own or to have the pupils make them. For example, a good normal distribution can be generated by putting nails in a board in such a way that when marbles are poured down it each marble has a probability of $\frac{1}{2}$ of going to the right of any given nail, and $\frac{1}{2}$ going to the left. An even simpler way to construct a normal curve is to fold a paper and pour salt (or some similar substance) over the paper toward the crease. There will be a normal curve on each half of the paper and the hollow between them will be an inverted normal curve.

Often, it will be easier for a pupil to calculate a probability if he can actually see the experiment happen, rather than just being told about it. For example, if the experiment has to do with drawing black and red balls out of urns that are chosen according to the results of rolling a die, it may be helpful actually to roll a die and draw the balls—at least in the first problem or two of this sort. In mathematics it is often desirable to call attention to the fact that the mathematics is supposed to be a description of the real world.

As an application of their knowledge of probability and statistics, it would be desirable for the pupils to conduct experiments near the end of the course and analyze their data. These experiments could be carried on in conjunction with a social studies class (for example, an opinion poll, a prediction of how the class election would come out, a survey of characteristics of certain graduates of the high school, etc.), a biology class (inherited characteristics of offspring of certain animals and plants, predicted behavior of certain animals in certain conditions, etc.), or an English class (mathematical analysis of lengths of words used by certain authors in certain types of writing, ages of individuals when they were most creatively productive, etc.). After carrying out the experiment, the experimenter would be expected to criticize his own experiment, and then it would be thrown open to others for comment, either on mathematical grounds or on nonmathematical assumptions.

### Exercises

1. What is the average of the following numbers?

$$2, 2, 2, 3, 4, 7, 18$$

(a) If you wished the average to appear small, would you use the mode, the mean, or the median?

(b) If you wished the average to appear large, would you use the mode, the mean, or the median?

2. (a) What is the range of the above set of data?

    (b) What is the mean absolute variation?

    (c) What is the standard deviation?

3. State and prove Chebyshev's Theorem.

4. If two honest dice are thrown and then thrown again, what is the probability that on at least one throw the total number of spots showing is exactly 7?

### Questions for Further Thought and Study

1. Read at least three statistical reports. Is there any reason to suppose that the reporter has an ax to grind? What information, if any, seems to be missing? Could you "prove" a different conclusion by leaving out some of the facts which are presented in the report? Is there any way you can suggest for improving the objectivity of the statistical report?

## REFERENCES

Goldberg, Samuel. *Probability, An Introduction*, Prentice-Hall, Englewood Cliffs, N.J., 1960. A clear, readable elementary mathematically sound introduction to probability.

Huff, Darrell. *How to Lie with Statistics*, W. W. Norton and Co., New York, 1954. See comments in chapter.

Kemeny, John G., J. Laurie Snell, and Gerald L. Thompson. *Introduction to Finite Mathematics*, Prentice-Hall, Englewood Cliffs, N.J., 1957. See comments on this and *Finite Mathematical Structures* in Chapters 8 and 10. Chapters 4, 6, and 7 are excellent for applications of probability and related branches of mathematics (e.g., game theory) and Chapter 7 of *Finite Mathematical Structures* is good for a more advanced look at probability.

Mosteller, Frederick, Robert E. K. Rourke, and George B. Thomas Jr. *Probability and Statistics*, Addison-Wesley, Reading, Mass., 1961. Used for the course in probability on Continental Classroom (and later revised and published in a hard cover), this book was designed to help teachers learn the mathematics necessary to teach a good course in high school probability and statistics.

Smith, David Eugene. *A Source Book in Mathematics*, 2 vols. Dover Publications, New York, 1959. See reference 5 in Chapter 4. Section IV (pp. 546–604) is on the beginnings of probability.

Commission on Mathematics. *Introductory Probability and Statistical Inference for Secondary Schools*, rev. preliminary ed., CEEB, New York, 1959. Before it went out of print, this was probably the best available textbook on probability and statistics for high school pupils. Perhaps a little too easy for very capable students.

# CALCULUS

Whether the calculus belongs in the high school mathematics curriculum is a subject of wide debate. A well-taught course in the calculus contains a great deal of excellent mathematics which is useful not only in the physical sciences and engineering but also in many recent applications to the social sciences. No person who has not studied the calculus may consider himself well educated in the natural sciences, and before long there may be some question whether he is well educated at all. In many respects, a good calculus course is the proper culmination to the elementary mathematics studied in high school.

However, the calculus is not an easy subject. Its full comprehension requires a firm understanding of the real number system. That the subject appears in this text does not signify a belief that calculus should necessarily be taught in the high schools. Its inclusion is a concession to the prevailing opinion that it cannot be ignored in a text of this kind.

Most leaders in mathematics education currently oppose the widespread teaching of the calculus in high school. Their principal argument is that a lack of time prevents adequately covering algebra, geometry, probability and statistics, and trigonometry while still leaving room for an effective one-year course in the integral and differential calculus. Although the Commission on Mathematics of the CEEB favors an advanced placement program for gifted pupils, it insists that they must first understand all of the work contained in the Commission's suggested course in Elementary Functions. To complete this work before the end of the eleventh year is a substantial accomplishment for all but the best mathematics students. Moreover, such a program does not include any work with probability and statistics nor more than a cursory study of analytic geometry in relation to demonstrative synthetic geometry and graphing in algebra. Any high school can be proud of its program if its pupils, after having completed the elementary functions course and a course in probability and statistics, have time for a careful study of analytic geometry before their graduation.

One problem which mathematics teachers have faced is that the general public, represented by the school administrator, has tended to believe that any high school that teaches calculus (no matter how bad the course, how unprepared the pupils or teachers, or how many better things might be done with the time) is doing an excellent job in mathematics education, and by implication, a high school that does not teach calculus is not doing as good a job. If a teacher is working in a community where this view prevails, it is partially his fault if the citizens and school administrators are not educated to see the folly of this point of view. We must learn to judge things by deeper and more appropriate considerations than their labels. The mathematics teacher must resist attempts to push students into a course in calculus (or anything else, for that matter) before they are ready for it.

Another popular opinion currently in circulation, especially among professional mathematicians, is the belief that there are no secondary school teachers who are capable of teaching a good course in calculus. Admitting that there may be many high school teachers of mathematics who would not feel comfortable in teaching a calculus course, we cannot resist the comment that a large number of high school mathematics teachers are better suited to teaching an elementary calculus course than the majority of college teachers whom the student is likely to face eventually. This comment applies not only to the first-year graduate students who teach freshman courses, but also to the renowned mathematician, author of many works on higher mathematics, who knows the course forwards and backwards, but teaches it backwards. Although some college teachers of calculus may have more mathematical understanding, there is considerable doubt of their understanding of people or how they learn. The dropout records for the first semester of calculus in any of our "better" institutions raises grave questions as to the effectiveness of the teaching of elementary calculus in the college.

If the colleges are failing to do a good job of teaching the calculus, does this mean that the high schools should take over? Of course not! What this implies, instead, for the high school curriculum is that if everything else has been completed, if sufficient time remains, and if a good teacher who has the proper background to teach calculus (at least one year of advanced calculus would seem to be a minimum requirement) can be found, there is no overriding argument against teaching the calculus in the high school. In other words, the calculus should not be taught in the high school because of its name nor should it be omitted in the high school for the same reason. More important considerations must be the factors behind the decision.

### Preparing for the Calculus

As the end of the high school program in mathematics approaches, a good high school teacher can do many things which will be well worth the pupil's time whether he goes on to take calculus or not.   One of the most important concepts that can be developed and that will be of great help to the pupil if he does continue into calculus is the concept of a limit. Although this concept is the most fundamental and important concept in calculus, it is common to hear a student who has just completed three semesters of calculus exclaim, "Oh, that's what a limit is! I never could figure out what they were talking about." If a student can begin the study of calculus with a good intuitive concept of limit, he has virtually won the battle. Further, if he has a good intuitive concept of limit plus a true understanding of a limit's formal definition, the calculus course should be one of his easiest. With this in mind, let us consider some of the topics that might help the pupil to understand the idea of limit.

### Sequences and Series

A sequence can be thought of as a function whose domain is the set of natural numbers ($\{1, 2, 3, 4, \cdot \cdot \cdot\}$), but before introducing so formal a definition, we should give the pupils a more intuitive notion of a sequence. Essentially, a sequence is a bunch or set of numbers in which order is important. To be technical about it, there is some question of how one goes about describing the order of a set of numbers. It is certainly not fair to "look at them," since one would be looking at numerals, not at numbers. This difficulty can be avoided by using the functional definition of a sequence, or it can simply be ignored as it has been by good mathematicians and teachers for hundreds of years. Probably the best tack is to talk about the set of numbers in listed order, but to mention that there is a more formal way of looking at it, namely, the functional definition.

Having mastered the definition, we can consider a few problems involving sequences. If the first three numbers in a sequence (in order) are 1, 2, 4, what is the fourth term (usually written "$a_4$")? How do we know it is 8, assuming that is what it is? Suppose we were told it was 7, could we justify the answer 7? What was added to the first term to get the second term? What was added to the second term to get the third? What should we add to the third term to get the fourth? Does it not make as much sense to add 1, then 2, and then 3, as to add 1, 2, and then 4? Although $2^n$, where $n$ is the number of the term, is a reasonable formula, so is $n^2/2 - n/2 + 1$, and the latter is really much simpler from many points of view. The moral of this paragraph is that finding the next term in a sequence may be a suitable question for an I.Q. test, but it is hardly appropriate for a mathematics course if a definite answer is thought to be right. A more interesting challenge might be, give a general formula for deriving the $n$th term of a sequence in which $a_1 = 1$, $a_2 = 2$, and $a_3 = 4$. The person with the most such formulas gets the highest grade on this question, assuming the formulas are correct.

Of course, if a rule is provided for finding the $n$th term of a sequence, then pupils ought to be able to find any given term without great difficulty.

Among the sequences we sometimes study, arithmetic and geometric sequences hold a special place. Suppose that in a sequence each term differs from the previous term by a constant number $d$, so that $a_2 = a_1 + d$, $a_3 = a_1 + 2d$, $a_4 = a_1 + 3d$, etc. Can we show that this condition is equivalent to the condition that the $n$th term is a linear function of $n$ (that is, there exists a $p$ and a $q$ such that $a_n = pn + q$)? The proof should be obvious, but in order to prove the conditions equivalent, we must show that each implies the other.

One of the interesting problems in an arithmetic sequence is to find the sum of the first $n$ terms. This is an intriguing exercise if the pupils are given a chance to try to figure it out rather than told how to find the answer. Probably the best procedure is to provide them with several specific sequences and suggest that they find the sum of some given number of terms of each of these and then try to generalize their procedure so that it will work for any arithmetic sequence.

A pertinent story, with which the reader is probably familiar, concerns Karl Friedrich Gauss (1777–1855), one of the greatest mathematicians of all time. When Gauss was very young his teacher gave the class the assignment of adding up the numbers from 1 to 100, inclusive, presumably to keep the class out of trouble while he did something else. In a moment or two, young Gauss stopped working on the problem and began looking around the room, or pulling the pigtails of the girl in front him, or whatever young German boys did at the time to indicate that they were not occupied with school work. The teacher walked over to check on him and found that Gauss had finished the problem correctly. He asked Gauss how he did it, and the reply indicated that Gauss had correctly derived a formula for finding the sum of the first $n$ terms of an arithmetic sequence. In effect, his procedure went something like this: pair 99 with 1, 98 with 2, 97 with 3, etc., until 51 is paired with 49. There are 49 100's plus the 100 at the end plus the 50 in the middle, and the result is 5050. A similar process can be used on any arithmetic sequence.

Another method, which does not have quite the same problem about a middle term as Gauss' procedure sometimes has, goes like this: take the average of the first and last terms, and replace each of these terms by that average. Clearly, the sum has not been changed. The average of the second and second to the last terms will be the same ($a_1 + d + a_n - d = a_1 + a_n$); hence replace each of them by $(a_1 + a_n)/2$ and continue the process until every term has been replaced by this average. Since each term has been replaced by $(a_1 + a_n)/2$, the sum is simply $n(a_1 + a_n)/2$ or, since $a_n = a_1 + (n - 1)d$, the sum of the first $n$ terms of an arithmetic sequence, in which the first term is $a_1$ and the difference between successive terms is $d$, is $(n/2)[2a_1 + (n - 1)d]$.

In a geometric sequence, there is some number $r$, which is equal to the quotient of any term, except the first, divided by the previous term. Thus, if $a_1$ is the first term, then $a_1r$ is the second term, $a_1r^2$ is the third term, $a_1r^3$ is the fourth term, etc., with $a_1r^{n-1}$ being the $n$th term. Now, suppose we were faced with the task of finding the sum of the first $n$ terms of a geometric sequence. Let us call the first term $a$ for simplicity of notation, and $r$ is the quotient of two successive terms. The sum $S_n$ of the first $n$ terms of the sequence is: $S_n = a + ar + ar^2 + ar^3 + \cdots + ar^{n-2} + ar^{n-1}$. What would be our first reaction when faced with the previous sum? Any normal pupil who has had the usual amount of work with factoring (or using the distributive law) will factor out (or undistribute) the $a$, getting

$$S_n = a(1 + r + r^2 + r^3 + \cdots + r^{n-2} + r^{n-1})$$

Now, there is a problem as to what to do next. However, if pupils have factored the difference of two $n$th powers before, they should have a clue as to how to proceed. They know (or should know) that $1 - x^n = (1 - x)(1 + x + x^2 + x^3 + \cdots + x^{n-2} + x^{n-1})$. Therefore (if $x \neq 1$),

$1 + x + x^2 + x^3 + \cdots + x^{n-2} + x^{n-1} = (1 - x^n)/(1 - x)$. Using this fact (with the $x$ replaced by $r$), they should find that $S_n = a(1 - r^n)/(1 - r)$.

Up to this point, there is no need for the limit concept. Now we come to a problem in which it is quite natural and rather exciting to consider limits. What happens to the formula $a[(1 - r^n)/(1 - r)]$ if $n$ gets very large? That depends on the number $r$. If $r$ is greater than 1, both numerator and denominator are negative so the quotient is positive; $r^n$ apparently gets large faster than $r$, and therefore, the whole quotient apparently gets very large. This is, of course, what we would expect if we considered the original sum

$$S_n = a + ar + ar^2 + ar^3 + \cdots + ar^{n-1}$$

Clearly, if $r$ is greater than 1, each successive term is greater than the previous one, and therefore $S_n$ seems to increase rapidly as the number of terms increases.

Suppose $0 < r < 1$, and for simplicity, we let $a = 1$. Then,

$$S_n = 1 + r + r^2 + r^3 + \cdots + r^{n-1}$$

Here each term is positive, but they continually get smaller. Let us consider the successive sums if $r = .5$.

$S_1 = 1$
$S_2 = 1 + .5 = 1.5$
$S_3 = 1 + .5 + (.5)^2 = 1.75$
$S_4 = 1 + .5 + (.5)^2 + (.5)^3 = 1.875$
$S_5 = 1 + .5 + (.5)^2 + (.5)^3 + (.5)^4 = 1.9375$
$S_6 = 1 + .5 + (.5)^2 + (.5)^3 + (.5)^4 + (.5)^5 = 1.96875$
$S_7 = 1 + .5 + (.5)^2 + (.5)^3 + (.5)^4 + (.5)^5 + (.5)^6 = 1.984375$
$S_8 = 1 + .5 + (.5)^2 + (.5)^3 + (.5)^4 + (.5)^5 + (.5)^6 + (.5)^7 = 1.9921875$
$S_9 = 1 + .5 + (.5)^2 + (.5)^3 + (.5)^4 + (.5)^5 + (.5)^6 + (.5)^7 + (.5)^8$
$\qquad = 1.99609375$
$S_{10} = 1 + .5 + (.5)^2 + (.5)^3 + (.5)^4 + (.5)^5 + (.5)^6 + (.5)^7 + (.5)^8$
$\qquad + (.5)^9 = 1.998046875$

What seems to be happening to the successive sums? Are the sums elements of a sequence? Does it seem as though any term of this new sequence will be greater than 2? As a matter of fact, is each term just halfway between the term preceding it and 2? If we start at one end of a room and walk halfway across, and then walk half the remaining distance, and then half of the remaining distance, and so on, will we ever get all the way across the room?[1] Then, does it seem that the sums of the geometric sequence will each be less than 2, but will continually be getting closer to 2? Will the sums also be less than 4 but continually getting closer to 4? In what way does 2 differ from 4 in this problem? Will the sums get as close to 2 as we like? That is, will there be a sum that is within .01 of 2? Name the least such sum. Will there be a sum that is within .001 of 2? $S_{11}$ happens to be the least such sum. Is there a sum that is within .0001 of 2? For any positive number (say $\epsilon$), no matter how small it may be, will there always be some sum within $\epsilon$ of 2?

For any number, say $\epsilon$, again, will there always be a sum that is within $\epsilon$ of 1? Name the sum that is always within $\epsilon$ of 1, no matter how small $\epsilon$ is. Why is 2 different from 1 in this problem? Besides the fact that 1 is one of the sums, is it true that once $n$ is greater than a certain number we can always be certain that $S_n$ is closer to 2 than $\epsilon$?

Here, then, is the beginning of a concept of limit. The $S_n$'s are said to approach 2 as $n$ gets very large if for any number ($\epsilon$), no matter how small, there is some number $N$ which is great enough so that whenever $n > N$, then $S_n$ is within $\epsilon$ of 2. In other words, there is an $S_n$ which is just as close to 2 as we would like it to be, and all of the $S_n$'s after that are at least as close.

Going back to the original formula for finding the sum of the first $n$ terms of a sequence, we find that for this sequence

$$S_n = \frac{1 - (\frac{1}{2})^n}{1 - (\frac{1}{2})} = \frac{1}{\frac{1}{2}} - \frac{(\frac{1}{2})^n}{\frac{1}{2}} = 2 - (\frac{1}{2})^{n-1}$$

If $n$ is very large, what kind of a number is $(\frac{1}{2})^{n-1}$? For example, if $n = 1000$, is $(\frac{1}{2})^{n-1}$ just slightly greater than 0? Does it seem as though we could make $(\frac{1}{2})^{n-1}$ as close to 0 as we wished simply by choosing $n$ great enough? In fact, does this formula for the sum seem to show that the sequence of $S_n$'s satisfies all of the conditions indicated in the previous paragraph. Then, again, we would say that as $n$ became very large, $S_n$ would approach 2. More formally, this would be written "limit $S_n = 2$," and would usually be read "the limit as $n$ approaches $n \to \infty$ infinity of $S_n$ is 2." When we begin to discuss the concept of limit, as in the beginning of any topic in elementary mathematics, it is desirable to be as informal as possible (without producing misconceptions, of

[1] A well-known variation on this has a professor asking a male student this question with a young lady at the other end of the room. The answer, purportedly is "No, but I'll get close enough for all practical purposes."

course), and therefore, to keep the notation of limit as well as the discussion at an informal level.

Notice that in this discussion, the word "series" has not been mentioned. We have considered various sequences, determined the sum of the first $n$ terms of several of these, and then examined the *sequence* of such sums to see if they approached a limit. In geometric sequences, if $0 < r < 1$, we found that as $n$ became very large, $S_n$ seemed to approach the limit $a/(1 - r)$. In a high school class, considerably more discussion of this idea would have preceded this conclusion. A series is usually thought of as an infinite sum, or the sum of all the elements of a sequence. However, defining an infinite sum is not easy; defining it in terms of limits, as we have, works well when there is a limit, but talking about an infinite sum that does not happen to be a number seems a little obscure. Of course, we all know what is meant by the sum $1 + \frac{1}{2} + \frac{1}{3} + \frac{1}{4} + \frac{1}{5} \cdots$ , and it is possible to discuss whether the sum of the first $n$ terms approaches a limit as $n$ gets very large, but if a pupil has been trained to look for technicalities, he might legitimately inquire as to the sort of an object this series is. It certainly is not a number, which excludes it from being a sum in the usual sense of the word. It can hardly be considered a numeral, and if it is an expression how can we talk about its sum? If we get bogged down in such a morass, we may manage to get out by contending that series notation is used to talk about limits of sums of sequences, and that when those limits do not exist, we say the series is divergent. Perhaps a better solution to the problem might be to avoid the word "series" completely in elementary mathematics courses, but unfortunately, this removes an often used word from the vocabulary of the pupils. Probably the best solution is simply to use "series" in the usual way and not worry about technicalities.

Having agreed that the limit of the sum of the first $n$ terms of a geometric sequence exists when $0 < r < 1$ (that is, a geometric series is convergent if $0 < r < 1$), the pupils may be interested in deciding whether there are other values of $r$ for which this is true. They may have the feeling that, since for negative $r$ alternate terms have an opposite effect, there should be "a greater number" of negative values of $r$ which produce convergent series than positive ones. A few simple experiments $(1 - 1 + 1 - 1 + 1 - 1 + \cdots$ , for example) will convince them that this is not the case, and they should agree quite readily that only for $|r| < 1$ does the sum of the first $n$ terms of a geometric sequence approach $a[1/(1 - r)]$ as $n$ gets large without bound.

There are many interesting examples of convergent infinite series with which pupils will already be familiar. As a matter of fact, every rational number has a convergent infinite series as part of its decimal representation. For example,

$$\tfrac{1}{3} = .3333 \cdots = \tfrac{3}{10} + \tfrac{3}{10} \cdot \tfrac{1}{10} + \tfrac{3}{10} \cdot (\tfrac{1}{10})^2 + \tfrac{3}{10} \cdot (\tfrac{1}{10})^3 + \cdots$$

A discussion of this matter would review ideas pertaining to the difference between rational and irrational numbers as well as reinforce the work with infinite geometric series.

## Other Limit Problems

There are other ways in which the concept of limit can be introduced into elementary mathematics without a full-fledged study of the calculus. One example was considered in Chapter 6, when the area of a circle was determined by an intuitive argument involving limits. Others have appeared at various places in this book, and will crop up in any ordinary high school mathematics program. If the pupils are introduced to a good sound, nonrigorous concept of limit in each of these cases, they will be relatively well prepared for the calculus. However, there are other places where limit ideas were skipped because they seemed too difficult. These might be reconsidered in a senior course in mathematics.

Historically, the most interesting discussion of limits, which is ordinarily skipped in elementary mathematics courses, is the discussion of incommensurable line segments. The discovery that there were such things as incommensurable line segments apparently shook the Pythagorean Society to its very foundations, and probably had a great deal to do with the beginnings of rigorous mathematical work in ancient Greece. The proof that the square root of 2 is irrational contains the essentials of the proof that there are incommensurable line segments. Two line segments are said to be commensurable if the length of one is an exact multiple of the other, or if both can be divided evenly into small segments such that the length of the small segments is the same for both lines. Thus, lengths of $2\tfrac{1}{3}$ inches and $4\tfrac{1}{8}$ inches are commensurable because the first can be divided into 56 lengths of $\tfrac{1}{24}$ inch, while the second can be divided into 99 lengths of $\tfrac{1}{24}$ inch. Saying that two segments are commensurable is equivalent to saying that if $a$ and $b$ are the lengths of the segments, then there is a rational number, $p/q$, such that $a = (p/q) \cdot b$. Here $p$ would be the number of segments into which the segment $a$ units long would be divided, and $q$ would be the number of segments into which the $b$ segment would be divided. If there are segments which are related by a factor of an irrational number (the side and diagonal of a square, for example), then these are incommensurable line segments.

The incommensurable problem was solved by the Greek mathematician Eudoxes. The solution is quite similar to later efforts to lay a careful foundation for the real number system. The usual idea of ratio no longer seemed to make sense if there were incommensurable line segments. However, Eudoxes solved this with the following definition of proportion.

Four magnitudes are in the same ratio, the first to the second as the third to the fourth, when, if any multiple whatever is taken of the first and the third (the same multiple of each) and also any multiple of the second and the fourth (the same multiple of each) then the multiple of the third exceeds, is equal to, or falls short of the multiple of the fourth, according as the multiple of the first exceeds, is equal to, or falls short of the multiple of the second. (Euclid V, Definition 5)

If we read this definition hurridly, it may seem obscure. However, if more careful consideration is given to the physical situation being described, it makes good sense. Imagine that Fig. 14.1 is a drawing of the intersection of a tiled wall and a tiled floor. Suppose that at the left end, the left sides of the tiles correspond precisely (both in the actual situation and in the drawing). How would we check to see if the drawing gives an accurate representation of the true ratio of the lengths of the tiles? First, we would probably look for another place where the side of a floor tile corresponds with the side of a wall tile. If we found such a place, we would simply count how many floor tiles there were between the two points and how many wall tiles, and if the numbers for the drawing were the same as the actual situation, we would conclude that the drawing was correct (assuming no other difficulties occurred, such as different-sized tiles, etc.).

But suppose there were no place, other than the beginning, where the sides of the tiles corresponded; the tiles go on forever, and there is only the one spot where endpoints correspond. Now what do we do? If we count out 11 wall tiles and find that the endpoint is just short of the endpoint for 14 floor tiles; if we then count out 8 wall tiles and find

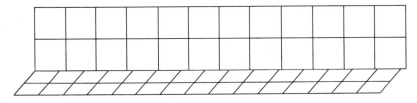

Figure 14.1

that this endpoint is just beyond the endpoint for 10 floor tiles, and if we continue this procedure until we have checked a large number of each "inequalities," observing that the picture and the actual situation always agree, will we not conclude that the picture is accurate? Now, read Eudoxes' definition again; this is exactly what he said we should do in such a situation.

What does all of this have to do with limits? This discussion is essentially one of completeness; for every point on a line there is a real number, and for every real number there is a point on the line. If such completeness exists in our number system, then it is clear—intuitively, at least—that every set of numbers which has an upper bound must have a least upper bound. That is, if every element of a set of numbers is less than or equal to a given number, there is a smallest number which is greater than or equal to every element of the set. Or geometrically, if all of the points of a set are to the left of some given point $(Q)$, there is a point $(P)$ such that every point of the set is to the left of $P$ or equal to $P$, and there is no point to the left of $P$ which also has the same property. As long as we are talking about points on a line, this should seem obvious, if the mass of words is not confusing; but with a set of numbers, it is not as obvious. For example, with the set of rational numbers, it is not true. The set of rational numbers whose squares are less than 2 does not have a least upper bound in the set of rationals, even though it has an upper bound. The property we are discussing is a property of the real numbers but not of the rational numbers; it is necessary to have this property if we are going to have limits of sequences when we would expect to have such limits.

There are many other activities which a senior in high school can carry on which will help to prepare him to understand the calculus. Approximating the value of $\pi$ by using inscribed and circumscribed polygons (not necessarily regular, but the perimeter of a regular polygon is easier to compute) is one example of using limits in a way which appeals to the intuition. More work with series and sequences is certainly appropriate. For example, various tests for convergence are well within the grasp of bright senior mathematics pupils. Such tests include: comparing terms with corresponding terms of another series that is known to converge (or not to converge); the ratio test which can be proved once geometric series have been considered (if $\lim_{n \to \infty} [(a_{n+1})/a_n]$ < 1, the series converges and if that limit is greater than 1, the series diverges, assuming that the terms are all positive; the proof is accomplished by choosing $r$ between the given limit and 1 and comparing the resulting geometric series with the given series); tests for alternating series; etc. The series definitions of trigonometric functions are interesting to study and will do no harm in helping the pupils to understand the concept of limit; and several limits $\left[ \text{such as } \lim_{x \to 0} \left( \sin \frac{x}{x} \right) \right]$ involving trigonometric functions can be profitably studied from an intuitive point of view.

Before leaving the topic of limits, we shall mention two well-known paradoxes associated with the concept. We do not mention these with the idea that they ought to be used in an intuitive introduction to limits, but as an example of something which ought *not* to be done in such an introduction.

The first of these is one of Zeno's paradoxes. Suppose Achilles can run ten times as fast as a certain tortoise. Suppose also that the tortoise has a head start of one unit and Achilles is trying to catch the tortoise. The race begins. Achilles covers the unit distance and finds that the tortoise is no longer there, but is one-tenth of a unit ahead; Achilles then runs the one-tenth of a unit only to find the tortoise is now one-hundredth of a unit ahead; next, Achilles runs the one-hundredth of a unit and finds the tortoise is one-thousandth of a unit ahead; etc. Therefore, since the tortoise is always ahead of Achilles (by one-tenth of the distance he used to be ahead), Achilles will never catch the tortoise.

The second paradox is illustrated in Fig. 14.2. In this problem, we are calculating the length of the diagonal of a square by use of limits. We begin by constructing perpendicular bisectors of $\overline{AB}$ and $\overline{BC}$, producing broken line $AEFGC$, which clearly has a length of two units if the side of the square is one unit in length. In a similar way, we produce broken line $AHIKFLMNC$ which also has length of two units. Then, broken line $APQRISTUFVWXMYZJC$ with length two units is created, and so on. It is clear that the broken lines are approaching the diagonal. It is also clear that the length associated with each broken line produced in this way will be two units. Therefore, the length of the diagonal of a square is twice the length of a side of the square.

What is wrong with these two examples? From a pedagogical point of view, they should probably not be considered either in a precalculus introduction to limits or in a beginning course in calculus. The fact is that Zeno's question, and others like it which he created, is generally credited with having set the calculus back about 2000 years. Two of the greatest mathematicians of all time did not really come up with a satisfactory answer to this question. Archimedes all but created the integral calculus, but his failure to answer Zeno's questions seem to have stopped progress completely along these lines. Newton did create the

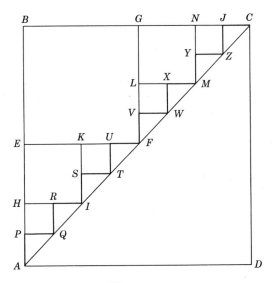

Figure 14.2

calculus (ignoring possible questions of priority raised by the followers of Leibnitz) but did not solve the questions raised by Zeno; he simply did not pay any attention to them. It was not until about 200 years later that the problem of a formal definition of limit was satisfactorily handled.

How, we might ask, can a high school senior or a college freshman, with relatively little training in mathematics be expected to solve problems that stumped some of the greatest mathematical minds in history? If the pupils cannot be expected to solve such problems, why bring them up? Of course, if the teacher is planning to explain in some detail what is wrong with the supposed paradoxes, the discussion is desirable, provided the students will understand both the problem and the solution. This criteria seems to indicate that such problems ought to wait until *after* at least two semesters of calculus. In any case, having these problems appear as exercises, without solution, in the first few pages of an elementary calculus book is highly inappropriate.

Zeno's paradox involves a confusion between the measure of an interval and the number of points it contains. His argument was aimed primarily at the concept of motion and is avoided in the modern definitions of limit which do not involve motion. The diagonal problem is also avoided by reasonable care in making definitions. It is true that individual points of the broken line can be made as close as we like to points of the diagonal, but the question has to do with lengths, and there is no evidence given that the length of the broken line approaches the length of the diagonal. In fact, there is considerable evidence that this is not the case.

The point is not that we should explain paradoxes carefully, but that there is no particular reason for bringing these up before the students are equipped to discuss them with some understanding.

## A Calculus Course

We have already mentioned that calculus is a college level course at present and will probably remain there for some time to come. It may be taught with great success to accelerated pupils by good teachers at the high school level, but for the majority of pupils (and teachers) it will remain a college course. Therefore, we shall not spend much time discussing a calculus course beyond the description of various desirable preliminaries. Among these preliminaries, as already mentioned, is a good course in analytic geometry beyond that studied in the plane geometry course. If such a course has not preceded the calculus, and a combined course is being taught, the analytic geometry should not be neglected as it often is in present-day courses entitled "Calculus with Analytic Geometry."

Limiting our consideration for a moment to the calculus itself, we find that the integral calculus seems to be more intuitive and therefore more easily studied before the differential calculus. This point of view is borne out historically, since Archimedes had developed many of the techniques of the integral calculus more than 2000 years ago. The concept of finding an area simply seems more natural than the concept of finding the slope of a tangent to a line or the rate of change of a function. Therefore, a calculus course ought to begin by allowing the students to find areas and volumes under curves by finding the limit of a sequence of sums, thus using the preliminary work mentioned. Then, the derivatives of polynomials can be considered. If this program is followed, the common procedure of defining (or apparently defining) an integral as an antiderivative will be avoided, and the fundamental theorem of calculus which links differentiation and integration will have real significance, as well as making computations of integrals much simpler.

Such a course would emphasize intuitive understanding which the teacher would attempt to develop along more rigorous lines until the student had a good understanding of the concepts and the need for rigorous statements in conjunction with it. However, if either rigor or understanding must be neglected, let us, by all means, neglect the former—for without understanding, rigor is quite empty. Applications are important and would occupy an important place in any calculus course, but the goal of being able to apply the calculus should not be so important that the pupils are taught *how* to differentiate and integrate without any understanding of the processes involved. Thus, a course in "cookbook" calculus is no more desirable than a course that is given over entirely to rigorous proofs and definitions. Rather, both the rigor and the applications should come in conjunction with the understanding, which ought to be the most important factor in teaching calculus or any other subject in mathematics.

## Teaching Hints

There are many things which students probably ought to know before they begin the formal study of calculus. Even when they know these things, they ought to be started out in a relatively informal way as they begin the study. If a good intuitive idea of limit has been developed before the beginning of the calculus class, that notion ought to be used to develop a concept of what is meant by an integral and a derivative. Then, at a later time, the subject of limits ought to be reconsidered, and put on a more formal basis for those who will benefit from such considerations. The intuitive understanding of the principles of calculus and the manipulatory aspects are easily comprehended and learned; it is the undue formalism that revolts many college students of calculus. This undue formalism is not desirable either for college students or for high school pupils and should be eliminated, if possible. This is *not* a plea for studying only the manipulatory aspects of calculus, or for learning in a "cookbook" style, but for a good, firm, intuitive understanding without necessarily bringing in deltas and epsilons near the beginning of the course. In fact, there is some reason to believe that if more familiar notation were used, some students would find it easier to follow the formal definition of limit when it did come. For example, $p$'s and $q$'s could be used instead of $\delta$'s and $\epsilon$'s. It may seem surprising, but people will often balk at understanding a relatively simple concept, simply because of a cumbersome or unfamiliar notation that is being used.

The first thing for a teacher to do to prepare for teaching a calculus course (assuming he has adequate preparation himself; if he does not he should not try to teach calculus) is to try to find a book that is comprehensible, and does not overstress formalism or manipulation. Unfortunately, there are too few calculus textbooks that develop a strong intuitive understanding of the calculus before going into either formal proofs or manipulations. Also, unfortunately, many of our "better" colleges and universities have adopted books that stress the formalism at the expense of both intuition and applications. In light of this, it may not be desirable for the teacher either to adopt the book he studied from or to go to the nearest college and use the book they are using.

## Exercises

1. Consider the sequence in which the first three terms (in order) are 1, 2, 4. Name at least three numbers which could be a fourth term of this sequence and justify the choice.

2. Show that if $a_n = pn + q$, where $n$ is a positive integer, then each term, $a_m$ of the sequence $(a_1, a_2, a_3, \ldots)$ is $n$ greater than the previous term $a_{m-1}$.

3. Prove the converse of the theorem in Exercise 2.

4. What is the sum of the first $n$ positive integers that are divisible by 3?

5. What is the sum of the first $n$ (positive) integral powers of 7?

6. Approximately what is the sum of the first 1000 powers of .7?

7. By approximately how much is your answer to number 6 in error (give a decimal approximation—you may use logarithms to find it if you like)?

8. Assuming that the theorem stated below has been proved, show that the ratio test for convergence of a series works.

THEOREM.    If $a_n \leq b_n$ for all elements (or all but a finite number of elements) of the two series $a_1 + a_2 + a_3 + \cdots$ and $b_1 + b_2 + b_3 + \cdots$, and if the second series is convergent, then so is the first.

9. What is $\lim\limits_{x \to 0} \left( \dfrac{\sin x}{x} \right)$? Prove it.

10. Graph $f(x) = \sin x$; $f(x) = x$; $f(x) = x - x^3/3!$; $f(x) = x - x^3/3! + x^5/5!$ on the same set of coordinate axes.

11. Graph $f(x) = \cos x$; $f(x) = 1$; $f(x) = 1 - x^2/2!$; $f(x) = 1 - x^2/2! + x^4/4!$ on the same set of coordinate axes.

12. If $f(x) = x - x^3/3! + x^5/5!$, what is $f'(x)$?

13. If $f(x) = 1 - x^2/2' + x^4/4! - x^6/6!$, what is $f'(x)$?

## Questions for Further Thought and Study

1. State and prove the fundamental theorem of calculus and discuss its importance in elementary calculus.

## REFERENCES

Allendoerfer, Carl B. "The Case Against Calculus," *The Mathematics Teacher*, **LVI** (November 1963), 482–485. Not, as the title seems to suggest, a condemnation of calculus, but rather Mr. Allendoerfer's opinion as to how, when, by whom, and to whom calculus ought to be taught. A thought-provoking article that should be read by anybody planning to teach calculus in the high school.

Courant, Richard, and Herbert Robbins. *What Is Mathematics?* Oxford University Press, New York, 1941. See reference in Chapter 9. Chapters 6 through 8 pertain to the foundations of calculus.

Dubisch, Roy (with Vernon E. Howes). *The Teaching of Mathematics*, John Wiley and Sons, New York, 1963. An excellent book on the teaching of advanced high school and elementary college mathematics. The style is informal, the ideas are thought provoking, and the bibliography is substantial. Topics covered include algebra, trigonometry and logarithms, analytic geometry, differential calculus, and integral calculus.

Randolph, John F. "Limits," *Insights into Modern Mathematics*, Twenty-third Yearbook of the National Council of Teachers of Mathematics, NCTM, Washington, D.C., 1957, pp. 200–240. A modern approach to limits leading to the differential and integral calculus.

Sawyer, W. W. *What Is Calculus About?* School Mathematics Study Group: New Mathematical Library 2, Random House, New York, 1961. An introduction to differential and integral calculus.

Smith, David Eugene. *A Source Book in Mathematics*, 2 vols., Dover Publications, New York, 1959. See reference in Chapter 4. The last section considers the beginnings of calculus.

National Council of Teachers of Mathematics. *The Twelfth-Grade Pre-College Mathematics Program*, NCTM, Washington, D.C., 1965. A compilation of nine speeches presented at a joint meeting of the Mathematical Association of America and the National Council of Teachers of Mathematics (50¢).

# TEACHING SECONDARY
# SCHOOL MATHEMATICS

Many aspects of mathematics are useful, enjoyable, and stimulating, and teachers have discovered that certain methods of teaching them can be most effective. Some of these subjects and methods have been presented in the course of this book; however, nothing here is intended to imply "this is the way to teach," or "this is what should be taught." Drawing on a variety of methods and teaching numerous subjects, many teachers have helped to educate good mathematicians and good citizens who are well versed in mathematics. It behooves each teacher to learn as much as possible about his subject, his pupils, and what able educators have said about the teaching of mathematics to pupils. Then he may begin to formulate, and constantly reformulate, his own ideas on teaching. In this way he can develop his own philosophy of mathematics education.

Despite the wide choice of subject and method available to the teacher of mathematics, we shall present a possible course of study for the secondary school mathematics program. For different situations in different schools with different teachers and pupils at different times, the course will vary greatly. No one textbook, no course of study, and no single method can be appropriate for all situations; since the beginning of formal education in this country, the idea of a National

Curriculum has been objectionable to educators, and with good reason. However, if the teacher has had an opportunity to examine someone else's idea of a course of study, it may help him to formulate his own. Other courses of study can be found in various reports mentioned in Chapters 1 and 2; probably the most pertinent is in the Report of the Commission on Mathematics of the College Entrance Examination Board.

Any series of textbooks incorporates a course of study worked out in great detail. The various experimental programs (such as SMSG or UICSM) also incorporate well-thought-out courses of study. An individual who is planning a course of study would do well to consult several of these sources.

The following course of study is designed for the average pupil who will study mathematics through the eleventh grade. He is average only in relation to the ever increasing percentage of the population attending high school. He is not average if the entire population is considered. Later we shall mention variations on this program which may prove useful for pupils of differing abilities.

## Seventh and Eighth Grade

The seventh and eighth grades are considered together because there is usually sufficient freedom at this level to develop an appropriate program which is not influenced by outside sources such as transferring of pupils to a different school, college entrance requirements, vocational education, etc. In these grades, the pupils should acquire a better understanding of arithmetic with considerable emphasis on properties of the rational number system. It is natural to use some algebraic symbolism in this study, but such symbolism should be employed only to help formulate general principles. The study of numeration systems other than base ten, and other systems such as a modular system, can be helpful in the understanding of the usual systems, but these are probably not worth studying for their own sake at the junior high level. The goal is better understanding of the rational number system and its subsystems.

A great deal of intuitive study of geometry ought to occur in the seventh and eighth grades. By the end of the eighth grade, the pupils should know most of the facts of two- and three-dimensional geometry. Formal proofs will not be presented at this level, but it is possible to develop a feeling for proof in both intuitive geometry and the study of number systems by asking pupils "why do you believe that statement is always true?" Many physical models can be used to help the pupils discover the facts of geometry, but pupils should begin to realize that a large number of examples is not enough to guarantee the invariable truth of a fact.

The method of associating numbers and points on a line in order to create a "number line" should be considered (or reconsidered), and the pupils should begin to learn to plot solution sets of simple conditions ($x = 4$, $x > 4$, $x \geq 4$, etc.). The number line can then be used, probably in the last semester of the eighth grade, to help develop the idea of negative numbers. Study of number systems would also help to establish which properties we want to maintain, and therefore, how operations ought to be defined for the new numbers.

Any pupil who spends several years in secondary school should know something about statistics and probability, and should learn how these subjects can be used and misused to report facts, predict events, make conclusions, etc. Junior high school seems a likely place to undertake this study since relatively little algebra, geometry, and trigonometry is needed to understand the basic ideas which are important in such a course, and the practice in arithmetic (disguised as the study of simple probability or statistics) is more palatable to youngsters in this form than in most others commonly used.

Throughout the seventh and eighth grades, as well as in later mathematics courses, considerable emphasis should be placed upon the pupils' creation of theorems (or statements which they think ought to be true) and subsequent proofs that the theorems are true. At the early stages, the statement of both the theorem and the proof ought to be quite informal, the understanding being of far greater importance than the form.

Problem solving should also be given considerable attention in the junior high as well as in later courses. Where possible, applications should be attempted from various branches of human endeavor, including the social sciences, the physical sciences, and the commercial arena. Again the understanding, not the form, should be emphasized. If it becomes necessary for the teacher to make the pupils memorize a particular form for solving a particular type of problem, either the pupils are not ready to solve that type of problem or they are not being taught well.

Of course, if, after understanding the problem and how to solve it, the pupils discover a shortcut for solving that type of problem, there would seem to be no objection to their learning the shortcut. We should not, however, allow the shortcut to replace understanding, since speed in solving problems is seldom the primary aim. This is especially true when the problem is not one the pupil will be trying to solve regularly at any time other than in a mathematics course.

Such traditional topics as ratio and percentage should also be studied in the seventh and eighth grades.

## Ninth Grade

Programs for the ninth-grade mathematics course throughout the country are surprisingly similar. In general, the subject matter includes the study of positive and negative numbers, solving of equations and systems of equations, manipulation of polynomials and rational expressions, some study of relations and functions, and at least the beginning of the study of real numbers. All of these topics are important, and if they have not been studied previously by the pupils, the ninth grade seems to be a good place to start them.

However, the list certainly cannot be considered complete. Any algebra course that does not include considerable work with inequalities and systems of inequalities is simply not appropriate for this day and age. A continuation of the informal proofs of the seventh and eighth grades is desirable, with a more formal type of proof possible and probably desirable in the ninth grade. Again, however, the emphasis should be on understanding and an intuitive feeling for the subject rather than upon form. Methods of manipulating polynomials and rational expressions can be justified at this level in terms of understanding of the real number system, since it is appropriate in the ninth grade to think of the replacement set for the variables as real numbers. Later, a more formal view of such expressions, in which no particular replacement set needs to be under consideration, can be used. This would not be suitable, however, for the ninth grade, nor even for the eleventh grade. The study of relations and functions should expand the pupils' understanding of graphic procedures; and a great deal of emphasis on two-dimensional graphs is desirable in the ninth grade.

Pupils intending to continue the study of mathematics will need a good understanding of quadratic equations and their solutions since there are many problems in geometry which lead to such equations. The study of real numbers at this level would concentrate on radicals, and this work would be reinforced in the geometry course.

Problem solving continues to be important in the ninth grade, and many applications of mathematical principles to actual problems should be explored. One application of particular interest to pupils which involves inequalities (considered in Chapter 10) is linear programming. Many other applications appear in various textbooks, and these should not be slighted. Without the applications, the algebra will seem hollow to most of the pupils—and rightly so. Very few pupils are going to become "pure mathematicians," and even they, though they may deny it, are interested in applications, if perhaps somewhat esoteric ones.

## Tenth Grade

At present, in the United States, tenth grade is usually given over completely to geometry. If this means that geometry and algebra are relegated to separate compartments and neither is to be mentioned while the other is being studied, this is not good practice. On the other hand, if algebra is used throughout the study of geometry, and the study of algebra depends in part on spatial conception, there is no reason for supposing that a full year devoted to geometry between two years of algebra is any less effective than a program in which geometry is studied for two or three days a week for two years with algebra's being studied for the other two to three days. Experiments in this country with so-called parallel courses in algebra and geometry have not been satisfactory in the past because the teachers managed to avoid mentioning any connection between the two, and often a teacher would like one subject more than the other and concentrate most of his (and the pupils') energy on that subject to the detriment of the other. The basic principle of relating algebra and geometry to each other is a good one, but the efforts in this direction have not been effective, and have produced other undesirable results. With this in mind, we propose a full one-year course in geometry for the tenth grade, while suggesting that some experimentation with variations might be tried. Since many other countries use the parallel system, such experiments might be set up on an international basis.

A course in geometry should include rather careful consideration of the concept of proof and mathematical structure in addition to the usual facts from plane and solid geometry and some introduction to the methods of analytic geometry. In studying the structure of the Euclidean axiom system, the possibility of changing some of the axioms and considering how results would be changed ought to be included. Although the formalism of modern correct Euclidean geometries would not be emphasized, it would certainly be mentioned in classes of brighter mathematics pupils. Algebra should be used wherever possible, both to show the connection between algebra and geometry, and to reduce the amount of forgetting between ninth- and eleventh-grade algebra.

## Eleventh Grade

If pupils have had a background in mathematics similar to that described here, they should be ready in the eleventh grade for a strong course in algebra and trigonometry. There will be need for some review of topics covered in earlier courses, but if the pupils really understood these topics at the time of study, and if they have had an opportunity to review them at various intervals, it should be possible to carry on this re-examination by considering the topics from a more advanced standpoint and also by studying more advanced topics. For example, the study of fields from a formal standpoint can serve to review information about mathematical structure, the natural number system, the system of integers, and the rational number system. This study can then be extended to clarify the properties of the real number system and to begin the study of the complex number system.

A good understanding of relations and functions can be developed further through the study of polynomial functions, logarithmic and exponential functions, circular functions, and other functions and relations. Circular functions lead naturally into a study of trigonometry, and various topics in the eleventh-grade course can be brought together in a unit on applications of trigonometry to complex numbers. Again, applications are important, but the pupils should not become so embroiled in calculations (with logarithms, or solving triangles, etc.) that they lose sight of the important general principles. As one of the important applications of trigonometry concerns vectors, it is particularly appropriate to consider the relation of trigonometry to complex numbers, since there is a close relationship between both and vectors.

If time permits, some consideration of series and sequences, the binomial theorem, permutations and combinations, analytic geometry, and linear algebra may be attempted. In most classes, however, the previously mentioned material keeps the pupils sufficiently occupied for a full, one-year, eleventh-grade course.

## Twelfth Grade

In the twelfth grade, any important material cited earlier, but not yet studied, should be considered before going on to new topics. All the material mentioned in the previous paragraph, with the exception of linear algebra, should be studied before any serious consideration can be given to the study of calculus, and a good course in probability and statistics (about 12 weeks) also ought to be introduced prior to the calculus for any pupils who may not study these subjects after the calculus.

Permutations, combinations, and the binomial theorem can be studied naturally in connection with probability, and the binomial theorem also has a natural association with sequences and series. Intuitive ideas of limits should be developed in connection with sequences and series, and it would be entirely appropriate to follow through some of the basic ideas of the integral calculus on an intuitive level at this time. Then a strong course in analytic geometry, at least nine to twelve weeks beyond that studied in the tenth grade, ought to round out the twelfth year of mathematics. This would include some idea of slope of a tangent to a curve and some intuitive idea of how, using limits, to find the slope of a tangent. It would not include a systematic development of the formulas of differential and integral calculus.

## Slow Learners

Whenever a particular classification seems relatively undesirable, there tends to be a flurry of attempts to think up a name that does not reflect its bad connotation. So it is with slow learners. The difficulty with this process is that it often results in an inappropriate name, and sometimes one which may be harmful. Pupils in slower classes have been called such things as "minnows" (the fast pupils being called whales), "the A group," "the C group," "the X group," "the under-achievers," "the noncollege bound," and many similar names. Although the first four names fool nobody, they at least have the advantage of not confusing the issues. The other two can, however, be actively harmful. "Underachiever" gives the strong impression that the pupil is lazy, and that if he just worked a little harder, everything would be all right. Although this may be true in some cases, it is certainly not true for all pupils who are not up to grade level in mathematics (or other subjects). In a similar way, "noncollege bound" or "noncollege capable" suggests that at the age of twelve or thirteen, we have decided what this individual will do with the rest of his life. Surely, no one who has studied the matter would be willing to suggest that a child who seems slow at age thirteen is necessarily going to be a failure; there are too many notable exceptions (for example, Winston Churchill, Albert Einstein).

Of course, "slow learner" is somewhat of a misnomer, since some pupils whom we might describe this way have not learned for some reason other than slowness. In many cases, they have learned a great deal, and very rapidly. It just happens that what they have learned does not happen to be mathematics (or any other academic subject). There are many reasons for a pupil's not knowing as much mathematics as others his age; part of the teacher's job is to find out what those reasons are. Hopefully, the teacher will not allow any preconceived label to affect his thinking on this matter.

Whatever we call them, it is true that some pupils are significantly behind their classmates in the learning of mathematics. It is also true that they are commonly put in a class by themselves. Although there have been many studies on homogeneous grouping, data resulting from these studies tend to be conflicting. There are many reasons for this: different grouping arrangements may be called "homogeneous," different things happen to the pupils once they are grouped, the gathering and analysis of statistics have been less than scientific in some cases, attitudes of teachers, school administrators, etc., have been different, and many other variables have crept in. However, it seems safe to say that when a good program of grouping is tried, and the teacher plans a program especially for the pupils with whom he is working, shutting out adverse factors, ability grouping can be useful in helping the teacher to do a more effective job of instruction.

Several things are important to remember when embarking on a program of grouping. First, the way in which the pupils are chosen for the groups is important. If the grouping is for a mathematics class, it seems only reasonable that mathematics should play a major role in determining to which group the pupil should be assigned. Although there is a positive correlation between achievement in mathematics and achievement in language arts, it is true that some pupils may be very good in the one, and quite poor in the other. It is also important to see that children are not put into the slow class because of discipline problems. Often, the worst discipline cases occur in children who are bright, but bored with what is going on in the class. To put such an individual into a class for slow learners will simply compound the difficulty. Well-motivated pupils who are intellectually challenged seldom become discipline problems.

Once a decision has been made as to the group to which a child belongs, the decision should not be looked upon as final and binding. If the pupil develops quickly under the new conditions, or if it turns out that a mistake was made, there should be some simple procedure for having him switched into a faster class. Finally, it is important that teachers not look upon the slow classes as a burden to be taken only if it cannot be avoided, and to be given to the teacher with least experience (or seniority) and least ability.

One of the first things to remember when teaching any class is that the class is made up of individuals. This is even truer with those who will be found in a class for slow learners. Not only will homogeneous grouping not make for equal abilities, it will hardly cut down at all on other variations which may exist among the children. In a slow group, about all we can take for granted (and this, only if the grouping has been done well) is that the pupils have all had some previous difficulty in learning mathematics.

Despite the wide variations, there are some characteristics which will be common to many of the pupils in a slow class. First, there will be many who have a short attention span. With this in mind, it is usually *not* a good idea to plan lessons in which the pupils must all give their undivided attention to the same topic for very long (usually, five to ten minutes is a long time to pupils with a short attention span).

A second factor which will be very common (even if the pupils are grouped according to mathematical achievement) is poor reading ability. If possible, the teacher should cut down as much as possible on the disadvantage a poor reader has. This means that there should not be long reading assignments, and class discussions should be used to cover (or recover) topics which the pupils may also read about.

Many of the children in slow classes are culturally deprived—at least in terms of the culture which is generally accepted by middle-class Americans. Some of these children will have rich cultures of their own, but it will be a different culture from that of the teacher and the authors of the textbooks. Thus, if the teacher can manage to make up problems that seem real in light of the child's culture, he is likely to generate far more interest than if he sticks to problems that seem real in light of his own culture. Of course, a great deal of effort would be required to do this. It undoubtedly would be desirable for the teacher to go and live among the people he intends to teach, and learn about them. In lieu of this, however, the teacher can ask the pupils to try to make up problems which *do* seem real to them, and which involve numbers. Over a period of years, quite a storehouse of problems could be accumulated in this way.

Some pupils in a slow class may have psychological problems. If these problems are serious, it may be desirable to request professional help. On the other hand, it may be that the child is simply emotionally starved—he needs somebody who likes him and appreciates him. Often a teacher can fill this role well. For example, a child from a broken home may need a father image; a male teacher may find that by giving him encouragement, high standards to live up to, and true affection, he can help the pupil immensely.

In light of the differences among children who are likely to be found in a slow mathematics class, it is difficult to set up hard and fast rules which will always work. However, there are several important points to consider.

Before beginning to teach, the teacher should begin by considering what he wants to accomplish. Does he want to prepare the pupils for the next test or for something more lasting? How are the pupils likely to use mathematics in the future? Will it help them to be better citizens? If so, how? Will it help them to hold better jobs? If so, what jobs, and what will be needed in those jobs?

If part of the goal is to help the pupils understand what is happening around them in the world, and to be more intelligent citizens, should not many of the problems come from newspapers and news magazines? Some teachers have found that an effective way to study large numbers is to have the class find places where such numbers are mentioned in papers (and elsewhere) and then discuss their meaning. For example, a city with a population of 100,000 is far different in size from a city with a population of 1,000,000. If the budget of a state is increased by $1,000,000, it will have far less effect on individuals than if the budget is increases $10,000,000. If a rocket must travel 28,000 miles, it will complete its trip more quickly than if it must travel 280,000 miles (assuming approximately the same speed), and so on. Newspapers and other periodicals can be used effectively not only to study numbers but also to provide simple, meaningful problems.

If part of the goal in teaching mathematics to pupils who are not very good in the subject is to help them hold jobs, perhaps it would be worthwhile to talk to local businessmen who may be hiring them and find out what sorts of abilities will be needed. Of course, the requirements may change later, but if one can get examples of problems that are solved in the local businesses, the pupils may find the problems more appealing.

If part of the goal of the mathematics course is to help the children be more intelligent consumers and use their incomes more efficiently, then such topics as insurance, income taxes, and installment buying may be appropriate. For college-bound pupils, it is generally assumed that the mathematics involved in such topics will not cause any serious problem, there are usually other issues involved for them. However, for slower pupils, and the pupils who will be dropping out of school shortly, a careful analysis of financial matters may be pertinent. Again, the problems should be as realistic as possible. Some children may be working, and need help figuring out their income tax; this would be a worthwhile expenditure of class time. Information on interest rates and expense of installment buying is easily available, and comparisons can be made in the classroom. When possible, it may be desirable to draw some general conclusions regarding what sort of financing seems the least expensive, what kind of insurance is most appropriate for certain circumstances, etc.

Such a program should be carefully coordinated with the work of other teachers. Often it will be found that the major difficulty in filling out an income tax form involves reading rather than arithmetic. In this case, perhaps the reading teacher should be consulted. Often, it will be possible to coordinate the mathematics lesson with the social science lesson. And it is quite natural to use mathematics in the home economics class (doubling or halving a recipe, designing clothes involving circles, parallel lines, and various other geometric figures, etc.), and the shop class.

In planning lessons for a slow class in mathematics, the teacher ought to remember that the pupils have had trouble with mathematics in the past, and have probably had some bad associations with arithmetic. It certainly does not seem appropriate to give them more of the same—only harder and more tedious. Many of the "General Mathematics" or "Practical Arithmetic" books that have been available in the past seemed to be based on the assumption that if children did not like arithmetic, they should be made to do more of it. If they had not learned it before it was not because the method was poor, but because they had not been forced to do enough work. Thus, we find in many books long columns of addition problems with no motivation. Many experiments which have been tried with slow pupils have shown that modern mathematics programs (designed for the "college capable") have been far more effective with these children than traditional books. Surely, this is damning the new programs with faint praise. Considering the available traditional books, one would expect almost anything to be more effective. Recently, there have been several imaginative, interesting, worthwhile books published for slow learners. There have also been various committees (for example, Committee on Mathematics for the Non-College Bound of the NCTM[1]) at work preparing materials for pupils who are not good at mathematics. This is an encouraging trend, and perhaps will lead to some really excellent materials for such classes. However, the teacher will still have to choose the materials that are most appropriate for his pupils.

In making decisions as to what to teach, the teacher should study the past experiences of the children. This is even more important for pupils who have not done well in the past than for average pupils. If their past experiences have been distasteful perhaps the teacher can find more interesting methods of attacking the ideas involved. Chapter 4 of this book contains some interesting ideas for the teacher who is trying to make arithmetic exciting.

In planning individual classes, it is desirable to present several com-

[1] This committee has written *Experiences in Mathematical Discovery*, designed for pupils with mathematical achievement between the 25th and 50th percentiles.

pelling topics in a given period, since the children can be expected to have short attention spans. Many suggestions for such topics can be found in some of the newer books, in reports of various projects, and in articles in the *Mathematics Teacher*. Since different pupils will react differently to different stimulants, it is desirable to have aids which depend on audio, visual, and kinestatic senses. Such objects as a physical number line, physical models of two- and three-dimensional figures, physical models of fractions and whole numbers (for example, Cuisenaire® Rods, etc.), adding machines, and so on will appeal to the children, especially if they are allowed to handle the models. In many cases, they will be able to make the aids themselves.

A bulletin board which is attractive and educational can be of considerable help to the children, and will maintain interest, especially if they have responsibility for it.[2] Films and film strips can attract interest and be educational if they are not overused. But, the children's own lives should provide a large portion of the material for the class. For example, so simple a procedure as guessing the relative volumes of a cylinder and a cone (of equal height and radius), and then actually finding them through physical means (pouring something from one to the other) will explain to the pupils why soda fountains always use conical rather than cylindrical cups—and the discussion should impress the fact itself upon their minds.

Much of what can be said about slow pupils can also be said about any pupils. Thus, much of what is said in this section is appropriate for other children; and much of what is said in the rest of the book may be appropriate for a teacher who is teaching slow learners. However, for slow learners, it is more important that the child be given serious consideration. It is imperative that the teacher not consider the job of teaching slow youngsters a burden, and that he not dislike them. On the contrary, he must like the children and have faith in them. He must encourage them to try (starting with easy problems)—and succeed. It is important that the pupil should learn that getting a wrong answer is not a crime. It is essential that the teacher value both the child and mathematics so that he can convince him of his own importance and the importance of mathematics.

## Mathematics for the Average and Below Average

Although the course of study proposed at the beginning of this chapter was intended for average pupils who take at least three years of

[2] The NCTM publishes a pamphlet by D. A. Johnson and C. E. Olander entitled *How to Use Your Bulletin Board*, which has many suggestions on where one may find bulletin board materials and how one may build effective displays.

high school mathematics, a large number of youngsters (close to 40 to 50%) fall between this group and the slow pupils discussed in the foregoing sections. For this sizable segment of the high school population, the regular course has to be slowed down considerably through the ninth grade. Some of the topics from informal geometry must be skipped, less emphasis need be placed on proofs, and much less algebra has to be completed by the end of the ninth grade. In the tenth grade, these pupils would study a less sophisticated version of geometry with relatively little discussion of the finer points: betweenness, non-Euclidean geometries, difficult proofs, etc. If these pupils take an additional year of mathematics in the eleventh grade, it could include more algebra (probably through quadratic equations), a sufficient amount of probability and statistics, and some numerical trigonometry. Here, too, applications would play an important role and there would undoubtedly have to be more practice exercises than with the fast pupils.

Many of these pupils can be expected to continue their education into college; below-average ability in mathematics does not necessarily exclude one from going to college. Such a program, therefore, should be acceptable to colleges to fulfill the common two-year requirement in mathematics for college entrance.

**Accelerated Program**

During the late 1950s it became fashionable to group pupils homogeneously in the early junior high school years and then to have fast classes either complete two years in one or skip an entire year of junior high school mathematics. This was at a time when most books and courses in junior high school mathematics had little mathematical content. Such a program may have been entirely appropriate at that time. However, with any good mathematics course now being used such a regimen would be sheer folly. Few pupils are able to skip an entire year of a well-thought-out mathematics program without serious damage to their education. If a pupil is able to do so, there is no reason to suppose that he could not do the same thing later on. In other words, if an acceleration program which involves skipping one year or combining two years of junior high school mathematics into one seems appropriate in one's school system, then one ought to give serious consideration to whether the junior high mathematics program is worth while for any of the pupils.

Yet, in large high schools, or large systems in which homogeneous grouping assigns pupils to schools (such as New York), there may be a sufficient number of good mathematics students in a school to justify having one class which is able to study the program suggested here (or a similar one) in five years or less. In such circumstances, and if the pupils really understand all of the material, including analytic geometry and limits (on an intuitive level), then, as suggested in the previous chapter, a good course in calculus can be given without apologies.

One final word of caution about homogeneous grouping: there will still be vast differences in ability within any one class even if the pupils are grouped as well as possible. Some teachers have the feeling that the differences are even more pronounced with homogeneous groups than with heterogeneous classes. With approximately similar abilities, the differences that remain within the class are more easily recognized than they would be if the whole range of abilities were included. However, homogeneous grouping is not a device to make the teacher's life easier, and does not do so. What homogeneous grouping does is to make it possible for the teacher to begin to cope with the remaining differences of ability in his class. Coping with such differences is still difficult, but since it is no longer an impossibility, it makes the teacher's job more rather than less difficult.

Of course, a good teacher would not make the mistake of trying to teach precisely the same things in the same ways to two classes of different ability, so no more needs to be said about that. However, it is surprising how many, otherwise good teachers, have the notion that the number of pages of the textbook they cover somehow measures their worth as a teacher. Thus, the teacher who is on Chapter 11 at Easter time is 10% better than the teacher who is on Chapter 10. What is even more amazing is that often *both* teachers act as though they believed that this was a good criterion. It is true that in order to avoid complete chaos in a school (with more than one mathematics teacher) certain minimums should probably be set up for the amount of material to which the pupils should be exposed in any given grade. These should be reasonable minimums and never thought of as speed records. As some good teacher once said, "it is not how much material you cover that is important, it is how much material you *uncover*."

## REFERENCES

Charosh, Mannis. *Mathematical Challenges*, National Council of Teachers of Mathematics, Washington, D.C., 1965. A collection of different and interesting problems (most of which have appeared in the *Mathematics Student Journal*) that are appropriate for junior high and high school pupils. The problems are divided according to the type of background expected. This is an excellent supplementary book (80¢).

National Council of Teachers of Mathematics. *Enrichment Mathematics for the Grades*, Twenty-seventh Yearbook, NCTM, Washington, D.C., 1963. See comments in Chapter 4. Could be very useful in helping "slow" junior and senior high pupils obtain a new perspective on mathematics.

National Council of Teachers of Mathematics. *Enrichment Mathematics for High School*, Twenty-eighth Yearbook, NCTM, Washington, D.C., 1963. Material not included in the usual secondary program. Should be useful in working with bright junior and senior high school youngsters. Excellent bibliography.

National Council of Teachers of Mathematics. *Experiences in Mathematical Discovery*, NCTM, Washington, D.C., 1966. Designed for pupils between the 25th and 50th percentiles. May be of some use to teachers of children below this level also.

Proctor, Amelia D. "A World of Hope—Helping Slow Learners Enjoy Mathematics," *The Mathematics Teacher*, **LVII** (February 1965), 118–122. An excellent article by a teacher who has worked with slow learners for some 25 years. Includes many practical suggestions such as games to play, teaching aids (individual kits for each pupil are described), methods of helping children with poor memories, books in which to find more suggestions, and a healthy, intelligent philosophy.

Woodby, Lauren G. *The Low Achiever in Mathematics*, U.S. Office of Education, Washington, D.C., 1965. Report of a joint NCTM-USOE conference. It includes papers presented at the conference, a summary of discussions and a set of recommendations for action. Available for 35¢ from the Superintendent of Documents, U.S. Government Printing Office, Washington, D.C.

# INDEX

Abacus, 124–125, 135

Abbott, Edwin A., 153 and n, 168

Abel, Neils Henrik, 278–279, 280, 296

Abelian group, 280

Abell, Theodore L., 56

Ability grouping, 405

Absolute value, defined, 263 and n

Academies, 2, 14

Acceleration, 9; program, 410–411

Accuracy, 65

Actuaries, 60

Adding machines, 34

Addition, 94, 258; associative law, 70–72, 94; cancellation law, 186; commutative law, 32, 70–72, 94, 240–241; complex numbers, 351; distributive law, 94; equivalence sets, 253–254; new numbers, 234; rational numbers, 239, 240; slide rule, 293–294; vectors, 345–349

Additive inverses, 237–238, 254

Adkins, Julia, 70 and n, 87

Adler, Irving, 54

Administration (profession), 31–32

*Administrative Responsibility for Improving Mathematics Programs*, 55

Administrators. *See* School administrators

Affine geometry, 357

Alaska, 367

"Aleph subzero," 222n

Algebra, 4, 6, 30, 37, 39, 91, 269–296, 397, 401, 403; advanced, 4, 6; applications, 401–402; relationship to arithmetic, 291; binomial theorem, 285–291, 374; creation, 30; curriculum, 7, 31; division algorithm, 128n; elementary, 188–189; elementary school, 31, 51; equations and word problems, 265–270; equivalent equations, 269; exponential and logarithmic function, 282–285; Europe, 51; fifth-degree equation, 278–279; fifth grade, 51; functional approach, 323; geometry, parallel courses, 402; groups, 279–282; history, 278; induction and binomial theorem, 285–291; inequalities, 270–278; linear, 33, 38, 295, 403; matrix, 350; modern, 279; presentation, 262; proofs, 278–282, 298; relationship to arithmetic, 291; set, 211; signed numbers, 263; solving triangles, 343; statistics, 378; structure, 279, 298; symbolism, 292; systems and proofs, 278–282; teaching hints, 291–294; texts, 24; understanding, 110; vs probability and statistics course, 358–359; word problems, 292

Algebraic geometry, 306

Algebraic inequalities, 33

Algebraic numbers, 243n

Algorism. *See* Algorithm

Algorithm, 292; defined, 92n

Allen, Frank B., 54

413

Allendoerfer, Carl B., 54, 396
American colonics, 1–2
American Federation of Teachers of the Mathematical and Natural Sciences, 7
*American Mathematical Monthly*, The, 12
American Mathematical Society (AMS), 5, 10, 12, 45
AMS. *See* American Mathematical Society
Analysis and geometry, 190–91
*Analysis of New Mathematics Programs*, 42–43, 55
Analytic geometry, 37, 306, 311, 382, 397, 402, 403, 404; precalculus, 394
Ancient history, 2
Ancient languages, 13, 14
Angle(s), 141; circles, relationship, 162; circular functions, 334–336; triangles, 155–157
*Appendices* (CEEB Commission on Mathematics), 37
Applications, 60, 400, 401
Applied mathematics, 7, 9
Arabic numeration system, 93, 124–125
Arabs, 30, 92n, 93
Archimedes, 24, 392, 394
Architecture, 7
Area, 145–153; circles, 161 and n; measure, 145
Arguments, implication or conditional, 199
Aristotelian logic, syllogism, 208
Arithmetic, 4, 91–112; algebra relationship, 291; basic facts, 94; checking operations, 118–119; division, 99–101; modular, 130; objects studied, 305; partial product, 95 and n; rational numbers and quotients, 239–240, 239n; sets, 211; signed numbers, 50; social, 31, 38; technical parts, 6; texts, 24; topics, 39
*Arithmetic Teachers*, The, 12
Arrowood, Charles F., 26
Artin, 357
Association of Colleges and Preparatory Schools of the Middle States and Maryland, 5
Associationist psychology, 80
Associative law, 91, 94, 131, 233, 238

Assumptions, 190n, 207, 210, 259; Euclid, 299–300, 302; graphing, 312; relationship to reality, 193
Astronomy, 323
Atomic physics, 143
Audiovisual aids, 83. *See* Visual aids
*Audiovisual Instruction*, 89
Ausubel, David P., 87
Average pupil, 399, 409–410
Averages, 359–360, 362
Axioms, 32, 33, 190 and n, 210; Euclid, 299, 303; geometry, 298; understanding, 226

Baldwin, George, 111, 138
Bar graph, 365
Bartnick, Lawrence P., 88
Base-ten numeration system, 34, 135. *See* Numeration systems
*Basic Geometry*, 303n, 321
Beatley, Ralph, 28, 303 and n, 321
Beberman, Max, 43, 45, 54, 69
Bechenbach, Edwin, 295
Beginning teachers, 69, 74, 85
Begle, Edward G., 46
Behavior, grades and, 66
Bellman, Richard, 295
Below average pupil, 409–410
Bentley, W. H. E., 160, 168
Berger, Emil J., 39, 88
Berkeley, California, 8
Betweenness, 142, 156, 309; assumptions, 307; concept, 302; Euclid, 300–301, 302
Bible, 1
Biconditional relation, 199–200, 205–206
Bigge, Morris L., 25
Binet, Alfred, 19
Binomial theorem, 403; algebraic viewpoint, 374; induction and, 285–291; probability, 374–375
Biological sciences, 229
Biology, 31; probability and statistics, 379
Biometrics, 31
Birkhoff, Garret, 295
Birkhoff, George D., 28, 303 and n, 309, 321
Blackboard and chalk, 76; geometry, 319; use of, 74–75, 81–82

Blocking, 22
Blumenthal, L. M., 321
Bond theory of learning, 16, 17–18, 20, 21, 24
Bookkeeping, 6
Boston English Classical School, 3–4
Boston Latin Grammar School, 2
Bourbaki group, 298n
Bruner, Jerome S., 52
Bulletin boards, 409 and n
Buswell, Guy Thomas, 25

Cajori, Florian, 26
Calculations, 361; numerical, 364
Calculators, 344; desk, 361
Calculus, 31, 37, 381–397, 403, 411; applications, 381, 395; course, 394–395; creation, 30; curriculum, 381–382, 394; limit concept, 383, 386–388, 389–394; manipulation, 395; preparation for, 383; real number system, 381; rigor, 394–395; sequences and series, 383–389; statement, 196–207; teaching hints, 395–396; textbooks, 395–396. *See* Differential calculus and Integral calculus
Cambridge Conference on School Mathematics, 41–42, 47, 182; "Report: Blueprint or Fantasy?," 54
"Cancel," 186–188
Cancellation laws, 186–187
Cantor, Georg, 222n, 223, 224, 246
Cardinal numbers, 134–135, 237
Carnegie Corporation, 43, 51
CASMT. *See* Central Association of Science and Mathematics Teachers
"Casting out nines," 118
Cayley, Arthur, 295
CEEB. *See* College Entrance Examination Board
Central Association of Science and Mathematics Teachers (CASMT), 12, 13
Certification, 89
Charosh, Mannis, 411
Chebyshev's Theorem, 361, 378
Checking arithmetic operations, 118–119
Chemistry, 31, 60
Child labor law, 20

Churchill, Winston, 404
Circles, 160–162; analogues, 317; area, 161 and n, 389
Circular functions, and trigonometry, 323-357, 403; angles, 334–336; complex numbers, 350–354; simple identities, 331–332; sine and cosine functions, 329–331; sum and difference formulas, 332–334; teaching hints, 354–355; triangles, solving, 336–344; vectors, 344–350; wrapping function, 324–329
Civil War, 4, 15
Clark, J. R., 27
Class participation, 66
Classroom: hints, in teaching and learning, 58–90; observers, 69
Clergy, 1, 2
Cleveland, Ohio, 11
Clock (face), 130, 136, 257
Closure, 130, 136, 233, 238, 242; principle, 72–73; vectors, 346–347
Code system, 125
Colburn, Warren, 14, 26; *First Lessons*, 3, 35
Cold War, 25
Colleagues, 84–85
College Entrance Examination Board (CEEB), 5, 36; Commission on Mathematics, 36–38, 308 and n, 317, 357, 370n, 381–382, 399, *Report*, 37–38, 345; Committee on Examinations, 36; creation, 36
College Entrance Examinations, preparation for, 36
College entrance requirements, 4, 56; Committee on, 6, *Report*, 28
Colleges: calculus, 382–383, 394; Committee on Undergraduate Program (CUPM), 49–50; curriculum, 256; discipline, 73; early, purpose, 2; mathematics: ability, 410, requirement, 410; teachers', 15; technical, 6. *See also* Junior colleges
Columbia University, Teachers College, 47
Columbus, Ohio, 8, 12
Combinations, 174. *See* Permutations
Commission on Post-War Plans, 11, 28

Commission on Secondary School Curriculum of the Progressive Education Association, 28
Commissions, mathematics education, 5–13
Committee of Fifteen, 7; "Provisional Report on Geometry Syllabus," 28
Committee of Ten, 5–6, 24; *Report on Secondary School Subjects*, 28
Committee on College Entrance Requirements, 6
Committee on Essential Mathematics for Minimum Army Needs, 10
Committee on Mathematics for the Non-College Bound, 408
Committee on Pre-Induction Courses in Mathematics, 10
Committee on Undergraduate Program in Mathematics (CUPM), 49–50
Committees, mathematics education, 5–13
Common school, 3. *See* Free school
Commutative group, 280
Commutative law, 91, 94, 233, 238; addition, 240–241; multiplication, 236; operation, 131
Complementary events (probability), 371
Complementation, of sets, 213
Complex numbers, 37, 38, 246–250, 259, 350–354; system, 134, 403; trigonometry, 403
Compulsory school law, 20
Computation, 17
*Computer Oriented Mathematics*, 12
Computers, 30, 31, 50, 52, 61, 256, 282; numeration systems, 119–120, 125; operators, 60
"Computers for School Mathematics," 88
*Computopics*, 88
Concepts, 37; children, 52; intuitive, 183; sets, 211–12; teaching, 39; verbalizing, 186
*Concepts of Algebra*, 138
*Concrete Approach to Abstract Algebra*, 296
Conditional events (probability), 371–372
Conditional probabilities, 179

Confidence limits, 376
Congruency theorems, 306
Conjectures, 73
Conjunctions, probability, 179
Conjunctive inference, 194
Continental Classroom, 295, 380
"Continuing Work of the Cambridge Conference on School Mathematics," 56
Continuous probability theory, 295
Contrapositive inference, 194, 195
Contrapositive proof, 194, 196, 209
Convention, 69, 70
Convergence, tests, 391–392
Convergent infinite series, 388–389
Converse, 308
Coordinate geometry, 38, 50, 311, 312–318; visual aids, 319
Coordinates, 38
Cosine function, 329–331
Cosines, law of, 338, 342, 343
Counting, 220–221; aids, 34; examples, 257–258; numbers, 237
Courant, Richard, 261, 357, 397
Covariance, analysis, 376
Crouch, Ralph, 111, 138
CUPM. *See* Committee on Undergraduate Program in Mathematics
Curriculum, 91; changes, 1; European, 51; improvement measures, 40ff.; influences on, 13; modern mathematics, 31, 35; National, 398–399; planning, 52–53; revolution, 39–40; wartime committees, 10–11. *See* CEEB *and under* subject *and* type of school
Curtis, Charles W., 321
Curve(s), 190–92; normal, construction, 378

Dame School, 1–2
Data, 370; organizing and reporting, 359–360; variability and reliability, 360–364
Daus, Paul A., 321
Davis, Robert B., 50, 51
Deans, Edwina, 55, 111
Decimals, 92, 114; repeating, 244–246
Dedekind, Julius Wilhelm Richard, 246
Deduction, 5; principle (logic), 195

Deductive reasoning, 37, 306
Definitions, 32, 69, 78, 210; geometry, 299
DeMoivre's Theorem, 353, 354, 357
DeMorgan's Laws, 206–207
*Designing the Mathematics Classroom*, 88
Detachment, rule of, 193–194
DeVault, M. Vere, 55, 70n, 90
*Development of Modern Education, The*, 26
Dewey, John, 22 and n, 26
Diagrams: Euler, 214n; Venn, 214 and n
Dice, 170–171; probability, 372–373
Die (singular of dice), 170
Dieudonne, Jean, 40, 297n, 304, 322
Differential calculus, 394, 397
Direct proofs, 194–195, 209
Discipline, 73–76, 405
"Discovery," 89
Discovery, emphasis on, 51
Discovery method (in teaching), 34–35, 39, 44, 50, 67–73; advantages, 68, 69, 74; examples, 70–73; purposes, 69; textbooks, 79
Disjunction, probability of, 179
Distribution(s), 360–362; binomial, 374; measuring "middle," 179; normal, 361–362, 378; population, 362; spread 179
Distributive law, 91, 94, 132, 233, 236, 238, 385; new number systems, 259; proof, 259
Divisibility, checks, 118–120
Division, 99–101, 257; fractions, 108–109; new numbers, 236; rules, 258
Divorces, *graph*, 365–367
Drop-outs, 73
Dubisch, Roy, *vi*, 138, 397
Duodecimal Society, 120

Earth satellite, 331
Eby, Frederick, 26
Economists, 60
Education: changes, 23; courses, purpose, 58; first formal, 1; mathematics, history, 1–25; philosophies, 13–15; progressive school, 22; public secondary, 4 (*see* High schools); transition, 48; universal compulsory, 2–3
Educational psychology, 8

*Educational Review*, 26
Educational Services, Inc., 51
Educators, 14–15, 52. *See also* under name
Egyptians, 268
Eighth grade. *See* Seventh and eighth grade
Einstein, Albert, 404
Elementary Functions course, 382
Elementary mathematics: language, logic and sets, 225; limit concept, 389
Elementary school: algebra, 51; curriculum, 31, 41–42, 49, 51–53, 91, 258, 259; discipline, 73; experimental programs, 48–49; "set theory" in first grade, 52–53; teachers, 48–49, training, 49–50; texts, 46
*Elementary School Journal*, 17 and n, 26
*Elementary School Mathematics*, 111; *New Direction*, 55
*Elements* (Euclid), 139, 290, 301, 302, 304, 321
*Elements of Algebra*, 261
Eleventh grade, 402–403
Eliot, Charles W., 5, 8
*Emerging Program of Secondary School Mathematics*, 54
Empty set, 213
Engineering, 60; calculus, 381; schools, 43
England, 2, 5, 6, 160, 297; U.S., 2
*Enrichment Mathematics for High School*, 90, 412
*Enrichment Mathematics for the Grades*, 412
Equality: defined, 134n; elementary mathematics, 251; rational numbers, 240; sets, 213–214
Equations, 38, 39, 262, 401; equivalent, 269; word problems, 265–270
Equipment, geometry, 157
Equivalence classes, 127–128, 250, 251–253, 256
Equivalence relation, 127, 199; properties, 250–254; sets, 250–251
Equivalent equations, 269
Equivalent systems, 269–270
Errors: measurement, 144–145, 363; probability, 363, 376; standard, 363–364

Euclid, 40, 139, 243, 297, 298, 321; contributions, 298; defense, 304–306; *Elements of Geometry*, 139, 298, 301, 302, 304, 321; errors, 298–304; parallel postulate, 160, 190
Euclidean axiom system, 402
Eudoxus, 246, 302, 321, 390, 391
Euler: diagrams, 214n; formula, 357
Europe, 14; schools, 38, 40, 51; teachers, 38
Evaluating pupils. *See* Grading
*Evaluation in Mathematics*, 90
*Everyday Arithmetic*, 17
Exceptional children, 19
Exner, Robert M., 114n, 209n, 229
*Experiences in Mathematical Discovery*, 408n, 412
Experimental elementary school mathematics programs, 48–49
Experimental programs, 5, 38, 42–43, 399, 402
Experimental psychology, 15, 24
Experimental secondary school programs, 42–43
Exponential functions, 282–285, 403

Factoring, 385
Factors, 39
Faculty psychology, 15, 16
Fadiman, Clifton, 59, 67n, 88
*Fantasia Mathematics*, 59, 67n, 88
Fehr, Henri, 6
Fehr, Howard F., 28, 55, 357
Fiction, mathematics, 59
Field(s), 133–134, 247, 279, 293, 403
Field trips, 76
Fiftieth percentile, 179
Film strips, 34, 76, 83, 409; geometry, 318
Films, 47, 51, 76, 83, 409; geometry, 318–319; reviews, 90
*Finite Mathematical Structures*, 229, 295, 380
*Finite Mathematics*, 295
Finite set, 212; definition, 224, 225
Finite systems, 126
*First Lessons*, 3
*Flatland: A Romance of Many Dimensions*, 153 and n, 168
"For all," 207–208

Forbes, Jack E., 80n, 88
Formal discipline, 7, 15
Formalism, 189–193, 208, 225, 230; calculus, 395; place of, 193
Foundations (of mathematics), 184
*Foundations of Geometry*, 302n, 321
*Foundations of Geometry and Trigonometry*, 357
Fractions, 107–110; cancellation, 186–188; rationalizing, 327
France, 5, 278
Franklin, Benjamin, 2, 14
Free school, 3
Free secondary schools, 3–4
Freitag, Arthur H., 138
Freitag, Herta T., 138
Froebel, Friedrich, 14–15, 26
Function: concept, 5, 217–218, 226; definition, 218–219, 226–227, 324; domain, 218; linear, 37, 282; ordered-pair definition, 226; range, 218; -relation, distinction, 219–220, 227
Functional analysis, 30
Functions and relations, 403
Fundamental Theorem of Algebra, 296

Galois, Evariste, 278–279, 296
Gambling, 170
Game theory, 30, 31, 61, 380
Games of chance, 169n, 170
Gauss, Karl Friedrich, 384–385
*General Survey of Progress in the Last Twenty-Five Years*, 27
*Geometric Inequalities*, 322
Geometric sequences, 384, 385–387, 388
Geometric transformations, 281, 295, 318
Geometric vectors, 322
Geometrics, 190
Geometry, 4, 27–28, 39, 226, 297–322, 401, 402; affine, 357; algebra, parallel courses, 402; analysis, 190; analytic, 322; assumptions, basic, 305; concepts, 156; coordinate, 37, 38, 50, 311–318, 319; course, 306–307; creation, 30; curriculum, 304–306; deductive, 6; definitions, 299; descriptive, 9; elementary school, 31; equipment for discovery, 157–160; Euclid, 190, 298–306; Europe, 51

Geometry, formal-informal, 139; high school course, 306–318; history, 304; incidence, 309–312; intuitive (*see* Intuitive geometry); junior high school, 139ff.; language, 210–211; new approach, 37; non-Euclidean, 192, 310–311, 311n, 322; nonmetric, 139–143; numbers, 258–259; objects studied, 305; original proofs, 320; physical models, 318; primary grades, 51–52; projective, 322; proofs, 298, 307, 320; real number system, 303, 304; reality, 318; rigor, 306; "sensed" angle, 339; sets, 211; solid, 31, 38, 164, 311–312; space, 139; spherical, 39, 311; syllabus, 7; synthetic, 311, 312; teaching, 5–6, 318–320; textbooks, 303–304; theorems, 305, 307–309; three-dimensional, 37, 317, 321; undefined words, 140; vectors, 345; visual aids, 318–319; world, relationship, 165–166. *See* Analytic geometry, Intuitive geometry *and* Plane geometry

*Geometry, Part One: Discovery by Drawing and Measurement*, 160, 168

Germany, 5, 6, 19; educators, 14–15

Gestalt psychology, 18, 19, 20

Gifted students, 41, 382

Glicksman, Abraham M., 321

Goals, teaching mathematics, 59–64

*Goals for School Mathematics*, 41 and n, 56–57

Gödel, Kurt, 184 and n

Gödel's Proof, 184 and n, 229, 230

Goldberg, Samuel, 380

Gould, S. H., 311n, 321

Grading and grades, 64–67, 258; changing, 67; organization, 8; scale, 65

Graduate students, as teachers, 382

Grammar school: curriculum, 5, 6, 8, 9, 11, 52–53

Graphic methods, 5, 7

Graphs (ing), 179, 271, 312; algebra, 292–293; bar, 365; "bell-shaped," 361–362; line, 365; picture, 369; sine and cosine functions, 331; two-dimensional, 401

"Great Books" movement, 13

Greece (Ancient), 30, 135, 303, 389, 390

Greenhill, Sir George, 6

Grouping: homogeneous, 86, 405, 410–411; program, 405

Groups, 293; algebra, 279–282

*Grube's Method of Teaching Arithmetic*, 27

Guessing, process of, 266–267

Guidance counselor, 86, 89

*Guidance Pamphlet*, 11

*Guide to the Use and Procurement of Teaching Aids for Mathematics*, 39, 88

*Guidebook to Departments in the Mathematical Sciences*, 89

Guthrie, Edwin R., 17–18

Hamilton, William R., 138, 295

*Harper's*, 377

Harvard College, 2, 5, 8; entrance requirements, 4

Harvard University, 303n

Hawaii, 367

Hawley, Newton S., 51

Heath, Sir Thomas L., 321

Hebrew alphabet, 222n

Henderson, Kenneth, 22n, 28

Herbart, Johann Friedrich, 15

Herbartian philosophy, 59. *See* Special Method in Arithmetic, 27

Herbert, Harriet B., 155n

*High School Mathematics Library*, 89

High schools, 4; algebra, 283, 293, attendance, 20; calculus, 381–383; curriculum, 60, 283, 306, 323, 344, 381–383, 401–404; geometry, 139, 306–318; library, 89; mathematics, teaching, 398-412; 1923 report, 8–9 -trigonometry integration, 323

Hilbert, David, 302–303, 309, 321–322

Hilgard, Ernest R., 17n

Hilton, Peter, 56

Hoffman, Walter, 88

Homework, 65–66, 75; textbook, 79–80

Homogeneous grouping, 86, 405, 410–411

Hoover, Kenneth, 2n, 27

*How to Lie with Statistics*, 369 and n, 377n, 380

*How to Solve It*, 23, 295

*How to Use Your Bulletin Board*, 409n

*How We Think*, 26

Howes, Vernon E., 397
Huff, Darrell, 369 and n, 377n, 380
Hull, Clark L., 17, 18
Hunt, Maurice P., 25
Hutchins, Robert M., 13
Hypotheses, testing, 376
Hypothetical syllogism, 194

Identical elements theory, 15–16, 26.
    See Thorndike
Identity elements, 132
"if and only if," 199–200, 308
"iff," 199–200
Illiteracy, 365
Imagination, 320
Implication, contrapositive form, 209
Incidence geometry, 309–312
Incommensurables, 302, 321, 389–390
Independent events (probability), 371
Indexes, 77
Indirect proofs, 194, 195, 209, 244. See
    Contrapositive proofs
Induction, 7, 285; principle (see Mathe-
    matical induction)
Inductive study, 14
Industry, 271; errors (probability), 363;
    statistics, 376
Inequalities, 39, 295, 401; algebra, 270–
    278; importance, 270–271; systems,
    401
Inference, 208–209; rules of, 193–196
Infinite number systems, 126
Infinite sets, 195, 218, 220–225, 227,
    294, 332; comparison, 221–223; defi-
    nition, 224–225
Infinite sum, definition, 388
Infinity, 220, 227, 232; symbol, 220
Ingenuity, 320
Initiative, 317
Insight, 18, 19
Insights into Modern Mathematics, 229,
    295, 311n, 321, 322, 397
Instruments, mathematical, 157–160
Insurance, probability, 170, 175–180
Integers, 126ff., 134, 233–242; applica-
    tions, 257–258; commutative law,
    131; construction, 251–257; identity
    elements, 132; set, 237; system, 403
Integral calculus, 392, 294, 397, 404

Intellectual Arithmetic Based Upon the
    Inductive Method of Instruction, 26
Intelligence, definition, 364
Intelligence scores. See I.Q.
Intelligence tests, 19, 364
International Commission, 6–7
International Congress of Mathemati-
    cians, 6
Interpolation, 178, 181, 338
Intersection, 142; sets, 213
Introduction to Finite Mathematics, 229,
    380
Introduction to Inequalities, 295
Introduction to Modern Algebra, 295
Introduction to the Foundations of Mathe-
    matics, 230
Introductory Probability and Statistical
    Inference, 37, 370, 380
Intuition, 225, 391; calculus, 394; fail-
    ures, 189–192; geometry, 306; mathe-
    maticians, 192
Intuitionists, 195
Intuitive concepts, 183
Intuitive geometry, 91, 139–168, 399–
    400; angles and triangles, 155–157;
    area, 145–153; betweenness, 142;
    circles, 160–162; discovery of facts,
    157–160; intersection, 142; measure-
    ments and formulas, 143–145; non-
    metric, 139–143; parallelograms, 149–
    150; prisms, 153–154; Pythagorean
    Theorem, 162–164; sets, 155; space,
    concepts of, 154; teaching hints, 164–
    166; textbooks, 160; trapezoid, 150–
    153; triangles, 147–149; volumes,
    153–155
Intuitive Geometry, 168
Inventiveness, 317
Inverses, 132–133, 247–248, 338
I.Q., 362–363
Irrational numbers, 37, 243n
Isomorphisms, 216–217, 224, 250, 254–
    255, 256
Iterative technique, 104

James, William, 15
Jefferson, Thomas, 2
Johnson, Donovan A., 39, 88, 409n
Joint Commission, 9–10, 28

Judd, Charles H., 20–21, 24, 25, 26, 27, 35
Junior colleges, 9; curriculum, 9, 11
Junior high schools, 8; algebra, 271; curriculum, 38–39, 44–45, 92, 232, 399–402, 410; discipline, 73; geometry, 139ff., 157, 307; homogeneous grouping, 410; modern mathematics, 31; 1923 report, 8–9; probability, 169–182, 370; statistics, 179, 180

Katona, George, 21, 26, 35, 62
Kazarinoff, Nicholas D., 322
Kelley, J. L., 295
Kemeny, John G., 56, 229, 295, 380
Kindergarten, 14–15, 91, 220–221; texts, 46
Klein, Felix, 5, 6
Kline, Morris, 56, 57

Language, 95n, 113–114; authors, 186; definitions, 210; importance, 265–266; logic and sets, 183–230; negations, use of, 189; purpose, 183; set, 33–34, 39, 157, 211; teachers, 186, 189; words, correct usage, 186–189
Language, logic and sets, 183–230; formalism, 189–193; infinite sets, 220–225; intersection, 213–215; logic, 193; negation, 196–197; notation, 212–213; proof and mathematical structure, 209–211; quantification, 207–209; relations and functions, 217–220; rules of inference, 193–196; sets, 211–217; statement calculus, 196–207; teaching hints, 225–227
Lasar rays, 140
Latin (language), 2
Latin Grammar School, 2
Law (profession), 31
"Law of probability," 181–182, 375–376
Laws, 3, 4, 20; mathematics, 91, 233, five basic, 259
Learning: bond approach, 16, 17; capabilities for, 52; methods, 80; subject controversy, 53; programmed, 80–81; theories, 17–19; transfer of, 8, 13–17, 20–21, 24. See Teaching and learning
Learning of Mathematics, Its Theory and Practice, 28

Leibnitz, Gottfried Wilhelm von, 393
Lemma, 243, 244 and n
Lesson Plans, 15, 59–64
Levi, Howard, 261, 304, 357
Library, 89
Limit(s), 291, 332, 397; concept, 227, 383, 386–392; definition, 393; intuitive idea, 395, 403–404; problems, 389–394; sequences, 391; trigonometric functions, 392
Line, 140, 141–143
Line graph, 365
Line segment, 140–143; incommensurable, 389–390
Linear algebra, 33, 39, 295, 403
Linear functions, 37, 282
Linear measure, 145
Linear programming, 30, 31, 275, 293, 295, 401
Lockard, J. David, 56
Locke, John, 26
Logarithms, 31, 282–285, 293, 323, 343–344, 397; applicability, 285; functions, 403
Logic, 2, 30, 32, 34–35, 39, 50, 69, 193, 206; biconditional, 199–200, 205–206; binary operations, 197–198, 199; deductive principle, 195; definition, 193; elementary mathematics, 209 and n; formal, and elementary set theory, 216–217, 224; implication, 199; negation, 196–197, 204; new numbers, 257; quantification, 207–209; sets, 211; statement formulas, 206–207; syllogism, 208; symbols, 196, 199, 200, 204–205, 208, 217; "thinking logically," 320; truth table, 200–204
Logic in Elementary Mathematics, 114n, 209n, 229
Logicians, 207, 214n
Long Way from Euclid, 322
Low Achiever in Mathematics, The, 412

MAA. See Mathematic Association of America
McCoy, Neal H., 295
McDonald, Blanche, 88
Machines, 264 and n
MacLane, Saunders, 295
McLaughlin, Katherine L., 17 and n, 26

McLellan, James, A., 26
McMurry, Charles H., 27
McShane, E. J., 229
Madison Project, 50–51, 70
*Main Currents in the History of Education*, 27
Mann, Horace, 3
*Manual on Certification Requirements for School Personnel in the U. S.*, 89
Maryland Project, 5, 160, 182
Massachusetts, education, 3
Matchett, Margaret S., 80n, 89
Mathematical Association of America, 8, 9, 10, 12–13, 46, 49, 397
*Mathematical Challenges*, 411
*Mathematical Education in the Americas*, 55
Mathematical induction, 285–288, 291, 294
Mathematical knowledge, body of, 298
*Mathematical Magpie, The*, 88
Mathematical structure, 32–33, 34, 38, 44, 45, 46, 160, 282, 293, 298, 403; proof, 209–211; textbooks, 78
Mathematical systems, 204; creating and expanding, 235; structure, 279
Mathematicians, 43, 46, 47, 50, 51, 52, 53, 60, 92n, 184, 222n, 295, 297, 302–303, 323, 384–385, 390, 392–393; algebra, 278–279, 291; assumptions, 210; calculus, teaching, 382; functions, 232–233; intuition, 192; reasoning, 193; work, 262; works, excerpts, 229–230. *See also* under name
Mathematics: abstraction and rigor, 192; applicability, 22; characteristics, 62; creative, 30, 31; described, 20; education (*see* Mathematics education); esteem, 59–60; foundations, 184; importance, 10, 31–32; learning qualifications, 320; nature of, 10; new developments, 30–32; purpose of teaching, 8, 58, 59–64; reality, relationship, 165, 379; supervisors, 39; topics, 32–33
Mathematics education, 381, 382; Committee of Fifteen, 7; Committee of Ten, 5–6; Committee on College Entrance Requirements, 6; committees and commissions, 5–13; history, 1–25

Mathematics education, International Commission, 6–7; Joint Commission, 9–10; 1923 report, 7–9; organizations, 11–13; PEA Committee, 9–10; philosophy, 398; psychology, 13–23; wartime committees, 10–11
*Mathematics for Elementary Teachers*, 111, 138
*Mathematics for High School, Introduction to Matrix Algebra*, 350
*Mathematics for Secondary School Teachers*, 182
*Mathematics in General Education*, 28
*Mathematics In-Service Education Program in Watertown Public Schools*, 70n, 90
*Mathematics Magazine*, 13
*Mathematics Student Journal, The*, 12, 411
*Mathematics Teacher, The*, 10, 11, 12, 28, 38, 54, 83, 87, 88, 89, 90, 396, 409, 412
*Mathematics Tests Available in the United States*, 39, 89
Matrix algebra, 350
May, Kenneth O., 89
Mayan civilization, 135
Mayor, John R., 45
Mean, 179, 359, 360, 361, 362; absolute deviation, 360–361
Measure theory, 30
Measurement, 363; and formulas, 143–145
Mechanical arts, 2
Median, 179, 359, 362
Medicine (profession), 31, 61
Memorization, 14, 15, 21, 33, 35, 65, 193, 320; faulty, 264; poor 412; -understanding gap, 23–24
Mensurational trigonometry, 323, 324
"Mental-discipline" philosophy, 13–14, 20; basis, 15
Meserve, Bruce E., 182
Method, modern mathematics emphasis, 34
Michigan, 4
Middletown Central School, Conn., 51
Millay, Edna St. Vincent, 297
"Minnemath," 47
Minnesota, 47; National Laboratory, 48

Minus sign, uses, 238

Mirkil, Hazelton, 295

Mode, 179, 359, 362

Models, 82

Modern mathematics, 1, 11, 29–57, 233; acceleration, 30–32; algebra for grade 5, 51; Cambridge Conference, 41–42; Commission of College Entrance Examination Board, 36–38; Committee on Undergraduate Program in Mathematics (CUPM), 49–50; defined, 29–30; discovery method, 34–35; effect on school curricula, 31; experimental elementary school mathematics programs, 48–49; experimental secondary school programs, 42–43; geometry for primary grades, 51–52; goals, 326; Madison Project, 50–51, 70; new methods, 34–35; new topics and sets, 33–34; O.E.E.C. Report and Synopsis, 40–41; opposition, 56; principles, 33; programs, and projects, 32–34, 47–48; reorganization and structure, 32–33; reports, 35–36; revolution in school mathematics, 39–40; School Mathematics Study Group, 45–47; Secondary School Curriculum Committee of the National Council of Teachers of Mathematics, 38–39; "set theory" in first grade, 52–53; "sets," 211; structure, 282; University of Illinois: Arithmetic Project, 51, Committee, 43–44; University of Maryland project, 44–45

*Modern View of Geometry*, 321

Modular arithmetic, 130

Modular number systems, 125, 135–136; field, 133–134

*Modus ponens*, 193, 194, 195

*Modus tollens*, 194, 195

Moore, E. H., 5, 27

Mosteller, Frederick, 380

Motion, concept of, 393

Movies, 34

Multiplication, 92–99, 257; associative law, 71–72, 94; binomials, 264–265; cancellation law, 186; commutative law, 71–72, 94, 131, 236; complex numbers, 351–352; distributive law, 33, 94, 236

Multiplication, equivalence sets, 253–254; new numbers, 235–236; rational numbers, 239, 240, 241; rules, 258; vectors, 349–350

Multisensory aids, 11

*Multisensory Aids in Teaching of Mathematics*, 82 and n, 155n, 168

Myers, Sheldon S., 39, 89

Nagal, Ernest, 184n, 229, 230

Names-objects, distinction, 113–114, 184–186

*National Association of Secondary School Principals Bulletin*, 45, 87–88

National Committee of Fifteen on Geometry Syllabus. *See* Committee of Fifteen

National Committee on Mathematical Requirements, 28; formation, 8; 1923 report, 7–9

National Council of Teachers of Mathematics (NCTM), 5, 9, 10–12, 46, 397; Committee on Mathematics for the Non-College Bound, 408; conferences, 39–40; film committees, 83; membership, 11–12; purpose, 11; Secondary-School Curriculum Committee, 38–39; -USOE Conference report, 412; *Yearbooks- First*, 27, *Third*, 27, *Fifth*, 27, *Seventh*, 28, *15th*, 28, *18th*, 82n, 155n, 168, *21st*, 21, *22nd*, 28, 295, *23rd*, 295, 311n, *27th*, 111–112, 412, *28th*, 412, *29th*, 56, 112

National Curriculum, 398–399

National defense, 10

National Defense Education Act (NDEA), 165, 318

National Education Association (NEA), 6, 7, 12; 38th Annual Meeting, 28

National Science Foundation, 39, 46, 51; Institute, 44

Natural numbers, 130, 237; system, 403

Natural sciences, 2, 6, 7, 32

*Nature of Number, The*, 138

Navigation, 9, 323

NCTM. *See* National Council of Teachers of Mathematics

NDEA. *See* National Defense Education Act

n-dimensional thinking, 153

NEA. *See* National Education Association

Negation, 196–197; logic, 204; use of, 189

Negative numbers, 231–232, 234, 400, 401; physical model, 236

Nelson, Leslie, 88

"Neoassociationist" psychology. *See* Stimulus-response

New England, 3, 4–5; Entrance Certificate Board, 4–5

New math. *See* Modern Mathematics

*New Methods in Arithmetic, The*, 27

New numbers, 231–232; addition, 234; annexing, 232–233; constructing from old, 250; division, 236; multiplication, 235–236; subtraction, 234–235; symbols, 233, 237

*New Thinking in School Mathematics*, 40 and n, 297n, 304n, 322

Newcomb, Simon, 5

Newman, James R., 184n, 229–230

Newton, Isaac, 30, 104, 392–393

Nightingale, A. F., 28

1923 report, 7–9, 24

Ninth grade, 401–402

Niven, Ivan, 261

Nonmetric geometry, 139–143

Normal school, 3

Norway, 278

Notation, 212–213, 395

NSF. *See* National Science Foundation

Null set, 213

Number line, 235, 236, 257, 258, 259, 400; inequalities, 271

*Number Stories of Long Ago*, 138

*Number Story, The*, 138

Number systems, 32, 33, 250, 399–400, 403; additive inverses, 237–238; annexing new numbers, 232–233; cardinal numbers, 237; completeness, 391; complex numbers, 246–250; counting numbers, 237; equivalence relations and sets, 250–251; expanding, 231–261: importance, 256, justification, 259, procedures, 232, 249–250, 255–256, purpose, 257; finite, 126; infinite, 126; integers, 126ff., 233–242, 257, construction, 251–257; modular, 125–135; natural numbers, 130, 237, 403

Number systems, negative numbers, 231–232, 234, 236, 400, 401; new numbers, 231–232, 238; number line, 235, 236, 257, 258, 259, 400; numeration systems, difference, 114; rational numbers, 134, 238–242, 403; real numbers, 46, 130, 134, 242–246, 303, 304, 381, 390, 403; reasons for studying, 136; structure, 279; teaching hints, 257–259; using, 256–257

Number theory, 134

*Numbers: Rational and Irrational*, 261

Numbers, 26, 70–71, 210; complex, 246–250; geometry, 258–259; measures, 145; numerals, distinction, 95, 185, 186; rational, 238–242, 243n; real, 130, 242–246, 401. *See* Number systems

Numeral-number, distinction, 95, 185, 186

Numeration systems, 39, 92, 93, 114–125; Arabic, 93–94; code, 125; number systems, difference, 114; place-value, 123; reaons for studying, 125; Roman numeral, 123–125, 136; tally, 123; teaching hints, 135–136

Nursing (profession), 61

Objects: -names, distinctions, 113–114, 184–186; symbols, confusion, 185

Observers (classroom), 69

O.E.E.C. *See* Organization for European Economic Cooperation

Olander, C. E., 409n

One-to-one correspondence, 221–223, 224; complex numbers, 249n; graphing, 312

Open sentences, 50

Operation, well-defined, 130–131

Opinion poll, 379

Optics, 355

Order, 271–272

Ordered pairs, 218–219, 255–256, 345; definition, 226

Organization for European Economic Cooperation (O.E.E.C.), 40–41, 297n, 304n, 322, 357; Report, 40–41

*Organizing and Memorizing*, 26

Oscilloscope, 331

Osgood, C. E., 21–22

Osgood, W. F., 7
Overhead projectors, 34, 82, 319

Page, David, 51
Paradoxes, 392–394
Parallel courses, algebra and geometry, 402
Parallel postulate, 160, 190, 310–311
Parallelograms, 149–150
Parents, 61, 83–84
Partial product, 95 and n
Pavlov, Ivan, 80
PEA. See Progressive Education Association
PEA Committee, 9–10
Pedagogy, 3
Pencils, automatic, 319
Percentage, 401
Periodicals, 12, 13
Permutations, 37, 172–175, 181; and combinations, 374, 403
Perry, John, 5, 7
Pestalozzi, Johann H., 3, 14, 15, 26, 27
Philosophy, 8, 13–15; of teaching, 10, 53
Physical examples (models), 76, 165, 235, 236; distributive law, 259; geometry, 318; new numbers, 236, 257; probability, 378
Physical sciences, 262, 400; calculus, 381; errors, probability, 363; inequalities, 271; mathematics, 47; vectors, 344
Physics, 31, 60, 181, 190, 344, 355; atomic, 143
Picture graphs, 369
Pigeons, 18
Pingry, Robert, 22n, 28
Place of Mathematics in Secondary Education, 28
Place-value numeration systems, 123
Plane, examples, 140, 141
Plane geometry, 38, 164, 298, 301, 307, 311–12, 317, 334–335; congruency theorems, 340; trigonometry, 340
Planning (teaching), 59–64
Plastic overlays (textbooks), 34
Plato, 13, 34, 67
Point, examples, 140, 141
Politics, 376, 377
Polya, George, 23, 230, 295

Polygons, 391
Polynomials, 403; derivation, 394; manipulation, 401
Population, 366–367; distributions, 362; school, 19–20
Positive numbers, 401
Postulate, 190n
Potts, E. W. Maynard, 160, 168
Power, Edward J., 27
Prenowitz, Walter, 322
Primary grades, geometry, 51–52. See Elementary schools
Prime numbers, 39
Principals, 85–86. See School administrators
Principles, 39
Prism, area, 153–154
Private schools, attendance, 20
Probability, 33, 37, 38, 39, 179, 180, 400; applications, 376–378; compound events, 179, 371; conditional 179, 371–372; defined, 182, 370–371; determining, 170; dice, 372–373; error, 363, 376; importance, 377–378; independent events, 371; insurance problems, 175–180; junior high school, 169–182; kits, 378; "law of," 181–182, 375–376; permutations, 172–175, 181; sets, 211; significance, 169–170; statistical inference, 358–380: applications, 376–378, ideas, emphasis on, 364, organizing and reporting data, 359–360, pictorial presentation, 365–369, teaching hints, 378–379, value of course, 358–359, variability and reliability, 360–364; statistics, 381, 382, 403; teaching hints, 180–182; two events, 372, 373–374
Probability, An Introduction, 380
Probability and Statistical Inference, 47
Probability and Statistics, 380
Problem(s): defined, 22–23; solving, 10, 22–23, 265, 266–267, 295, 400, 401; types, 65–66. See Equations and word problems
Proctor, Amelia D., 412
Professions, 31–32, 60–61
Professors, 4, 12
"Programmed Instructional Materials —Past, Present, and Future," 80n, 88

Programmed learning, 24, 76, 80–81
Programmed materials, 46
*Programmed Learning and Mathematical Education*, 89
Programming, 18; linear, 30, 31, 275, 293, 295, 401
Progressive education, 67–68
Progressive Education Association (PEA), 9; Committee on the Function of Mathematics in General Education, 9, 22
Progressive movement, 22
*Promising Practices for Elementary and Secondary School Teachers*, 56
Proof(s), 192, 243–244, 255–256, 298, 401; construction, 193; contrapositive, 194, 196, 209; deductive, 285; definition, 193; developing, 192–193; direct, 194–195, 209; indirect, 194, 195, 209, 244; induction, 285; informal, 160, 209; inequalities, 272; introducing, 226; and mathematical structure, 209–211; methods, 244 (*see* Mathematical induction); theorems, 210–211. See Rules of Inference *and under* subject
Proportion, definition, 390, 391
"Proposal for the High School Mathematics Curriculum," 56
Pseudo-indirect proofs, 194. *See* Contrapositive proofs
*Psychological Foundations of Education*, 25
Psychologists, 364
Psychology, 45, 80; associationist, 80; educational, 8; experimental, 15, 24; formal discipline, value, 7; gestalt, 18, 19, 20; mathematics education, 13–23. *See also* Thorndike
*Psychology of Arithmetic, The*, 16 and n, 27
*Psychology of Number, The*, 26
PTA, 83
Public schools, 3
Pupils, 58, 66, 70, 73, 412; average, 399; evaluation (*see* Grading); gifted, 19, 41, 382; grouping, 405; problem, 76; types, 358, 404–410. *See* Slow learner
*Purchase Guide for Programs in Science and Mathematics*, 88

Puritans, 1, 2
Pythagoras, 321
Pythagoreans, 243
Pythagorean Society, 389
Pythagorean Theorem, 162–164, 243, 305, 311, 325, 327; original proofs, 320; physical model, 318

Quadratic equations, 401
Quadratic functions, 37
Quality control, 30, 60
Quantification, 207–209
Quantifiers, 208
Quaternions, 138, 295, 296
Questions, 69, 70

Radicals, 401
Radical symbol, 248n
Radio, educational, 76
Randolph, John F., 397
Randomness, 376
Ratio(s), 26, 109–110, 401
Rational expressions, 401
Rational numbers, 238–242, 243n; definition, 240; system, 134, 403
Ray, 141, 142–143
Reality, 318; assumptions, relationship, 193; mathematics relationship, 379
Real number system, 46, 130, 134, 242–246, 303, 304, 381, 390, 403
Real numbers, 130, 242–246, 401
Reasoning, 17
Recorde, Robert, 112
Reeve, W. D., 27, 28
Reflective thinking, 22
Regression lines, coefficients, 376
Reid, Constance, 322
"Relation of Special Training to General Intelligence," 26
Relation(s), 37; concept, 217–218; definition, 206, 218; domain, 218; equivalence, and sets, 250–251; functions, 217–220, 401, difference, 219–220, 227; range, 218
Reliability, and variability, of data, 360–364
"Remedial" pupils, 358. *See* Slow learners
*Reorganization of Mathematics in Secondary Education*, 28

Repeating decimal, 244–246
Replacement set, 213
"Report to the International Congress of Mathematicians," 56
Research, 31, 32
Retardation, 9
"Reviews of films," 90
Revolution in School Mathematics, The, 12, 40, 42, 54
Rhode Island, 3
Rice, J. M., 25–26
Richard, Jules, 184
"Richard Paradox," 184
Rigor, 226, 306, 394–395. See Proofs
Rings, 293
Robbins, Herbert, 261, 357, 397
Robinson, Edith, vi
Roman numerals, 123–125, 136
Rome (Ancient), 124, 135
Rome, Italy, 6
Rosenbloom, Paul, 47, 48
Rosskopf, Myron F., 21, 27, 28, 114n, 209n, 229
Rote drill, 38
Rourke, Robert E. K., 380
Rule of detachment, 193–194, 195
Rules of inference, 193–196
Russell, Bertrand, 184
Russell's Paradox, 184

Sampling, 376
Sawyer, Warwick W., 51, 296, 397
Schaaf, William H., 89
School administrators, 39, 85–86, 382, 405
School Mathematics Study Group (SMSG), 45–47, 143, 160, 182, 350, 399
Schools: early types, 1–4; Europe, 38, 40, 51; grade organization, 8; population, growth, 19–20. See under type of school
School Science and Mathematics, 28
Schorling, Raleigh, 27
Schult, Veryl, 39, 56
Science, 2; curricula, 13; probability, 170; statistics, 376
Scientific American, 248
Scientific induction, 285
Scientific Foundations of Education, 27

Scores, true, 363–364
Seating chart, 74
Secondary Mathematics, A Functional Approach for Teachers, 357
Secondary schools, 4-5, 6, 7, 9–11; curriculum, 4-5, 6, 7, 9–11, 36–38, 44; Europe, 40–41; experimental programs, 42–43; free, 3–4; grades (7–12), 399–404; periodicals, 12, 13; teaching, 5, 398–412; texts, 46. See High schools and Junior high schools
"Second Revolution in Mathematics," 54
Seeley, Levi, 27
Selected Topics in the Teaching of Mathematics, 27
Sequence, 291; arithmetic, 384–385; definition, 383–384; limits, 391; series, 383–389, 404
Series, 291; definition, 388; sequences, 403
Set language, 33–34, 39, 157, 211
Set theory, 30, 211; creation, 33; elementary, and formal logic, 216–217, 224; first grade, 52–53
Set(s), 33, 37, 39, 211–217; complementation, 213; concepts, 211–212; defined, 212; equality, 213–214; equivalence relations, 250–251; finite (see Finite set); infinite (see Infinite set); integers, 237; intersection, 213; isomorphisms, 216–217; naming, 212; null or empty, 213; relations and functions, 217–220; replacement, 213; Russell's Paradox, 184; subsets, 213; symbol, 212–213, 217; terminology, 155; union, 213; universe, 213; Venn diagram, 214 and n
Seventh and eighth grade, 399–401
Shop mathematics, 9
"Sign learning," 19
Signed numbers, 263
Significance tests, 376
Significant Changes and Trends in the Teaching of Mathematics Throughout the World Since 1910, 27
Simon, Théodore, 19
Sine: and cosine functions, 329–331; curve, 323; law of, 337
6-3-3 grade organization, 8

Skills, 37
Skinner, B. F., 17, 18
Slide rule, 282, 293–294
Slow learners, 81, 168, 404–409, 412; probability and statistics, 358
Smith, David E., 6, 7, 27, 112, 138, 261, 296, 322, 380, 397
SMSG. *See* School Mathematics Study Group
*SMSG—The Making of a Curriculum*, 57
Snell, J. Laurie, 229, 295, 380
Sobel, Max A., 182
Social arithmetic, 31, 38
Social sciences, 31, 32, 61, 229, 381, 400; error probability, 363; inequalities, 271
Social studies, 379
Society, 31–32, 36, 53
Society for Industrial and Applied Mathematics, 12
Socrates, 34, 35
*Socrates and the Slave*, 67 and n
Socratic Method, 67, 68
Solid geometry, 31, 38, 164, 311–312
*Source Book in Mathematics*, 112, 138, 261, 296, 322, 380, 397
Soviet Union, 37
Space, concepts of, 154
Space geometry, 139
Space perception, 38
Spanish texts, 47
*Special Method in Arithmetic*, 27
Spherical geometry, 311
"Spiral approach," 42
Sputnik, 10, 29
Square roots, 101–107; proofs, 243, 244
Standard deviation, 360–361, 363
Standard error, 363–364
Standards: college entrance requirements, 4–5; intelligence measurement, 19
Stanford Elementary School, 51
Stanford University, 23, 46, 51
Statement calculus, 196–207
Statement formulas (logic), 206–207
Statistical inference, 33; probability, 358–380

Statistics, 9, 31, 37, 39, 60, 61, 177, 400; applications, 376—378; cause-and-effect relationship, 368–369; course, 364; divorce, 365–368; graphs, 365–368; homogeneous grouping, 405; ideas, emphasis on, 364; importance, 377–378; interpretation, 358; junior high school, 179, 180; misconceptions, 368, 369; organizing and reporting data, 359–360; pictorial presentation, 365–369; probability, 370–376; variability and reliability, 360–364
Stimulus-response (or bond) theory of learning, 17–19, 24, 80
Stone, Marshall H., 56
Student teaching, 58
*Studies in Mathematics, Vol. II—Euclidean Geometry Based on Ruler and Protractor Axioms*, 321
*Studies in Mathematics Education*, 43
Structure. *See* Mathematical structure
Subject matter, presentation, 15
Subsets, 213
Substitute teachers, 59
Subtraction, 234–235, 257, 258
*Successful Classroom Control*, 88–89
Sum and difference formulas, 332–334
"Summary of Current Tendencies in Elementary School Mathematics as Shown by Recent Textbooks," 26
*Summary of Educational Investigations Relating to Arithmetic*, 25–26
*Supervisor of Mathematics; His Role in the Improvement of Mathematics Instruction*, 39
Suppes, Patrick, 51, 52
Surface areas, calculating, 154
Surveying, 9
*Survey of Modern Algebra*, 295
Switzerland, 6, 14
Syllogism, 208
Sylvester, J. J., 5, 297
Symbolism, 69, 136, 208, 262, 265, 266, 292
Symbols, 208, 259, 305; algebraic, manipulation, 262; inequalities, 271; infinity, 220; logic, 196, 199, 200, 204–205, 208, 217; new numbers, 233, 237; object, confusion, 185; radical, 248n; rational numbers, 241; relation, 250; sets, 212–213, 217
Syracuse University, 50

Systems: isomorphisms, 216–217; and proofs, algebra, 278–282
*Synopses for Modern Secondary School Mathematics*, 357
Synthetic geometry, 311, 312

Tally system, 123
Tangent(s), 404; law of, 343, 344, 355
Tannery, J., 5
Taxes, 4
Teachers: administrator, 85–86; beginning, 58–59, 68, 74, 85; calculus, 382; characteristics, 58, 85; colleagues, 84–85; discovery method (*see* Discovery method); elementary school, 48–50; European, 38; graduate students, 382; language, 186, 189; parents, 83–84; periodicals, 12–13; shortage, 56; slow learners, 405; substitute, 59; training, 3, 7, 43–44, 49–50
Teachers' colleges, 15
Teaching: advances, timing, 24–25; aims, 7–9, 24; algebra, 6; beginning, 69, 74, 85; characteristics, 67; decompartmentalization, 6, 9; materials, 50; mathematical structure, 282; mathematics, purpose of, 59–64, 193; methodology, 5, 11, 14, 16, 20, 24, 34–35, 67–73 (*see also* Discovery method); new developments, 92; nineteenth century, 5; organizations, 12; philosophy, 13–15, 53; profession, 31, 61; recommendations, 39; secondary schools, 5, 398–412; "spiral approach," 42; student, 58; team (*see* Team teaching); theories, 15, 17–19. *See* Education *and* Teaching and learning
Teaching aids, 34, 76, 77–80
Teaching and learning: classroom hints, 58–90; discipline, 73–76; discovery approach, 67–73; grading, 64–67; lesson plans, 59–64; people, 83–86; programmed learning, 80–81; teaching aids, 76; textbooks, 77–80; visual aids, 81–83
Teaching machines, 18, 24, 34, 76, 80
"Teaching Machines or What?", 80n, 89
*Teaching of Algebra, The*, 28
*Teaching of Mathematics*, 397

Team teaching, 34
Technical colleges, 6
Technology, 37, 38
Television, 34; educational, 76
Temperature, 257, 258
Tenth grade, 402
Terminating decimal. *See* Repeating decimal
Testing, 45, 47, 48
Tests, 64–65, 89, 90, 391–392; convergence, 391–392; grades, 64; intelligence, 19, 364; significance, 376; true score, 363–364
Textbooks, 3, 14, 17, 24, 42, 46, 77–80; advantages, 77, 79; algebra, 263; authors, 79; calculus, 395–396; courses, 399; definitions, 217; discovery approach, 79; geometry, 303–304; intuitive geometry, 160; junior high school, 45; language, 185–186; plastic overlays, 34; programmed materials, difference, 81; selection, 77–79; set language, 34; structure, 78; traditional, 263–264; using, 79
Theorems: creation, 400; geometry, 298; lemma, 244 and n; proving, 210–211; sequence (geometry), 307–309
Theories, of learning, 17–19
*Theories of Learning*, 17n
"there exists at least one," 207–208
Thermometer, 257
"think logically," 320
*Third New Science and Mathematics Curricula*, 56
Thomas, George B., Jr., 380
Thompson, Gerald L., 229, 295, 380
Thorndike, Edward L., 8, 15–17, 18, 20, 21, 24, 27, 29, 62, 80
Tolman, Edward C., 18–19
Topology, 30, 31, 322
Tornow, Gene, 70n, 90
Town school, 2
Townsend, E. J., 302n, 321
Training, transfer of, 20–21, 24, 320. *See* Learning
Transcendental numbers, 243n
Trapezoid, 150–143
Triangles, 147–149, 210–211; angles, 155–157; proof, 195; solving, 336–344
Trigonometry, 4, 6, 38, 322, 397, 403; applications, 403; astronomy, 323; circular functions, 31, 37, 323–357

Trigonometry, complex numbers, 350–354; congruence theorem, 307; functional approach, 323; geometric viewpoint, 318; identities, 331–332, proving, 207–208; plane geometry, 340; purpose of study, 323 ; right-triangle approach, 31; sense of the angle, 339; sine and cosine functions, 329–331; solving equations, 207; solving triangles, 336–344; tables for angles, 338; vectors, 344–350; wrapping function, 324–329, 354–355

True score, definition, 364

*True Story*, 377

Truth sets, 50

Truth table, 200–203, 204

Turing, 230

Twelfth grade, 403–404

*Twelfth-Grade Pre-College Mathematics Program*, 397

*Twentieth Century Mathematics for the Undergraduate Preparation of Elementary School Teachers*, 112

UICSM. *See* University of Illinois Committee on School Mathematics

UMMAP. *See* University of Maryland Mathematics Project

"Underachiever," 404

Understanding, 24, 61, 62, 264–265; algebra, 262; calculus, 394–395; emphasis on, 51, 91–92, 125; importance, 186, 188, 395, 400; intuitive, 225; transfer, 62

Union, sets, 213

Uniqueness, vectors, 347

Unit, planning, 63

Unity, of mathematics, 355

Universal compulsory education, 2–3

Universe, 72, 213, 214n

University of Illinois Committee on School Mathematics, 43–44, 51, 69, 399

University of Maryland Mathematics Project, 44–45

"Unlearning," 22

*U.S. Bureau of Education Circular of Information, No. 3*, 26

Van Engen, Henry, 28, 112

Variability: measures, 360; and reliability of data, 360–364

Variables, 50

Variance, analyis, 376

Vaughn, Herbert, 43, 45

Vectors, 33, 38, 39, 41, 296, 344–350, 357, 403; addition, 345–346; algebra, 322; definition, 345; spaces, 296, 322, 357; teaching methods, 345

*Vectors in Three-Dimensional Geometry*, 321

Venn, John, 214n

Venn diagram, 214 and n

Virginia, 2

Visual aids, 34, 81–83, 318–319, 409

Volume measure, 145

Volumes (intuitive geometry), 153–155

von Neumann, John, 229, 230

Walker, Robert J., 321

War Policy Committee, 10

War Preparedness Committee, 10

Wartime committees, 10–11

Wave motions, 323, 331

Webster College, 50

Weierstrass, Karl Theodor, 191–192

Weiss, Thomas M., 2n, 27

*Were We Guinea Pigs?*, 26

Wertheimer, Max, 19

Wesleyan University, 51

*What Is Calculus About?*, 397

*What Is Mathematics?*, 261, 357, 397

Wilder, Raymond L., 230

Willoughby, Stephen S., 70n, 73n, 89, 90

Woodby, Lauren G., 412

Wooten, William, 57

Words: correct usage, 186–189, 225–226; definitions, 210; problems, 65–70, 292

*World of Mathematics, The*, 184n, 229–230

World War II, 10, 25, 32, 59

Wrapping function, 324–329, 354–355; defined, 324

Yale University, 46

Yearbooks, 12

Young, J. W. A., 7

Yugoslavia, 41

Zant, James H., 57

Zeno, 299

Zeno's Paradoxes, 392–394